ARTHURIAN STUDIES XCII

LOCAL PLACE AND THE ARTHURIAN TRADITION IN
ENGLAND AND WALES, 1400–1700

ARTHURIAN STUDIES

ISSN 0261-9814

General Editors
Norris J. Lacy
Cory James Rushton

Previously published volumes in the series
are available at https://boydellandbrewer.com/

Local Place and the Arthurian Tradition in England and Wales, 1400–1700

Mary Bateman

D. S. BREWER

© Mary Bateman 2023

All rights reserved. Except as permitted under current legislation no part of this work may be photocopied, stored in a retrieval system, published, performed in public, adapted, broadcast, transmitted, recorded or reproduced in any form or by any means, without the prior permission of the copyright owner

The right of Mary Bateman to be identified as the author of this work has been asserted in accordance with sections 77 and 78 of the Copyright, Designs and Patents Act 1988

The publishers are grateful to the Vinaver Trust for generously providing a subvention towards the production costs of this volume

First published 2023
D. S. Brewer, Cambridge
Paperback edition 2026

ISBN 978 1 84384 658 1 (hardback)
ISBN 978 1 84384 770 0 (paperback)

D. S. Brewer is an imprint of Boydell & Brewer Ltd
and of Boydell & Brewer Inc.
website: www.boydellandbrewer.com

The publisher has no responsibility for the continued existence or accuracy of URLs for external or third-party internet websites referred to in this book, and does not guarantee that any content on such websites is, or will remain, accurate or appropriate

A CIP catalogue record for this book is available from the British Library

Contents

List of Illustrations	vi
Acknowledgements	vii
Introduction: Place and the defence of Arthur	1
1. 'Thise were his places and his habitacions': Arthur *in situ* in the fifteenth century	33
2. Contentious places: Reconciling Arthurian places in the fifteenth century	89
3. The best of the west: John Leland's West Country Arthur	137
4. Locating Arthur in England and Wales: John Leland, John Prise, and Elis Gruffydd	171
5. Placing Arthur in William Camden's *Britannia*	216
Coda: Arthur's local renaissance?	261
Bibliography	269
Index	315

Illustrations

Maps

1.	Map of Arthurian locations discussed in Chapter 2	136
2.	John Leland's Arthurian places	170
3.	John Prise's Arthurian places	214
4.	Elis Gruffydd's Arthurian places	215
5.	William Camden's Arthurian places	260

Figures

1.	*Panel 1b in the Great East Window of York Minster*	48
2.	Cotton MS Titus A XIX f. 107v	71
3.	MS Lat. Hist. A. 2 (*magna tabula*), page 1	82
4.	MS Lat. Hist. A. 2 (*magna tabula*), page 1 (detail)	83
5.	Cotton MS Titus A XIX, f. 19r	84
6.	Detail from frontispiece of Camden, *Britain* (1610)	235
7.	Arthur's Cross, from Camden's *Britain* (1607)	241

Acknowledgements

In writing this book, I was very fortunate to be supported financially through several sources. I am grateful to the Arts and Humanities Research Council and the University of Bristol Alumni Foundation for generously funding the earliest stages of this research. This book has been greatly improved by the inclusion of a number of images, and I extend my gratitude to the Vinaver Trust for providing financial support to ensure this could happen.

This book could not have been written without the tireless support, unending patience when deadlines were stretched, and minute advice on early drafts from Caroline Palmer, Ad Putter, and Robert Gossedge.

Others have given their time, expertise, and attention to my work, helping me to bring this book into being. I must therefore extend my thanks to Helen Cooper, Leah Tether, Sebastiaan Verweij, Benjamin Pohl, Adrian Ailes, and George Ferzoco for offering valuable feedback on my work. Thanks are also due to Erik Kooper, James Carley, Richard Utz, Trevor Russell Smith, Claire Macht, Sarah Peverley, and Lily Hawker-Yates for kindly sharing their expertise and feedback.

Finally, I must thank those who have given generous moral, practical, and emotional support. First and foremost, this includes my husband Maxwell, who provided not only loving support and patient proof reading, but also assisted with the unenviable task of indexing this book. I am also grateful to my family, especially Helen Smith, Patrick Bateman, and Rosie Cox, for their support and patience.

Introduction: Place and the defence of Arthur

Places are powerful. Even when we visit the settings for works of fiction, we find ourselves suspending our disbelief. Several literary geographies have sparked successful tourism industries: Thomas Hardy's Wessex, for example, or the Brontës' home in Haworth.[1] Literary tourism has a surprisingly long history: a fifteenth-century continuation of *The Canterbury Tales* which describes the pilgrims' experience after arriving at Canterbury Cathedral appears to have been composed by a monk at the cathedral responsible for administering St Thomas Becket's shrine (and perhaps guiding visiting pilgrims).[2] Of course, Chaucer's *Tales* were not the key motivation for pilgrims travelling to Canterbury, but the existence of this text suggests that on-site interpreters responsible for choreographing pilgrims' experiences were engaging with the Cathedral's literary connotations. Recognisable stories can illuminate our experiences of particular places.

In the same vein, sites associated with King Arthur continue to attract visitors. Across the English and Welsh landscape, Arthur's name keeps appearing: as W. H. Dickinson observes, 'only the Devil is more often mentioned in local association than Arthur'.[3] At Glastonbury, Arthur has been swept up into the town's thriving New Age tourist economy, and his purported grave site at Glastonbury Abbey, discovered in 1191, is no longer the only site of Arthurian interest in the town. Visitors climb Glastonbury Tor, now associated widely with the Avalon of Arthurian tradition, and drink from the waters of the Chalice Well said to have sprung from the Holy Grail buried somewhere nearby.[4] Likewise, Tintagel,

---

[1] W. J. Keith, 'Thomas Hardy and the Literary Pilgrims', *Nineteenth-Century Fiction*, 24 (1969), 80–92; D. C. D. Pocock, 'Haworth: The Experience of Literary Place', in *Geography and Literature: A Meeting of the Disciplines*, ed. William E. Mallory and Paul Simpson-Housley (Syracuse, NY: Syracuse University Press, 1987), pp. 135–44; Nicola J. Watson, *The Literary Tourist: Readers and Places in Romantic Victorian Britain* (New York: Palgrave Macmillan, 2006), pp. 106–28; pp. 174–200.

[2] Laura Varnam, *The Church as Sacred Space in Middle English Literature and Culture* (Manchester: Manchester University Press, 2018), pp. 7–8; Peter Brown, 'Journey's End: The Prologue to the Tale of Beryn', in *Chaucer and Fifteenth-Century Poetry*, ed. Julia Boffey and Janet Cowen (London: Kings College Centre for Late Antique and Medieval Studies, 1991), pp. 143–74.

[3] W. H. Dickinson, *King Arthur in Cornwall* (London: Longmans Green, 1900), p. vi.

[4] Marion Bowman is the primary authority on the pull of New Age spirituality at Arthurian Glastonbury: see 'Drawn to Glastonbury', in *Pilgrimage in Popular*

associated with King Arthur since at least the twelfth century, remains one of English Heritage's most visited sites. Arthur is unquestionably the key draw: in 2010, interviews conducted with visitors to Tintagel Castle demonstrated that visitors reacted with discomfort to attempts to disrupt their suspended disbelief in Arthur.[5] Today, Tintagel is more than just the castle; James Noble memorably described the integrated Arthurian tourism experience at Tintagel in the 1990s as 'the best of English Twinkie', enumerating the various Arthur-themed museums, hotels, restaurants, and souvenir shops lining the streets of the town.[6]

While Arthur's tourist appeal today is obvious, the long history of Arthurian tourism is less well-recognised. From at least the fourteenth century, and perhaps even earlier, custodians of religious and secular sites with Arthurian connections carefully curated their sites' histories for the benefit of their visitors. This book pays attention to these localised experiences of Arthur and their considerable impact, direct and indirect, on the changing shape of Arthur in the popular imagination through the centuries. Studies in recent decades have shed light on the real-world geographies written into Arthurian texts, from Geoffrey of Monmouth's *Historia regum Britanniae* (1136) to Sir Thomas Malory's *Morte Darthur* (c. 1470).[7] I begin with the places themselves by asking what qualities they exhibited (and indeed continue to exhibit) that strengthened their visitors'

Culture, ed. Ian Reader and Tony Walter (London: Palgrave Macmillan, 1993), pp. 29–62; 'Arthur and Bridget in Avalon: Celtic Myth, Vernacular Religion and Contemporary Spirituality in Glastonbury', *Fabula*, 48.12 (2007), 16–32; 'Going with the Flow: Contemporary pilgrimage in Glastonbury', in *Shrines and Pilgrimage in the Modern World: New Itineraries into the Sacred*, ed. Peter Jan Margry (Amsterdam: Amsterdam University Press, 2008), pp. 241–80; 'Restoring/Restorying Arthur and Bridget: Vernacular Religion and Contemporary Spirituality in Glastonbury', in *Vernacular Religion in Everyday Life: Expressions of Belief*, ed. Marion Bowman and Ulo Valk (London: Routledge, 2012), pp. 328–49. See also Roberta Gilchrist, *Sacred Heritage: Monastic Archaeology, Identities, Beliefs* (Cambridge: Cambridge University Press, 2020), pp. 176–218.

[5] Hilary Orange and Patrick Laviolette, 'A Disgruntled Tourist in King Arthur's Court: Archaeology and Identity at Tintagel, Cornwall', *Public Archaeology*, 9.2 (2010), 85–107 (p. 96).

[6] James Noble, 'Tintagel: The Best of English Twinkie', in *King Arthur in Popular Culture*, ed. Elizabeth S. Sklar and Donald L. Hoffmann (Jefferson, NC: McFarland, 2002), pp. 36–44.

[7] Examples include Michelle R. Warren, *History on the Edge: Excalibur and the Borders of Britain, 1100–1300* (Minneapolis, MN: University of Minnesota Press, 2000); Robert Allen Rouse and Cory James Rushton, 'Arthurian Geography', in *The Cambridge Companion to the Arthurian Legend*, ed. Elizabeth Archibald and Ad Putter (Cambridge: Cambridge University Press, 2009), pp. 218–34; Dorsey Armstrong and Kenneth Hodges, *Mapping Malory: Regional Identities and National Geographies in Le Morte Darthur* (London: Palgrave Macmillan, 2014); Jamie McKinstry, *Middle English Romance and the Craft of Memory* (Cambridge: D. S. Brewer, 2015), pp. 45–68.

impressions of Arthur's reality. In the early fifteenth century religious institutions used their Arthurian connections to defend their own prestige and antiquity to the public. A century later, Arthurian defenders were invoking these sites in order to shore up the impression that Arthur had truly existed. In the sixteenth century, Arthurian scepticism was being aired more openly by writers of English history such as Polydore Vergil, prompting a new kind of Arthurian writing to emerge: the Arthurian defence, exemplified in texts such as John Leland's *Assertio inclytissimi regis Arthurii regis Britanniae* [An assertion of the most famous Arthur, King of Britain] (1544) and John Prise's *Historia Britannicae Defensio* [A defence of the British History] (1573). The authors of these defences turned to Arthurian places as proof of Arthur's existence, harnessing the rhetoric of such places to defend Arthur's reality in conjunction with more traditional textual authorities. For the visiting public of the fifteenth and sixteenth centuries, as for tourists today, Arthur could be experienced quite differently on-site at abbeys, churches, or castles than he could through the medium of text alone. Encountering a space in which Arthur was said to have been crowned, buried, or to have held court gave a sense of reality and dimension to Arthur's history. Fundamentally, this book argues that the power of place has been essential to the development of Arthurian tradition in England and Wales, and particularly in making Arthur's existence seem more believable.

The key sources of this book fall into two categories. Both source types evince the various ways in which Arthur has been emplaced from the later Middle Ages through to the seventeenth century. Because this is a book about the power of place, the first type of source we will encounter in this book is locative in nature: architecture, the inscribed artefacts designed to be consumed on site at Arthurian places, stained glass windows, and the less tangible 'tour guiding' that went on at Arthurian sites. These sources are broadly my earliest. While a study of Arthurian localisation could easily begin before 1350, visitor experiences appear to have been more effectively choreographed from the late fourteenth to early fifteenth centuries, or at least there is more material evidence for such choreography surviving from this period. This was a time when a large number of religious houses underwent a great restoration of some sort.[8] Buildings were renovated, and the oldest parts of their fabric were

---

[8] See, for example, the discussion of the great restoration of St Bartholomew's church in Varnam, *The Church as Sacred Space*, p. 62; and of Sherborne Abbey in Arthur L. Salmon, *Dorset* (Cambridge: Cambridge University Press, 1910), p. 94. Other examples include renovations carried out at St Albans, Crowland, Evesham, Glastonbury, York, Ramsey, and Worcester. See James G. Clark, 'Selling the Holy

re-incorporated and centred to emphasise the institutions' antiquity.[9] At the same time, historical and legendary material was transferred from chronicle manuscripts hidden away in institutional libraries to innovative, accessible formats such as *tabulae*, window glazing schemes, tapestries, and wall paintings, many of which were designed specifically to be consulted by pilgrims and mediated by clerks or monks acting as guides. It is possible that this kind of guided visitor experience had a longer history, but there is limited physical and textual evidence that survives from earlier periods. Surviving evidence suggests that Arthur, and his fellow legendary British kings, were popular subjects for guided on-site experience in the later Middle Ages. Arthur might come to be associated with a particular site for various reasons. Sometimes, physical or thematic proximity might be enough to fit a location into an existing Arthurian geography. Many places, however, were already powerful before their association with Arthur – topographically striking, politically significant, or visibly ancient – and it is perhaps unsurprising that powerful, affective places should become connected with one of Britain's most powerful legendary figures.

The second type of source I will be using might be described, very broadly, as textual. The endurance of Arthurian places in the public imagination relied upon various human actors responsible for carefully cultivating, interpreting, and publicising such places. Yet while this began with the *in situ* interpretations of site custodians, visitors to Arthurian sites, too, were essential in managing and interpreting Arthurian locations, fitting such places into their own frameworks of knowledge and writing them into textual works. Locative sources alone – stained glass, *tabulae*, and evidence of tour guiding – do not give much insight into how carefully managed Arthurian sites actually affected their visitors, and thanks to the ravages of the Reformation (and quite simply of time) many examples of locative Arthurian sources do not survive at all. Fortunately, some of the individuals who experienced Arthurian sites in person left us texts that describe their impressions of Arthur and his places. The latter half of this book deals with several such writers, demonstrating how their impressions of Arthurian sites, either through personal

---

Places: Monastic Efforts to Win Back the People in Fifteenth-Century England', in *Social Attitudes and Political Structures in the Fifteenth Century*, ed. Tim Thornton (Stroud: Sutton, 2000), pp. 13–32.

[9] At Glastonbury, twelfth-century building materials and stained glass were re-incorporated into the renovations of the fourteenth and sixteenth centuries. This, and other examples from elsewhere, is described in Gilchrist, *Sacred Heritage*, pp. 151–52.

experience or through reading the accounts of other visitors, proved crucial in defending Arthur's existence. These works vary significantly in form, including notebooks never intended for publication, chronicles, dedicated Arthurian defences, and chorographies.[10] They range in date from the mid-fifteenth to the seventeenth centuries. This was a period of Arthurian instability. While the much-maligned Polydore Vergil only went so far as to suggest that untruths existed *within* Arthur's story, William Caxton had insinuated several decades earlier in the preface to his edition of Malory's *Morte Darthur* (1485) that some held Arthur to have never existed at all.[11] It has been debated whether or not the 'dyuers men' Caxton enigmatically identifies as Arthurian sceptics – or indeed the 'noble and dyuers gentylmen' he claimed to have pushed for the *Morte*'s publication – represent real people, or are merely straw opponents in Caxton's shrewd marketing strategy.[12] Certainly, Arthur had always had his doubters: Caxton may have been thinking of writers such as Ranulf Higden and Alfred of Beverley, both of whom drew attention to the lack of references to Arthur in the works of Gildas and Bede, or of even earlier Arthurian sceptics such as the acid-tongued William of Newburgh.[13] In any case, Caxton's introduction suggests that by the late fifteenth century Arthur's very existence was being widely questioned, enough to justify the publication of a defensive counterargument. Although the earliest works discussed in this book are not explicitly framed as Arthurian defences, we should nevertheless consider the environment of emerging Arthurian scepticism in which they were produced, and the impact that this environment might have had on their representation of Arthurian places.

In writing this book, I am attempting to understand and trace, for the first time, the history of the local Arthur: from carefully managed

---

[10] The 'chorography', a systematic description of a place, is defined and discussed below in Chapter 5.

[11] Caxton's preface in Thomas Malory, *Works*, ed. Eugène Vinaver (Oxford: Clarendon Press, 1977), pp. xiii–xv (p. xiv).

[12] Scepticism as to the actual existence of these men is expressed by Russell Rutter, 'William Caxton and Literary Patronage', *Studies in Philology*, 84 (1987), 440–70; N. F. Blake, 'Caxton Prepares His Edition of the *Morte Arthur*', in *William Caxton and English Literary Culture*, ed. N. F. Blake (London: Hambledon, 1991), pp. 199–212. See also Catherine Batt, *Malory's Morte D'Arthur: Remaking Arthurian Tradition* (London: Palgrave, 2002), pp. 38–42. An alternative view is put forward by S. Carole Weinberg, who suggests that Malory's *Morte* may have been brought to Caxton's attention by Anthony Woodville: S. Carole Weinberg 'Caxton, Anthony Woodville, and the Prologue to the Morte Darthur', *Studies in Philology*, 102.1 (2005), 45–65.

[13] Antonia Gransden, *Legends, Traditions and History in Medieval England* (London: Hambledon, 1992), pp. 24–25.

sites like Glastonbury Abbey and Dover Castle into the notebooks of itinerant site visitors, chronicles, tailor-made defences of Arthur, and ultimately the ambitious *fin de siècle* chorographies produced at the turn of the seventeenth century that fundamentally shape our impression of Arthurian localities today. This book could not have been written without the important groundwork laid by scholars such as Richard Utz, Robert Rouse, Cory Rushton, and Catherine A. M. Clarke, all of whom have had something to say about Arthurian geographies.[14] Those who have broken ground in challenging the periodisation of the medieval and the modern, such as Margreta de Grazia and Helen Cooper, have also paved the way for a treatment of the local Arthur and his medieval and early modern continuities.[15] Previous interest in the local Arthur includes several gazetteers of Arthurian locations, and since the early 1990s there have been a number of more focused studies that shed light on the cultural impact of a select number of Arthurian places in specific geographical areas such as Cornwall, Wales, and Glastonbury.[16]

---

[14] Richard Utz, 'Hic Iacet Arthurus? Situating the Medieval King in English Renaissance Memory', in *Studies in Medievalism XXXI: Memory and Medievalism*, ed. Karl Fugelso (Cambridge: D. S. Brewer, 2006), pp 26–40; Rouse and Rushton, 'Arthurian Geography'; Catherine A. M. Clarke, *Literary Landscapes and the Idea of England, 700–1400* (Cambridge: D. S. Brewer, 2006). See also Ad Putter and Kate McClune, 'The Geographies of Later Medieval Arthurian Literature in England and Scotland', in *La matière arthurienne tardive en Europe 1270–1530*, ed. Christine Ferlampin-Acher (Rennes: Presses Universitaires de Rennes, 2020), pp. 1049–58.

[15] Margreta de Grazia, 'The Modern Divide: From Either Side', *Journal of Medieval and Early Modern Studies*, 37.3 (2007), 453–67; Helen Cooper, *The English Romance in Time: Transforming Motifs from Geoffrey of Monmouth to the Death of Shakespeare* (Oxford: Oxford University Press, 2004); Helen Cooper, *Shakespeare and the Medieval World* (London: Arden Shakespeare, 2010); Helen Cooper, 'The Origins of the Early Modern', *Journal for Early Modern Cultural Studies*, 13.3 (2013), 133–37. See also *Medieval into Renaissance: Essays for Helen Cooper*, ed. Andrew King and Matthew Woodcock (Cambridge: D. S. Brewer, 2016).

[16] Such gazetteers include Geoffrey Ashe, *A Guidebook to Arthurian Britain* (London: Longman, 1980); Caitlin Green, *Arthuriana: Early Arthurian Tradition and the Origins of the Legend*, 2nd edn (Louth: Lindes Press, 2021). On Arthur in the South-West and Cornwall, see O. J. Padel, 'Some South-Western Sites with Arthurian Associations', in *The Arthur of the Welsh* (Cardiff: University of Wales Press, 1991), pp. 227–48; O. J. Padel, 'The Nature of Arthur', *Cambrian Medieval Celtic Studies*, 27 (1994), 1–31; and Oliver J. Padel, 'Cornwall and the Matter of Britain', in *Arthur in the Celtic Languages*, ed. Ceridwen Lloyd-Morgan and Erich Poppe (Cardiff: University of Wales Press, 2019), pp. 263–80. On Arthur's connections with Glastonbury, see *Glastonbury Abbey and the Arthurian Tradition*, ed. James Carley, 2nd edn (Cambridge: D. S. Brewer, 2001). On Arthurian associations in Wales, see Scott Lloyd, *The Arthurian Place Names of Wales* (Cardiff: University of Wales Press, 2017); Scott Lloyd, 'Arthurian Place-names of Wales', in *Arthur in the Celtic Languages*, ed. Ceridwen Lloyd-Morgan and Erich Poppe (Cardiff: University of Wales Press, 2019), pp. 231–44.

However, there has been no comprehensive attempt to trace or theorise the emergence of a local Arthur in the popular imagination – the Arthur that survives most obviously today, attached to hillforts, earthworks, ruins, towns, and castles. There is a new history of Arthur to be told, one comprising a collection of local histories; by picking up this thread and following it, it becomes clear that local places – cities, monasteries, natural landscapes – have been and remain essential to the longevity and allure of the Arthurian legend to this day, and that the local Arthur has distinctly medieval roots.

Defining the local

For many, the idea of the local Arthur immediately brings to mind the innumerable theories of Arthurian enthusiasts regarding the places where the 'real' King Arthur had his seat or battled his opponents.[17] These connotations might explain why scholars so far have been hesitant to focus their attentions squarely on Arthur's local iterations. When it comes to Arthur's places, we remain captivated, even though scholarly consensus today concludes that Arthur probably never existed.[18] Nonetheless,

---

[17] In addition to the seemingly unending flow of new publications on the subject, the question of locating the 'real' Arthur dominated Arthur scholarship in the nineteenth and early twentieth centuries; for example, see William Forbes Skene, *Four Ancient Books of Wales*, 2 vols (Edinburgh: Edmonston and Douglas, 1868); J. S. Stuart Glennie, *Arthurian Localities: Their Historical Origin, Chief Country and Fingalian Relations with a Map of Arthurian Scotland* (Edinburgh: Edmonston and Douglas, 1869); Dickinson, *King Arthur in Cornwall*; J. Cuming Walters, *The Lost Land of King Arthur* (London: Chapman and Hall, 1909).

[18] Contemporary scholarship largely follows the sharp advice of David Dumville: 'there is no historical evidence about Arthur; we must reject him from our histories and, above all, from the titles of our books'. David Dumville, 'Sub-Roman Britain: History and Legend', *History*, 62 (1977), 173–92 (p. 188). Dumville was responding to publications such as John Morris's *The Age of Arthur* (London: Weidenfeld and Nicolson, 1973) and Leslie Alcock's *Arthur's Britain: History and Archaeology AD 367–634* (London: Allen Lane, 1971). Dumville's conclusion is accepted and amplified in Thomas Charles-Edwards, 'The Early Welsh Arthurian Poems', in *The Arthur of the Welsh*, ed. Rachel Bromwich, A. O. H. Jarman and Brynley F. Roberts (Cardiff: University of Wales Press, 1991), pp. 15–32. There are two notable exceptions to this sceptical approach: Geoffrey Ashe, who argues that Arthur was really 'Riotamus', a Romano-Britain (Geoffrey Ashe, 'The Origins of the Arthurian Legend', *Arthuriana*, 5.3 [1995], 1–24); and Andrew Breeze, who argues the case for a Strathclydian Arthur or 'Artorius', largely on an onomastic basis (Andrew Breeze, 'The Early Welsh Cult of Arthur: Some Points at Issue', *Studia Celtica Posnaniensia*, 1.1 [2016], 1–13). Whilst a firm rebuttal of Breeze's theory would be most welcome, Ashe's 'real' Arthur has since been disputed by several scholars: see O. J. Padel, 'Recent Work on the Origins of the Arthurian Legend: A Comment', *Arthuriana*, 5.3 (1995), 102–14; R. W. Hanning, '*Inventio Arthuri*: A Comment on the Essays of Geoffrey Ashe and D. R. Howlett', *Arthuriana*, 5.3 (1995), 96–100. The debate as to

Arthur continues to inspire perennial claims from truth-seekers as to his real identity and his authentic locations, remaining (along with Robin Hood) one of the British legendary figures who we are most ready to believe existed.[19] It is not my intention to discover whether or not Arthur existed nor to make claims about where we might find him. The purpose of this book is rather to examine the process by which Arthur became associated with local places, and the ideological uses to which Arthur's geography was subsequently put in defending his existence. My aim is not to uncover what Arthur's places are, but rather what they can do. In order to achieve this, it is first necessary to clarify what I mean when I speak of the local Arthur.

Powerful places have played an important part in the Arthurian tradition from its earliest inception: we might observe, for example, the distinct Wirral topographies of *Sir Gawain and the Green Knight* (c. 1350–1400), the concentration of Arthurian places in Geoffrey of Monmouth's native south-west Wales in the *Historia regum Britanniae* (c. 1136), or the topographical Arthuriana in the ninth-century *Historia Brittonum*. There is, however, a sudden spate of material and textual evidence recording real-world (rather than literary) experiences of specific Arthurian sites surviving from the later Middle Ages, and for this reason it is largely the period between c. 1350 and 1700 on which this book is focused, and particularly the fifteenth and sixteenth centuries. Previous scholarship has tended to situate this particular vision of the local Arthur slightly later, in the landscape folklore consciously collected by antiquarians between the sixteenth and nineteenth centuries. Often, this local Arthur is imagined in contrast to the grander imperial figure of the Middle Ages and early Tudor period, and he is sometimes parsed as less important, with this period representing a low point in the history of Arthur's waxing and waning significance. The early modern period has been described in Arthurian scholarship as an Arthurian 'barren age' or 'nadir',[20] a time

---

Arthur's existence is summarised in N. J. Higham, *King Arthur: Myth-Making and History* (London: Routledge, 2002), pp. 1–9; and most recently in P. J. C. Field, 'King Arthur: Hero or Legend?', in *The Arthurian World*, ed. Victoria Coldham-Fussell, Miriam Edlich-Muth, and Renée Ward (London: Routledge, 2022), pp. 25–34.

[19] A survey of almost 3,000 British teenagers in 2008 found that King Arthur was the mythical figure most commonly considered to have existed: 65 per cent of respondents believed so, whilst 47 per cent believed Richard the Lionheart to be fictional. Aislinn Simpson, 'Winston Churchill Didn't Really Exist, Say Teens', *The Telegraph*, 4 February 2008, www.telegraph.co.uk/news/uknews/1577511/Winston-Churchill-didnt-really-exist-say-teens.html [accessed 7 February 2020].

[20] Alan Lupack, 'The Arthurian Legend in the Sixteenth to Eighteenth Centuries', in *A Companion to Arthurian Literature*, ed. Helen Fulton (Oxford: Blackwell, 2012), pp. 340–54 (p. 340); E. van der Ven-Ten Bensel, *The Character of King Arthur*

when Arthur 'ceases to be important' or remains accommodated only in 'a minor and local role'.[21] The implication seems to be that in the face of increasing scepticism Arthur was forced to retreat to local places, just as the Britons were said to have 'retreated to Cornwall and Wales, the western parts of the kingdom' according to Geoffrey of Monmouth.[22]

The association of the local with the unimportant or the parochial calls to mind contemptuous attitudes towards local history that have only lately begun to shift. Local histories have previously been dismissed as unimportant, and the work of the local historian snubbed as inadequately rigorous. John Beckett argues that the marginalisation of local history as 'parochial, antiquarian, and not "proper" history' has its roots in the increasingly professionalised and nationally focused histories of the nineteenth century.[23] These national histories still influence the way that we think about the practice of studying and writing history today, and the study of the Arthurian tradition in particular. Grand iterations of Arthur – Arthur as king, Arthur as emperor, Arthur as national symbol – have proven far more popular as research subjects than more localised visions of Arthur.[24]

(Amsterdam: H. J. Paris, 1925), pp. 169–74. See also Stephen Knight, *Arthurian Literature and Society* (London: Palgrave Macmillan, 1983), p. 149.

[21] Christopher Dean, *Arthur of England: English Attitudes to King Arthur and the Knights of the Round Table in the Middle Ages and Renaissance* (Toronto: University of Toronto Press, 1987), p. 107; Higham, *Myth-Making and History*, p. 241. See also David N. Klausner, 'The Historical Arthur: Dryden's Great Leap Backwards', *Restoration: Studies in English Literary Culture, 1660–1700*, 34.1–2 (2010), 21–32.

[22] '[T]he remnants of the Britons had retreated to Cornwall and Wales, the western parts of the kingdom' (Secesserunt itaque Britonum reliquiae in occidentalibus regni partibus, Cornubiam uidelicet atque Gualias). Geoffrey of Monmouth, *The History of the Kings of Britain: An Edition and Translation of De Gestis Britonum (Historia Regum Britanniae)*, ed. Michael D. Reeve and trans. Neil Wright (Woodbridge: Boydell, 2007), pp. 257–58.

[23] John Beckett, *Writing Local History* (Manchester: Manchester University Press, 2007), pp. xi–xii, pp. 70–80.

[24] On the Tudors' interest in Arthur, see Roberta Florence Brinkley, *Arthurian Legend in the Seventeenth Century* (London: Cass, 1932), pp. 1–25; Richard Koebner, '"The Imperial Crown of this Realm": Henry VIII, Constantine the Great, and Polydore Vergil', *Bulletin of the Institute of Historical Research*, 26.73 (1953), 29–52; E. B. Millican, *Spenser and the Table Round*, 2nd edn (London: Cass, 1967), pp. 7–36; David Starkey, 'King Henry and King Arthur', *Arthurian Literature*, 26 (1998), 171–96; Pamela Tudor-Craig, 'Iconography of the Painting', in *King Arthur's Round Table: An Archaeological Investigation*, ed. Martin Biddle (Woodbridge: Boydell, 2000), pp. 285–333; Stewart Mottram, '"An Empire of Itself": Arthur as Icon of an English Empire, 1509–1547', *Arthurian Literature*, 25 (2008), 256–73. There is also a wealth of scholarship on Arthurian propaganda under earlier monarchs. Some examples include R. S. Loomis, 'Edward I, Arthurian Enthusiast', *Speculum*, 28 (1953), 114–27; Jonathan Hughes, *Arthurian Myths and Alchemy: The Kingship of Edward IV* (Stroud: Sutton, 2002); *Edward III's Round Table at Windsor: The House of the Round Table and*

The implied local–national dichotomy is problematic, not least because our modern notions of national, regional, and local identity categories do not map easily onto the premodern British archipelago. Several modernist scholars (most notably Benedict Anderson, whose imagined communities are discussed below) assert that there was no concept of nationhood at all prior to the eighteenth century, while others identify the emergence of national consciousness with early modernity.[25] There is divergence among medievalists, and although many have since offered a corrective to Anderson there is no consensus as to whether this should be done on Anderson's own terms – the temporal goal posts simply moved backward – or whether those terms are themselves inadequate for discussions about nation in the premodern British Isles.[26] The enormous variety of linguistic, ethnic, and political affinities within premodern Britain (and, indeed, the complicated relationships that these affinities engendered with other peoples and places – the use of the

---

the *Windsor Festival of 1344*, ed. Julian Munby, Richard Barber, and Richard Brown (Woodbridge: Boydell, 2007); Martin Aurell, 'Henry II and Arthurian Legend', in *Henry II: New Interpretations*, ed. C. Harper-Bill and N. Vincent (Woodbridge: Boydell, 2007), pp. 365–94; Christopher Michael Berard, 'Edward III's Abandoned Order of the Round Table Revisited: Political Arthurianism After Poitiers', *Arthurian Literature*, 33 (2016), 70–109; Christopher Michael Berard, *Arthurianism in Early Plantagenet England* (Woodbridge: Boydell, 2019). Other scholars take a broader view on Arthur's value as a sovereign symbol. See, for example, Patricia Clare Ingham, *Sovereign Fantasies: Arthurian Romance and the Making of Britain* (Philadelphia, PA: University of Pennsylvania Press, 2001). For a discussion of Arthur's use as a national symbol in medieval Scotland, see R. James Goldstein, *The Matter of Scotland: Historical Narrative in Medieval Scotland* (Lincoln, NE: University of Nebraska Press, 1993).

[25] *Nationalism*, ed. Elie Kedourie (London: Hutchinson, 1960); Ernest Gellner, *Nation and Nationalism* (Oxford: Blackwell, 1983); Benedict Anderson, *Imagined Communities: Reflections on the Origin and Spread of Nationalism*, 3rd edn (London: Verso, 2006); E. J. Hobsbawm, *Nations and Nationalism Since 1780: Programme, Myth, Reality* (Cambridge: Cambridge University Press, 1990). Proponents of an early modern inception include Richard Helgerson, *Forms of Nationhood: The Elizabethan Writing of England* (Chicago, IL: Chicago University Press, 1992); Claire McEachern, *The Poetics of English Nationhood, 1590–1612* (Cambridge: Cambridge University Press, 1996); and Cathy Shrank, *Writing the Nation in Reformation England, 1530–1580* (Oxford: Oxford University Press, 2004).

[26] The debate is characterised as one of 'discontinuity' and 'continuity with the past' in Ardis Butterfield, *The Familiar Enemy: Chaucer, Language, and Nation in the Hundred Years War* (Oxford University Press, 2009), p. 30. The rebuttals to Anderson are many, and include Thorlac Turville-Petre, *England the Nation: Language, Literature, and National Identity, 1290–1340* (Oxford: Clarendon Press, 1996); Derek Pearsall, 'The Idea of Englishness in the Fifteenth Century', in *Nation, Court and Culture: New Essays on Fifteenth-Century English Poetry*, ed. Helen Cooney (Dublin: Four Courts Press, 2001), pp. 15–27; *Imagining a Medieval English Nation*, ed. Kathy Lavezzo (Minneapolis, MN: University of Minnesota Press, 2004); and Armstrong and Hodges, *Mapping Malory*, pp. 11–13.

French language in England, for example) have led some to suggest that difference or variety, rather than unity, was essential to the construction of nation at this time.²⁷ Other scholars suggest that finding points of mutuality helped the varied inhabitants of the medieval and early modern British Isles to generate a sense of unity and perhaps (among the English, at least) a nascent national consciousness. This might be *literal* common ground in the form of shared landscapes and geographies (as Kathy Lavezzo, Laura Ashe, and Catherine A. M. Clarke attest) or, more figuratively, a shared language, king, or common Other against whom a collective identity might be built.²⁸ Most important, for my purposes here, is the suggestion of an ambivalent relationship between local and regional identities and the national imaginary: while some have argued that smaller scale communities and regions 'complicate any effort to locate a medieval English nation', others have clearly demonstrated that regional identities in the Middle Ages could work in tandem with and perhaps even towards a national consciousness.²⁹ This all suggests that local Arthurian places could be powerful building blocks in imaginative

---

[27] Andrew Galloway, 'Latin England', in *Imagining a Medieval English Nation*, pp. 41–95 (p. 59); Ardis Butterfield, 'National Histories', in *Cultural Reformations: Medieval and Renaissance in Literary History*, ed. Brian Cummings and James Simpson (Oxford University Press, 2010), pp. 33–55 (p. 39); Kathy Lavezzo, 'Nation', in *A Handbook of Middle English Studies*, ed. Marion Turner (London: Wiley, 2013), pp. 363–78 (pp. 368–69).

[28] Clarke, *Literary Landscapes*; Laura Ashe, *Fiction and History in England, 1066–1200* (Cambridge: Cambridge University Press, 2007); Kathy Lavezzo, *Angels on the Edge of the World: Geography, Literature, and English Community, 1000–1534* (Ithaca, NY: Cornell University Press, 2006); Galloway, 'Latin England', p. 51. On the importance of language to national thinking, see Turville-Petre, *England the Nation*, p. 11; Robert Bartlett, *The Making of Europe: Conquest, Colonization and Cultural Change 950–1350* (London: Penguin, 2003), pp. 198–202; Butterfield, 'National Histories', p. 36 (although Butterfield's stance is that this is complicated by the Latin and French of England). On the importance of the king to nationalist ideology in medieval England, see Geraldine Heng, 'The Romance of England: Richard Coer De Lyon, Saracens, Jews, and the Politics of Race and Nation', in *The Postcolonial Middle Ages*, ed. Jeffrey Jerome Cohen (New York: Palgrave Macmillan, 2000), pp. 135–71 (p. 139). On oppositional models of identity formation (that is, the creation of a common Other), see Thomas H. Crofts and Robert Allen Rouse, 'Middle English Popular Romance and National Identity', in *A Companion to Medieval Popular Romance*, ed. Raluca L. Radulescu and Cory James Rushton (Cambridge: D. S. Brewer, 2009), pp. 79–95 (p. 83); Jeffrey J. Cohen, *Of Giants: Sex, Monsters, and the Middle Ages* (Minneapolis, MN: Minnesota University Press, 1999), pp. 132–33; Siobhain Bly Calkin, *Saracens and the Making of English Identity: The Auchinleck Manuscript* (London: Taylor and Francis, 2013); Mary Bateman, 'The Native Place of That Great Arthur: Foreignness and Nativity in Sixteenth-Century Defences of Arthur', *Arthurian Literature*, 35 (2019), 152–72.

[29] Lavezzo, 'Nation', pp. 365–66; Clarke, *Literary Landscapes*, pp. 67–68; Turville-Petre, *England the Nation*, p. 143. See also Robert W. Barrett Jr, *All England: Regional Identity*

nation-building, given that they could represent both shared geographies and a shared king (and sometimes, as I suggest in Chapter 4, were co-opted against a perceived common enemy).

We might therefore think of the relationship between the local and national spheres in terms of how place is imagined, rather than simply framing the two terms oppositionally. Although medievalists have been quick to disagree with Benedict Anderson regarding the emergence of national thought, Anderson's work has nevertheless provided rich ground for investigating the possibility of a premodern national consciousness through his idea of the nation as an imagined community. For Anderson, the nation is 'imagined' because 'the members of even the smallest nation will never know most of their fellow-members, meet them, or even hear of them, yet in the minds of each lives the image of their communion'.[30] No individual can experience or visualise a nation in its entirety and all at once. This is why mnemonic national symbols have developed through history: in the modern era this has included the flag, the map logo, the national anthem.[31] These latter phenomena are all the products of modernity, enabled by mass communication, although this is not to say that rapid, wide-scale communication was unknown in the Middle Ages: the speed and breadth with which news spread of the 1191 discovery of Arthur's 'grave' at Glastonbury Abbey has led at least one scholar to theorise a campaign of pamphlet distribution.[32] In the premodern period, local places could also operate effectively as mnemonics for 'imagined communities' of larger scales, and it is partly my aim in this book to demonstrate how local places came to be publicised so widely and effectively by Arthur's defenders, with the aim of also defending whatever collective identity Arthur represented to them. Though local places may not be created from scratch for the purposes of mnemonic function, like the examples listed above, Arthurian sites were carefully managed and reshaped over time to adapt them to this purpose.[33] Local places can also be powerful mnemonics

---

and Cheshire Writing, 1195–1656 (Notre Dame, IN: University of Notre Dame Press, 2009); Armstrong and Hodges, *Mapping Malory*, p. 11.

[30] Anderson, *Imagined Communities*, p. 6.

[31] Gabriella Elgenius, *Symbols of Nations and Nationalism: Celebrating Nationhood* (London: Palgrave Macmillan, 2011), p. 1.

[32] Antonia Gransden, 'The Growth of the Glastonbury Traditions and Legends in the Twelfth Century', in *Glastonbury Abbey and the Arthurian Tradition*, pp. 29–54 (p. 50).

[33] Two examples discussed below are Winchester and Stirling (pp. 133–34). Both places were used as the symbolic hearts of England (by Edward I) and Scotland (by David II) respectively, and both monarchs made artificial 'Arthurian' constructions to support the impression of the legendary king's connection with each site.

for trans- and sub-national communities as well as the nation, for 'all communities larger than primordial villages of face-to-face contact (and perhaps even these) are imagined' according to Anderson.[34] While Anderson was concerned primarily with the idea of the nation, imagined communities can take many forms.[35]

Local places (which *can* be experienced face-to-face, even if such experiences are mediated in some way) therefore contribute to the formation of 'imagined communities' of all sizes and varieties. As such, the importance of Arthurian places to various kinds of 'imagined communities' (local, regional, national, historic), and the interrelation between these communities, cannot be overstated. Communities of different scales rely on each other for definition. As Doreen Massey asserts in her discussion of localism and globalism, local places are not simply 'victims of the global' nor 'politically defensible redoubts *against* the global'; rather, it is in the sphere of local places that 'globalisation is produced: the moments through which the global is constituted, invented, coordinated. They [local places] are "agents" in globalisation.'[36] For these reasons, to speak of the emergence of the local Arthur as a retreat away from the national is inaccurate.

If the local is not the antithesis of the national, then what is it? Experiences of place are an important component of how I define the local Arthur, the subject of this book. Locality suggests familiarity, and the process by which an individual becomes familiar with an Arthurian location is reflexive. Visitors to Arthurian sites experience such places quite differently depending on many factors – their emotions, political affiliations, or sense of personal and collective identity – and a site's custodians will be similarly influenced when it comes to how they interpret an Arthurian place. At the same time, powerful places are capable of inspiring and perhaps even shaping a sense of individual or collective identity, as the impact of Arthurian places on the construction of an emergent sense of early modern "Britishness" makes clear.[37] My approach to the local in this book, then, aligns with Arjun Appadurai's definition of locality as 'relational and contextual [...] constituted by a series of links between the sense of social immediacy, the technologies of

---

[34] Anderson, *Imagined Communities*, p. 6.
[35] See, for example, Helen Fulton, 'Regions and Communities', in *The Oxford Handbook of Medieval Literature in English*, ed. Greg Walker and Elaine Treharne (Oxford: Oxford University Press, 2010), pp. 515–39.
[36] Doreen Massey, *For Space* (London: SAGE, 2005), p. 101.
[37] See Chapters 4 and 5 below.

interactivity, and the relativity of contexts'.[38] This definition of locality-as-familiarity intersects with various theories of place prevalent within the study of human geography. Yi-Fu Tuan distinguishes space from place based on how humans fill it with meaning: 'what begins as an undifferentiated space becomes place as we get to know it better and endow it with value'.[39] Place familiarity occurs when someone has come to know a place in their own way: either through living their daily lives in and around it, through repeated visits, or perhaps by experiencing a certain location through many affective textual encounters. Tuan associates place with 'pause', suggestive of a settled idea of a location's value, and space as 'that which allows movement', which indicates freedom.[40] This duality is echoed by Michel de Certeau, though framed in terms of how individual practice subverts the strictures of planned places: 'space is a practiced place. Thus the street geometrically defined by urban planning is transformed into a space by walkers.'[41] In other words, a managed Arthurian site might be interpreted in such a way as to encourage a certain collective response to it – a settled, familiar sense of place as Tuan defines it – but, in reality, every visitor will navigate these sites differently, and come away with their own sense of how they fit in with their existing worlds. Although Tuan's place-as-pause and de Certeau's practiced place appear to come from quite different angles, they both indicate a process of becoming familiar with a location. Repeating the same routes through a city, stopping to take in the stained glass of a cathedral, or simply reading about a site's history through the medium of text prior to a personal visit allows an individual to get to know a place, and to orient it (or re-orient it, in de Certeau's case) towards their own sense of self. For a place to feel local, it must feel intimately familiar.

Places are therefore locations that have become meaningful, functioning as symbolic reminders for other collective identities: a people group, a region, or a nation. This means that the local and national iterations of Arthur are not diametrically opposed, nor are they mutually exclusive; rather, they are mutually supportive. Local Arthurian places function as mnemonics for larger imagined communities.

---

[38] Arjun Appadurai, 'The Production of Locality', in *Modernity at Large: Cultural Dimensions of Globalization* (Minneapolis, MN: University of Minnesota Press, 1996), pp. 178–204 (p. 178).
[39] Yi-Fu Tuan, *Space and Place: The Perspective of Experience* (Minneapolis, MN: University of Minnesota Press, 1977), p. 6.
[40] Tuan, *Space and Place*, p. 6.
[41] Michel de Certeau, *The Practice of Everyday Life*, trans. Steven Rendall (Oakland, CA: University of California Press, 1984), p. 117.

Contested places

If local places are crucial to the construction of conceptually larger units, such as the nation, it is understandable that places are not neutral, and can be contested. Regardless of how the custodian of a space manages it in order to try and influence the experiences of those who move through it, spaces can be navigated and interpreted differently depending on the values and intentions of whoever is experiencing them. The contested nature of space is perhaps especially true for locations connected with Arthur, a figure associated with different kinds of identity. To return to the example of Tintagel, the intense Arthurianisation of Tintagel town has not been without controversy. Within the debate, Arthur has been framed variously as either a local Celtic hero or an anglicised symbol of British unity.[42]

Historically, too, Arthur himself, and therefore the places connected with him, were heavily contested. As scepticism surrounding parts of Arthur's story grew around the turn of the sixteenth century, Arthur's defenders moved quickly to locate what they saw as Arthur's real places. The areas drawn out for Arthur differed depending on the agendas and identities of the people creating them. I do not mean to suggest that the motives for locating Arthur in any particular region were conscious and cynical, but rather that there might be other factors at play – other kinds of absolute belief, ideologies, identities – that might cause an individual to believe in some Arthurian places more readily than others. For Arthur's defenders, the construction of Arthurian regions was also a powerful strategy for shoring up the believability of Arthur's existence, but the realism of Arthur's places is supported by other kinds of constructed realities. In fact, to defend Arthur's existence, to make Arthur seem nearer at hand and more real, was also to defend whatever personal or collective identities Arthur was seen to represent, identities that may have felt under threat in the rapidly shifting political landscape of the British Isles during the 1500s. As Yi-Fu Tuan puts it, 'to strengthen our sense of self the past needs to be rescued and made accessible'.[43] For the Welsh chronicler Elis Gruffydd, for example, Arthur's places were predominantly to be found in northern Wales, centred around Gruffydd's own native places. On the other hand, the West Country was drawn out as a valid space for Arthur by antiquaries in support of a united England and Wales, like Leland. The

---

[42] Orange and Laviolette, 'A Disgruntled Tourist', passim; Amy Hale, 'Representing the Cornish: Contesting Heritage Interpretation in Cornwall', *Tourist Studies*, 1.2 (2001), 185–96.
[43] Tuan, *Space and Place*, p. 187.

South-West provided the ideal location, not only because Glastonbury – the least contested of Arthur's places – could be placed at its centre, but also because this area sat at the gateway between England and Wales and was therefore a prudent space in which to cultivate the impression of an ancient united Britain.

While a south-western Arthurian region might have sprung up and flourished within the particular learned communities investigated in this book, it must nevertheless be reasserted that Arthurian regions are not singular and concentric but plural and overlapping. Although my focus is predominantly Arthurian localities in late medieval and early modern South-West England and Wales, it would be equally possible to discuss how Arthurian regions in the North of England and Scotland were formed, or in Cornwall specifically, or more broadly in Western Europe. Regions, in this sense, are perhaps the most imaginative and flexible kind of imagined communities: they can be large or small; they can overlap; and they can shift and change across time depending on who is imagining them, and for what purpose.

Arthur's defenders differed not only in terms of where they located Arthur on account of their individual political and cultural allegiances, but also in where they located the source of the attack on Arthur. Many of the writers discussed in this book were invested, to a greater or lesser extent, in supporting the impression of Arthur's historicity because they were also invested in what Arthur symbolised to them. For the fifteenth-century chronicler John Rous, Arthur's magnificence went hand-in-hand with promoting Rous' own locality in Warwick. Others saw in Arthur the pinnacle of England's historic victories over the French or the Scots. For John Leland, John Prise, and William Camden Arthur represented a unified Britain; and the Welsh chronicler Elis Gruffydd saw Arthur as a sophisticated historic British king who vanquished both English and continental foes. For many, the biggest threat to Arthur's historicity was the Urbino-born humanist Polydore Vergil (c. 1470–1555), whose criticisms of Britain's mythical foundation and history seemed to strike at the heart of Britain's very existence.[44] Polydore was characterised by his respondents, and indeed by some modern scholars, as an explicit doubter of Arthur's very existence, even though he never expressed such doubts.[45] This is due in no small part to Polydore's status as an Italian:

---

[44] Polydore's criticisms, and the xenophobic responses to them, are discussed more fully in Chapter 4.

[45] James P. Carley, 'Polydore Vergil and John Leland on King Arthur: The Battle of the Books', *Interpretations*, 15.2 (1984), 86–100. See also Arthur B. Ferguson, *Utter Antiquity: Perceptions of Prehistory in Renaissance England* (Durham, NC:

for his contemporary critics he represented Rome's historic and present threats to Britain's independence and antecedence; and scholars such as Denys Hay characterise Polydore as a 'man of letters', an embodiment of the Italian humanistic Renaissance and the healthy scepticism that came with it.[46]

In order to grasp what was at stake in Polydore's perceived attack on British history, it is important to explain what exactly is meant by the term 'Britain', both here and throughout this book. Britain as it exists today is also imagined, not only in the terms set by Benedict Anderson but also because it is a reconstitution of many other past Britains.[47] This causes us some issues of terminology: what do we mean by 'Britain' or 'British'? Britain is not a fixed but an unstable unit that has changed over time, and indeed questions of devolution suggest that it may change again.[48] This book touches upon various Britains, and we should not imagine them as interchangeable: though related, they are separate constructions.[49] 'The British History' refers specifically to the version of Britain put forward by Geoffrey of Monmouth.[50] Geoffrey of Monmouth's *Historia regum Britanniae* [History of the Kings of Britain] (1136) describes Britain's history and foundation myths, beginning with its foundation by Brutus and spanning the reigns of the legendary British kings, ending

---

Duke University Press, 1993), pp. 84–105. Contemporary assertions of Polydore's Arthurian disbelief include Denys Hay, *Polydore Vergil: Renaissance Historian and Man of Letters* (Oxford: Clarendon Press, 1952), p. 158; Higham, *Myth-Making and History*, p. 236; Philip Schwyzer, 'Archipelagic History', in *The Oxford Handbook of Holinshed's Chronicles*, ed. Paulina Kewes, Ian W. Archer, and Felicity Heal (Oxford: Oxford University Press, 2013), pp. 593–608 (p. 596). Correctives to this view have been offered in Christopher Dean, *Arthur of England*, pp. 20–21; David A. Summers, 'Re-fashioning Arthur in the Tudor Era', *Exemplaria*, 9.2 (1997), 371–92 (pp. 378–79); and James P. Carley, 'Arthur and the Antiquaries', in *The Arthur of Medieval Latin Literature*, ed. Siân Echard (Cardiff: University of Wales Press, 2011), pp. 149–78.

[46] Denys Hay, *Polydore Vergil*, passim.
[47] Anderson, *Imagined Communities*, p. 6.
[48] The changing shape of Britain is explored in *Uniting the Kingdom? The Making of British History*, ed. Alexander Grant and Keith J. Stringer (London: Routledge, 1995).
[49] On the shifting conception of Britain from the twelfth to the seventeenth centuries, see Alan Maccoll, 'The Meaning of "Britain" in Medieval and Early Modern England', *Journal of British Studies*, 45.2 (2006), 248–69.
[50] On 'The British History', see Philip Schwyzer, 'British History and "The British History": The Same Old Story?', in *British Identities and English Renaissance Literature*, ed. David J. Baker and Willy Maley (Cambridge: Cambridge University Press, 2002), pp. 11–23; J. G. A. Pocock, 'British History: A Plea for a New Subject', *The Journal of Modern History*, 47.4 (1975), 601–21; R. R. Davies, *The Matter of Britain and the Matter of England: An Inaugural Lecture Delivered before the University of Oxford on 29 February 1996* (Oxford: Clarendon Press, 1996).

with Cadwallader.⁵¹ Arthur is a major focus of the *Historia*, and Geoffrey's work represents the earliest detailed description of Arthur's reign that survives. The idea of Britain for much of the Middle Ages hinged upon Geoffrey's text. There is also the revivalist Britain that began to emerge in the fifteenth and sixteenth centuries, which referred back to Geoffrey's Britain. I distinguish between this reconstituted Britain and the Anglo-Welsh state in this book because the former is only an idea (or ideal), whereas the latter is an administrative unit. The idea of Britain as a contemporary (rather than a historic) unit emerged gradually over the course of two centuries, perhaps as a result of political union (rather than as a precursor to it). As Armstrong and Hodges have pointed out, 'groups [that] share the same sovereign [may] begin to imagine themselves as a community', although the thought of a shared Arthurian origin would have contributed significantly to this conceptual unification.⁵² Another issue is that Britain as we know it today refers to more than just England and Wales. To use the term Britain to refer to the Anglo-Welsh union of the mid-sixteenth century risks anachronism because it ignores Scotland's joining of the Union in the early eighteenth century, an event which falls outside the temporal remit of this book. Wherever I have used 'Britain' or 'British' as a descriptor, I intend it as the authors of my source texts would have understood it in their own terms. For Galfridian sceptic William Camden, Britain meant a revival of the Roman *Britannia*. For Galfridian defender John Leland, Britain implied the realm founded by Brutus.

In addition to the changing shape of Britain over time, we are also confronted with the problem that 'British' is frequently used as a lazy shorthand for 'English'. In his field-changing plea for a different approach to British history, J. G. A. Pocock used the term 'British history'

> for lack [...] of a better term – to denote the plural history of a group of cultures situated along an Anglo-Celtic frontier and marked by an increasing English political and cultural domination.⁵³

Pocock called for a more pluralist, less Anglocentric approach to thinking about and writing British history, one which synthesises different perspectives and focuses on the points of connection and

---

⁵¹ Geoffrey's text is widely known as *Historia regum Britanniae* (1136), and I use this title throughout this book as it remains the most widely recognised. However, this was likely not how the text was originally known: Michael Reeve and Neil Wright have found that it was more commonly known as *De gestis Britonum* for much of the Middle Ages. See Geoffrey of Monmouth, *The History of the Kings of Britain*, passim.
⁵² Armstrong and Hodges, *Mapping Malory*, p. 11.
⁵³ J. G. A. Pocock, 'British History: A Plea for a New Subject', p. 605.

conflict between the various people groups of the British Isles. Pocock's plea has led to a heightened awareness of what has now been termed the 'British Problem', and a more pluralist approach in the writing of British history since its time of writing.[54] In response to Pocock's plea, the following pages are not restricted to Arthurian places considered from the perspective of English writers; instead, I draw on the works of writers from England and Wales with diverse ideas about their own identities, taking into account intersections between their political, linguistic, and ethnic affiliations. The West Country and Wales, the area on which this book is focused, represents a point of contact and contestation between two distinct British cultures, and especially during the sixteenth century. Although the transportive power of place continues to operate within virtually all imagined communities, Arthurian geography is imagined very differently depending on who is doing the imagining (and in what contexts). For example, those in favour of Anglo-Welsh political union under Henry VIII might see themselves as English, Welsh, British, or some combination of these. They might also identify to a greater or lesser extent with the Britons and the Briton language. Until the mid-sixteenth century, the Britons (and indeed the British) were largely treated as a historic people group distinct from the contemporary *Walliae* or Welsh. On the other hand, the Briton language was seen as a still-living language spoken by the Welsh.[55] Neither were these identities – English, Welsh, British, Briton – fixed. Arthur's defenders had multiple national, transnational, and subnational identities, and were capable of conceiving of and performing these identities differently in diverse contexts.[56] As Doreen Massey has argued, 'the identities of place are always unfixed, contested and multiple'.[57]

These dynamics are especially important to bear in mind when we consider how Arthurian regions were imagined at this time in

[54] Stewart Mottram, 'Empire, Exile, and England's "British Problem"': Recent Approaches to Spenser's *Shepheardes Calendar* as a Colonial and Postcolonial Test', *Literature Compass*, 4.4 (2007), 1059–77. A recent study which demonstrates this approach is Victoria Flood's *Prophecy, Politics and Place in Medieval England: From Geoffrey of Monmouth to Thomas of Erceldoune* (Cambridge: D. S. Brewer, 2016).
[55] See Philip Schwyzer, 'The Age of the Cambro-Britons: Hyphenated British Identities in the Seventeenth Century', *Seventeenth Century*, 33.4 (2018), 427–39.
[56] Andrea Ruddick, '"Becoming English": Nationality, Terminology, and Changing Sides in the Late Middle Ages', *Medieval Worlds*, 5 (2017), 57–69. See also Helen Fulton, 'Class and Nation: The English in Late-Medieval Welsh Poetry', in *Authority and Subjugation in Writing of Medieval Wales*, ed. Ruth Kennedy and Simon Meecham-Jones (London: Palgrave Macmillan, 2008), pp. 191–212.
[57] Doreen Massey, *Space, Place, and Gender* (Minneapolis, MN: University of Minnesota Press, 1994), p. 5.

England and Wales. The very term 'region' is fraught with associations of parochiality and marginalisation, and it should be used with care, particularly within the context of English and Welsh cultural geographies in the sixteenth century.[58] This period marked a major shift in the relationship between Wales and England, and a time of conscious regional self-fashioning in the context of cartographical developments and the emergence of the chorography.[59] The sixteenth century also saw regional divisions within Wales itself change dramatically. At the beginning of the century, Wales remained divided into two broad areas: the Principality in the north-west and south-west, which had long since been annexed to the English crown; and the March, an area comprising individual lordships operating independently of the crown, and running in a broad arc from north to south dividing Wales from England.[60] This division appears to have influenced how regional identity within Wales was articulated in the later Middle Ages, often in bilateral relation to other kinds of identity beyond Wales itself. Emily Dolman's analysis of the ancestral romance *Fouke de Fitzwaurin* (c. 1325–40), a text connected intimately with the March, suggests that the text is characterised by a strong sense of overlapping identities at different scales – both local and pan-insular, with the March conceived as 'the keystone that joins England and Wales, yoking together the [whole island] into a single geopolitical unit'.[61] Two centuries after *Fouke* was written, the Acts of Union (1536 and 1542) were passed annexing the whole of Wales to England, a development driven not only by regional pressures, such as a perceived need to bring law and

---

[58] The *Oxford English Dictionary* offers several definitions for 'region'; one identifies it as a 'the parts of a country outside the capital or chief seat of government. C.f. Province.' 'region, n.', *Oxford English Dictionary* Online (Oxford University Press, 2009), https://oed.com/view/Entry/161281?redirectedFrom=region (accessed 13 July 2020). The issue of regionality is discussed within the context of early modern Scotland in Sebastiaan Verweij, *The Literary Culture of Early Modern Scotland: Manuscript Production and Transmission, 1560–1625* (Oxford: Oxford University Press, 2016), p. 12.

[59] This increased focus on the region became even more pronounced in the seventeenth century; see Daniel Cattell and Philip Schwyzer, 'Introduction: Visions of Britain', *The Seventeenth Century*, 33.4 (2018), 377–91 (p. 383 and passim).

[60] In the North-West, the Principality included Anglesey, Caernarfon, and Merioneth; in the South-West, Carmarthen and Cardigan. Flintshire, which had been acquired by the English crown slightly later, sat under the jurisdiction of the Justice of Chester. On the Principality and March in the sixteenth century, see Glanmor Williams, *Renewal and Reformation: Wales c. 1415–1642* (Oxford: Oxford University Press, 1993), pp. 31–55, including a map of Principality and March at p. 33.

[61] Emily Dolmans, 'Locating the Border: Britain and the Welsh Marches in Fouke Le Fitz Waryn', *New Medieval Literatures*, 16 (2016), 109–34 (p. 112). See also Emily Dolmans, *Writing Regional Identities in Medieval England: From the* Gesta Herwardi *to* Richard Coer de Lyon (Cambridge: D. S. Brewer, 2020) at p. 102.

order to the Marches, but also international ones, such as the threat of foreign invasion via the coasts of Wales.[62] The Marcher territories were swept away, re-established as the new counties of Monmouth, Brecknock, Radnor, Montgomery, and Denbigh, with some parts absorbed into existing counties such as Shropshire and Gloucestershire.[63] The Acts brought Wales, as a whole, under the control of the English crown, and in the decades following the annexation Wales was repeatedly invoked in literature and culture as a distinct but important part of the Britain that began to emerge during the course of the century. Norman Jones and Daniel Woolf sum this up effectively in their analysis of Camden's *Britannia* (1586), a vision of Britain that effectively folded the Welsh counties in with their English equivalents: 'the sum, while greater than the parts, was also constituted by the parts; the treasure was in the details'.[64] In discussing how various actors imagined Arthurian regions in the sixteenth century, this context of a newly formed Anglo-Welsh state cannot be ignored, not least because Arthur could represent both a hero of the Welsh who would one day return to their aid, and also a symbol of pan-British empire with his power base in England.[65]

The power of place

For Arthur's defenders, their other affinities – political, cultural, or otherwise – were crucially linked to proving Arthur's existence: Arthur's historicity was a matter of importance because if Arthur was only a figure of fable, then the various ideals that he symbolised could also be brought into question and perhaps even dismantled altogether. Yet the question remains as to *why* Arthurian places were so appealing, not only to Arthur's most avid defenders such as John Leland and John Prise, but also more sceptical writers like Raphael Holinshed (and even, indeed, in our own sceptical present). The familiarity of Arthurian places was crucial to their ability to foster belief: as a place becomes more familiar through experience, it grows more capable of impressing the things it symbolises – both historic and ideological – as a *reality* into the mind of whoever is experiencing it.

---

[62] Williams, *Renewal and Reformation*, p. 266.
[63] Ibid.
[64] Norman L. Jones and Daniel Woolf, *Local Identities in Late Medieval and Early Modern England* (New York: Palgrave Macmillan, 2007), p. 221.
[65] The so-called Breton Hope – the belief in Arthur's return – is first attested in English and continental sources, rather than Welsh texts, from the twelfth century. It had, however, made its way into vaticinatory poetry in Wales by the sixteenth century. See Berard, *Arthurianism*, pp. 300–02; Ingham, *Sovereign Fantasies*, p. 61.

Cognitive theory can help us to understand the power of place to suspend disbelief, or to support 'make-believe'.[66] Richard Utz, one of the few scholars to have theorised the early modern treatment of Arthurian places, draws on the work of Eviatar Zerubavel to illustrate how places can enable a sense of connection with the distant past.[67] In *Time Maps*, Zerubavel outlines a process which he calls 'mnemonic bridging', consisting of

> strategies we normally use to help us create and maintain the illusion of historical continuity [...] different bridges we build – physical, calendrical, iconic, discursive – in an effort to 'connect' the past and the present.[68]

Zerubavel's 'mnemonic bridges' encapsulate a broad range of phenomena: anniversaries, for example (calendrical); constructing statues or painting portraits (iconic); or naming something after a particular historical figure (discursive). 'Physical' mnemonic bridges form an expansive sub-category, but places are of primary importance:

> one of the most effective ways of bridging the gap between noncontiguous points in history is by establishing a connection that allows them to almost literally touch one another [...] constancy of place is a formidable basis for establishing a strong sense of sameness.[69]

The description of two discrete points in history becoming seemingly proximal – 'almost literally touch[ing] one another' – suggests a quasi-spiritual dynamic to experiencing 'constancy of place' that echoes the notion of 'thin places'. Popular in New Age spirituality (contemporary Glastonbury might well be described as a thin place by some), thin places have been described rather poetically as locations 'where one's nerve

---

[66] The term 'make-believe' was first theorised by J. R. Morgan in 'Make-believe and Make Believe: The Fictionality of the Greek Novels', in *Lies and Fiction in the Ancient World*, ed. Christopher Gill (Liverpool: University of Liverpool Press, 1993), pp. 175–229. The concept has more often been used in discussions of the unspoken contract of suspended belief between an author of fiction and their reader, both of whom understand the work's status as a fiction. This terminology becomes more problematic when applied to Geoffrey of Monmouth's *Historia* and its reception, a text often dismissed as a 'fiction' but not exhibiting any signs that its author intended for it to be received as such. See D. H. Green, *The Beginnings of Medieval Romance: Fact and Fiction, 1150–1220* (Cambridge: Cambridge University Press, 2000), pp. 11–13.

[67] Utz, 'Hic Iacet Arthurus?', passim.

[68] Eviatar Zerubavel, *Time Maps: Collective Memory and the Social Shape of the Past* (Chicago, IL: University of Chicago Press, 2003), p. 8.

[69] Zerubavel, *Time Maps*, pp. 40–41.

endings are bare. People make pilgrimages to thin places, places where gods have made their mark on the land.'[70] Places are 'thin' when there is a sense of the otherworld being within reach – be it the fairy world, the spirit world, the realm of angels, or what you will. In the case of locations where something once took place in history (or is thought to have taken place), the thinness is rather a thinness of time.

The literary chronotope is also helpful for thinking about the power of Arthurian places. Mikhail Bakhtin defines the chronotope in terms of the particular relationship between time and space that takes shape in different literary genres. Bakhtin's description of the 'chronotope of the castle' or 'castle time' is markedly similar to Zerubavel's comments about 'constancy of place'. Bakhtin distinguishes castle time from the chronotope of the road, which he identifies with the questing knights of medieval romance. The chronotope of the road sees time and space marching together in tandem and wrapping around the physical location of the hero on the move. Or, as Robert Rouse puts it, 'this manner of theorising how space is revealed – or perhaps constructed – subjugates physical and geographical space to chivalric exploit, and to the needs and desires of the chivalric classes'.[71] Castle time, on the other hand, instead implies a gulf between sameness of space and temporal difference:

> The castle is the place where [...] the traces of centuries and generations are arranged [...] in visible form as various parts of its architecture, in furnishings, weapons, the ancestral portrait gallery [...] and finally legends and traditions animate every corner of the castle and its environs through their constant reminders of past events [...] the traces of time in the castle do bear a somewhat antiquated, museum-like character.[72]

---

[70] Ann Armbrecht, *Thin Places: A Pilgrimage Home* (New York: Columbia University Press, 2009), p. 87. The concept of thin places has had more impact in the fields of theology, medicine, and social care than it has in literary and historical studies. See, for example, Jeanne Merkle Sorrell, 'Listening in Thin Places: Ethics in the Care of Persons with Alzheimer's Disease', *Advances in Nursing Science*, 29.2 (2006), 152–60; Laura Béres, 'A Thin Place: Narratives of Space and Place, Celtic Spirituality and Meaning', *Journal of Religion and Spirituality in Social Work: Social Thought*, 31.4 (2012), 394–413. A literary exception is Laura Dabundo, 'Maria Edgeworth and the Irish "Thin Places"', in *New Essays on Maria Edgeworth*, ed. Julia Nash (London: Routledge, 2006), pp. 193–98.

[71] Robert Rouse, 'Walking (between) the Lines: Romance as Itinerary/Map', in *Medieval Romance, Medieval Contexts*, ed. Rhiannon Purdie and Michael Cichon (Cambridge: D. S. Brewer, 2011), pp. 135–48 (p. 142).

[72] Mikhail Bakhtin, 'Forms of Time and of the Chronotope in the Novel: Notes towards a Historical Poetics', in *The Dialogic Imagination: Four Essays*, ed. Michael Holquist, trans. Jay Wright (Austin, TX: University of Texas Press, 1981), pp. 84–258.

The tangible sameness of space inherent in 'castle time' is crucial in providing a sense of continuity with the past. Although Bakhtin's chronotopes are framed as distinctly literary phenomena – he points to the Gothic novel *The Castle of Otranto* as an example of castle time – the idea of the chronotope clearly has application for framing *any* kind of narrative.[73] As Sarah Bowden and Susanne Friede have recently argued, all textual representations of space can be considered narratives: 'every space as depicted in a literary work is a narrated space, even in the case of more ostensibly "functional" texts'.[74] I would go further to suggest that even those who visited Arthurian sites at first hand in the premodern era encountered spaces that were mediated and therefore narrated, sometimes literally in the form of textual *tabulae* or personal guides. Even the Arthurian associations of places that were not actively interpreted on site such as Cadbury Castle (at least as far as we know) would have been encountered by those visiting in textual or oral narration before or after their visit – otherwise their Arthurian connections would simply have gone unremarked. To segue Bakhtin's ideas with Zerubavel's, it is perhaps the coming together of two types of space-time experience that made personally visiting an Arthurian place so affective: on the one hand, the individual and immediate experience of physically walking around an Arthurian site in person, redolent of Bakhtin's 'road' chronotope and de Certeau's city walkers creating 'practiced place'; and, on the other, the exhibition of slices of deep history in the same space – shared history and shared space – as a kind of castle–chronotope experience.

The 'noncontiguous points in history' that Zerubavel describes indicate a gap which can only ever be imaginatively elided, a rupture in time that appears to close but does not. The numinosity of Arthurian sites depends on this rupture, and it is this paradoxical dependence that generates the emotive potential of Arthurian places as sites of yearning, places of both remembering and forgetting. In his monumental work *Les lieux de mémoire*, Pierre Nora collated a vast number of what he called

---

[73] Other scholars have stepped outside the bounds of the textual altogether to identify Bakhtinian chronotopes with diverse lived experiences: see John Cook, 'Events Set in Amber: Bakhtin's "Chronotope of the Castle" as Solidified Space-Time', *Australian Slavonic and East European Studies*, 28 (2014), 51–70; J. B. Richland, 'Sovereign Time, Storied Moments: The Temporalities of Law, Tradition, and Ethnography in Hopi Tribunal Court', *PoLAR*, 31.1 (2008), 8–27; J. Lawson, 'Chronotope, Story, and Historical Geography: Mikhail Bakhtin and the Space-Time of Narratives', *Antipode*, 43.2 (2011), 384–412.

[74] Sarah Bowden and Susanne Friede, 'Introduction: Sacred Space and Place in Arthurian Romance', *Arthurian Literature*, 36 (2021), 1–12 (p. 4).

INTRODUCTION   25

'*lieux de mémoire*' ('places' or 'realms of memory').[75] Nora distinguishes between 'history' and 'memory', claiming that *lieux de mémoire*

> occur at the same time that an immense and intimate fund of memory disappears, surviving only as a reconstituted object beneath the gaze of critical history [...] our intellectual, political, historical frameworks are exhausted but remain powerful enough not to leave us indifferent; whatever vitality they retain impresses us only in their most spectacular symbols. [...] [*Lieux de mémoire* are] fundamentally remains, the ultimate embodiments of a memorial consciousness that has barely survived in a historical age that calls out for memory because it has abandoned it.[76]

In other words, *lieux de mémoire* are fragments. The subconscious impulse to fill in the gap between past and present, to imaginatively reconstruct the comings and goings of Arthur's court on top of a hillfort, relies upon the existence of the gap itself. *Lieux de mémoire* are called into being when something seems to have been irretrievably lost. These fragments can be locative – an earthwork, or a fragment of inscribed stone rebuilt into a castle hallway. They can also take other forms. Nora points to 'the irrevocable break marked by the disappearance of peasant culture, that quintessential repository of collective memory', and indeed oral fragments are something that Arthur's antiquarian defenders seek to recover from the people living around the base of Cadbury camp or near the assumed site of the battle of Camlan.[77] Nora's diverse *lieux de mémoire* – and indeed Zerubavel's various 'mnemonic bridges' – help us to make sense of the interest of Arthur's defenders in places and other fragments (rather than in narrative histories).

Later in the same chapter, Zerubavel describes another kind of mnemonic bridge: relics and memorabilia. Zerubavel outlines the similar importance that 'relics', which Zerubavel defines in the loosest of terms, can have as tools for group nostalgia. Although these objects are portable and not fixed in place, they can still '[help] provide some physical continuity, which is why they are indeed used [...] for storing memories'.[78] Zerubavel compares relics and memorabilia to 'ruins and historic buildings' in terms of the 'quasi-tangible contact with the past'

---

[75] David P. Jordan, 'Introduction', in Pierre Nora, *Rethinking France: Les Lieux de Mémoire: Volume 1 The State*, ed. David P. Jordan (Chicago, IL: University of Chicago Press, 2001), pp. xxiii–xxxiv (p. xxv).
[76] Pierre Nora, 'Between Memory and History: Les Lieux de Mémoire', *Representations*, 26 (1989), 7–24 (p. 12).
[77] Nora, 'Between Memory and History', p. 7.
[78] Zerubavel, *Time Maps*, pp. 43–44.

that they can conjure.[79] The rhetorical similarities between relic and ruin are borne out in the dual premodern definition of monument as both a commemorative construction and a physical historical text in manuscript form; as early as the seventh century, Isidore of Seville wrote that 'histories are called "monuments" (*monumentum*), because they grant a remembrance (*memoria*) of deeds that have been done'.[80] Relics and memorabilia operate not only as mnemonics for the past but also for powerful places in the present, and early modern Arthurian defenders tend to use relic-like objects associated with Arthur in conjunction with Arthurian places to foster the impression of Arthur's reality. Following E. M. R. Ditmas' earlier study, Robert Rouse and Cory Rushton's *The Medieval Quest for Arthur* (2005) catalogues the various Arthurian relics of the later Middle Ages.[81] Places do play a part in Rouse and Rushton's argument, but they suggest that

> only when a site attracted Arthurian relics to itself, and when the location of an Arthurian object attracts the legend to its physical location, does it become of importance to our [i.e. Rouse and Rushton's] discussion. The present book does not focus on Arthurian sites.[82]

I take the opposite view. Arthurian relics are imbued with significance by the places in which they were said to have originated: the places are the source of the numinosity, not the objects. I agree with Laura Varnam's assessment that sacred spaces are 'contagious', investing sanctity in the people, objects, and other places that they come into physical or metaphysical contact with.[83] Although Varnam's arguments relate specifically to sacred spaces in a religious sense, alluring figures such as Arthur also had the potential to redraw the landscape around them. Arthur's defenders made use of relic-like objects as mnemonics for Arthurian places – for example, John Leland's imagining of a Glastonbury origin for Arthur's seal (then housed at Westminster), or William Camden's insistence on situating Arthur's lead cross within its physical environment at Glastonbury. Sometimes, relics provide a means of allowing Arthurian places to be invoked at a spatial remove. Arthurian 'relics' need not be encountered in person: they can be equally arresting

---

[79] Zerubavel, *Time Maps*, p. 44.
[80] Isidore of Seville, *The Etymologies of Isidore of Seville*, ed. Stephen A. Barney et al. (Cambridge: Cambridge University Press, 2006), 1.41, pp. 66–67.
[81] E. M. R. Ditmas, 'The Cult of Arthurian Relics', *Folklore*, 75.1 (1964), 19–33; Robert Rouse and Cory Rushton, *The Medieval Quest for Arthur* (Stroud: Tempus, 2005).
[82] Rouse and Rushton, *The Medieval Quest for Arthur*, p. 19.
[83] Varnam, *Church as Sacred Space*, pp. 6–7.

when presented visually as illustrations on the page. However, these relics are always orientated towards their locative origins (real or imagined).

To return to the idea of Arthurian regions, the contagious nature of sacred spaces can explain how the impression of such areas could build up over time. The *Oxford English Dictionary*'s anatomical and medical definition for 'region' is most illustrative of what I mean: 'an area of the body [...] defined by surface landmarks, proximity to an organ, vascular supply, innervation, etc.'[84] This encapsulates the organic qualities of Arthurian geographies: an Arthurian region emerges as locations with imposing topographical, historical, or political qualities act as a 'vascular supply' of sorts, supplying the surrounding area with meaning and causing new 'surface landmarks' to generate. This spatial clustering chimes with Laura Varnam's observations about sacred spaces: 'the characteristic that [they] share' is their 'ability to organise and redraw the map of the surrounding space. Sacred spaces are magnetic and attractive.'[85] Major Arthurian sites like Glastonbury function in this way, drawing in other Arthurian sites toward themselves and prompting new Arthurian associations to pop up in the surrounding landscape. We can imagine this as a concentric heat map: immediately surrounding Glastonbury there is the Tor, Wearyall Hill, Pomparles bridge, and Beckery.[86] More recently, the Chalice Well and Holy Thorn have been added to this list.[87] Slightly further afield there is Brent Knoll, Polden, and Cadbury; further still in one direction lies Caerleon, and in another Tintagel and the proposed Camlan location near Padstow.[88]

It is at these sites of 'vascular supply' that this book begins: Arthurian sites as they were managed in the later Middle Ages. This book is broadly chronological, and my opening chapter begins in the fourteenth and fifteenth centuries by exploring how physical, on-site experiences of Arthurian places were shaped and experienced during this period. This forms an appropriate starting point for this book because late medieval Arthurian site management continued to influence the Arthurian tradition

---

[84] 'region, n.', *Oxford English Dictionary* Online (Oxford University Press, 2009), https://oed.com/view/Entry/161281?redirectedFrom=region (accessed 13 July 2020).
[85] Varnam, *The Church as Sacred Space*, p. 7.
[86] The Arthurian associations of these places are discussed later at pp. 51–52 (Glastonbury Tor); p. 52 (Wearyall Hill); pp. 137–38 (Pomparles Bridge); p. 52, p. 75 (Beckery).
[87] On the Chalice Well, see below at pp. 62–63; and on the Holy Thorn, see Adam Stout, *Glastonbury Holy Thorn: Story of a Legend* (Glastonbury: Green and Pleasant, 2020), passim.
[88] Arthur gifts Brent and Polden to the abbey according to Adam of Damerham's *Chronicle* (1291); see Dean, *Arthur of England*, p. 10. On Padstow and Tintagel, see below at p. 164; p. 260.

both directly and indirectly long after the sites in question had ceased to operate. In the later Middle Ages, it was not so much Arthur that needed defending, but rather the religious houses that invoked him. Monastic communities faced something of a crisis in the fourteenth century. The rise of the Wycliffite and Lollard movements did irreparable damage to the stability of established religious orders.[89] Rather than retreating into their institutions and closing the doors, as some scholars have suggested, English monks did quite the opposite, selling their ongoing relevance to a visiting public (that is, to pilgrims) by invoking the antiquity and eminence of their institutions through public-facing materials including glazing schemes, plaques, and tablets (sometimes called by their Latin name, *tabulae*).[90] The last were prototypes of the modern-day museum information board, functioning as the common ground between place and text and providing mutual authentication for both. Some of the best-preserved physical examples of Arthurian windows, tablets, and plaques come from York Minster and Glastonbury Abbey. Though there is evidence for early Arthurian tourism elsewhere – Cirencester and Dover, for example – the comparative wealth of physical materials and visitors' accounts that survive for Glastonbury and York enable us to pinpoint the parts of these sites' local Arthurian histories that became subsumed into broader textual tradition. Site visitors played a vital part in this transmission, for inquisitive guests made notes during their visits. The information they copied was often intended for use in larger projects, some never completed, others sadly lost.[91] One historian in particular, John Hardyng, appears to have used material from local Arthurian sites such as St Paul's and Glastonbury to write his influential Metrical Brut

---

[89] Clark, 'Selling the Holy Places', p. 15.
[90] Clark, 'Selling the Holy Places', pp. 15–16. The notion of a worldly 'retreat' is put forward by the following authors (all cited in Clark, 'Selling the Holy Places', p. 16 n. 8): Eamon Duffy, *The Stripping of the Altars: Traditional Religion in England, c. 1400–c. 1580* (New Haven, CT: Yale University Press, 1992); Christopher Harper-Bill, 'Dean Colet's Sermon and the Nature of the Pre-Reformation Church', *History*, 73 (1988), 191–210 (pp. 194–97); Christopher Harper-Bill, *The Pre-Reformation Church in England*, 2nd edn (London: Longman, 1996), pp. 40–42; R. N. Swanson, *Church and Society in Late Medieval England* (Oxford: Blackwell, 1989), pp. 82–88; pp. 268–96.
[91] Some have suggested that William Worcester's *Itineraries* were intended to furnish a major topographical description of Britain. See, for example, Jan Broadway, *'No historie so meete': Gentry Culture and the Development of Local History in Elizabethan and Early Stuart England* (Manchester: Manchester University Press, 2006), p. 18. A further work composed by Worcester that may have emerged from his itinerant researches is *Anglorum antiquitates* [the antiquities of England], as the later antiquarian John Bale calls it. Sadly, the work does not survive. It is listed in John Bale, *Index Britanniae Scriptorum*, ed. Reginald Lane Poole and Mary Bateson (Oxford, 1902), pp. 116–17.

Chronicle. Hardyng's *Chronicle* impacted the writing of other major texts, from Thomas Malory's *Morte Darthur* to medieval and early modern historiographies and even the works of Shakespeare.[92]

As local Arthurian histories were increasingly absorbed into broader textual traditions, a problem arose in Arthur's geography that needed addressing: the issue of Arthurian place duplication. The prestige that Arthur could give to cities, castles, cathedrals, and abbeys meant that many places claimed Arthurian connections. Some of these Arthurian places seem, at first glance, to be in competition with each other, such as the multiple cities of the legion attested in various fifteenth-century texts as the seat of Arthur's court. Whilst this book's opening chapter addresses how custodians' management of Arthurian sites influenced Arthur's localisation, Chapter 2 considers the bigger picture by identifying how multiple competing Arthurian place claims were subsequently reconciled and consolidated in the fifteenth century through the medium of text. Some locations' claims to an Arthurian connection suggest long and well-documented histories, while others appear more obscure, perhaps representing new associations or even long traditions that had been maintained orally. When considered together, these competing places exhibit a set of characteristics that made them ripe for inclusion in Arthur's multifarious geography.

Despite attempts to make sense of the mass of Arthurian place claims, Arthur's geography did not seem believable, and in the more openly sceptical climate of the sixteenth century this quickly became a problem for Arthur's champions. Particularly in Geoffrey of Monmouth's *Historia*, there is an unevenness of focus that proved problematic for the question of Arthur's reality. Too much attention was paid to Arthur's continental conquests, many of which lacked supporting textual authorities. At the same time, Arthur's native places required sharper definition. Geoffrey's *Historia* does not discuss long periods of peace in detail, and romance authors – seen as less credible by those writing and critiquing Arthur's history in the sixteenth century – were quick to fill in these intervals with quests and adventures. My third chapter considers how one of Arthur's most influential defenders, John Leland, addressed this issue by drawing

---

[92] E. D. Kennedy, 'Malory's Use of Hardyng's *Chronicle*', *Notes & Queries*, 16 (1969), 167–70; E. D. Kennedy, 'Malory's Use of Hardyng's *Chronicle*: A Reconsideration', *West Virginia Philological Papers*, 54 (2011), 8–15. Hardyng's influence on historical writing from the fifteenth to seventeenth centuries is explored throughout this book. For Shakespeare's use of Hardyng's *Chronicle*, see Alicia Marchant, 'John Hardyng's Scotland: Emotional Geographies and Forged Histories in the Fifteenth Century', in *Historicising Heritage and Emotions: The Affective Histories of Blood, Stone and Land*, ed. Alicia Marchant (London: Routledge, 2019), pp. 51–66 (pp. 62–63).

out an enduring Arthurian region in the West Country, a region which would be picked up by Leland's inheritors such as William Camden and Michael Drayton. Geoffrey of Monmouth's *Historia* provides a geographical blueprint for Leland, whose defence of Arthur had in fact started life as a defence of Geoffrey's text; but Leland adapted the *Historia*'s Arthurian geography by shifting Arthur's centre from Caerleon in south-east Wales to Cadbury in Somerset. Cadbury also made sense geographically because of its proximity to Glastonbury, and Leland may have settled on it partly due to the logic of this geographical association. Leland refocused Arthur's geography around Cadbury, adding detail at this new Arthurian centre. At the same time, Leland shifted focus away from the distant edges of Arthur's world. This created a sense of perspective for Leland's readers, placing them directly at the centre of Arthur's realm.

Where Chapter 3 focuses on the Arthurian region imagined by John Leland, Chapter 4 takes a more comparative approach by considering how Arthur's geography was constructed differently by three sixteenth-century writers with different ideas about how Arthur related to their own identities: John Leland (c. 1503–1552), John Prise (c. 1501–1555), and Elis Gruffydd (1490–1552). By the turn of the sixteenth century many writers saw a need to defend Arthur's existence, a need that intensified after the composition of Polydore Vergil's *Anglica Historia* in 1513. Local Arthurian places were considered valuable evidence in defending Arthur. Whilst some saw the attack on Arthur as Italian in origin, others – such as the Welsh chronicler Elis Gruffydd – considered the English to be the real threat to the British History. As well as locating the threat to Arthur differently, these authors also differed in terms of where they located Arthur's authentic places. Only Gruffydd wrote his defence in Welsh, and Gruffydd is the only of these men to have constructed a local Arthurian geography centred around North Wales. Prise, a Welshman who nevertheless saw England as his adopted home, favoured an Arthurian geography shared more evenly between England and Wales, though he connected several holy houses in South Wales with valuable and ancient manuscript evidence for Arthur's reality.

My final chapter rehabilitates William Camden as an Arthurian defender, discussing the role he played in further developing an Arthurian geography in the West Country and Wales inherited from John Leland. Though Camden is often associated with the 'new' antiquarianism that peaked in the late sixteenth to early seventeenth centuries, his historical approach shares much in common with the earlier sources discussed in this book. The narrative that separates Camden's antiquarian work from his medieval and sixteenth-century forebears is therefore open to challenge. Reconsidering Camden in light of medieval continuities raises important questions about his attitude towards Arthur. Previous scholars have expressed doubt about Camden's interest in Arthur, tending to characterise Camden as impartial at best.[93] Yet the editorial decisions of Camden and his publishers show that he was not only interested in Arthur, but endeavoured to support the impression of Arthur as a real historical king. Camden's approach to achieving this lay in his shrewd use of local Arthurian places. Although Camden's predecessors such as Leland also used local places in defence of Arthur, they were not successful because of the structural qualities of their defences. Camden succeeded where others had failed because of the geographical organisation of his text, which reinforced the impression of a believable Arthurian region centred around the West Country and Wales. By embedding carefully manipulated poetic fragments into his descriptions of Arthurian places, Camden created the impression of virtual Arthurian monuments, textual imitations of their physically inscribed cousins. If Arthur's doubters uprooted Arthur by bringing his places into question, Camden was the first to really succeed at putting him back.

When we read the history of Arthur's places as a whole, tracing the narrative from site visits to textual encounters and back again, and from the medieval to the modern, two things become clear. First, and most fundamentally, the mnemonic power of place as Zerubavel describes it – the feeling of actually experiencing an Arthurian location – has been crucial to supporting belief in Arthur.[94] Second, the places of Arthur have been under almost constant negotiation and re-negotiation by those who manage, experience, and write about them: the history of Arthurian places is therefore also a study of the people captivated by those places. These agents' impressions of Arthur's locations were shaped by individual agendas, be it the generation of institutional prestige, the affirmation of local, regional, or national identities, the support of a particular political vision, or the attempt to recover pre-Dissolution spaces after their ruination. The narratives of Arthur's places have therefore been consistently shaped and reshaped, textual and material threads worked by many hands and pulled in different directions depending on the weavers' individual motivations. At the heart of this process lay a connection between the textual or narratological on the one hand, and the material or spatial on the other. Enduring Arthurian narrative histories,

[93] Higham, *Myth-Making and History*, p. 238; Blaire Zeiders, 'The Arthurian Book in Print: Reading the Debts and Desires of the Early Modern English Nation' (unpublished doctoral thesis, University of Wisconsin-Madison, 2013), pp. 40–41.
[94] Discussed above at p. 22–25.

such as Geoffrey of Monmouth's *Historia regum Britanniae*, had the power to spawn new Arthurian place associations. In contrast, a place's material qualities, if powerful enough, could supersede individual motivations and fill textual lacunae, stamping a location newly, or more enduringly, on the Arthurian map. Leland and Camden's powerful descriptions of Cadbury Castle gave birth to a new and enduring Camelot; and Elis Gruffydd, though dismissive of oral traditions of a sleeping Arthur under a hill near Glastonbury, nevertheless describes Arthur's burial at Glastonbury as a historic reality because of Glastonbury's persuasive Arthurian materialities. I will return to Glastonbury frequently throughout this book for this very reason, and it is at Glastonbury itself, virtually speaking, that I will begin.

1
'Thise were his places and his habitacions': Arthur *in situ* in the fifteenth century

Thenne to procede forth in thys sayd book, whyche I dyrecte vnto alle noble prynces, lordes and ladyes, gentylmen or gentylwymmen, that desyre to rede or here redde of the noble and Ioyous hystorye of the grete conquerour and excellent kyng, Kyng Arthur, somtyme kyng of thys noble royalme thenne callyd Brytaygne [...][1]

William Caxton's preface to his edition of Thomas Malory's *Morte Darthur* sets two complementary iterations of Arthur side-by-side. The first is Arthur the imperial symbol, the 'grete conquerour and excellent kyng [...] of thys noble royalme thenne callyd Brytaygne'. The second is the Arthur of local places. On the one hand, Caxton tells us that he has been implored to write the history and deeds of Arthur by an unnamed array of 'noble and dyuers gentylmen of thys royame' for reasons of national pride.[2] Caxton's unnamed petitioners, upset that Caxton has ignored Arthur in favour of other Worthies in his prior publications, argue that he should have instead prioritised Arthur as 'a man borne wythin this royame and kyng and emperour of the same'.[3] After Caxton's retort that there are some men who think 'there was no suche Arthur', the unnamed gentlemen defend their position by turning to a number of Arthurian sites and objects across the English and Welsh landscape:

Fyrst, ye may see his sepulture in the monasterye of Glastyngburye [...] And in dyuers places of Englond many remembraunces ben yet of hym and shall remayne perpetually, and also of his knyghtes: first, in the abbey of Westmestre, at Saynt Edwardes shrine, remayneth the

---

[1] Malory, *Works*, pp. xiii–xv (p. xiii).
[2] Ibid.
[3] Malory, *Works*, pp. xiii–xiv. The 'Nine Worthies' were nine figures representing paragons of chivalry in the later Middle Ages. They are often seen represented in architecture, and include three Christians (Arthur, Godfrey of Bouillon, Charlemagne); three pagans (Alexander the Great, Julius Caesar, Hector of Troy); and three Jews (King David; Joshua; Judas Maccabeus). On the Nine Worthies, see Horst Schroëder, *Der Topos der Nine Worthies in Literatur und bildender Kunst* (Göttingen: Vandenhoeck & Ruprecht, 1971). By 1485, Caxton had already published the deeds of another Christian worthy, Godfrey of Bouillon.

prynte of his seal in reed waxe [...] item, in the castel of Douer ye may see Gauwayns skulle & Cradoks mantle; at Wynchester, the Rounde Table; in other places Launcelottes swerde and many other thynges. [...] And yet of record remayne in wytnesse of hym in Wales, in the toune of Camelot, the grete stones & meruayllous werkys of yron lyeng vnder the grounde, & ryal vautes, which dyuers now lyuyng hath seen.[4]

Together, these sites form a coherent vision of a historic Arthur, incorporating several prominent Arthurian settings, objects, and their associated legends and connecting them with real-world locations: the ruins of Arthur's court in Wales at Caerleon or Caerwent, identified here as 'Camelot' in line with Malory's romance toponyms; Arthur's grave at Glastonbury;[5] his seal at Westminster and his Round Table at Winchester; and Gawain's skull and Caradoc's mantle in Dover Castle.[6] The passage seems to convey a sense of urgency, a pressing need to communicate these local Arthurian histories to readers who may not have yet been able to visit themselves. We cannot know whether Caxton or his petitioners (if they existed at all) *truly* believed in Arthur.[7] They may simply have been resisting scepticism – or perhaps indulging in 'make-believe' – because of their attachment to the myth of Arthur. What is clear from Caxton's preface is that specific Arthurian places played a crucial role in supporting the *impression* of Arthur's reality in the fifteenth century, offering believable anchor points in the form of real places just as some aspects of Arthur's narrative were being brought into question.

Caxton's preface demonstrates that a variety of localised Arthurian histories had gained a wider platform by 1485, and were beginning to

---

[4] Caxton, 'Preface', p. xiii.

[5] On whether Caxton had Caerleon or Caerwent in mind, see below at p. 123.

[6] Caxton, 'Preface', pp. xiii–xiv. Caradoc's connection with Dover may have been strengthened by local historiography at Dover; see below at pp. 68–69. Thomas Gray offers an alternative location for Caradoc's mantle in *Scalacronica*, in which Gray states that the mantle was transported to Glastonbury before being refashioned into a priest's robe. See Richard Moll, *Before Malory: Reading Arthur in Later Medieval England* (Toronto: University of Toronto Press, 2003), p. 51.

[7] The question as to whether or not medieval people believed in Arthur is discussed in relation to Caxton's preface in Danièle Cybulskie, 'Did Medieval People Believe in King Arthur?', *Medievalists.net*, www.medievalists.net/2016/07/did-medieval-people-believe-in-king-arthur/ [accessed 27 June 2020]. See also William A. Kretzschmar, 'Caxton's Sense of History', *The Journal of English and German Philology*, 91.4 (1992), 510–28. I concur with Christopher Dean's conclusion that 'despite [medieval historians'] inclusion of material they must have recognized as fictional [...] most medieval historians who described Arthur's reign believed that there was a hard core of truth in the story' (Dean, *Arthur of England*, p. 9). Dean's discussion of medieval and Renaissance belief in Arthur appears at pp. 3–31.

be used collectively to bolster the impression of Arthur's credibility as it began to be questioned more widely. This chapter traces the transference of these local histories in the fifteenth century from carefully choreographed visitor experiences at Arthurian sites – cathedrals, abbeys, and castles where visitors learned about the sites' connections to Arthur – to widely disseminated works, such as Caxton's edition of the *Morte Darthur*. The crucial transmission point was the site visitors themselves, and in the following pages I focus on how Arthurian sites affected their visitors and made their way into broader texts. On-site Arthurian experiences were not simply immediate, personal encounters whose influence did not stray beyond their respective locations. Rather, as the works of Caxton and Hardyng demonstrate, site visitors carried the memories (and sometimes the notes) of their locative experiences with them after they left, using their own encounters with local Arthurian places to inform their subsequent writings, and in turn effect a broader impact on their readers. Many of these projects were of great national significance: works dedicated to English history, often framed as British through the context of the Brut tradition detailing Britain's legendary foundation by Brutus of Troy.[8] This demonstrates the crucial role that local places and their histories could play in the construction of a national consciousness. By gathering together and publishing local Arthurian histories, these writers helped to strengthen the impression of Arthur as a national symbol.

On-site histories

Tour guides and tabulae

Changes in the production and reception of local history had a major impact on its development during the fifteenth century. Monks and other religious played a central role in the production of local history writing in the later Middle Ages. According to Antonia Gransden,

> as the monks and other religious abandoned their role as the main chroniclers of national events, they turned more and more to local history. They wrote monographs on local history, and devoted an increasing amount of page space to local affairs in their annals.[9]

---

[8] See Margaret Lamont, 'Becoming English: Ronwenne's Wassail, Language, and National Identity in the Middle English Prose *Brut*', *Studies in Philology*, 107.3 (2010), 283–309.
[9] Antonia Gransden, *Historical Writing in England*, 2 vols (London: Routledge, 1982), II, p. xiii.

In contrast, the practice of 'keeping a monastic chronicle, in the sense of a full-scale narrative combining general and local history' was virtually abandoned during the fifteenth century.[10] This shift in focus was largely driven by the need to emphasise the anteriority and prestige of one's own religious house, hoping to curry royal favour and increase visitor footfall. Competition between the different houses led each institution to carve out its own historical niche, some in the pre-Conquest period, others further back still in the expansive caves of The British History.[11] Perhaps as a result of this shift in local historiographical praxis, pilgrimage to local holy places increased during the fifteenth century just as visits to far-flung locations such as Jerusalem and Rome were in decline.[12]

During the course of the fourteenth and fifteenth centuries, local histories were transferred from chronicles to new formats that were more accessible to a visiting public, such as *tabulae* or tablets.[13] A kind of precursor to the informative panels that we see today in modern museums, historical *tabulae* appear to have been especially popular for display in cathedrals and monasteries.[14] This transfer was perhaps due, in part, to a growing need for religious houses to defend their existence to the public and themselves: not only were *tabulae* geared towards public consumption, but also to fostering imaginative or devotional engagement with the physical environment of the sites in which they were displayed.[15] Medieval *tabulae* were large boards inscribed with text, or with parchment affixed to them, that could be hung up on display or secured to the wall in religious houses, churches, and elsewhere.[16] Other *tabulae* were made

---

[10] Gransden, *Historical Writing in England*, II, p. 388.
[11] On the cultivation of legendary local histories – Galfridian and otherwise – at religious houses, see Gransden, *Legends, Traditions and History*, passim.
[12] Claire Macht, 'Changes in Monastic Historical Writing Throughout the Long Fifteenth Century', in *The Fifteenth Century XVI: Examining Identity*, ed. Linda Clark (Woodbridge: Boydell, 2018), pp. 1–26 (p. 22).
[13] Macht, 'Changes in Monastic Historical Writing', pp. 1–26.
[14] Macht, 'Changes in Monastic Historical Writing', p. 13.
[15] Macht, 'Changes in Monastic Historical Writing', p. 25. See also Clark, 'Selling the Holy Places', passim.
[16] There have been several studies of medieval *tabulae*. See Gordon Gerould, 'Tables in Medieval Churches', *Speculum*, 1 (1926), 439–40; Gransden, *Historical Writing*, II, pp. 494–95; Jeanne Krochalis, 'Magna Tabula: The Glastonbury Tablets', in *Glastonbury Abbey and the Arthurian Tradition*, pp. 435–567; Richard Marks, 'Picturing Word and Text in the Late Medieval Parish Church', in *Image, Text and Church, 1380–1600: Essays for Margaret Aston*, ed. Linda Clark, Maureen Jurkowski and Colin Richmond (Toronto: PIMS, 2009), pp. 162–88; Michael Van Dussen, 'Tourists and Tabulae in Late-Medieval England', in *Truth and Tales: Cultural Mobility and Medieval Media*, ed. Fiona Somerset and Nicholas Watson (Columbus, OH: Ohio State University Press, 2015), pp. 238–54; Conrad Rudolph, 'The Tour Guide in the Middle Ages: Guide Culture and the Mediation of Public Art', *Art*

of stone. Only three examples of wooden *tabulae* are known to survive – two from York Minster, one from Glastonbury known as the *magna tabula* (or 'great tablet'): both examples are discussed further below. We know from the writings of early antiquarians that there were similar examples at numerous other locations.[17]

Tabulae must once have been very widespread in England's churches, cathedrals, and monasteries: the now-destroyed church of St Christopher-le-Stocks in London contained twelve *tabulae* alone.[18] The Christopher-le-Stocks *tabulae* contained material intended to support devotional practices, a common function for *tabulae* and particularly those that hung in parish churches.[19] Others – especially those on display in cathedrals and monasteries – were historical in nature. *Tabulae* were especially useful as vessels for the history and legends of the places in which they were exhibited, and Arthurian material was not an unpopular choice. All three surviving *tabulae* contain Arthurian material. There were further Arthurian *tabulae* in Cornhill (London), Colchester, and Dover Castle.[20]

Bulletin, 100.1 (2018), 37–67; Macht, 'Changes in Monastic Historical Writing'; Kathryn Kerby-Fulton, *The Clerical Proletariat and the Resurgence of Medieval English Poetry* (Philadelphia, PA: University of Pennsylvania Press, 2021), pp. 243–77 and passim; and, most recently, David Mason, 'Writing on the Wall: Chronicles Written for Public Display at St Paul's Cathedral, London', *The Medieval History Journal*, 26.1 (2023), 23–56.

[17] The most up-to-date lists of known *tabulae* appear in Claire Macht, 'Changes in Monastic Historical Writing', pp. 14–20; and John Clark, 'The King Lucius Tabula in St Peter Upon Cornhill Church, London', paper given at the Medieval and Tudor London Seminar, Institute of Historical Research, 2011 (revised 2014), available online, www.academia.edu/6553953/The_King_Lucius_tabula_in_St_Peter_Upon_Cornhill_church_London. To these, we can add a few more examples. The first is a *tabula* at Hyde Abbey at Winchester, observed by John Rous, which contained information about the foundation of Oxford University. The second is a *tabula* which hung in Tavistock church in the late fifteenth century. William Worcester copied its contents, five lines of verse encouraging hopefulness in times of despair. Worcester also describes a *tabula* on display St Henry's Chapel in the Carmelite Friary at Yarmouth, which detailed the life of St Henry, the English-born bishop of Uppsala, Sweden. John Rous, *Joannis Rossi Antiquarii Warwicensis Historia Regum Angliae*, ed. Thomas Hearne, 2nd edn (Oxford: Sheldonian Theatre, 1745), p. 96; William Worcester, *Itineraries*, ed. John H. Harvey (Oxford: Clarendon Press, 1969), pp. 112–13; pp. 186–87.

[18] Marks, 'Picturing Word and Text', pp. 164–65.

[19] Other devotional examples include the *tabulae* at St Stephen Walbrook in the City of London; see Marks, 'Picturing Word and Text', p. 164; Macht, 'Changes in Monastic Historical Writing', p. 24.

[20] The text from the Cornhill *tabula* is preserved in John Stow's *Survey of London*, ed. C. L. Kingsford (Oxford: Oxford University Press, 1908), p. 174, p. 423. On the Cornhill *tabula*, see John Clark, 'The King Lucius *tabula*'. Arthur was also mentioned in lists of great kings in the *tabula* of St John the Baptist Church in Colchester, Essex (see Oxford Bodleian Library MS Gough Essex 1). Dover Castle's *tabula* is described in

A further example that has previously gone unnoticed was described by John Leland in the sixteenth century. After describing the history of Caerleon in Wales and its association with Arthur, Leland claims that this information 'is testified in very ancient tablets, which I recently saw affixed to the columns of temples in Wales' (antiquissimis tabulis, quas ego nuper in Cambria vidi columnis templorum adfixas [...] testantibus).[21] There is also an alternative to the *tabula* explanation: Caerleon was rich in ancient inscribed fragments during the sixteenth century, some of which were incorporated into more recent buildings, and it may be these inscribed stones that Leland had in mind.[22] Of course, given the lack of specifics regarding these tablets' location and contents, and the absence of the claim in Leland's final defence published in 1544, it is possible that Leland's claim to have read these tablets himself is an exaggeration.

There are not many sources that tell us how *tabulae* were commissioned and made, but there are some important exceptions. The tablets on display at St Paul's state that London laymen had a hand in setting up and restoring *tabulae*.[23] Two more examples, both from the Diocese of York, give us further insight into *tabulae* production. The text on one of the two surviving York Minster *tabulae* partly describes the process of the tablet's creation, and its intended purpose to preserve and publicise the histories hidden away in the minster's archival holdings.[24] The largest *tabula* opens:

Camden's *Britannia* from the 1607 edition onwards. It described Caesar's invasion at Dover, Arviragus' reputed fortification of the castle, and a battle between King Arthur's men and certain rebels. See William Camden, *Britannia* (1607), pp. 241–43, sigs Z5r–Z6r; William Camden, *Britain*, trans. Holland (1610), p. 342, sig. Ff2r. I am grateful to John Clark for drawing my attention to this example.

[21] John Leland, 'Codrus sive laus et defensio Gallofridi Arturii contra Polydorum Vergilium', in *Joannis Lelandi Antiquarii de rebus Britannicis Collectanea*, 6 vols (Oxford, 1715; London, 1770, 1774), V, pp. 2–10 (pp. 5–6), translation mine.

[22] Bishop Francis Godwin of Llandaff (1562–1633) took a serious interest in these Caerleon fragments, and was responsible for introducing them to his contemporary William Camden. See Jeremy Knight, 'Welsh Stones and Oxford Scholars: Three Rediscoveries', *Bulletin of the Institute of Classical Studies*, 44.S75 (2000), 91–101.

[23] Mason, 'Writing on the Wall', p. 31.

[24] The York Minster *tabulae* survive as York, York Minster Archives, L1/1; and a copy of a third York Minster *tabula* concerning the miracles of St William survives as Oxford, Bodleian Library, Bodleian MS Dodsworth 125 at f. 132. The surviving tablets are described in J. S. Purvis, 'The Tables of the York Vicars Choral', *The Yorkshire Archaeological Journal*, 41 (1966), 741–48; N. R. Ker, *Medieval Manuscripts in British Libraries* (Oxford: Clarendon Press, 1977), IV, pp. 825–26. For the text of the York *tabula*, see James Raine, *The Historians of the Church of York and Its Archbishops*, 2 vols (London: Longman, 1886), I, pp. 450–51.

> Hic Eboracensis temple, metropolis, urbis,
> Ecclesiaeque statum praesens pandit Tabulatum.
> [...] Haec ex archivis de multis paucula scripsi;
> Ne lateat latebris Tabula sic publice fixi [...]
> Ecclesiae jura noscas ut carime plura,
> Plenius in Tabula scribitur historia.
>
> [The present Table displays the state of the Temple of York, the metropolis, the City and the Church. [...] These small matters I have written from many archives, and have fixed them thus publicly lest they remain hidden in concealment. [...] That you may know the laws of the Church, the history is written more fully in the Table.][25]

The text of another metrical chronicle, also produced within the York Diocese, states that it, too, had been written in order to furnish a *tabula*. The text of the *Aliud Chronicon Metricum* claims that it had originally been started by John of Allhallowgate, a member of the Ripon Minster vicars choral in the late fourteenth century, to provide material for a set of tablets.[26] The chronicle was picked up again almost a century later, apparently by a priest from the same church, and continued until the archiepiscopate of William Booth who was then living (d. 1464).[27] The involvement of John of Allhallowgate and his continuator in producing the *Aliud Chronicon Metricum* supports Kathryn Kerby-Fulton's suggestion that vicars choral and other chantry priests were likely to have been closely engaged in the interpretation, the maintenance, and perhaps even the production of *tabulae* texts.[28]

Whilst the modern museum equivalents sometimes go sadly unread, we know that literate visitors engaged with *tabulae* texts in the later Middle Ages. Some guests even made copies. During a visit to Hyde

---

[25] York, York Minster L1/1. Text from Raine, *The Historians of the Church of York*; translation in Purvis, 'The Tables', p. 742. Subsequent citations are taken from Raine's edition; translations are Purvis's unless otherwise stated.

[26] The text reads: 'our predecessor John de Hallowgate made accessible to us in writing through his tablets the memory of blessed antiquity to the knowledge of later ages, concerning the ordination and succession of certain bishops of York [...]' (Reserante nobis in scriptis suis tabulatis quadam predecessor nostro, Johanne de Allhallowgate, felicis antiquitatis memoriam ad posteritatis notitiam, de ordinatione et quorundam successione Episcoporum Eboracensium [...]). 'Aliud chronicon metricum ecclesiae Eboracensis', in *The Historians of the Church of York*, ed. James Raine, pp. 464–87 (p. 464); partially cited in Kerby-Fulton, *The Clerical Proletariat*, p. 260. Translation mine.

[27] Kerby-Fulton, *The Clerical Proletariat*, ibid.

[28] Kerby-Fulton, *The Clerical Proletariat*, pp. 260–305, passim.

Abbey, John Rous claims to have seen 'an ancient *tabula*, whose copy I took from thence and [now] have' (antiqua tabula, cujus copiam inde habui & habeo).[29] Rous (c. 1420–92) was employed as a chantry priest at Guy's Cliffe in Warwickshire, and at least one of his known works, the *Historia regum Angliae* (c. 1486), was commissioned to provide information on illustrious historical figures for commemoration in the form of statues at St George's Chapel in Windsor. It is therefore possible that his interest in interpretative materials such as *tabulae* was professional, rather than simply personal. Further evidence of *tabulae* copying can also be found in British Library Cotton Titus A.XIX, a composite manuscript of densely packed quires. One of these quires has been dubbed 'the Glastonbury Quire' because it contains extensive Glastonbury material which Krochalis has shown to have been partially copied from the *magna tabula* displayed at Glastonbury, or from a direct copy thereof (probably with no more than one degree of separation).[30] The compiler appears to have been drawn to material gathered from *tabulae*. Elsewhere in the manuscript there is material copied from the tablets at York Minster, as well as a description of a *tabula* on display in the Holy Basilica in Rome.[31] A number of other manuscripts contain transcriptions taken from *tabulae* displayed at St Paul's Cathedral.[32] Site visitors copied from other architectural texts, too. One manuscript – British Library MS Royal 20 B.XV – appears to have been copied from Arthur's epitaph at Glastonbury (f. 109).[33] Both Cotton Titus A.XIX and Royal 20 B.XV were copied in the mid- to late-fifteenth century, and indeed most manuscripts copied from *tabulae* date from this period.[34] By this point, the rise of a professional clerical class and the ready availability of writing materials had led to the emergence

---

[29] Rous, *Historia regum Angliae*, p. 96.

[30] The so-called Glastonbury Quire runs ff. 16–23. For an extensive description of the manuscript, see Jeanne Krochalis and Alison Stones, *The Pilgrim's Guide: A Critical Edition*, 2 Vols (London: Harvey Miller, 1998), I. In Cotton Titus A.XIX the *magna tabula* texts do not appear in the same order that they do on the tablets but have been arranged alphabetically, which supports the possibility of a single intermediary copy, though Krochalis suggests that no more than a single intermediary is possible (*The Pilgrim's Guide*, I, pp. 131–32).

[31] Cotton Titus MS A.XIX, ff. 6–11; f. 12v. See Krochalis and Stones, *The Pilgrim's Guide*, I, p. 135; Krochalis, 'Magna Tabula', p. 439.

[32] The copies are listed in Mason, 'Writing on the Wall', pp. 41–43.

[33] Michelle P. Brown and James P. Carley, 'A Fifteenth-Century Revision of the Glastonbury Epitaph to King Arthur', in *Glastonbury Abbey and the Arthurian Tradition*, pp. 193–203. See also Neil Wright, 'A New Arthurian Epitaph', in *Glastonbury Abbey and the Arthurian Tradition*, pp. 205–09.

[34] Macht, 'Changes in Monastic Historical Writing', pp. 14–20.

of travel diary writing and itinerant antiquarianism, which may explain the increase in *tabula* transcriptions in informal notebooks.[35]

Of course, not all guests at *tabulae* sites would have been literate or proficient in Latin. Some locations chose to display *tabulae* in English, or with rich illustration, so that guests might peruse it themselves.[36] Others however, including Glastonbury and York, exhibited densely packed, unillustrated *tabulae* written in Latin. Less accessible examples such as these would have been communicated to most guests through the mediation of chantry priests, vicars choral, or monks acting as guides.[37] This would have ensured that even visitors who could not read Latin would still have access to the text (albeit mediated access), which may have been read or summarised aloud. There is precedence for such guiding activity at various sacred and legendary sites. At Thomas Beckett's shrine in Canterbury, a monk was always employed to direct visitor experience and watch for theft: the Sacrist would have overseen and perhaps trained these guide staff.[38] At York, the vicars choral were expected to learn the material contained in the *tabulae* by heart, perhaps for the purpose of guiding guests;[39] and they could be issued fines for failing to attend to the pilgrims' needs.[40] When Margery Kempe visited York Minster, she was guided through the cathedral by John Kendale, a member of the vicars choral responsible for 'informing her as a pilgrim and visitor about the Minster's history and saints' cults'.[41]

---

[35] Shayne Aaron Legassie, *The Medieval Invention of Travel* (Chicago, IL: University of Chicago Press, 2017), pp. 133–41 for the emergence of late medieval travel diarists travelling to the Holy Land; pp. 165–226 for the application of this approach closer to home in Europe after 1350. Examples of itinerant diarists' notes include the notebooks of William Worcester (Cambridge, Corpus Christi College MS 210), William Wey (Oxford, Bodleian Library MS Bodl. 565); John Curteys (Oxford, Bodleian Library MS Bodl. 487); John Leland, *Itineraries*, ed. Lucy Toulmin-Smith, 5 vols (London: George Bell, 1906–10). See Macht, 'Changes in Historical Writing', pp. 14–20.

[36] Macht, 'Changes in Monastic Writing', pp. 21–22.

[37] Macht, ibid.; Rudolph, 'The Tour Guide in the Middle Ages', passim.

[38] Rudolph, 'The Tour Guide', pp. 41–43. Most recently, a new discovery of a Florentine merchant's notebook has illuminated the guided pilgrim experience at Canterbury in considerably more detail. Chiara Capulli and Raffaele Danna, 'Ughi's *Viaggio di Fiandra ed Inghiterra*: A Florentine Merchant Experiences Sacred Space in Canterbury, 1444 – analysis of a previously unknown autograph diary', International Medieval Congress (Leeds, 1 July 2019); John Jenkins, 'Modelling the Cult of Thomas Becket in Canterbury Cathedral', *Journal of the British Archaeological Association*, 173 (2020), 100–23.

[39] *A Book of British Kings 1200BC–1399AD*, ed. A. G. Rigg (Toronto: PIMS, 2000), p. 3.

[40] Kerby-Fulton, *The Clerical Proletariat*, p. 247.

[41] Kerby-Fulton, *The Clerical Proletariat*, ibid.

Arthur was not the only legendary figure to draw in pilgrims at religious sites: there is evidence of tour guiding at Guy's Cliffe in Warwickshire, a location associated with Guy of Warwick.[42] According to the story of Guy's life, the romance hero retired to Guy's Cliffe at the end of his days to live as a hermit. The glamour of romance clearly made Guy's Cliffe an enduringly magnetic destination: as late as 1642, visitors were still flocking to the site to see Guy of Warwick's cave, chapel, and wells.[43] John Rous, the chantry priest at Guy's Cliffe in the late fifteenth century, petitioned for the employment of two 'pore men' at the chantry, revealing the kinds of responsibilities that this work might entail:

> [...] hyt were ful conuenient, youe that hit plesyd, sum good lord or lady to fynd in the same place [i.e. at Guy's Cliffe] ij pore men that cowd help a prest to syng on of them to be there continually present weryng hys pilgrime habit **and to show folk the place** and theyr habitacion myght be ful wel set over hys caue in the roke.[44]

This provides a rare and fascinating glimpse of how the fifteenth-century guide might have looked. Rous's suggestion that the 'pore man' on guide duty should be 'weryng hys pilgrime habit' and seemingly living 'over hys caue in the roke' may even indicate that the guide was intended to embody Guy of Warwick himself. This possibility of a wholly immersive experience for chantry visitors reflects the interpretative praxis of contemporary heritage sites. Anyone who has grown up the vicinity of Glastonbury today probably knows someone who worked as a costumed monk guide at Glastonbury Abbey during the summer months. Rous's statements seem to suggest that chantry priests like himself were responsible not only for maintaining *tabulae*, as Kerby-Fulton has argued, but also for coordinating other kinds of interpretative activities within the spaces for which they were responsible.[45] It would seem that Rous's petitions were successful; reflecting back on the establishment of the Guy's Cliffe 'pore men', Rous claims that this was inspired by a similar example at Winchester, and though the responsibilities and

---

[42] For a comparison of Guy of Warwick's status with King Arthur's, particularly in visual culture, see David Griffith, 'The Visual History of Guy of Warwick', in *Guy of Warwick: Icon and Ancestor*, ed. Rosalind Field and Alison Wiggins (Cambridge: D. S. Brewer, 2017), pp. 110–32; Nicholas Orme, 'Place and Past in Medieval England', *History Today*, July 2008, pp. 25–30.

[43] Robert Crane, 'The Vogue of *Guy of Warwick* from the Close of the Middle Ages to the Romantic Revival', *Publications of the Modern Language Association*, 30 (1915), 125–94.

[44] John Rous, *The Rous Roll*, ed. Charles Ross (Gloucester: Sutton, 1980), no. 22, emphasis mine.

[45] Kerby-Fulton, *The Clerical Proletariat*, pp. 260–305.

behaviours of these Winchester 'pore gentylmen' is unknown Rous provides valuable information on who was responsible for instigating the developments there:

> [Neville] endowid his place of Gybclyf with more lyuolede for mo prestys and poer Gentilmen [...] and inremembrance of seynt Gy he wold haue had a certen of pore gentylmen found ther as were at seynt Cros of Wynchestre by the fundacon of maister herre beauford cardynal and bishop of Wynchestre brodur to kyng herre the foruth wich place was endowid with forfet lyuelode of the Eorl of Salisbury [...][46]

This suggests that the 'pore men' at Guy's Cliffe were increased by Richard Neville in remembrance of 'seynt Gy', and in imitation of Bishop Henry Beaufort's installation of a similar group at Winchester.

Just before describing the 'pore gentylmen' guides of Guy's Cliffe, John Rous recounts Richard Neville's plans to have an image of Sir Guy painted in the chapel, presumably to enhance the multimedial experience of visiting pilgrims.[47] This exemplifies another strategy that sites used to communicate their histories with guests (literate or otherwise): by drawing out connections between the text of *tabulae* and other architectural and artistic features, site custodians could create what Van Dussen has identified as a kind of metaphorical electrical circuit, a 'closed loop of interaction with an architectural space'.[48] *Tabulae* often formed just one part of a programme of visual and architectural installations which were designed to work in tandem – either to support devotional practices or imaginative engagement with site histories. In his late fifteenth-century *Historia regum Angliae*, Rous describes a tapestry at St Albans which depicted an episode from the site's legendary history:

> Eventually, another King Offa descending from that line learned in a vision of how the foundations of the monastery of St Albans had been built. He splendidly endowed it with magnificent possessions, and most commendably he elevated the true relic of the blessed first

---

[46] John Rous, *The Rous Roll*, no. 57.

[47] 'Thys noble lord [Richard Neville] was purpsid to have endowed his place of Gybclyf [...] by the avys of oder lordys sturryng hym so to doo and to let peynt Sir Gyes Image [...]' Rous, *Rous Roll*, no. 22. John A. A. Goodall points out that 'the only other almsmen of gentle status in the kingdom were the Poor Knights of the Royal College of St George at Windsor', which suggests that the expansions proposed at Guy's Cliffe were extremely ambitious in scale. John A. A. Goodall, 'The Chantry Chapel at Guy's Cliffe, Warwick', in *Coventry: Medieval Art, Architecture and Archaeology in the City and its Vicinity*, ed. Linda Monckton and Richard K. Morris (London: Routledge, 2011), pp. 304–17 (p. 306).

[48] Van Dussen, 'Tourists and Tabulae', p. 248.

martyr, [St] Alban, translating it from a lowly to a fine reliquary. This is set forth in the very same place in the book of the Abbots' lives, and a much longer version has been taken down in writing verbatim from the noble memory of Richard Neville Earl of Warwick at his direction. In the said abbey, the abbot's hall is even until this day still decorated with cloth [telling] the same history, as I myself have seen.

(Tandem alius rex Offa ab eo lenealiter descendens visione doctus senobium Sancti Albani a fundamentis construxit, possessionibus magnifice dotavit, & corpus ipsius almi prothomartyris Albani in nobili scrineo ab humili in altum laudabiliter transtulit. Istum processum eodem loco libro de gestis abbatum vidi, & multo longiori processu verbatim abiinde scriptus illustris memoriae Ricardo Nevel comiti Warwici erat directus. In dicta eciam abbathia aula abbatis in pannis cum eadem historia usque hodie decoratur, & egomet vidi.)[49]

The abbot's hall at St Albans was not a private space, and was used to accommodate guests as early as the eleventh century.[50] As well as royals and other dignitaries, religious houses also hosted learned guests in such spaces; William Worcester was entertained in the abbot's hall at Glastonbury when he visited the abbey in the late fifteenth century.[51]

Arthurian multimedia at York Minster

Of course, stained glass was an essential component of visitors' media experience at many religious houses, and glazing schemes could readily be designed for consumption alongside *tabulae* (or vice versa). At St Paul's Cathedral, the legend of King Lucius and the holy rood was displayed on a *tabula* hanging near the tomb of John of Gaunt before the Rood at the North Door, in the direct line of sight of a window above showing details from the same story.[52] The interpretative scheme at St Paul's was completed with further *tabulae* along the ambulatory, beside shrines, and next to the graves of prominent figures; some examples

---

[49] Rous, *Historia Regum Angliae*, pp. 64–65.

[50] The abbot's hall at St Albans, and its use for accommodating guests, is described in Julie Kerr, *Monastic Hospitality: The Benedictines in England, c. 1070–c. 1250, The Administrative Structure* (Woodbridge: Boydell, 2007), pp. 80–85.

[51] Worcester, *Itineraries*, pp. 260–61.

[52] Macht, 'Changes in Monastic Historical Writing', pp. 20–21. The text is partially copied in British Library Harley MS 565 at f. 2v, and is also mentioned in John Hardyng's chronicle; see British Library MS Lansdowne 204, f. 42r, quoted in Felicity Riddy, 'Glastonbury, Joseph of Arimathea, and the Grail in John Hardyng's Chronicle', in *Glastonbury Abbey and the Arthurian Tradition*, pp. 269–84 (p. 278).

even cross-referenced each other.⁵³ Van Dussen has found evidence to suggest that a Bohemian traveller who travelled from Prague to London, visiting Westminster and St Paul's, took notes from various *tabulae* on display there.⁵⁴

A similar interplay between Arthurian media was employed at York Minster, where a clear and cohesive historical scheme embedding Arthur in the minster's history survives across extant *tabulae*, tablet texts, and stained glass in the cathedral. Together, these media tell the story of the minster's first foundation and subsequent Christian restorations during its early pseudo-history. Arthur, we are told in both the larger tablet and John of Allhallowgate's *Aliud chronicon metricum*, was the British king who oversaw the third restoration of the minster to Christianity, and the installation of Piramus as the third Archbishop of the See. The first figures to be named in the *Aliud chronicon metricum* are the three earliest Christian kings of Britain to have re-founded the minster, and the York archbishops in place during each of their respective reigns. These kings are listed in order, as if to aid memorisation:

> Of the four Archbishops of York in the time of the Britons, it should in fact be known that those who follow were the archbishops of the Metropolitan See of York during the time when Christianity endured through Pope Eleutherius. [...] Archbishop Fagan was the first of these in the time of King Lucius. The second archbishop there was Samson in the time of King Aurelius Ambrosius. The third archbishop was Piramus, or Priamus, in the time of King Arthur.

> (De quatuor archiepiscopis Eboracensibus tempore Britonum revera sciendum est quod isti sequentes fuerunt archiepiscopi sedis metropolis Eboracensis tempore quo perduravit dicta Christianitas per papam Eleutherium [...] Primus in ea sede fuit archiepiscopus Faganus praedictus in tempore Lucii regis. Secundus ibidem archiepiscopus fuit Samson in tempore Aurelii Ambrosii regis. Tertius archiepiscopus Piramus, alias Priamus, in tempore Arthuri regis.)⁵⁵

This sequence is repeated in the larger of York's surviving *tabulae*, where rubricated headings further support the memorability of this series of kings. Lucius, Aurelius Ambrosius, and Arthur are introduced in three consecutive sections under the following rubrics:

---

⁵³ Mason, 'Writing on the Wall', passim and p. 36.
⁵⁴ Van Dussen, 'Tourists and Tabulae', pp. 245–47.
⁵⁵ Raine, *The Historians of the Church of York*, p. 467.

On the first foundation of the Church of York and the consecration of the archbishop[56]

(De prima fundatione ecclesiae Eboracensis et consecratione archiepiscopi)

On the second restoration of the Church of York by King Aurelius and Archbishop St Sampson[57]

(De secunda reparatione ecclesiae Eborum per regem Aurelium et Sanctum Sampsonum archiepiscopum)

On the third restoration by King Arthur and Archbishop Piramus[58]

(De tertia reparatione per regem Arthurum [et] per Piramum archiepiscopum)

In the second and third rubrics, the kings are named alongside their respective York archbishops. Only the first heading does not mention the name of the archbishop installed by King Lucius: Faganus is not named here as York's first archbishop, as he is in the *Aliud Chronicon Metricum*. Instead, the tablet follows Geoffrey of Monmouth's *Historia* by focusing on Pope Eleutherius, Fagan, and Damian as the key Christian figures of influence in Britain during King Lucius' reign.[59]

This trio of early kings and their accompanying churchmen – Lucius and the first archbishop (perhaps Faganus), Aurelius and Sampson, Arthur and Piramus – closely reflects the glazing scheme of the Great East Window. While there has been some disagreement as to where exactly the large *tabula* was displayed, with suggestions ranging from Bedern Hall where the vicars choral were housed to the main body of the Minster church itself, it is quite possible that it hung within the vicinity of the Great East Window.[60] Even if it did not, we know that its contents were

[56] Raine, *The Historians of the Church of York*, p. 447. Translation mine.
[57] Raine, *The Historians of the Church of York*, p. 449. Translation mine.
[58] Raine, *The Historians of the Church of York*, p. 450. Translation mine.
[59] Geoffrey of Monmouth, *The History of the Kings of Britain*, 4.72, pp. 86–88; Raine, *The Historians of the Church of York*, p. 448, l. 61 (Faganus and Damianus); p. 449, l. 82 (Eleutherius).
[60] Purvis and Harrison suggest it hung in the Vicars Choral; see Purvis, 'The Tables of the York Vicars Choral', pp. 741–48; Frederick Harrison, *Life in a Medieval College: The Story of the Vicars-Choral of York Minster* (London: J. Murray, 1952), p. 64. Barrie Dobson previously argued for a hanging site in the main cathedral for the benefit of visiting pilgrims, a view shared by Kathryn Kerby-Fulton; but more recently Dobson has suggested the table might instead have hung in the Bedern. See Barrie Dobson, 'The Later Middle Ages 1215–1500', in *A History of York Minster*, ed. G. E. Aylmer and Reginald Cant (Oxford: Clarendon Press, 1977), pp. 44–109 (p. 108, n. 227); 'The English Vicars Choral: An Introduction', in *Vicars Choral at English Cathedrals*, ed. Richard Hall and David Stocker (Oxford:

recounted to visiting guests by guides. The Great East Window, installed between 1405 and 1408 after almost five decades of renovations to the minster including the *tabulae*'s production, sets out a carefully planned iconographic scheme divided into clear and distinct layers. The bottom row of panels depicts figures particular to the minster's history, split into two halves with secular rulers on the left side and saints and bishops on the right. Each half runs chronologically from left to right, and the halves are divided by a middle panel where Bishop Walter Skirlaw appears (d. 1406), the bishop who held the See when the window was created. Panel 1b, captioned 'fundantes reges britonum' (founding kings of the Britons), features the figures of King Aurelius and King Lucius, both labelled (see Figure 1). A third unlabelled figure is clearly intended to represent King Arthur, appearing above Arthur's most ubiquitous heraldic arms.[61] This identification makes sense within the context of this row of glazing and with the panel's caption, as well as the *tabula* and *Aliud chronicon metricum*. Panel 1f, the chronological counterpart to 1b appearing to the right of the Skirlaw panel, features Sampson, Eleutherius, and Piramus, the three Christian figures associated with the minster's history during the reigns of Aurelius, Lucius, and Arthur respectively.[62] If the large *tabula* was indeed displayed within sight of the Great East Window, visitors could take in the textual history and visual iconography together. If it was displayed elsewhere and interpreted to guests orally by a guide, as others have suggested, these visitors could enjoy a running commentary as they viewed the window.

The examples of Arthurian multimedia at York Minster show clear signs of being designed with a mnemonic function in mind. Not only do the *tabula*, the *Aliud chronicon metricum* and the Great East Window reiterate the same material, this material is repeated across these media in the same memorable clusters: three kings, three bishops, three periods

---

Oxbow Press, 2005), pp. 1–10; Kerby-Fulton, *The Clerical Proletariat*, p. 369 and p. 367, n. 53.

[61] Panel 1b, The Great East Window, https://stainedglass-navigator.yorkglazierstrust.org/window/great-east-window/panel/1b [accessed 12 March 2022]. On Arthur's arms, see Gerard J. Brault, *Early Blazon: Heraldic Terminology in the Twelfth and Thirteenth Centuries*, 2nd edn (Woodbridge: Boydell, 1997), pp. 44–46. The Arthurian arms of three gold crowns on blue, two over one, that appears in the York Minster glazing also appear elsewhere in English stained glass, such as the examples in the ante-chapel of All Souls College Oxford and St Mary's Hall in Coventry. See C. E. Pickford, 'The Three Crowns of King Arthur', *Yorkshire Archaeological Journal*, 38 (1954), 373–82 (p. 375). I am grateful to Sheri Chriqui for sharing her expertise on Arthur's heraldry.

[62] Panel 1f, The Great East Window, https://stainedglass-navigator.yorkglazierstrust.org/window/great-east-window/panel/1f [accessed 12 March 2022].

Figure 1. Panel 1b in the Great East Window of York Minster. Showing (L–R) Aurelius, Lucius, and Arthur. Taken by The York Glaziers Trust, reproduced by kind permission of the Chapter of York.

of Christian revival in York. Eviatar Zerubavel refers to this type of repetition as a means of remembering history in terms of 'mnemonic typification'.[63] History becomes schematised: the narrative reiterated across the discrete media at York Minster essentially boils down local, national and universal Christian histories to their most basic points of connection, all of which come together in the location of the minster itself.

[63] Zerubavel, *Time Maps*, pp. 24–25.

More precisely, it is the very act of creating the window, tablets, and chronicle that pulls these different histories together and publicises them, calling this particular vision of the past into being. This coming together is rendered literally in the Great Window, in which Bishop Skirlaw, the figure who oversaw the window's production, is placed at the very centre of his row of panes, acting as a point of connection between the secular and sacred, local and universal figures, all connected with York, who radiate outwards on either side.

Experiencing Arthur on-site: Glastonbury Abbey

Arthur in Avalon

If Arthur played an important role in York Minster's history, he was absolutely central to the history of Glastonbury Abbey. It is clear from Glastonbury's surviving *magna tabula* ('great tablet') and from descriptions of visual culture and guided experiences at medieval Glastonbury that the abbey placed Arthur at the heart of its visitors' experience.

Glastonbury's association with Arthur is complex and long-standing. He appears to have already been closely bound up with the sacred space of the Abbey and its territory when Caradoc of Llancarfan wrote his *Life of Gildas* (c. 1130–50), a text written around the same time that Geoffrey of Monmouth immortalised Arthur in his *Historia regum Britanniae*.[64] Likely commissioned by Glastonbury Abbey monks, the *Life* describes the conflict that develops between King Arthur and King Melwas after the latter kidnaps Guinevere and steals her away to his court at Glastonbury. The kings are ultimately reconciled by the Glastonbury abbot who makes them promise never again to 'violate the most sacred place nor even the districts adjoining the chief's seat'.[65] Though Glastonbury is not mentioned in Geoffrey of Monmouth's *Historia regum Britanniae* (c. 1136), the text would become crucial to Glastonbury's Arthurian story some sixty years later when, in 1191, Arthur's grave was reportedly discovered in the abbey grounds. According to the earliest record of the discovery in Gerald of Wales' *De instructione prinicipis* (c. 1193), Gerald describes

---

[64] Geoffrey of Monmouth referred to Caradoc as a 'contemporary' (contemporaneo); see Geoffrey of Monmouth, *The History of the Kings of Britain*, 9.208, pp. 280–81. On the dating of Caradoc's text, see J. S. P. Tatlock, 'Caradoc of Llancarfan', *Speculum*, 13.2 (1938), 139–52; Gransden, *Legends, Traditions, and History*, p. 162; C. N. L. Brooke, *The Church and the Welsh Border in the Central Middle Ages* (Woodbridge: Boydell, 1986), p. 42.

[65] Antonia Gransden, 'The Growth of the Glastonbury Traditions', p. 40; Caradoc cited in Adam Stout, 'Savaric', pp. 105–06.

how the bodies of Arthur and Guinevere were found buried between two stone pyramids, along with a lead cross bearing the following inscription:

> Here lies buried the glorious King Arthur with Guenevere his second wife, in the isle of Avalon
>
> (Hic iacet sepultus inclitus rex Arthurus cum Wenneuereia vxore sua secunda in insula Auallonia)[66]

'Avalon' is a place name taken from Geoffrey of Monmouth's *Historia regum Britanniae*, and refers to 'the isle of Avalon' (insula Avallonis), where Geoffrey claims Arthur was taken at the end of his life.[67]

That Glastonbury should have become associated with Arthur's Avalon is perhaps unsurprising, not only because of Arthur's appearance in earlier Glastonbury texts such as Caradoc's *Life of Gildas* but also because the Abbey carefully fostered an image as an abundant island in the years before and after the 1191 discovery.[68] More detailed descriptions of Avalon written later in the twelfth and thirteenth centuries likewise identify Avalon with the 'insula pomorum' (island of fruit trees, or apple trees according to Gerald of Wales), describing it as an abundant and fertile island, a *locus amoenus* inhabited by healing women.[69] This was probably a move on the part of the Abbey to assert their significance over and above England's other religious houses, and to drum up royal favour in the wake of several difficult decades involving a disastrous fire and dwindling financial investment.[70] It may also be suggestive that the abbey saw itself as a microcosm for the nation, which was imagined at this time as a fantasy of an entire, remote, and fecund island. As both Catherine

---

[66] Gerald of Wales, *Giraldi Cambrensis Opera*, ed. J. S. Brewer, James F. Dimock, and George F. Warner, Rolls Series 21, 9 vols (Cambridge: Cambridge University Press, 2012), VIII, p. 127. Translation mine. In Gerald's later work, *Speculum Ecclesiae* (c. 1216), he gives a second account, which places more emphasis on his own eyewitness testimony of the grave discovery and his handling of the lead cross; and further accounts of the disinterment were made by Ralph of Coggeshall (c. 1223), Glastonbury monk Adam of Damerham (c. 1275–1300), and the chronicler of Margam Abbey (c. 1234). All reports are cited in E. K. Chambers, *Arthur of Britain* (London: Sidgwick & Jackson, 1927), pp. 233–82. See also Gransden, 'The Growth of the Glastonbury Traditions', especially pp. 43–46.

[67] Geoffrey mentions 'Avallon' twice: as the site where Arthur's sword Caliburn was forged (Geoffrey of Monmouth, *The History of the Kings of Britain*, 9.147, pp. 198–99); and also as the location where Arthur was taken to heal following his final battle at Camlan (Geoffrey of Monmouth, *The History of the Kings of Britain*, 11.178, pp. 252–53).

[68] Clarke, *Literary Landscapes*, pp. 69–79.

[69] James Wade, *Fairies in Medieval Romance* (London: Palgrave Macmillan, 2011), pp. 39–71. See also Aisling Byrne, *Otherworlds: Fantasy and History in Medieval Literature* (Oxford: Oxford University Press, 2016), pp. 119–29.

[70] Clarke, *Literary Landscapes*, p. 68.

Clarke and Aisling Byrne have pointed out, Glastonbury's island self-fashioning effectively framed the abbey as a local mnemonic for the broader nation, using the very landscape of the abbey and its surrounds to draw connections between the local, national, and universal Christian spheres.[71] If the presence of the name Avalon on the inscribed cross and its appearance in Geoffrey's text lent credibility to the 1191 discovery, it was the very land itself at Glastonbury, carefully cultivated to match the abundant Avalonian isle of Geoffrey of Monmouth's *Vita Merlini* (c. 1150), that made Arthur's grave seem truly believable, a Zerubavelian 'constancy of place' that managed to cut not only across time, but also across the worlds of romance, chronicle, and the real abbey site.[72]

Fomenting an impression of Glastonbury as the isle of Avalon was no doubt greatly assisted by the imposing silhouette of Glastonbury Tor. The tor is a dramatic hill on the outskirts of Glastonbury that dominates the local skyline, and would once have risen as an island above the local wetlands before they were drained by the monastery in the early Middle Ages.[73] At its top is St Michael's Tower, a remnant of a chapel of St Michael built in the fourteenth century to replace a much earlier wooden church; Glastonbury's fourteenth-century chronicler John of Glastonbury claimed the oratory had been built by Britain's earliest Christian missionaries, Fagan and Deruvian, and that this oratory had been rediscovered by Saint Patrick.[74] Today, the tor is connected with all manner of myths, legends, and belief, and is broadly associated with the Isle of Avalon.[75] Medieval texts do not tend to link the tor directly with Avalon; this honour generally goes to the main abbey precinct on account of the 1191 disinterment. There are, however, one or two tantalising exceptions. Morgan ('le Fay' in later textual tradition) has been associated with Avalon since at least 1151, when Geoffrey of Monmouth described her residing there as a healer in his later and lesser-known text, the *Vita Merlini* (1151).[76] The Glastonbury Quire of Cotton Titus A.XIX and a further Glastonian manuscript, MS Bodley 622 (c. 1300–50), contain an early description of the Chapel

---

[71] Clarke, *Literary Landscapes*, pp. 67–89; Byrne, *Otherworlds*, p. 126.
[72] Cited above at pp. 22–26.
[73] Roberta Gilchrist and Cheryl Green, *Glastonbury Abbey: Archaeological Investigations, 1904–79* (London: Society of Antiquaries of London, 2015), p. 54.
[74] Gilchrist and Green, *Glastonbury Abbey*, p. 56; Krochalis, 'Magna Tabula', p. 488 n.; Gransden, 'The Growth of the Glastonbury Traditions', p. 40.
[75] Marion Bowman, 'Procession and Possession in Glastonbury: Continuity, Change and the Manipulation of Tradition', *Folklore*, 115.3 (2004), 273–85 (pp. 274–75); Bowman, 'Going with the Flow', p. 256. See also Stout, *Glastonbury Holy Thorn*, pp. 94–126.
[76] The *Vita* associates Morgan with Avalon and the island of apples (*insula pomorum*) for the first time, characterising her as a skilled healer rather than the 'Fee' of later texts. See Wade, *Fairies*, p. 12.

Ride story known as the *Quedam narracio de nobili rege Arthuro*, itself a reworking of an episode from *Perlesvaus*.[77] This episode describes Arthur falling asleep and experiencing a dream vision in which an angel appears to him and instructs him to go to a hermitage at Beckery (or Hearty, another island within the Abbey's Hides, in MS Bodley 622), ultimately leading to the Virgin Mary gifting him a crystal cross that is later added to Glastonbury Abbey's relic collection and adopted into Arthur's new coat of arms. Later versions of this story say that Arthur had his dream at a 'monastery of holy virgins' (monasterium sanctarum virginum) 'within the island of Avalon, at Wearyall' (intra insulam Auallonie in Wirale).[78] But the version in Cotton Titus A.XIX's Glastonbury Quire and in Bodley MS 622 instead claims that Arthur fell asleep in

> the chamber of his sister (whose name was Morgan, known as the Faye), situated on top of the mount right next to Wearyall [Hill]
>
> (camera sororis sue nomine morgan cognomento la faye sita supra montem proximum iuxta Wirehall)
>
> (Cotton Titus MS A.XIX, ff. 16v–17r)

This is unquestionably Glastonbury Tor: there are no other hills 'right next to' Wearyall Hill which could be described as a 'mount'; and St Michael's Chapel is similarly described as 'montane capelle' (the chapel on the mount) in the *magna tabula* (Oxford, Bodleian Library, MS Lat. Hist. A. 2, tablet page 4 [bottom]). Given that the *Quedam narracio* seems to have originated at Glastonbury – James Carley has suggested it was adapted from *Perlesvaus* at the abbey itself – this suggests the abbey was keen to foster its association with Avalon in the early fourteenth century.[79] At least two Welsh texts from the fourteenth and fifteenth centuries respectively, the *Llyfr Arfau* and *Darogan yr Olew Bendigaid*, also include a version of this episode, and both locate it at Glastonbury.[80]

Following the remarkable discovery of 1191, the news of Arthur's grave spread rapidly.[81] Soon after the excavation the bones claimed to

---

[77] James P. Carley, 'A Glastonbury Translator at Work: *Quedam Narracio de nobili rege Arthuro* and *De Origine Gigantum* in their Earliest Manuscript Contexts', in *Glastonbury Abbey and the Arthurian Tradition*, pp. 337–46.

[78] See, for example, John of Glastonbury, *Cronica sive antiquitates Glastoniensis Ecclesie/The Chronicle of Glastonbury Abbey: An Edition, Translation and Study of John of Glastonbury's Cronica of c.1342*, ed. James P. Carley (Woodbridge: Boydell, 2009), pp. 76–77.

[79] Carley, 'A Glastonbury Translator at Work', passim.

[80] Ceridwen Lloyd-Morgan, 'From Ynys Wydrin to Glasynbri: Glastonbury in Welsh Vernacular Tradition', in *Glastonbury Abbey and the Arthurian Tradition*, pp. 170–72.

[81] The speed at which this news was spread may, according to some scholars, suggest that a pamphlet may have been shared; see Gransden, 'The Growth of the

be Arthur and Guinevere were entombed at the choir end of the Great Church before the high altar, the most sacred part of the abbey, reserved for its founders.[82] Although John Leland describes the tomb as having been relocated on at least two occasions, he probably encountered the original monument when he visited in 1530.[83] The tomb, a black marble 'chest' sarcophagus supported by a lion at each corner, looks to have been designed in an intentionally archaic style, modelled on classical sarcophagi and seemingly geared towards aligning Arthur with the ancient Saxon kings buried in the abbey.[84] Pilgrims would have seen a carved image of Arthur at the foot of his tomb and inscriptions for Arthur and Guinevere at the monument's east and west end, along with an inscription for Abbot Henry of Sully that helps us to date the monument to c. 1200.[85] Arthurian inscriptions at the tomb may have included epitaphs and other poetic fragments that were updated throughout the tomb's history; a series of different epitaphs for Arthur have been discovered, and one visitor, William Worcester, noted down yet another fragment of verse praising Arthur in notes taken *in situ* beside the tomb during his 1480 visit.[86] Material fragments were also displayed at the tomb site, perhaps only on special occasions; Adam of Damerham wrote that when Edward I and his queen visited in 1278 the skulls of Arthur and Guinevere were shown at the tomb 'for the veneration of the people'.[87]

As a result of the grave discovery, there was a sudden explosion in references to Glastonbury in Arthurian texts in the late twelfth and thirteenth centuries, and by 1250 this had led Joseph of Arimathea, Glastonbury, and Arthur to be connected in romance literature.[88] Perhaps

---

Glastonbury Traditions', p. 50; see above at p. 12.
[82] Gilchrist and Green, *Glastonbury Abbey*, p. 61.
[83] Gilchrist and Green, *Glastonbury Abbey*, pp. 61–62.
[84] Gilchrist and Green, *Glastonbury Abbey*, p. 62; Phillip Lindley, *Tomb Destruction and Scholarship: Medieval Monuments in Early Modern England* (Donington: Shaun Tyas, 2007), p. 141.
[85] Gilchrist and Green, *Glastonbury Abbey*, p. 61.
[86] The verse extract appears in Worcester's *Itineraries*; see Cambridge, Corpus Christi College MS 210, p. 218; Worcester, *Itineraries*, pp. 298–99. On Arthur's changing epitaphs, see John Withrington, 'The Arthurian Epitaph in Malory's *Morte Darthur*', in *Glastonbury Abbey and the Arthurian Tradition*, pp. 211–48; Michelle Brown and James P. Carley, 'A Fifteenth-Century Revision of the Glastonbury Epitaph to King Arthur', in *Glastonbury Abbey and the Arthurian Tradition*, pp. 193–203; and Neil Wright, 'A New Arthurian Epitaph', in *Glastonbury Abbey and the Arthurian Tradition*, pp. 205–09.
[87] Cited in Charles T. Wood, 'Guenevere at Glastonbury: A Problem in Translation(s)', in *Glastonbury Abbey and the Arthurian Tradition*, pp. 83–100 (p. 86).
[88] Joseph of Arimathea first features in Grail romance in Robert de Boron's *Joseph d'Arimathie* in the late twelfth century, which describes Joseph's journey west to 'vaus d'Avaron'; and in the *Estoire del Saint Graal* (c. 1215–30) Joseph's travel takes

as a result of this burst in literary production, interpolations were added to William of Malmesbury's history of the abbey, *De antiquitate Glastonie Ecclesie*, between c. 1230 and 1250. William's text, composed c. 1129–39, had not originally made any connections between Arthur and the abbey, though it did assert that Glastonbury had been founded early during the reign of King Lucius. The thirteenth-century interpolations brought William's history up-to-date by connecting Arthur with Glastonbury and claiming Joseph of Arimathea as the abbey's apostolic founder, rather than the unknown figures sent to convert Britain during King Lucius' reign according to William's original text.[89]

Some of the Arthurian material interpolated into William of Malmesbury's *De antiquitate* has no clear source, such as a story of Yder's fatal fight with a giant at 'Frog Mountain, now called Brent Knoll' (montem Ranarum, nunc dictum Brentecnol), which results in Arthur giving lands to the abbey.[90] This tale may have been of more than a passing interest to the abbey's monks, for by the fourteenth century abbey visitors would have also seen the remains of 'Iderus filius Nuti' (Yder son of Nut) alongside a number of other objects relating to secular abbey founders and kings, displayed atop a nearby tomb in the choir adjacent to Arthur's.[91] William's interpolator says that the Frog Mountain episode can be read in 'the deeds of the most illustrious King Arthur'

---

him, explicitly, to Britain, starting a line of Grail keepers that would continue until the time of Arthur. Lagorio, 'The Evolving Legend of St Joseph of Glastonbury', in *Glastonbury Abbey and the Arthurian Tradition*, pp. 55–81.

[89] William of Malmesbury, *The Early History of Glastonbury* [*De antiquitate Glastonie Ecclesie*], ed. John Scott (Woodbridge: Boydell, 1981), referred to henceforth as *De antiquitate*. The Arthurian interpolations occur throughout but especially at the end of ch. 1 (pp. 46–47), ch. 5 (pp. 52–53), part of ch. 31 (pp. 82–84), and ch. 34 (pp. 86–89).

[90] William of Malmesbury, *De antiquitate*, pp. 86–88. The episode is later incorporated into John of Glastonbury's *Cronica*, though John relocates the site of the battle with the giant to the mountain of Areynes in North Wales, and instead makes nearby Brent Knoll in Somerset one of the gifts of land that Arthur bestows upon the Abbey after the incident. See John of Glastonbury, *Cronica sive antiquitates Glastoniensis Ecclesie/The Chronicle of Glastonbury Abbey: An Edition, Translation and Study of John of Glastonbury's Cronica of c.1342*, ed. James P. Carley (Woodbridge: Boydell, 2009), pp. 76–77, henceforth cited as *Cronica*. The association between Brent Marsh/Brent Knoll and the 'frog mountain' location may have been a story that the monks shared with guests; in the English edition of *Britannia* William Camden states: 'by that moory or fenny-country Brenmarsh, that runneth out verie farre, which the Monkes of Glastenburie interpreted to be the Counttey of Fen frogges, like as the little towne Brentknoll there, which signifieth Frog-hill'. Of course, Camden may simply have taken this from the *magna tabula*, William's *De antiquitate*, or John's *Cronica*. William Camden, *Britain*, trans. Philemon Holland (London: George Bishop and John Norton, 1610), STC (2nd edn) 4509, p. 230.

[91] Julian M. Luxford, *The Art and Architecture of English Benedictine Monasteries, 1300–1540: A Patronage History* (Woodbridge: Boydell, 2005), p. 170.

(in gestis illustrissimi regis Arturi), and Carley, Nitze, and Jenkins all suggest that this tale may share a now-lost source with the Anglo-Norman romance *Yder*.[92] That such sources have not been preserved is unsurprising given the poor survival rate of insular romance texts and their manuscripts.[93] Other Arthurian interpolations made to *De antiquitate* have clearer precedents, however, such as a section at the end of chapter 1 also attributed to 'the book of the deeds of the famous King Arthur' (liber de gestis incliti regis Arturi), which refers to episodes seemingly taken from three Vulgate romances.[94]

We shall return later to the tantalising question of possible lost Arthurian texts at Glastonbury. Clearly, the abbey was making shrewd use of its Arthurian connections in this period to raise its profile, but what can be said for guided experiences of Glastonbury's Arthurian history at this time? There is little textual evidence that tells us how guests' experiences of Arthurian Glastonbury might have been managed prior to the fourteenth century. There may be an interesting exception in the form of Oxford Bodleian Library MS Laud Misc. 750, a Glastonbury manuscript that has been described as a belt book: that is, a long and slender manuscript designed to be portable, attached to the belt of whomever would be consulting it. Most belt books of this date tend to include material such as medical recipes for travelling doctors. Unusually, this example gives a potted summary of the abbey's history, detailing the saints and kings buried at the abbey and its relic collections, material that would later be contained in Glastonbury's *magna tabula*.[95] Krochalis has suggested that this belt book might have been useful for monk guides, and perhaps it is an indication of the kinds of tour guiding that took place

---

[92] William of Malmesbury, *De antiquitate*, pp. 86–87. Concerning the possibility of a shared lost source with *Yder*, see Carley's analysis in John of Glastonbury, *Cronica*, p. 284 n. 116; *Le Haut Livre du Graal: Perlesvaus*, ed. William A. Nitze and T. Atkinson Jenkins, 2 vols (Chicago, IL: University of Chicago Press, 1932–37), II, pp. 303–06. *Yder* survives in a single incomplete manuscript, Cambridge University Library MS Ee.4.26; for a study and edition, see *The Romance of Yder*, ed. and trans. Alison Adams (Cambridge: D. S. Brewer, 1983).

[93] A recent study employed a model from ecology that suggested that Middle English heroic and chivalric narratives have fared particularly poorly, with only around 4.9 per cent surviving. See Mike Kestemont et al., 'Forgotten Books: The Application of Unseen Species Models to the Survival of Culture', *Science*, 375 (2022), 765–69.

[94] William of Malmesbury, *De antiquitate*, pp. 46–47. The interpolations made to *De antiquitate* are repeated in John of Glastonbury's *Cronica*, and an analysis of the extract's sources is provided by James Carley (ed.) in John of Glastonbury, *Cronica*, p. 279, n. 75.

[95] Both Jean Krochalis and Conrad Rudolph argue convincingly that this may have been used by guides at Glastonbury. Krochalis, 'Magna Tabula', p. 437; Rudolph, 'The Tour Guide', pp. 45–46.

at Glastonbury Abbey at a much earlier period, around a century before the installation of the *magna tabula*. As this manuscript predates the *magna tabula*, it may suggest that *tabulae* were constructed not only to shape the guiding activities of monks and other site custodians, but that they might themselves be carefully shaped around the bodies of knowledge already being compiled and shared orally by tour guides.

Romance and history

The interpolations made to William's text demonstrate that by 1250, Arthurian romances were functioning as authorities for Glastonbury's apocryphal legends.[96] Based on what survives, however, Arthur's Glastonbury grave lacked supporting chronicle evidence at this time that explicitly placed Arthur at Glastonbury. The interpolations to William's *De antiquitate* may have been made because the chronicle, which lacked references to Arthur and Joseph of Arimathea, was no longer adequate as a historic source for the Abbey's illustrious history by c. 1230.[97] William's interpolator seems to use only romances and the grave itself as sources for his Arthurian additions. Even if the Avalon of the Vulgate romances was associated with Glastonbury at this stage, providing some textual support for the inscription on the cross cited by Gerald of Wales, the vague topographical and onomastic qualities of these early romances made them unsuitable tools for grounding Arthurian legends in the real site at Glastonbury. The untethered fluidity of quest romance topographies would not be effectively disrupted until the fifteenth century, when the toponyms of romance were layered with real-world equivalents by writers like Malory and Hardyng – Avalon for Glastonbury, or Winchester for Camelot.[98] These romance toponyms were far too suggestive of the untethered and ahistoric chronotope of the knight on the road, which undermined the sense of deep time and sameness of space – Bakhtin's

---

[96] I use the term 'apocryphal' because Joseph of Arimathea's story originates from the *Gospel of Nicodemus*. French verse translations of the *Gospel* were circulating in the thirteenth century, and at least one surviving manuscript is authored in Anglo-Norman. See Richard O' Gorman, 'The *Gospel of Nicodemus* in the Vernacular Literature of Medieval France', in *The Medieval Gospel of Nicodemus: Texts, Intertexts, and Contexts in Western Europe*, ed. Zbigniew Izydorczyk (Tempe, AZ: Medieval and Renaissance Texts and Studies, 1997), pp. 103–31 (p. 105).

[97] *De antiquitate*, p. 35.

[98] Meg Roland, 'The Rudderless Boat: Fluid Time and Passionate Geography in (Hardyng's) Chronicle and (Malory's) Romance', *Arthuriana*, 22.4 (2012), 77–94. See also Cooper, *The English Romance in Time*, pp. 67–73.

'castle time' – that the Abbey monks were keep to cultivate.[99] In other words, to make Glastonbury's Arthurian claims appear more believable the monks of Glastonbury Abbey would need to provide Arthur's grave with some kind of support – physical or textual – that could transpose Arthur from the drifting space/time of romance to the physical castle space/time of the Abbey grounds. From the mid-fourteenth century, the physicality of the Glastonbury site and its Arthurian connections would begin to be exploited more effectively, and its local histories brought to a wider audience.[100] The first step was the commissioning of a new chronicle for Glastonbury, one that included details about Arthur and Joseph of Arimathea that had been lacking in William of Malmesbury's earlier attempt. John of Glastonbury's *Cronica sive Antiquitates Glastoniensis Ecclesie* (c. 1342) achieved this by rooting Arthur firmly in the geography and history of Glastonbury Abbey, making several original contributions to Glastonbury's Arthurian legends. John, like the unknown *De antiquitate* interpolators, likely had other sources at his disposal that are now lost to us. Distinctly local in focus, the *Cronica* brought together all the strands of the Glastonbury legends – Arthurian and apocryphal – into one place, weaving together the narratives of Joseph of Arimathea and Arthur into a coherent whole. Though the *Cronica* includes material borrowed from Arthurian romance, John nevertheless alters some of his source matter to downplay its romance elements: for example, the version of the Chapel Ride incident, based on the *Quedam narracio*, does not mention Morgan's chamber as its source does.[101] That the references to Morgan were edited out supports the idea that the monks felt a need to pull the abbey away from its romance associations and towards a more realistic iteration of its Arthurian connections.

The *Cronica* is marked by a distinct focus on the sanctity of the physical land at Glastonbury. It contains the earliest mention of a prophecy in muddled Latin attributed to a Merlin-esque figure named 'Melkin' claiming that Joseph of Arimathea had brought the blood and sweat of Christ to Glastonbury in two cruets, and that they were buried there beside him.[102] The implication is that Glastonbury is not only holy because of its Christian anteriority, but physically sanctified through

---

[99] Bakhtin, 'Forms of Time', p. 98; p. 244.
[100] Lagorio, 'The Evolving Legend', pp. 217–18; James Carley, introduction in *Glastonbury Abbey and the Arthurian Tradition*, p. 6.
[101] John of Glastonbury, *Cronica*, 76–77.
[102] John of Glastonbury, *Cronica*, pp. 29–31. For an edition and loose translation of Melkin's prophecy, see James P. Carley, 'Melkin the Bard and Esoteric Tradition at Glastonbury Abbey', *The Downside Review*, 99 (1981), 1–17 (pp. 3–4).

these buried relics. The *Cronica* even tells of a sultan in the Holy Land who frees a prisoner on the agreement that he is brought a glove full of holy earth back from Glastonbury, where Joseph was buried.[103] The abbey's twelve hides, lands belonging to the abbey since as early as the Domesday book, are also described at length, their boundaries and antiquity exaggerated.[104] From its opening folios, the *Cronica* draws an immediate connection between Glastonbury's twelve apostolic founders and these twelve hides of land:

> In the thirty-first year after the Lord's Passion, twelve of the disciples of St Philip the apostle, among whom Joseph of Arimathea was chief, came into this land and brought Christianity to King Arviragus, although he refused it. They nevertheless obtained from him this place, with its twelve hides of land; here, they constructed the first church in this kingdom [...]
>
> (Anno post passionem Domini tricesimo primo duodecim ex discipulus Sancti Philippi apostoli ex quibus Ioseph ab Arimathia primus erat in terram istam uenerunt, qui regi Aruirago renuenti Christianitatem optulerunt. Tamen locum istum cum duodecim hidis terre ab eo inpetrauerunt, in quo [...] primam huius regni construxerunt ecclesiam)[105]

The patterning of twelve here – twelve disciples and twelve hides – performs a mnemonic function, reinforcing the connection between local Glastonian, British (in the Galfridian sense), and universal Christian histories in much the same way as the recurring trios of kings and bishops used in the Arthurian media at York Minster. The *Cronica*'s careful cataloguing of the local land in its descriptions of the hides forms a stylistic precursor to the chorographical work of John Leland and William Camden in the sixteenth century. This was common practice in the historiography of monastic institutions from the 1100s, but Glastonbury seemed particularly keen to emphasise the importance of its land. The hides are vital to John's *Cronica*: only after the landscape has been introduced in his opening chapters can he turn his attentions to the saints and relics associated with Glastonbury. By the time John was writing, the

---

[103] John of Glastonbury, *Cronica*, pp. 33–35.

[104] The hides are also described (and similarly exaggerated) in the interpolations added to *De antiquitate* in the thirteenth century. William of Malmesbury, *De antiquitate*, chs 72 and 73, pp. 148–52; John of Glastonbury, *Cronica*, chs 3 and 4, pp. 12–16. On the historic boundaries of the hides, see Stephen C. Morland, 'Glaston Twelve Hides', in *Glastonbury, Domesday and Related Studies*, ed. Stephen C. Morland (Glastonbury: Glastonbury Antiquarian Society, 1991), pp. 61–84; Lesley Abrams, *Anglo-Saxon Glastonbury: Church and Endowment* (Woodbridge: Boydell, 1996), pp. 126–27.

[105] John of Glastonbury, *Cronica*, pp. 2–3.

land at Glastonbury had evidently become as important as the figures associated with it – and was crucial to anchoring its mythological figures more firmly in the Abbey's surrounding geography.

The *Cronica* survives in seven manuscripts, and perhaps unsurprisingly given its focus on local landscape, it seems to have predominantly been produced and circulated locally.[106] At least four of the seven manuscripts were probably copied in Glastonbury.[107] C was likely composed at the abbey under Abbot Chinnock in the late fourteenth century; *A* is written in the hand of Thomas Wason, a prior at Glastonbury from c. 1493; and *P* was copied by (or for) William Wyche, a monk at the abbey in 1497.[108] Although the author of *V* is unknown, the text also incorporates sections from the interpolated version of William of Malmesbury's *De antiquitate*. It places extra emphasis on St Patrick and on Arthur's epitaph, which is moved from the middle of the text to the end. A catalogue of Glastonbury abbots is also appended. Given this information, I would suggest that this manuscript also originated in Glastonbury. Of the other three manuscripts, *T* was likely owned by the church at Damerham, part of the abbey's estates, and *B* was the property of Edward Bisse (c. 1588–1647) of nearby Wells.[109] *B1* is a seventeenth-century copy collated from several of the earlier surviving witnesses.

Though the text dates to around 1340, only one surviving manuscript dates to the fourteenth century, likely produced under Abbot John Chinnock as part of the Abbey's marketing drive between c. 1375 and 1390; the other six witnesses date to the late fifteenth or early sixteenth centuries. In the interim period, the *Cronica* was mainly consumed indirectly via the *magna tabula*, an enormous book-like *tabula* on display at the abbey in which fragments of John's *Cronica* were exhibited selectively alongside other texts for the benefit of the abbey's visitors.[110]

---

[106] The manuscripts in question are Cambridge, Trinity College, MS R. 5. 16 (711), known as C (c. 1375–90); Oxford, Bodleian Library, MS Ashmole 790, copied circa 1500 (A); Princeton, Princeton University, MS Robert Garrett 153, dated to 1497 (P); London, British Library MS Cotton Tiberius A.5, late fifteenth- to early sixteenth century (T); London, British Library MS Cotton Vespasian. 22, a fifteenth-century codex (V); Oxford, Bodleian Library MS Bodl. 854, written in the second half of the sixteenth century (B); plus a seventeenth-century copy of the various manuscripts, Oxford Bodleian Library MS Bodl. 957 (B1). A thorough description of the manuscript witnesses is provided by James Carley in John of Glastonbury, *Cronica*, pp. xi–xx.

[107] John of Glastonbury, *Cronica*, pp. xi–xx.

[108] John of Glastonbury, *Cronica*, pp. xi–xiv.

[109] John of Glastonbury, *Cronica*, p. xviii; Henry Lancaster, 'Edward Bisse (c. 1588– by 1647), History of Parliament Online, www.historyofparliamentonline.org/volume/1604-1629/member/bisse-edward-1588-1647 [accessed 2 August 2018].

[110] For a full description, edition, and study of the *tabula*, see Krochalis, 'Magna Tabula'.

Historical media at medieval Glastonbury

The Glastonbury *magna tabula* is one of the earliest known examples of medieval *tabulae*, produced just after Abbot Chinnock's refurbishments in 1382 and certainly before the end of his abbacy in 1420.[111] Chinnock's extensive renovations formed part of a campaign to boost visitor footfall and therefore the abbey's status and bankability.[112] Held today at the Bodleian Library (MS Lat. Hist. A. 2), the *tabula* comprises a large hollow wooden box, over three feet tall, with two hinged wooden 'pages' inside upon which parchment has been pasted. These pages, arranged in loosely chronological order, contain a potted summary of Glastonbury's secular and sacred mythologies: material concerning the myths of Arthur and Joseph of Arimathea, as well as information regarding other saints and relics connected with Glastonbury.

The first tablet page is the most obviously Arthurian section of the *tabula*. It opens with a condensed extract from the Latin apocryphal *Gospel of Nicodemus* concerning Joseph of Arimathea and his coming to Britain. This is immediately followed by some episodes taken from Arthurian romance – the Vulgate *Lancelot*, the *Quest del Saint Graal*, and the *Estoire del Saint Graal*. Next comes Melkin's prophecy, followed by excerpts about Joseph of Arimathea from Peter Riga's versified bible. The next item comprises four lines of verse concerning Joseph's journey to Glastonbury claimed to have been taken from a chronicle about King Arviragus (discussed further at the end of this chapter). The first tablet page closes with two pieces of genealogical material linking Joseph of Arimathea and his family with Arthur and Gawain. Tablet page 2 contains various extracts on the early history of the abbey, from its apostolic foundation to the abbey's connection with Saint Patrick, whose charter appears in full on tablet page 3 along with information on Glastonbury's other important saints, relics, and records of miracles. Tablet 4 focuses on illustrious figures buried at Glastonbury, with information about Glastonbury's onomastic origins at the end of the tablet page: the story of Glasteing and his brothers, and a list of Glastonbury's many alternative

---

[111] Krochalis, 'Magna Tabula', pp. 463–64

[112] Chinnock would later go on to use the Joseph of Arimathea foundation myth (outlined at length in the *magna tabula*) to justify the abbey's primacy at a national synod; later, the legend would be presented before four church councils to argue for the anteriority of England's Christian past. See Lagorio, 'The Evolving Legend of St Joseph', passim. Felicity Riddy, 'John Hardyng in Search of the Grail', in *Arturus Rex: Acta Conventus Lovaniensis 1987*, ed. Willy Van Hoecke, Gilbert Tournoy, and Werner Verbeke, (Leuven: Leuven University Press, 1991), II.

names. Tablet page 5 is concerned with the abbey's built environment and the history of its founding and reparation. The sixth and final tablet page contains three items: a brief reiteration of the saints buried at the abbey; information on St Michael's chapel and on the burial of Joseph of Arimathea; and, finally, a list of indulgences.

Throughout the *tabula*, the material appears to have been arranged and sometimes altered to centre Arthur and his world at Glastonbury, and in fact Arthur appears slightly out of chronological order in item 2 on the first tablet page, perhaps due to his status as the Abbey's star attraction.[113] The theme of Arthurianisation continues on tablet 4, where the illustrious figures listed are broadly arranged from greater to lesser, from saints to archbishops and eventually through to lesser nobles – with Arthur 'and other kings' (et aliis regibus) appearing in second place, after the saints.[114] The opening item on the first *tabula* page, an abbreviated extract borrowed from *The Gospel of Nicodemus*, is doctored to include two figures from the *Estoire del Saint Graal*, Nasciens and Mordrains, reflecting changes made to the same material in John's *Cronica*. The item that follows, which refers to material taken from Arthurian romance, is also in John's *Cronica*. It proclaims that the 'book of the deeds of glorious King Arthur' (gesta incliti Regis Arthuri) bears witness to Joseph of Arimathea coming to Britain with his son Josephes; this is seemingly also based on the *Estoire*. The passage claims, however, that this narrative can be found

> in the part of the book where a hermit explains to Gawain the mystery of a fountain which keeps changing taste and colour [...] It is also reported practically at the beginning of the quest for the vessel which is there called the Holy Grail, where the White Knight explains to Galahad, son of Lancelot the mystery of a miraculous shield which he enjoins him to carry and which no one else can bear, even for a day, without grave loss.

> (uidelicet ubi quidam heremita exponit Walwano misterium cuiusdam fontis: saporem et colorem crebro mutantis. [...] Item in sequentibus in inquisicione uasis quod ibi uocant sanctum graal: idem refertur fere in principio. Ubi albus miles exponit Galaat filio Lanceloth misterium cuiusdam mirabilis scuti quod eidem deferendum commisit quod nemo alius sine graui dispendio ne una quidam die poterat portare.)[115]

---

[113] Krochalis, 'Magna Tabula', p. 465.
[114] Krochalis, 'Magna Tabula', p. 474.
[115] Krochalis, 'Magna Tabula', p. 482. The translation is James Carley's from his edition and translation of John of Glastonbury's *Cronica*, in which the same material appears. John of Glastonbury, *Cronica*, p. 52.

The exchange with the hermit appears in the Vulgate *Lancelot*, while the shield story features in the *Estoire* and the *Queste del Saint Graal*.[116] These excerpts are intriguing: given the vast romance material on which to draw, why has the compiler chosen to mention these particular episodes? While the Glastonbury interest is self-evident in the first reference to Joseph and his son, the reasons for the second item's inclusion are less immediately obvious. In the Vulgate *Lancelot*, the hermit in question makes it clear that the fountain's mutable qualities are due to the miraculous interventions of Joseph of Arimathea and his son, Josephes, shortly after their coming to Britain.[117] It is easy to see how this tale might be identified with Glastonbury's two springs – the red spring, whose red waters have a distinctive iron-rich taste, and the white spring, both of which are key tourist attractions in Glastonbury today: according to contemporary Glastonbury lore, these springs emerged when Joseph planted his two cruets containing Christ's blood and sweat.[118] If the compiler did indeed have Glastonbury's two springs in mind when selecting this episode for reference, it provides another example of the very land at Glastonbury being invoked to bring together local, universal Christian, and national spheres in the Abbey's tourist media. The springs are not mentioned in the *tabula*, of course, which is perhaps unsurprising given the unorthodoxy of such material within a religious context; but this is not to say that a guide, expanding on the material contained in the *tabula*, might not have pointed out the connection.

Smoke stains visible on the *tabula* suggest that this remarkable object would have been on display at the abbey for visitors to peruse, and it appears to have still been on display when Henry VIII's commissioners came.[119] Even after this point, it may have continued to be accessed by antiquaries, albeit not on site at Glastonbury; by the turn of the seventeenth century it was in the possession of Lord William Howard (1563–1640) of Naworth Castle in Cumberland.[120] Lord Howard was evidently deeply

---

[116] John of Glastonbury, *Cronica*, p. 279.
[117] Cited in Carley, ed., John of Glastonbury, *Cronica*, p. 279 n.
[118] Stephanie Mathivet, 'Alice Buckton (1867–1944): The Legacy of a Froebelian in the Landscape of Glastonbury', *History of Education*, 35.2 (2006), 263–81 (p. 276). Bizarrely, the actor Nicolas Cage, who lives near Glastonbury, recounted this piece of local lore in a 2019 interview, demonstrating its ongoing appeal: 'For me it was all about where was the grail? […] Is it at Glastonbury? […] If you go to Glastonbury and go to the Chalice Well, there's a spring that does taste like blood. […] legend has it that in that place was a grail chalice, or two cruets rather, one of blood and one of sweat.' Laura Bradley, 'Nicolas Cage Lived *National Treasure* by Searching for the Holy Grail', *Vanity Fair*, 7 August 2019.
[119] Gilchrist and Green, *Glastonbury Abbey*, p. 63; Krochalis, 'Magna Tabula', p. 459.
[120] James Ussher, *Britannicarum Ecclesiarum Antiquitates* (Dublin: Societatis Bibliopolarum, 1639), p. 16.

interested in the work of contemporaries like William Camden and Robert Cotton, and seems to have maintained a collaborative relationship with them, providing Camden with copies of various inscriptions for inclusion in *Britannia*, and accommodating Camden and Cotton during their tour of northern England in 1599.[121] It is not clear how the *tabula* made its way from the abbey into the hands of Lord Howard.

The spatially interactive visitor experience at Glastonbury was augmented further after 1400, and perhaps during the abbacy of Richard Beere, when a new kind of *tabula* was appended to a 'very ancient column' (columna vetustissima) said to have been erected by St David on the site where the old apostolic church was rumoured to have stood.[122] The item in question was an octagonal brass plaque of 237 x 158 millimetres, inscribed with a curious mixed script not paralleled on any surviving English brasses.[123] In the seventeenth century, James Ussher reported having seen the brass in the home of 'D. Thomas Hughes, knight' in nearby Wells.[124] Although the plaque does not survive, a facsimile was published by Henry Spelman in 1639, giving us an insight into its dimensions, script, and content.[125] The inscription states that the column to which it was attached was located in the same space as the original apocryphal church at Glastonbury apparently founded by Joseph of Arimathea. Based primarily on John of Glastonbury's *Cronica* and the interpolated *De antiquitate*, the plaque's inscription situates the object in its spatial context by referring deictically to 'this column' (hec columpna):

> And lest the site or size of the earlier church should come to be forgotten because of such additions, he [St David] erected this column on a line drawn southwards through the two eastern angles of the same church, and cutting it off from the aforesaid chancel. And

---

[121] Richard Ovenden and Stuart Handley, 'Howard, Lord William (1563–1640), Antiquary and Landowner', *The Oxford Dictionary of National Biography* (Oxford: Oxford University Press, 2004). Krochalis points out that Howard must have had the tablets between his possession of Naworth in 1603 and Ussher's publication of *Antiquitates* in 1639. Krochalis, 'Magna Tabula', p. 459. Camden and Cotton's trip, and the other sketches provided by Lord Howard, corresponds with expanded Arthurian material added to the 1607 enlarged edition of *Britannia*.

[122] John A. Goodall, 'The Glastonbury Abbey Memorial Plate Reconsidered', in *Glastonbury Abbey and the Arthurian Tradition*, pp. 185–92 (p. 185).

[123] For a description and study of the plaque, see Goodall, 'The Glastonbury Abbey Memorial Plate Reconsidered'.

[124] Ussher, *Britannicarum Ecclesiarum Antiquitates*, p. 16. This is a significant detail given that Arthur's lead cross epitaph was reportedly last seen in the possession of 'Mr Chancellor Hughes, at Wells', though this claim has never been verified. See J. Whitaker, *The Life of Saint Neot* (London: Joseph Stockdale, 1809), p. 39 (n.)

[125] Henry Spelman, *Concilia, decreta, leges, constitutiones in re ecclesiarum orbis Britannicis* (London: Richard Badger, 1639), I, pp. 7–10. The facsimile is at pp. 8–9; it is reproduced more clearly in Goodall, 'The Glastonbury Abbey Memorial Plate', p. 186.

its length was 60 feet westward from that line, its breadth was truly 26 feet; the distance from the centre of this pillar from the midpoint between the aforesaid angles, 48 feet.

([...] Et ne locus aut quantitas prioris ecclesie per tales augmentationes obliuioni tradetur: erigitur hec columpna in lineo per duos orientales angulos eiusdem ecclesie uersus meridiem protracta & predictum cancellum ab ea abstindente. Et erat eius longitudo ab illa lineo uersus occidentem .lx. pedum, latitudo uero eius .xxvi. pedum distancia centri istius columpne a puncto medio inter predictos angulos .xlviii. pedum.) [126]

Here, the plaque gives very specific information about the placement and dimensions of the Old Church in relation to the existing site, commemorating the former church and prompting its readers to imaginatively reconstruct the surrounding space in their minds in response to the apparent petition of a forward-looking St David. The inscription is clearly commemorative ('and lest the site or size of the earlier church should come to be forgotten [...]'). The impulse here might even be considered antiquarian according to Angus Vine's definition of antiquarianism as a 'dynamic, recuperative, resurrective response to the past' that is 'essentially imaginative'.[127] Moreover, by claiming that the 'ancient column' to which the plaque was affixed had been erected by St David, a saint venerated at Glastonbury and said to have been King Arthur's uncle, different layers of Glastonbury's pseudo-history were brought together into a single experience.[128] Abbey visitors were called to superimpose multiple visions of the abbey's past spaces onto its present site, retracing the commemorative gestures of figures imagined to have come before them such as St David, and pre-empting the antiquarians who would go on to engage in similar restorative exercises of the imagination over a century later.[129]

The *magna tabula* and brass plaque must have formed part of a carefully managed 'closed circuit' of media within the abbey grounds geared towards visitors.[130] We do not know exactly how this circuit would have looked, although David Mason has reconstructed a similar scheme

---

[126] Text and translation from Goodall, 'The Glastonbury Abbey Memorial Plate', pp. 188–90.

[127] Angus Vine, *In Defiance of Time: Antiquarian Writing in Early Modern England* (Oxford: Oxford University Press, 2010), p. 3. Antiquarianism is discussed below at pp. 218–20.

[128] Geoffrey of Monmouth claimed St David as Arthur's uncle; see Geoffrey of Monmouth, *The History of the Kings of Britain*, 9.158, pp. 214–15.

[129] For example, Glastonbury visitor John Leland; see his similarly reconstructive description of Cadbury Castle below at pp. 152–61.

[130] Krochalis, 'Magna Tabula', p. 464.

that once existed within the space of St Paul's Cathedral in the later Middle Ages.¹³¹ There must have been a formidable schema of *tabulae* at Glastonbury, however; a Glastonbury accounts roll for 1403 states that a tree was cut down to make fourteen wooden *tabulae* in that year alone.¹³² Though it is not known where exactly the *magna tabula* was displayed within the abbey, it is clear from its contents that the brass plaque must have been displayed at the site of the Old Church upon which the Lady Chapel had been constructed. Other developments at the abbey made around the time the plaque was erected, probably under Abbot Beere, allowed pilgrims to get even closer, physically and affectively, to the Old Church that the Lady Chapel had been built to replace after the 1184 fire.¹³³ William Good, who lived at Glastonbury Abbey as a young acolyte before fleeing to Rome during the reign of Elizabeth I, recalls a subterranean sanctuary ('sacellum subterraneum') beneath the abbey church.¹³⁴ This sanctuary was located close to Joseph of Arimathea's reputed burial site, according to Good, although he admits that there was some disagreement at the abbey as to whether Joseph lay buried there or rather in Montacute some fifteen miles distant.¹³⁵ A commonplace book from Glastonbury dating to c. 1450 includes a verse epitaph for Joseph of Arimathea; John Withrington has tentatively suggested that this may have been intended to furnish Joseph's tomb if the saint's bones were ever discovered, and we might speculate that the subterranean sanctuary was intended for their translation if such a find were made.¹³⁶ In this sanctuary, Good tells us, a stone statue of Joseph ('imago saxea') was erected for the benefit of visiting pilgrims.¹³⁷ Archaeological excavations confirm that a subterranean chapel had indeed been dug out of the clay beneath the Lady Chapel.¹³⁸ Visitors could descend into the crypt, perhaps after reading the brass plaque, and encounter the figure of

---

[131] The examples at St Paul's included a 'topographical tablet' giving information on the cathedral's dimensions; a 'great tablet', whose universal, national, and local histories echo the material seen in Glastonbury and particularly York's great tablets; a shorter chronicle tablet. These three examples adorned the ambulatory, whilst more specific examples punctuated the cathedral space, gathered around particular tombs and shrines. Mason, 'The Writing on the Wall', passim.

[132] Krochalis, 'Magna Tabula', p. 464.

[133] Lindley, *Tomb Destruction*, p. 141.

[134] J. Armitage Robinson, *Two Glastonbury Legends* (Cambridge: Cambridge University Press, 1926), p. 67; Carley, 'The Discovery of the Holy Cross of Waltham', in *Glastonbury Abbey and the Arthurian Tradition*, pp. 303–08 (p. 306); Jean-Guy Gouttebroze, 'Melkin et Les Treize Boules de Cristal', *Journal of the International Arthurian Society*, 6.1 (2018), 70–94 (p. 79).

[135] James P. Carley, 'The Discovery of the Holy Cross', p. 306.

[136] Withrington, 'The Arthurian Epitaph', p. 238.

[137] Gouttebroze, 'Melkin et Les Treize Boules de Cristal', p. 79.

[138] Gilchrist and Green, *Glastonbury Abbey*, p. 66.

Joseph illuminated by candlelight, which must have made a dramatic impression. From here, an underground passage led out of the crypt to the south, taking pilgrims along a route to an associated well of St Joseph that appears to have predated the abbey itself, and which may have called to mind the miraculous fountain whose story is hinted at on the *magna tabula*.[139] The physical movement of visitors downward into the sanctuary functioned powerfully as an embodiment of the descent into deep time. Yi-Fu Tuan has shown that, from the perspective of the upright human body, space and time are oriented along horizontal and vertical axes, along which 'the past is behind and "below"'.[140] The effect of stepping down into Joseph's sanctuary, then, particularly after reading the brass plaque, was of moving temporally and spatially forward into the past.

Good's assertion that this sanctuary was located near Joseph's reputed burial site seems to indicate that the crypt and statue were constructed, in part, to fulfil the muddled prophecy attributed to Melkin concerning the burial location of Joseph and his two cruets of Christ's blood and sweat.[141] In around 1450, Joseph was also included in the glazing scheme of All Saints Church in Huish Episcopi, some twelve miles distant, complete with the two cruets in hand described by 'Melkin': this clearly demonstrates the contagious qualities of sacred space for spreading out into a local area. An account made by William Worcester, who visited Glastonbury Abbey shortly before the plaque and underground sanctuary are likely to have been built, also suggests that the sanctuary was built to fulfil the prophecy attributed to Melkin. Having just visited the Great Church, describing the dimensions of its nave, the situation of the choir including Arthur's tomb, and the reredos, Worcester moved next into the adjoining Lady Chapel – the building beneath which the underground sanctuary would be built some two decades later. From here he seems to have had a plain view of two hollow cross containers that once housed the purported remains of Arthur and Guinevere, as well as Joseph's rumoured burial site:[142]

---

[139] Gilchrist and Green, *Glastonbury Abbey*, p. 66, p. 384, p. 435. The well and crypt were excavated in 1991–92 and again in 2013. See Philip Rahtz, *Glastonbury* (London: Batsford, 1993), pp. 85–87; Stewart Brown, 'Glastonbury Abbey St Joseph's Crypt archaeological evaluation 2014', unpublished report for the Trustees of Glastonbury Abbey (Glastonbury, 2014). On the miraculous fountain, see above at pp. 61–62.

[140] Tuan, *Space and Place*, p. 35.

[141] Gouttebroze, 'Melkin et Les Treize Boules de Cristal', passim. Melkin's prophecy is discussed elsewhere in this book at pp. 78–80. For more on Melkin and his prophecy, see Carley, 'Melkin the Bard'; James P. Carley, 'John of Glastonbury and Borrowings from the Vernacular', in *Interstices: Studies in Middle English and Anglo-Latin Texts in Honour of A. G. Rigg*, ed. Richard Firth Green and Linne R. Mooney (Toronto: University of Toronto Press, 2004), pp. 55–73.

[142] These containers were surely not claimed as the bones' original coffins; the earliest reports describe Arthur as having been discovered in a hollowed-out oak. The

On each side are 7 large windows, and opposite to the second window on the south side in the the churchyard are two stone crosses hollowed out where they stored King Arthur's bones, and where Joseph of Arimathea lies [buried] in a 'bifurcated line'.

(Et in qualibet latere sunt 7 fenestre magne
Et ex opposito secunde fenestre ex parte meridionali sunt in cimiterio due cruces lapidee concauate vbi ossa Arthuri Regis recondebant vbi in linea bifurcata iacet Josephus ab Arimathia)[143]

The 'bifurcated line' marks a clear reference to Melkin's prophecy, which states that Joseph lies buried on a 'linea bifurcata' close to the southern corner of the Old Church along with the two cruets.[144] This may suggest that, by this point, Glastonbury's monk-guides were communicating the details of Melkin's prophecy to visitors. What exactly is meant by the 'bifurcated line' is not clear, and scholars have puzzled over the muddled Latin of the prophecy;[145] but the consistency with which those who visited Glastonbury describe this information suggests the abbey monks had clarified the meaning of the prophecy within the context of the physical space where Joseph's resting place was said to be. A church lection that routinely precedes John's *Cronica* in its extant manuscripts states that St David added a new chapel to the west of the old wattle church, marking the join between old and new buildings on the northern side with a pyramid and the southern side with a platform.[146] This join may represent the 'bifurcated line' of Melkin's prophecy as it was understood and interpreted in late medieval Glastonbury, and it is possible that the platform or pyramid were still visible when Worcester visited. This chimes with the specifics given in the brass plaque about its orientation relative to the original position of the Old Church, and with Worcester's account.

---

bones had undergone a number of translations over the years, and the graveyard crosses might represent temporary containers that held the bones at some stage; see Wood, 'Guenevere at Glastonbury', pp. 83–100.

[143] Cambridge, Corpus Christi College MS 210, p. 218; *Itineraries*, pp. 298–99. I have diverged from Harvey's translation here where he translates the final clause as '[...] and where in a different direction (?) lies Joseph of Arimathea'. Worcester's text has been written to echo the wording of Melkin's prophecy.

[144] 'Et iacet in linea bifurcata iuxta meridionam angulum oratorii cratibus preparatis super potentem adorandam virginem'. Carley translates this as: 'And he lies on a forked line close to the southern corner of the chapel with prepared wattle above the powerful venerable Maiden [...]'. Carley, 'Melkin the Bard', p. 3.

[145] Some of the theories as to the meaning of 'linea bifurcata' are discussed in Carley, 'Melkin the Bard', passim.

[146] Carley, 'Melkin the Bard', p. 9.

Antiquarians at fifteenth-century Glastonbury: William Worcester and John Hardyng

Glastonbury's fifteenth-century visitors would thus have encountered a site whose historic space was carefully mediated through *tabulae*, guides, and architecture. This may explain why six of the seven surviving witnesses of John of Glastonbury's *Cronica* date from the fifteenth century onwards, after the *magna tabula* and brass plaque had been erected. The sudden spate of witnesses copied from Glastonbury manuscripts (and the *tabula*) in the fifteenth century suggests that the interests of literate visitors were being accommodated. When William Worcester made enquires after specific texts in Glastonbury, such as the 'Acts of Arthur' (actibus Arthuri Regis), he was obligingly shown a 'list of certain acts of the Emperor from the book of Geoffrey of Monmouth' by 'Dom Murelege, a monk' (billam de certis actibus Imperatoris de libro Gaufridi Monumentensis).[147]

Glastonbury was not the only site keen to share its Arthurian histories with visitors. Similar strategies were employed at secular institutions such as Dover Castle, another Arthurian location known to have displayed a *tabula* detailing Arthur's local exploits. John Leland provides a fascinating insight into Dover's Arthurian tourism experience which can be helpfully compared with Glastonbury. In his *Itinerary* Leland describes seeing 'Guenevere's chamber, Arthur's hall, and the bones of Gawain' at Dover Castle (Camera Guaenorae, Aula Arturii, et ossa Walwani).[148] In both the early version of his Arthurian defence and also his work on famous men, Leland describes his experience of being shown these Arthurian places and objects by Dover's castellans, as well as two texts: a book of Dover's 'civil history' (in libro de Civili historia) and the Dover annals (Annales), the latter of which Leland describes excitedly as a 'newly-found little book on the antiquities of Dover' (nuper inveni historiolam de antiquitate Dovarensi), a 'worke sauouring of antiquitie [which] makes mention of Caradocus' (opus antiquitatem redolens meminere Carodoci).[149] Whilst the exact nature of these texts is uncertain, a Dover chronicle copied c. 1475–1525 describes Arthur's Hall:

> King Arthur, who greatly improved Dover Castle, in which he once built a hall that is still called Arthur's Hall.

---

[147] Worcester, *Itineraries*, pp. 261–62; pp. 292–93.
[148] Leland, *Itineraries*, IV, p. 55.
[149] John Leland, *De Uiris Illustribus = On Famous Men*, ed. and trans. James P. Carley (Oxford: The Bodleian Library, 2010), pp. 316–17. Leland, 'Codrus', p. 7. John Leland, *A Learned and True Assertion*, trans. by Richard Robinson (London, 1582), STC (2nd edn) 15441, sig. E1v (hence *Learned*); John Leland, *Assertio inclytissimi Arturii Regis Britanniae* (London, 1544), STC (2nd edn) 15440, sig. D1r (hence *Assertio*).

([...] Rex Arthurus qui multum emendauit Castum Doverrum in quo fecit quondam aulam qui uocatur hodietenus Arthureshalle.)[150]

Any guest could be shown Arthur's Hall, Guenevere's chamber, or Gawain's bones by the castellans, but more learned visitors such as Leland could be shown textual holdings such as these that corroborated these histories.

Where the notebooks of learned antiquarian guests do survive it can be difficult to know when exactly they record material from library holdings, *tabulae*, or oral guides. During William Worcester's visit to Glastonbury Abbey, he noted down six lines of verse regarding Joseph of Arimathea's coming to England. Apparently made *in situ* as Worcester explored the space of the abbey church, Worcester attributes the lines to 'Godefridus de gestis Britonum', the name by which Geoffrey's *Historia* was known for much of the Middle Ages, though the lines do not come from the *Historia*.[151] The final couplet, shown in bold here, is unique to Worcester and to one other source:

> There enters Avalon a party of twelve men:
> Joseph, the flower of Arimathea, is chief of them;
> Josophes, Joseph's son, accompanies his father
> And to these with ten others the rights of Glastonbury are appropriated.
> **"To the Britons I went after I had buried Christ,**
> **Came to Glastonbury, taught the Britons, took my rest".**
>
> (Intrat Aualloniam duodena caterua virorum
> Flos Arimathie Joseph est primus eorum
> Josophes ex Joseph genitus patrem comitatur
> Hiis aliisque decem, ius Glastonie propriatur
> **"Ad Britones iui postquam Christum sepeliui**
> **Glastoniam veni Britones docui requieui".**)[152]

Worcester divides the final couplet from the first four lines with a line and paraph indicator, though there is no change of ink. The first-person voice implies that Joseph is speaking.

Where did Worcester find this fragment of verse? While the first four lines appear in John of Glastonbury's *Cronica* and on the *magna tabula*, Worcester could not have taken the final couplet from these sources, as they do not include it.[153] The *magna tabula* and John's *Cronica* attribute

---

[150] London, British Library Cotton MS Vespasian B.XI, f. 73r. Underlined text indicates expanded abbreviations.
[151] Worcester, *Itineraries*, pp. 296–97; Cambridge, Corpus Christi College MS 210, p. 217.
[152] Ibid.
[153] John of Glastonbury, *Cronica*, pp. 50–51; Krochalis, 'Magna Tabula', p. 484.

these lines to 'some chronicles on the subject of King Arviragus' (quibusdam cronicis ubi agitur de rege Arvirago), an attribution repeated by later antiquaries.[154] However, the versions in John's *Cronica* and the *magna tabula* lack the final couplet in which Joseph appears to speak ('Ad Britones [...] docui requieui'). The only other place where the sestet appears in full is in the margin of a metrical chronicle contained in Cotton MS Titus A.XIX, the manuscript mentioned earlier containing *tabulae* texts and a Glastonbury Quire. This chronicle – sometimes referred to as the chronicle of John Stafford or *Stafford's Chronicle* – varies considerably from manuscript to manuscript, with a commentary often appearing in the margins tailored to the locality of each individual witness.[155] Given that the remainder of Cotton Titus A.XIX evinces material closely related to Glastonbury and York, it is possible that the sestet comes from a Glastonbury version of *Stafford's Chronicle*.[156] The *Chronicle* is essentially a metrical adaptation of Geoffrey's *Historia regum Britanniae*, which explains why Worcester attributes it to Geoffrey and why the sestet's opening lines are repeatedly ascribed to a chronicle about Arviragus (Arviragus would, of course, be included in an adaptation of the *Historia*). The sestet does not normally appear in *Stafford's Chronicle*, but the Cotton Titus copy contains the full six lines, written vertically in the margin, bracketed, and apparently not planned as part of the main text although it accords metrically (see Figure 2). *Stafford's Chronicle* does not appear in the Glastonbury section of the codex, suggesting that the influence of Glastonbury material in this manuscript extends beyond the limits of the Glastonbury Quire itself.[157]

---

[154] Both James Ussher and Richard Robinson, Leland's translator, likewise attribute these lines to chronicles about Arviragus. Robinson claims that the chronicles about Arviragus had been given to him by Stephen Batman, who Robinson claims held 'Auncient records written at Aualonia'. See Robinson's preface to 'A Learned Assertion' in *The famous historie of Chinon of England, together with The Assertion of King Arthure*, ed. William Edward Mead, Early English Text Society, Original Series 165 (Oxford: Oxford University Press for the Early English Text Society, 1925), pp. 12–13; James Ussher, *Britannicarum Ecclesiarum* (Dublin: Societatis Bibliopolarum, 1639), pp. 15–16.

[155] Rigg, *A Book of British Kings 1200BC–1399AD*, p. 14. See also Jacob Hammer, 'Une version métrique de l'*Historia Regum Britanniae* de Geoffroy de Monmouth', *Latomus*, 2.2 (1938), 131–51.

[156] See Krochalis's discussion of the Glastonbury and York associations of the manuscript in Krochalis and Stones, *The Pilgrim's Guide*, I, pp. 136–39. Krochalis suggests some possible channels as to how York scribes might have obtained Glastonbury material at p. 132.

[157] The marginalia appears at f. 107v; see Krochalis, 'Magna Tabula', p. 471. Most of the Glastonbury-specific material in Cotton Titus A.XIX is contained in 'The Glastonbury Quire' (ff. 16–31); see Krochalis, 'Pilgrim's Guide', pp. 136–39 and Michael Lapidge, 'Additional Manuscript Evidence for *De vera historia de morte Arthuri*', *Arthurian*

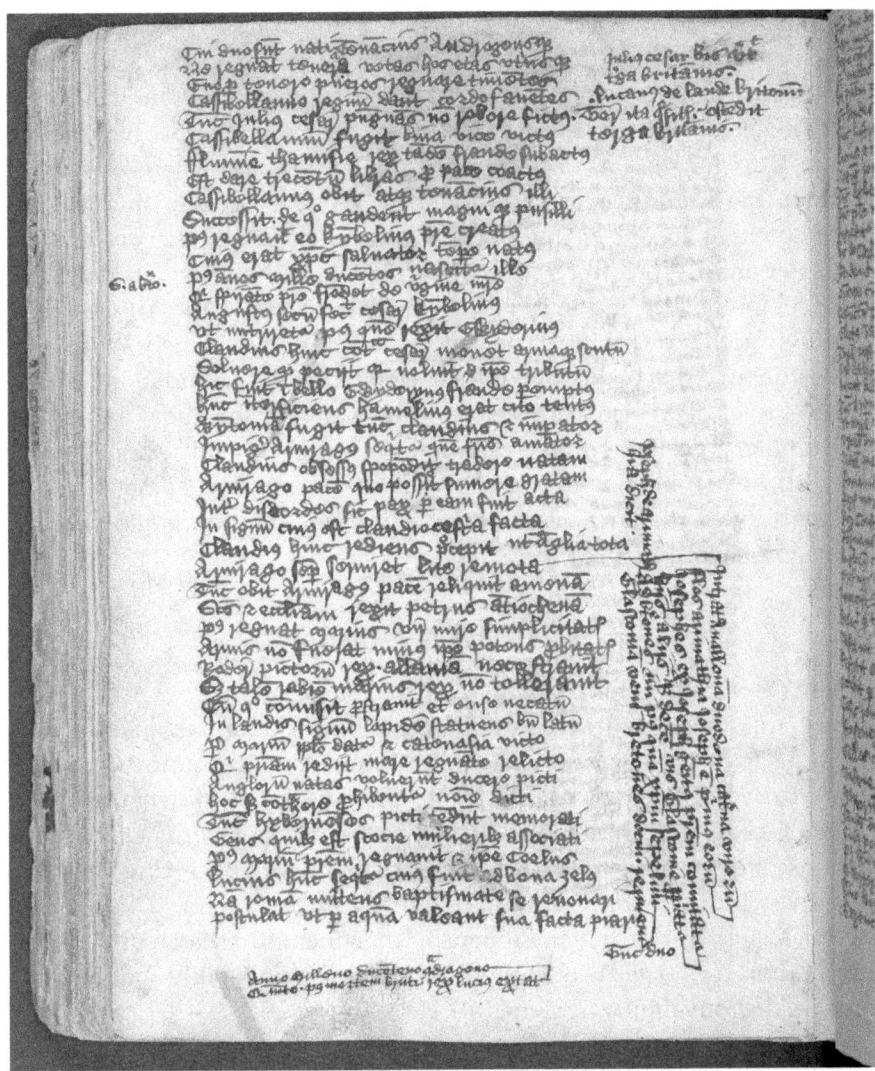

Figure 2. Sestet on Joseph of Arimathea added to the margin of Stafford's Chronicle in Cotton MS Titus A.XIX, f. 107v. © British Library Board.

The marginal hand adds the note 'Joseph of Arimathea speaks' (Joseph de Arimathea dicit) to the sestet's final couplet, echoing the paraph indicator in Worcester's notes. As well as the sestet, other

---

Literature, 2 (1982), 163–68. In fact, the first four lines of the sestet also appear earlier in Cotton Titus A.XIX in the Glastonbury Quire at f. 19r; this shorter four-line version was likely copied from the *magna tabula* (or a direct copy of it).

marginalia surrounding *Stafford's Chronicle* in the Cotton Titus manuscript implies a connection with Glastonbury Abbey's internal space – the verse epitaph for Arthur in the margin at f. 109r, for example. The hand that copied *Stafford's Chronicle* was also responsible for the *tabulae* material in Cotton Titus A.XIX. This raises the question of how and where Worcester obtained the same sestet at Glastonbury. While Worcester might have come across it in one of the abbey's textual holdings, the position of the sestet amid Worcester's *in situ* description of the abbey church, and the focus on *tabulae* and epitaphs by the sestet's copyist in Titus A.XIX, suggests another possibility. The majority of the notes taken by Worcester at Glastonbury reflect the kind of material frequently included in *tabulae*. For example, details concerning the dimensions of the abbey buildings echo similar information on a tablet displayed in St Paul's Cathedral.[158] The full sestet may therefore have been on display somewhere at Glastonbury, perhaps on one of the many *tabulae* that once adorned the abbey and have since been lost.

John Hardyng's Chronicle

While Worcester's notes partially replicate his experience of Glastonbury Abbey and other Arthurian locations, other itinerant figures, such as John Hardyng (c. 1377–1464), left no notes. We cannot therefore be certain about their experiences of particular places, nor even whether they visited sites such as Glastonbury in person. Hardyng's work nevertheless demonstrates a marked interest in Glastonbury Abbey and striking overlaps with material local to Glastonbury, such as John's *Cronica* and the *magna tabula*. Hardyng's propensity for itinerant research and taking information from *tabulae* elsewhere supports the possibility that he may have carried out similar activities at Glastonbury.

Although Hardyng was active considerably earlier than the other writers discussed in this book, his metrical *Chronicle* was a key source for many of them, and especially on the subject of Arthurian Glastonbury. Later figures encountered Hardyng's *Chronicle* in one of its two original manuscript forms or in the 1543 print edition, which included Richard Grafton's continuation.[159] John Rous had read it in manuscript form,

---

[158] Mason refers to it as the 'topographical tablet'; Mason, 'Writing on the Wall', passim. The St Paul's *tabula*, copied in MS Harley 565 at ff. 2r–v, describes in detail the height, length, and width of St Paul's in feet, and the ground space it covered in acres (f. 2r). Worcester gives the same details about the Abbey Church and the Lady Chapel at Glastonbury; see *Itineraries*, ed. Harvey, pp. 296–99.

[159] John Hardyng and Richard Grafton, *The chronicle of Ihon Hardyng* (London: Richard Grafton, 1543), STC (2nd edn) 12767.

citing it directly in *Historia regum Angliae* and in his lost work on Britain's ancient universities.[160] John Leland was likely familiar with the manuscript version; the fact that the second half of Leland's work on illustrious men *De viris illustribus* (1543) mentions Hardyng makes it likely that Leland knew Hardyng's *Chronicle* before its publication in print.[161] Later antiquarian John Dee also owned a copy of the 1543 Grafton edition.[162] The *Chronicle* exists in two versions. The vast 'Lancastrian' version was presented to Henry VI in 1457. The later and much condensed 'Yorkist' version was presented to Richard of York shortly before his death in 1460, and Hardyng may have also given a copy to Edward IV in May 1463.[163] The Yorkist version formed the basis for Richard Grafton's 1543 edition. Throughout the *Chronicle*, Hardyng justifies his own authority through his eyewitness testimony of both textual and physical sources. He assures us several times that he has 'seen' the chronicles, books, muniments, and letters he describes.[164] He knows the bones of St Andrew are held in

---

[160] Rous cites Hardyng as an authority on Corineus and Gogmagog in his *Historia regum Angliae*, pp. 19–20. Leland copied extracts from Rous's lost *De antiquitate academiarum Britannicarum* (On the antiquity of the universities of Britain). In these extracts Rous observes: 'Mewinus historicus, cujus mentio est apud Joannem Hardingum historicum, qui Mewini autoritate scribit, Josephum fuisse Avalloniae' (The historical Mewin is mentioned in the writings of the historian John Hardyng, who writes under Mewin's authority of Joseph's coming to Avalon). John Leland, *Itineraries*, II, p. 167.

[161] John Stow owned the manuscript copy of the longer chronicle (British Library MS Lansdowne 204), to which he contributed extensive marginalia. See Colin C. G. Tite, '"Lost or Stolen or Strayed": A Survey of Manuscripts Formerly in the Cotton Library', *British Library Journal*, 18.2 (1992), 107–47 (p. 126); Sarah L. Peverley, '"A Good Exampell to Avoide Diane": Reader Responses to John Hardyng's Chronicle in the Fifteenth and Sixteenth Centuries', *Poetica*, 63 (2005), 1–18 (pp. 3–4). Leland identified Hardyng's 'Mewyn' as John of Glastonbury's 'Melkin' and copied from the short form of Hardyng's *Chronicle*: see John Leland, *Commentarii de scriptoribus Britannicis*, ed. A. Hall, 2 vols (Oxford: Theatro Sheldoniano, 1709), I, p. 42; John Leland, *Joannis Lelandi Antiquarii de Rebus Britannicis Collectanea*, ed. Thomas Hearne, 6 vols (London: William and John Richardson, 1770), III, pp. 425–26; Leland, *De uiris illustribus*, I, pp. 66–69. I thank James Carley for sharing with me his notes made in preparation for the second volume of his edition of *De uiris illustribus*, which is forthcoming.

[162] John Dee held a copy of the 1543 edition of Hardyng which was auctioned at Sotheby's on 29 October 2009, complete with Dee's marginalia and autograph; see Julian Roberts and Andrew G. Watson, *John Dee's Library Catalogue* (November 2009 update), item 1686, www.bibsoc.org.uk/sites/www.bibsoc.org.uk/files/John%20Dee%27s%20Library%20Catalogue%204.pdf [accessed 1 August 2018].

[163] The 1457 version survives in a single manuscript, British Library MS Lansdowne 204, while the later Yorkist versions survives in sixteen manuscripts. See C. L. Kingsford, *English Historical Literature in the Fifteenth Century* (New York: Burt Franklin, 1927), pp. 143–44.

[164] John Hardyng, *The Chronicle of John Hardyng, Together with the Continuation by Richard Grafton*, ed. Henry Ellis (London, 1812), p. 22; p. 361.

'Brigthricke', Scotland, because 'there in dede I was, and haue it seen'.[165] In 1424, when Hardyng was sent to Rome 'at the instance and writing' of the cardinal of Winchester, he consulted 'the great Chronicle of Trogus Pompeyus', provided to him for 'daily inspection and description'.[166]

Though Hardyng's life's work was largely spent trying to prove England's sovereignty over Scotland, his interests were not limited to Scotland. His *Chronicle* also reveals a detailed awareness of Glastonbury Abbey and its history. In fact, his attention to Glastonbury may be related to his obsession with Scotland. The primacy of the Glastonbury church and the presence of Welsh and Irish saints there, coupled with Melkin's writings denigrating the Scots (according to Hardyng, at least), would have made Glastonbury a valuable place to go hunting for sources to justify English sovereignty over the rest of Britain.[167] Given Hardyng's use of his own travel experiences in support of his writing, and that Arthurian sites were sharing their histories and libraries with literate visitors in the fifteenth century, it is certainly possible that Hardyng visited Glastonbury, perhaps even making use of the sources in its library or the *magna tabula* when constructing his *Chronicle*. It was fairly usual for *tabula* material to function as sources for historiographers, or even for *tabulae* texts to be incorporated directly into chronicles (or rather *back* into them, as chronicles were often the sources for *tabulae* in the first place).[168] Indeed, Hardyng had used at least one *tabula* as a source before; in one copy of Hardyng's *Chronicle*, MS Lansdowne 204, a marginal gloss summarises a legend relating to a crucifix hanging at St Paul's 'as is comprised in a table afore the Rode at Northdore and in a story in a window byhynde the sayd Rode'.[169]

---

[165] *The Chronicle of John Hardyng*, ed. Ellis, p. 188.
[166] Cited in *The Chronicle of John Hardyng*, ed. Ellis, p. vii.
[167] E. D. Kennedy, 'John Hardyng and the Holy Grail', *Arthurian Literature*, 8 (1989); *The Chronicle of John Hardyng*, ed. Ellis, pp. 86–87.
[168] Macht provides two examples from the *Chronicle* of the abbots at Fountains: see Macht, 'Changes in Monastic Writing', p. 23. Another interesting case is the printed book *The Shrine at Walsingham*, part of which seems to have been copied from a *tabula*, as the text refers to itself at one point as 'this table'. Cited in Alexandra Da Costa, 'Marketing the Shrine: Printed Pilgrimage Souvenirs, Guides, and Advertising', *Journal of the Early Book Society*, 16 (2013), 85–100 (p. 89). David Mason has also cited numerous examples of London chroniclers, such as John Cok and Robert Fabyan, who used the St Paul's *tabulae* as sources; see Mason, 'Writing on the Wall', pp. 38–40.
[169] Lansdowne MS 204, f. 42r, quoted in Riddy, 'Glastonbury, Joseph of Arimathea, and the Grail', p. 278. It should be noted that the rubrics and glosses in the Lansdowne copy of Hardyng's *Chronicle* are not necessarily Hardyng's own as they were added at a later date, though Felicity Riddy still believes they are Hardyng's doing; see Riddy, 'Glastonbury, Joseph of Arimathea, and the Grail', p. 271 n.

The text of Hardyng's gloss can be verified against British Library Harley MS 565, copied from the *tabula* in question.[170]

Whilst it is impossible to prove that Hardyng visited Glastonbury personally, the 1460 *Chronicle* suggests an improved acquaintance with Glastonbury's local history and built environment. This corresponds with other changes made in the later chronicle that might suggest a research-gathering trip in southern England, including a detail about a literal *tabula*: King Arthur's Round Table, which Hardyng claims 'hangeth yet' in Winchester.[171] This is apparently the earliest attestation to the existence of the physical tabletop that has hung on display there until the present day; P. J. C. Field has argued that Hardyng must have seen the table in person, and if Hardyng did indeed make such a trip then Glastonbury might readily have been included in his itinerary.[172] Like John of Glastonbury before him, John Hardyng took pains to transmute the undefined places of Arthurian romance into definitive real-world locations within the abbey's boundaries. In John of Glastonbury's *Cronica*, the chapel ride episode from the romance *Perlesvaus* is relocated to the hermitage of St Mary Magdalene at Beckery.[173] Similarly, John Hardyng identifies the Black Chapel of the Vulgate *Mort Artu* as the Lady Chapel at Glastonbury Abbey, which he must have known about when he wrote the earlier version of his chronicle. Compare the relevant passages in the earlier and later versions of the *Chronicle*:

> [earlier version]
> Kynge Arthure than so wounded mortal
> Was led forth thane to Avalon fulle sore
> To lechen thare his woundes pryvely
> Whare than he dyed and byried was right thore
> As yit this day ys sene and shalle evermore
> Within the chirche and mynstere of Glastyngbyry
> In tombe rialle made sufficiantly.
> [...]

---

[170] London, British Library MS Harley 565. See Mary-Rose McLaren, *The London Chronicles of the Fifteenth Century: A Revolution in English Writing* (Cambridge: D. S. Brewer, 2002), p. 103.
[171] *The Chronicle of John Hardyng*, ed. Henry Ellis, p. 164.
[172] P. J. C. Field, 'Searching for Camelot', *Medium Aevum*, 87.1 (2018), 1–22 (p. 1), pp. 8–9.
[173] John of Glastonbury, *Cronica*, pp. 76–79; *Le Haut Livre du Graal*, II, pp. 105–20. Other Glastonbury-specific versions of this story (which may even predate John's *Cronica*) localise it further by claiming that Arthur experiences his dream while sleeping atop Glastonbury Tor (see below at p. 159). Whilst the passage in John's *Cronica* is similar in form to the *Perlesvaus* extract, Nitze establishes that *Perlesvaus* was not John's direct source, but that the two texts must share a common Latin original, now lost.

> De quo Merlinus dicit inter prophecias suas exitus eius erit
> dubius et quidam propheta Britonum fecit pro epitaphio
> super tumbam suam versum istum: Hic iacet Arthurus rex
> quondam rexque futurus.[174]
> Bot of [Arthur's] dethe the story of Seynt Grale
> Sayth that he dyed in Avalon fulle fayre
> And byried there his body was alle hale
> Within the Blake Chapelle whare was his layre
> Which Geryn made whare than was grete repayre
> For Seynt Davyd, Arthurs uncle dere,
> It hallowed had in name of Mary clere.[175]

> [later version]
> Kynge Arthure than in Aualon so diede,
> Wher he was buried beside a chapell faire,
> **Which nowe is made and fully edifiede,**
> **Weste fro the mynstre churche of grete repaire**
> **Of Glastonbury**, where nowe he hath his laire –
> But than it was called **the Black Chapell**
> **Of Oure Lade**, as cronyclers can tell.[176]

In the *Mort Artu*, Girflet (renamed Geryn in Hardyng's *Chronicle*) takes the wounded Arthur to the Black Chapel after his battle with Mordred. Hardyng manipulates his source here to align the Black Chapel with the legendary Old Church at Glastonbury. The passage taken from the earlier version of Hardyng's *Chronicle* shows he already had some knowledge of Glastonbury's history, but this knowledge was imperfect. He is aware that Arthur's 'tomb rialle' appears '[w]ithin the chirche and mynstere of Glastyngbyry', and either Hardyng or his rubricator cites an epitaph for Arthur naming him 'rex quondam rexque futurus' (the once and future king). Yet as far as we know, the epitaph Hardyng cites was not displayed at Glastonbury – hardly surprising, given that the grave discovery at Glastonbury worked to counter the narrative of Arthur's return. A number of other texts claim the epitaph was displayed at Glastonbury, and it may be that one of these was Hardyng's

---

[174] 'Of whom Merlin says in his prophecies that his departure shall be doubtful, and a certain Briton poet made this verse for an epitaph over his tomb: "Here lies King Arthur, the once and future king."' Translation mine. The underlined text appears as a rubricated chapter heading.

[175] John Hardyng, *John Hardyng's Chronicle: Edited from London British Library MS Lansdowne 204*, ed. Sarah Peverley and James Simpson, TEAMS (Kalamazoo, MI: Medieval Institute Publications, 2015), http://d.lib.rochester.edu/teams/publication/simpson-pevereley-hardyng-chronicle [accessed 30 July 2018], 3.3843-49.

[176] *The Chronicle of John Hardyng*, ed. Henry Ellis, p. 147, emphasis mine.

source.[177] Arthur's Glastonbury burial was certainly common knowledge by this stage, and Hardyng would have already been familiar with it when writing the first version of his *Chronicle*. The extract in the later version, however, exhibits spatial qualities which imply a more intimate knowledge of the location where the grave was discovered ('beside a chapell' rather than 'within it'; 'west fro the mynstre churche'). Moreover, while Hardyng was clearly already familiar with the story that St David ('Arthurs uncle dere') had restored the abbey church – knowledge perhaps taken from William of Malmesbury's *Gesta regum Anglorum* – Hardyng had specific knowledge of the abbey's more recent renovation history, and of the precise location of the alleged grave site, by the time that he wrote the later *Chronicle*.[178] The *magna tabula* communicates the details of abbey renovations, and the notes of John Leland also suggest that such information was communicated to abbey guests.[179]

The 'Chapel of Our Lady' is mentioned elsewhere by Hardyng. The earlier version of Hardyng's *Chronicle* names 'Mewytryn' as the piece of land given to Joseph of Arimathea by King Arviragus, 'whare that he [Joseph] lyeth men say and hath his byry'.[180] 'Mewytryne' is also known as 'Glassynbyry' and 'the Ile of Avalon'.[181] Later, Hardyng tells us that the 'herte in golde preserved' of Galaad and the 'sepulture and very monument | Whare Josep lyeth of Aramathy' are 'enterde at Avaloun I rede'.[182] These statements imply that Hardyng had heard (or read) of Glastonbury and its connections with Joseph of Arimathea but had not visited in person when he composed the earlier version of his chronicle in 1457. In the later 1460 chronicle Hardyng becomes even more specific:

> And howe Galaad [then] at his deth [Arthur] prayed
> His herte to bury, beside kyng Eualake,

---

[177] These texts include Robert Thornton's manuscript containing the *Alliterative Morte Arthure*; an English rhymed chronicle (known as *Arthur*) contained in a manuscript from Bath; and some copies of Lydgate's *Fall of Princes* (c. 1438). On this epitaph, see Withrington, 'The Arthurian Epitaph in Malory's *Morte Darthur*', passim.

[178] Both Gerald of Wales' *Life of St David* and the earlier *Life* authored by Rhigyfarch claim that Glastonbury was one of twelve churches built by St David; but William of Malmesbury claims that the saint had a vision of an earlier church on the site, and decided to rebuild it. See James Carley's introduction in John of Glastonbury, *Cronica*, pp. xxxix–xl.

[179] The *magna tabula* describes the 1382 renovation of St Michael's chapel. In his *Itinerary*, John Leland describes the detailed information communicated to him concerning the Lady Chapel's renovations. Krochalis, 'Magna Tabula', p. 521; Leland, *Itineraries*, I, pp. 289–90.

[180] John Hardyng, *Chronicle*, ed. Simpson and Peverley, 2.825, 2.2625, 2.2612G, 2.2632–3.

[181] John Hardyng, *Chronicle*, ed. Simpson and Peverley, l. 825, 2625, 2612G, 2632.

[182] John Hardyng, *Chronicle*, ed. Simpson and Peverley, 3.3153–66.

> And duke Saraphe, in golde thus arrayed,
> Where they be buryed beside Ioseph their make;
> And thus muche he prayed you to do for his sake,
> In the chapel of our Lady, Chrystes mother,
> At Glastenbury, with dyuers sayntes other.[183]

Hardyng makes a number of small but significant changes to this material in the later version of his *Chronicle*. Here, Joseph and Galaad's burial is situated quite clearly at Glastonbury rather than Avalon, excising the extract of its romance toponym. Two further names are added, however, from the world of romance: Evalake and Saraphe, also known by their baptised names Mordrains and Nasciens, who appear in the *Estoire del Saint Graal* and under their Christian names in the doctored *Nicodemus* extract in the *tabula* and John's *Cronica*. Hardyng is also far more precise here about where exactly Joseph and his fellows are buried. If he had indeed visited the abbey, Hardyng would have learned all about Joseph's rumoured burial in the Old Church from the guiding monks and the *tabula*, though the plaque and subterranean sanctuary were later developments. The specificity of detail shown in the later *Chronicle* may tempt us to speculate whether Hardyng's interest in Glastonbury was sufficiently piqued to encourage him to consult further Glastonbury material, or perhaps even visit the site in person.

There are other clues in Hardyng's text that suggest he may have consulted Glastonbury sources directly, perhaps even at Glastonbury itself. Hardyng describes Joseph's bringing to Britain the 'two fyols fulle of the swete to sayne | of Jhesu Cryste as rede as blode of vayne'.[184] This is a very early reference to Melkin's prophecy. While several other fifteenth-century manuscripts appear to have copied the prophecy from the *tabula* directly, these mostly postdate Hardyng's reference.[185] Hardyng probably copied his material on Melkin from a written source, as he

---

[183] *The Chronicle of John Hardyng*, ed. Ellis, p. 136.

[184] *John Hardyng's Chronicle: Edited from London British Library MS Lansdowne 204*, ed. Sarah Peverley and James Simpson, TEAMS (Kalamazoo, MI: Medieval Institute Publications, 2015), http://d.lib.rochester.edu/teams/publication/simpson-pevereley-hardyng-chronicle [accessed 30 July 2018], 2.2615-16.

[185] See John of Glastonbury, *Cronica*, p. 279 n. 76. A fifteenth-century hand has added the prophecy to a flyleaf of a manuscript from Glastonbury Abbey's medieval library, Cambridge, Trinity College MS R.5.33, f. 1r. It also occurs in two other fifteenth-century manuscripts which appear to have been copied from the *magna tabula*: British Library MS Cotton Cleopatra C.X, f. 98; and British Library MS Arundel 220, f. 274. On the latter, see Peter Fleming, 'Making History: Culture, Politics and *The Maire of Bristowe is Kalendar*', in *Reputation and Representation in Fifteenth Century Europe*, ed. Douglas L. Biggs, Sharon D. Michalove and Albert Compton Reeves (Boston, MA: Brill, 2004), pp. 289–316 (p. 293, n. 24).

mistakenly refers to the prophet as 'Mewyn' in both the long and short versions of the *Chronicle*.¹⁸⁶ This misnomer suggests that Melkin and his prophecy were not well-known beyond the immediate Glastonbury area at this stage. Hardyng describes 'Mewyn' as a 'Bryton chronicler' and 'wyse poete [...] that florisht so ful longe afore Merlyne', a description which echoes the heading introducing Melkin's prophecy in John of Glastonbury's *Cronica* and the *magna tabula*: 'Ista scriptura inuenitur in libro Melkini: qui fuit ante Merlinum' (this extract is found in the book of Melkin, who was before Merlin).¹⁸⁷ Although Hardyng appears to have misremembered or miscopied Mewyn's name, he is quite clear in associating him with Glastonbury. 'Mewytryne' is the place, Hardyng tells us, where Mewyn composed his 'boke'.¹⁸⁸ This seems to be a garbled form of Ynyswitrin, a legendary pseudonym for Glastonbury appearing in John of Glastonbury's *Cronica* ('Ynyswytryn'), the interpolated *De antiquitate*, and the *magna tabula* ('Ynswitrin').¹⁸⁹ Hardyng appears to read 'Mewyn' as the namesake for 'Mewytryn', an onomastic practice common in the work of early antiquaries.¹⁹⁰ 'Mewytryn' has been altered throughout to 'Ineswytryne' in at least one of the later short *Chronicle* witnesses, British Library MS Harley 661.¹⁹¹ Felicity Riddy has pointed out that the similarity between anglica 'lk' and 'w' may explain Hardyng's

---

[186] Riddy, 'Glastonbury, Joseph of Arimathea and the Grail in John Hardyng's Chronicle', p. 320. Riddy also states that 'Mewyn' is only mentioned in the Short Chronicle (pp. 318–20), but in fact he is mentioned in both versions, though in the longer Chronicle the emphasis seems to be placed more on 'Mewytryne' the place, rather than 'Mewyn' its namesake. 'Mewyn' is mentioned in the short chronicle: Hardyng, *Chronicle*, ed. Ellis, pp. 84–85, pp. 86–90, pp. 131–8, p. 136. In the long chronicle, 'Mewyn' is named at l. 822 (*John Hardyng's Chronicle*, ed. Peverley and Simpson). John Leland, who made use of Hardyng's *Chronicle*, would later remark upon Hardyng's misnaming of Melkin in *De uiris illustribus*, I, pp. 66–69 (no. 25).

[187] *The Chronicle of John Hardyng*, ed. Ellis, p. 132; John Hardyng, *Chronicle*, ed. Simpson and Peverley, 3.821-24. John of Glastonbury, *Cronica*, pp. 54–55; Krochalis, 'Magna Tabula', p. 470.

[188] Hardyng, *Chronicle*, ed. Simpson and Peverley, 3.825, 2625, 2612G, 2632.

[189] Richard Moll, 'Another Reference to John Hardyng's "Mewyn"', *Notes and Queries*, 245 (2000), 497–98; John of Glastonbury, *Cronica*, pp. 10-11; Krochalis, 'Magna Tabula', p. 510; William of Malmesbury, *De antiquitate*, p. 52.

[190] An astonishing example of onomastic squirreling occurs in John Rous's *Historia regum Angliae*. Rous also takes a close interest in the historical figures behind place names, and is similarly ready to bend and alter names to fit his needs: Geoffrey of Monmouth's 'Guthelin' becomes 'Gutheleon', whom Rous associates with 'Caer Leon', which he places at Warwick. See Rous, *Historia regum Angliae*, p. 69.

[191] See Richard Moll, 'Another Reference to John Hardyng's "Mewyn"', *Notes and Queries*, 245 (2000), 497–98 (p. 297). Riddy suggests that the changes to Harley 661 may have been made by a circumspect scribe. Riddy, 'Glastonbury, Joseph of Arimathea and the Grail', p. 319; p. 329, n. 35.

misspelling of Melkin.[192] Neither the *magna tabula* nor any of the existing manuscripts for John's *Cronica* use an anglicana script; but it is possible that other copies once existed. Hardyng's notes do not survive, and we cannot therefore draw any conclusions about their contents or script. It is possible, however, that Hardyng may be looking back on his notes and misreading them, particularly if he had copied a large volume of material from disparate sources on a variety of subjects during his itinerant visits and returned to them later. This possibility is complicated by the presence of the spellings 'Mewynus' for Melkin and 'inswytryn' (which might readily be mistaken for 'mewytryn', especially if sigma 's' was used) for Ynyswitrin in the version of the prophecy contained in British Library Cotton MS Cleopatra C.IV, where there is also reference made to Melkin's 'book'.[193] This compilation of prophecies and other material, put together by London canon lawyer William Swann in the 1440s or 1450s, contains various extracts relating to medieval *tabulae*, including examples from Glastonbury, Ripon, and York.[194] It also features texts relating to Anglo-Scottish relations, such as the *Second Scottish Prophecy* (c. 1350–1400), which would of course have been of interest to a figure like Hardyng. Whether Hardyng saw this manuscript or not is impossible to know, but it may explain how the misreadings of 'Mewyn' for Melkin and 'Mewytryn' for Inswytryn came to exist.

If Hardyng did not encounter the *magna tabula* or John's *Cronica* in person, it is also possible that he procured his Glastonbury details via a related Glastonian text. James Simpson and Sarah Peverley suggest an interpolated chronicle or a romance.[195] This is indeed a possibility: John Leland, visiting Glastonbury Abbey in 1533, describes having found 'in Glastonbury's library an ancient fragment of Melkin's *Historia*' from

---

[192] Riddy, 'Glastonbury, Joseph of Arimathea and the Grail', p. 320.

[193] 'Note that King Arviragus, a pagan Briton, after the incarnation of Jesus Christ, granted the island of Avalon (which in the language of the Britons is called Inswytryn) to Joseph of Arimathea. Mewynus, who was before Merlin and recorded various events from the time of the Britons in his book, says the following...' (Nota quod Rex Arviragus paganus britonis post incarnacionem ihesu Christi concessit ioseph ab arimathia insula aualonis qui britanice inswytryn uocatur. Mewynus qui ante merlinum fuit inter cetera gesta de tempore britonum in libro suo hec dicit). Then follows the prophecy. London, British Library Cotton MS Cleopatra C. IV, ff. 87v–88r; transcription in Krochalis, 'Magna Tabula', p. 483 n.

[194] The manuscript is a composite, and only the section containing Mewynus' prophecy (alongside other prophetic material) dates to the 1440s–50s. This manuscript also contains copies of the *Aliud chronicon* and the metrical chronicle that adorned York's *tabula*, both discussed above. Krochalis suggests its contents were copied from *tabulae* (Krochalis, 'Magna Tabula', p. 438). For more on this manuscript, see Lesley Coote, *Prophecy and Public Affairs in Later Medieval England* (York: York Medieval Press, 2000), pp. 157–94.

[195] John Hardyng, *Chronicle*, ed. Simpson and Peverley, 2.2611-47, n.

which he claims to have taken notes which he used in the composition of *De uiris illustribus*.[196] There are certainly a suspicious number of unfamiliar texts related to Glastonbury that Hardyng cites as authorities. In the earlier *Chronicle*, Hardyng attributes his description of Joseph's coming to Britain and his receipt of the twelve hides of land by King Arviragus to 'the book of Joseph of Arymathi lyfe and of his governance'.[197] Later, when describing a unique version of the Galahad shield story alluded to in the *tabula* and John's *Cronica*, Hardyng asserts that the episode was 'writton' by 'Josep off Aramathy | That holy knight with God fulle welle beloved | As by his werkes it is welle sene and proved'.[198] Elsewhere, Hardyng mentions a 'book of Josep of Arymathie' said to contain 'what the reule of ordour of Saynt Graal was', information which Hardyng assures us can also be found in 'a dialogue that Gildas made, *De Gestis Arthuri*'.[199] This attribution echoes the 'Gestis regis Arthuri' named as the source behind the romance interpolations in *De antiquitate*, item 2 on the *tabula*'s first page, and in John of Glastonbury's *Cronica*. James P. Carley has suggested that Hardyng's 'gestis' may represent an actual source, 'some sort of compendium concocted at Glastonbury separate from John's chronicle (but into which it was partially incorporated)'.[200] It may be significant that Hardyng's *Chronicle* shares a number of details with Richard Pynson's 1520 edition of Joseph of Arimathea's *Lyfe*, a text which may have been created for distribution to those visiting Glastonbury.[201] Furthermore, some versions of the Vulgate Prose Merlin claim that Joseph of Arimathea's son, also named Joseph, composed an Arthurian history identical to Blaise's book – a 'book of Joseph', albeit a different Joseph.[202]

---

[196] John of Glastonbury, *Cronica*, p. liv; Leland, *De uiris illustribus*, I, pp. 66–69.

[197] Hardyng, *Chronicle*, ed. Peverley and Simpson, 2.2613G. Peverley and Simpson point out that Wynkyn de Worde's *Nova Legenda Anglie* (1516) was interpolated with similar material.

[198] Hardyng, *Chronicle*, ed. Peverley and Simpson, 3.3084-86.

[199] Hardyng, *Chronicle*, ed. Simpson and Peverley, 3.3114-5G. Unfortunately (or perhaps fortunately?), this probably does not mean a valuable now-lost work of Gildas's: many works have been misattributed to Gildas, including Geoffrey of Monmouth's *Historia regum Britanniae*. See Sjoerd Levelt, 'Citation and Misappropriation in Geoffrey of Monmouth's *Historia Regum Britannie* and the Anglo-Latin Historiographical Tradition', in *Citation, Intertextuality and Memory in the Middle Ages and Renaissance*, ed. Giulino Di Bacco and Yolanda Plumley (Liverpool: Liverpool University Press, 2013), II, pp. 137–47.

[200] James P. Carley, 'Arthur in English History', in *The Arthur of the English*, ed. W. R. J. Barron (Cardiff: University of Wales Press, 2001), pp. 47–57 (p. 54); see also Moll, *Before Malory*, pp. 188–89.

[201] On the possibility of a connection between Pynson and Wynkyn's Joseph texts and the Glastonbury *tabula*, see Da Costa, 'Marketing the Shrine', passim.

[202] Ceridwen Lloyd-Morgan, 'Later Hybrid Narrative Texts in Middle Welsh', in *Arthur in the Celtic Languages*, ed. Ceridwen Lloyd-Morgan and Erich Poppe (Cardiff: University of Wales Press, 2019), pp. 203–13 (p. 206).

Figure 3. The first page of the magna tabula. MS Lat. Hist. A. 2, page 1. Bodleian Libraries, Oxford.

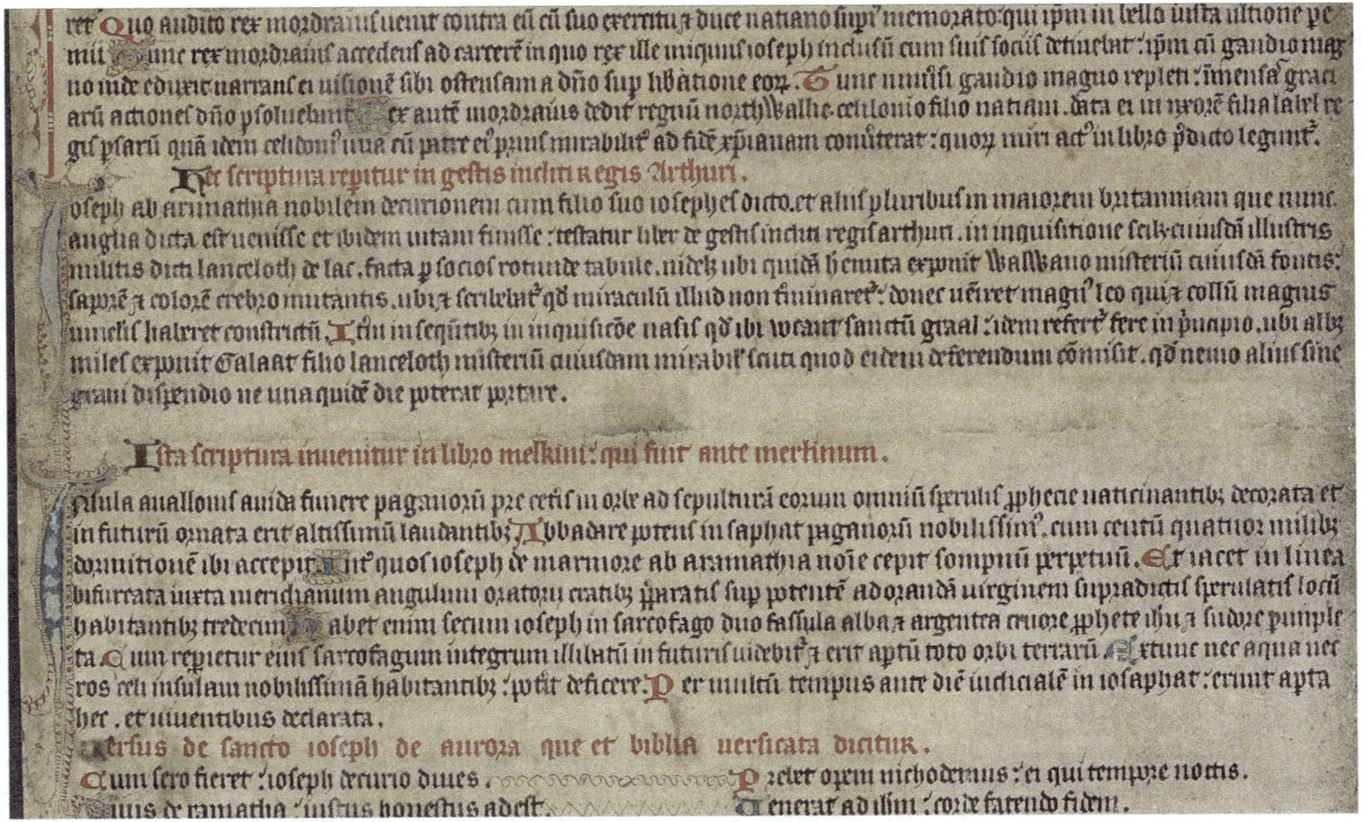

Figure 4. Detail showing rubrics and page design from the magna tabula. MS Lat. Hist. A. 2, page 1. Bodleian Libraries, Oxford.

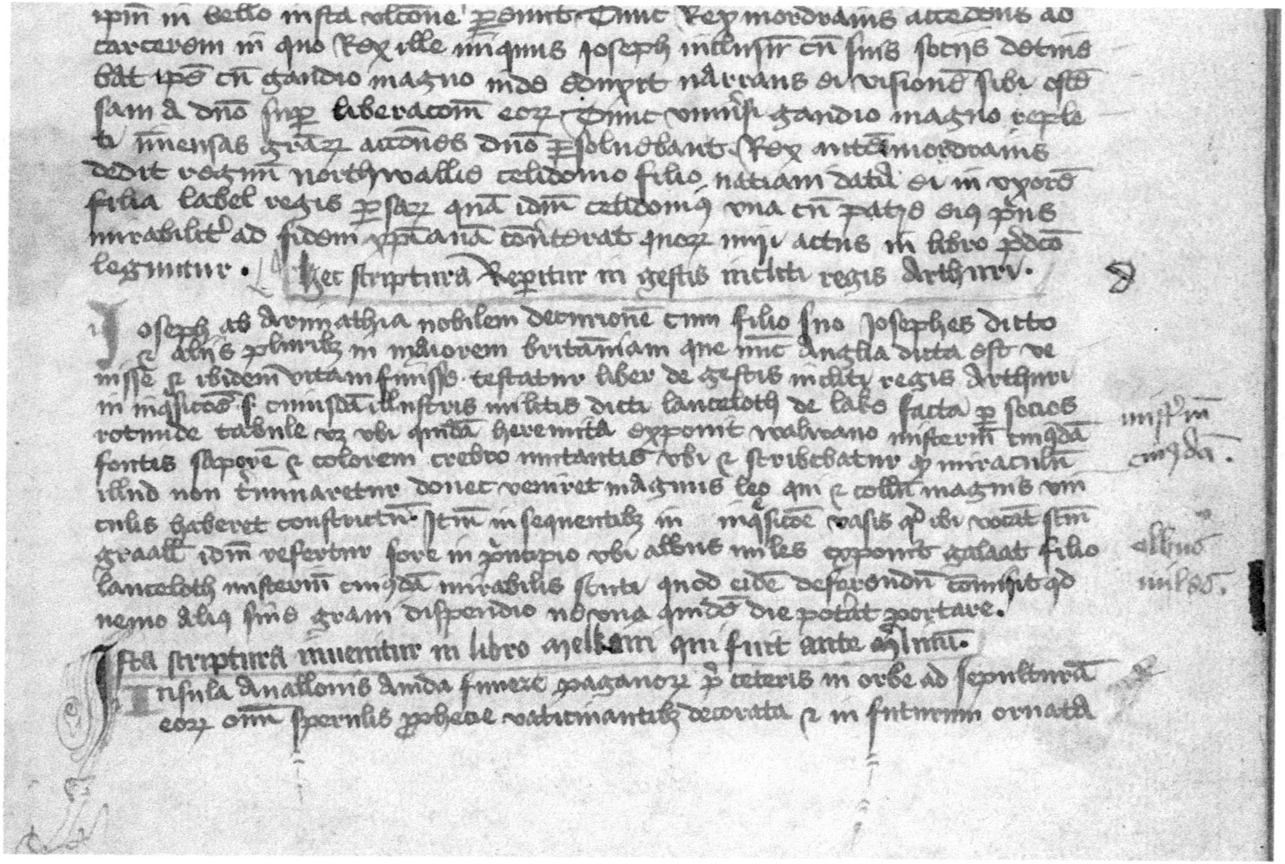

Figure 5. Detail showing the page design of a copy taken from the magna tabula contained in Cotton MS Titus A.XIX, f. 19r. © British Library Board.

Whilst it is possible that Hardyng encountered these unknown texts through a now-lost compendium text, Hardyng's ideas about the contents of the 'book of Josep' and the 'Gestis' may be a result of simple misreading, just as he may have misread the name Melkin. Other scholars have suggested Hardyng may have used John's *Cronica* as a source, but there remains something to be said concerning the sequence of material in both the *Cronica* and the *magna tabula* that may explain some of Hardyng's puzzling references to these unknown works.[203] To illustrate this, we need to turn for a moment to the text and page design of the *tabula* itself. Much of the material in the *tabula* also appears in John of Glastonbury's *Cronica*, and it is also possible that Hardyng had found it there. The first tablet-page begins with a rubric for item 1: 'here begins the treatise of St Joseph of Arimathea' (incipit tractatus de sancto Ioseph ab Arimathia).[204] If Hardyng had indeed taken his material directly from the *magna tabula*, we might expect this 'tractatus' to summarise the 'book of Josep' that Hardyng mentions throughout his *Chronicle*. Item 1 is in fact taken from the *Gospel of Nicodemus*, cropping its source to focus squarely on Joseph and adding further detail about his coming to Britain. However, the extract on the *tabula* does not concern the 'reule of the ordour of Saynt Graal' or Galahad's shield episode, both of which Hardyng attributes to Joseph's 'book'.[205] The *Nicodemus* extract does contain some suggestively Arthurian characters apparently taken from the *Estoire del Saint Graal*, and it is tempting to wonder what Arthurian material may have occupied the rest of the text.[206] Following the *Nicodemus* extract on the *magna tabula*'s first page, and also in John's *Cronica*, is item 2, with the title rubric 'this passage is found among the *Gestis incliti Regis Arthuri*' (hec scriptura reperitur in gestis incliti Regis Arthuri). Item 2 relates Joseph's journey to Britain, followed by a reference to the story of Galahad and the shield. Once again, Hardyng attributes the shield story to a book written by Joseph of Arimathea, perhaps the same 'book of Josep' he mentions elsewhere.

The first tablet-page of the *tabula* therefore presents these textual extracts one after another, and the page design is such that one could misread item 2 as a continuation of item 1 – a possibility that becomes

---

[203] See, for example, Carley, 'Melkin the Bard'; John of Glastonbury, *Cronica*, pp. lii–lx; Riddy, 'Glastonbury, Joseph of Arimathea, and the Grail'; John Hardyng, *Chronicle*, ed. Simpson and Peverley, 2.2611 n.

[204] Krochalis, 'Magna tabula', p. 477; John of Glastonbury, *Cronica*, pp. 46–47 (including English translation). The following quotations in this paragraph are taken from Krochalis, 'Magna Tabula', pp. 470–71; pp. 477–82.

[205] See Carley, 'Arthur in English History', p. 54.

[206] The characters in question are Mordrains, Nasciens, Joseph's son Josephus, and Celidoine and his wife. Krochalis, p. 445; John of Glastonbury, *Cronica*, pp. 50–51.

more likely if Hardyng were working from a copy of the *tabula* or the *Cronica*, where these extracts appear in sequence. On the *tabula*, item 2 is introduced with a rubric, but there is no clear line break between items 1 and 2 as there is between items 2 and 3 (see Figures 3 and 4). Considering what we know about the order, contents, and page design of the *magna tabula*, it is possible that Hardyng is making a series of misreadings or misunderstandings of a copy made from the *tabula* that can be summarised as follows:

1. Hardyng is mistakenly reading the Arthurian romance references in item 2 as a continuation of item 1 (that is, material taken from the 'book of Joseph')
2. Rather than reading item 2's rubric as the introduction of a new item that presents fresh material from a different source (the *Gestis*), Hardyng instead assumes it to be announcing a second source where the reader can also learn about these matters – that is, 'and these things, mentioned in the book of Joseph, are also mentioned in the *Gestis*' – an observation of intertextuality or shared evidence, rather than the introduction of a new text.

In other words, it is plausible that Hardyng may have read 'tractatus de sancto Ioseph ab Arimathea' and assumed that it encompassed items 1 and 2. This would explain why Hardyng attributes the shield story to Joseph's book. Hardyng may have read from a copy of John's *Cronica*, directly from the *tabula*, or, more probably, from a hastily written copy. Cotton MS Titus A.XIX provides an example of what a *tabula* copy may have looked like, replicating and amplifying the features of the *tabula*'s page design (see Figure 5). Although the rubrics for items 2 and 3 in Cotton MS Titus A.XIX are both included, item 2 is inset from the body of text and lacks a large initial.[207] Even if a copy preserved elements of the *tabula*'s original page design, the mention of a new source, even if in passing, might be enough to warrant rubrication. In chronicle manuscripts, sources are often rubricated, as well as proper names and the opening titles for new sections. It is easy to see how Hardyng might have mistaken this type of rubric for one acting as a subtitle for a new section.

This does not explain Hardyng's attribution of the 'reule of ordour of Saynt Graal' to Joseph's book, however. Either we must accept that

[207] British Library, Cotton MS Titus A.XIX, f. 19r; see Figure 5.

Hardyng concocted the 'reule' himself, perhaps based on the pre-existing Round Table oath as Simpson and Peverley have suggested, or that he found it in a now-lost text.[208] We are brought back to the tantalising question of Hardyng's ghost sources, and to the related question of whether Hardyng would have consulted such a lost text himself at Glastonbury. Both of these questions are impossible to answer, and we can only offer speculative suggestions based on how Hardyng expanded his Glastonbury material coupled with what we know about how the abbey accommodated its guests. One final example from Hardyng's text is illuminated by both questions. In his telling of the Galahad shield story, Hardyng (or his source) recasts the narrative as a 'castle-time' chronotope centred on Glastonbury. In the *Estoire* Galahad learns about the shield's back story, including its creation by Joseph of Arimathea's son Josephes, from a mysterious 'White Knight'.[209] In Hardyng's retelling, it is the 'holy men' at Avalon (associated elsewhere by Hardyng with Glastonbury) who share this information with Galahad having found it 'wreton' 'in bokes', and show him the shield along with a spear and sword.[210] Hardyng may have found this version of the story in some lost work, perhaps at Glastonbury as Carley has suggested, although in the later version of Hardyng's *Chronicle* there are no 'holy men'; Galahad happens upon the artefacts and book himself left at an eerily silent Avalon.[211] The earlier *Chronicle* demonstrates an awareness of how the abbey monks at Glastonbury might share their stories and objects with visiting guests, while the later telling presents a vision of Galahad himself consulting the 'book of Josep' at Avalon. If Hardyng did visit Glastonbury and consult the collections there, as he did with other chronicles in Rome and elsewhere, the later version of the *Chronicle* indicates that he envisioned himself retracing the steps (and pages) of Galahad who had come before him.

When thinking about the question of Hardyng's sources, it is worth remembering that the immediate intercessions of any tour guides at medieval Glastonbury are also, in their way, lost texts. As William Good's statements concerning Joseph of Arimathea's rumoured burial site suggest, there might be disagreement about Glastonbury's legends and history even among the monks themselves. Although the physical presence of the *magna tabula* in the abbey church ensured some cohesion in terms of how Glastonbury's narrative was told there were evidently

---

[208] Hardyng, *Chronicle*, ed. Simpson and Peverley, 3.3115 n.
[209] Summarised by Carley in John of Glastonbury, *Cronica*, p. 279.
[210] Hardyng, *Chronicle*, ed. Simpson and Peverley, 3.3052-61.
[211] *Hardyng's Chronicle*, ed. Ellis, p. 135.

more than enough gaps – especially among the *tabula*'s less orthodox Arthurian material, far less expansive than the preceding excerpt from the *Gospel of Nicodemus* – for a willing guide to elaborate on the *tabula*'s contents if they so wished. To return to the ideas of space and place introduced at the beginning of this book, we might think of Glastonbury's physical tourist media – its plaque and *tabula* – as Yi-Fu Tuan's place-as-pause, or in terms of the carefully planned cities illustrated by Michel de Certeau: an attempt to demarcate the narrative boundaries required to transform a neutral space into a place filled with value. On the other hand, Glastonbury's shadowy tour guides, more akin to de Certeau's city walkers, could disrupt such careful planning, or at the very least find their own ways to navigate through the material set out for them.

In conclusion, institutions with strong Arthurian connections, such as Glastonbury Abbey, evidently managed the experiences of their visitors with care. Multiple media forms were balanced to immerse guests in the sites' histories, and it is clear from the notes of Worcester and more complete works like Hardyng's *Chronicle* that these histories were not simply left on site. Rather, site visitors took these histories with them, whether in physical notebooks or simply as memories of *tabulae* and glazing schemes. Visitors pursuing important projects were accommodated even more fully by being given access to institutional libraries at sites both secular (Dover Castle) and sacred (Glastonbury Abbey), libraries that held locally tailored chronicles and perhaps other lost texts. Although it is not possible to prove whether or not Hardyng visited Glastonbury himself, his works point to the undeniable broader impact of local Arthurian site histories well beyond their immediate localities by the later Middle Ages. By this stage, Arthurian sites had become embroiled in issues of national interest, such as Hardyng's suzerainty efforts.

Hardyng appears to have improved his familiarity with Glastonbury Abbey's history in the interim between the composition of his earlier and later *Chronicles*, and given the condensed nature of the later *Chronicle* Hardyng must have had good reason to sharpen his focus on the history and space of Glastonbury. The abbey is not, however, the only Arthurian location named by Hardyng in his *Chronicle*, and some of the other places he connects with Arthur are far more idiosyncratic. The following chapter considers how Hardyng and his contemporaries imagined Arthur's most important places, and the ways in which they reconciled an increasingly crowded and sometimes contradictory Arthurian map.

2
Contentious places: Reconciling Arthurian places in the fifteenth century

In order to appreciate the connections between localised, *in situ* experiences of Arthur in the fifteenth century and the local Arthur handed down by later antiquarians such as John Leland and William Camden, it is crucial to understand the sheer number of Arthurian localities available to Arthur's early modern defenders, and the ways in which those defenders consolidated, reconciled, and managed such a wealth of Arthurian place claims. As the previous chapter demonstrated, the fourteenth and fifteenth centuries were characterised by Arthurian sites communicating their local histories to interested visitors, some of whom noted them down in travel diaries or perused the holdings of the on-site libraries. This was the first step in the emergence of a local Arthur; by the fifteenth century, there were a very large number of places across England, Wales, and Scotland claiming a connection to Arthur in some way, and visitors to Arthurian localities in this period, such as William Worcester and John Hardyng, often visited a significant proportion of them. This multiplicity means that the local Arthur in the fifteenth century would have been hard to miss.

For those invested in defending Arthur's reality and purging his history of some of its less credible elements, these Arthurian locations needed to be sorted through. The enormous range of Arthurian place claims that existed by this stage – some of which were contradictory – laid the groundwork for those writing about Arthur in the sixteenth century to locate Arthur wherever they thought most appropriate. Later chapters of this book will analyse the different regions carved out for Arthur by his early modern defenders according to their own affiliations and interests; but before we come to these it is important to grasp the vast number of possible places in which Arthur might be located.

This chapter therefore pulls together the competing Arthurian place claims that were current in the fifteenth century, and suggests reasons as to why some sites were contested while others were not. Some of these place claims are obviously contradictory, sometimes the product of civic, episcopal, or local competition (largely over unidentifiable obsolete toponyms from ancient texts).[1] Others, however, are less contentious than they initially seem. Locations claimed as Arthur's court or the site of his Round Table, for example, are accepted as plural. Sometimes Arthurian toponyms are not fought over, but rather shared out. The City of Legions is one such example: several candidates were put forward by the end of the fifteenth century, but these do not seem to contradict each other. Rather, it was broadly accepted by this point that there must have been many such legionary cities, and the events in the lives of Arthur and his contemporaries could readily be split between them all.

The chapter concludes by suggesting how and why certain places may have been incorporated into Arthur's geography. First, onomastics (and indeed pseudo-onomastics, or misread onomastics) had a part to play; for example, the presence of a place name in existing texts featuring Arthur, such as Geoffrey's *Historia*, or apparent similarities between obsolete and contemporary toponyms. The presence of other major Arthurian places nearby could perform a generative function, spawning new associations in the immediate area and sometimes even forming new Arthurian microregions. Material culture was also an important factor in Arthurian place attributions: the presence of visibly ancient remains such as earthworks, foundations, or inscribed rubble incorporated into more recent buildings; unusual topographies; or apparently Arthurian artefacts such as the Winchester Round Table. The political significance of a particular location could also play a crucial role in its 'Arthuring'.

A minor but interesting illustrative example combining many of these elements – striking topography, political significance, prior appearance in Arthurian texts, 'contagious' Arthurian places nearby – is the network of caves situated beneath the city of Nottingham. The Nottingham cave network is man-made, carved out of the sandstone beneath the city from the early Middle Ages and perhaps earlier.[2] In the Auchinleck manuscript, a fourteenth-century interpolation made to the *Short English Metrical*

---

[1] On the political potential for onomastics, see *Critical Toponymies: The Contested Politics of Place Naming*, ed. Lawrence D. Berg and Jani Vuolteenaho, 2nd edn (London: Routledge, 2016).

[2] In his *Life of Alfred* (893), Asser records Welsh and Latin place names for Nottingham, 'Tig Guocobauc' and 'Speluncarum Domus', which translate to 'house of caves'. See Gareth Davies, David Knight, Scott C. Lomax and Christopher Loveluck, 'From "House of Caves" to Nexus of Central England: Nottingham, c. AD 650–1250 – Future Research Directions', *Transactions of the Thoroton Society of Nottinghamshire*, 123 (2019), 55–76 (pp. 66–67). On the caves' historic use and dating, see A. C. Waltham, 'Crown Hole Development in the Sandstone Caves of Nottingham', *Quarterly Journal of Engineering Geology*, 26.4 (1993), 243–51.

Chronicle (apparently a very popular form for the expression of local Arthurian histories) claims that these caves were carved out by Lancelot in an attempt to hide Guenevere.³ Seemingly the earliest reference to the pair's infidelity in Middle English, it is striking that this reference dates to c. 1331, just a year after Edward III had besieged Nottingham Castle where his mother, Isabella of France, had taken refuge with her paramour Roger Mortimer.⁴ As Richard Moll points out, Nottingham Castle had previously been associated with the Dolorous Garde, Lancelot's castle, in Rauf de Boun's *Le Petit Bruit* (c. 1309); and although the story of the caves is seemingly original to the Auchinleck interpolation, the nearby castle's association with the Dolorous Garde may have helped to call the cave tradition into being.⁵ In this case, then, Arthurian narrative provided a way of reflecting on more recent political events that had occurred at Nottingham, while the distinct topography of the caves functioned as a 'mnemonic bridge' capable of drawing past and present together.⁶

On the basis of textual evidence alone, the tradition connecting Lancelot and Guinevere's affair with the Nottingham Caves does not appear to have spread any more broadly than this single interpolation. This may be because the caves were not immediately familiar beyond the local area, or else because this episode belongs more to the realm of continental Arthurian romance than insular Arthurian historiography; the Auchinleck *Short English Metrical Chronicle* is, after all, anomalous within the chronicle tradition in including Lancelot and Guinevere's affair in its account of Arthurian history. For those defending Arthur's existence in the fifteenth century, distinguishing a believable geography for Arthur was a priority, and this meant downplaying places associated with romance whilst simultaneously drawing out a believable, historical Arthurian geography and reconciling contradictory place claims. In order

---

³ *An Anonymous Short English Metrical Chronicle*, ed. Ewald Zettl, Early English Text Society, Original Series 196 (London: Early English Text Society, 1935), Auchinleck additions at pp. 70–71.

⁴ The parallels between history and legend are identified in Helen Cooper, 'Lancelot, Roger Mortimer and the Date of the Auchinleck Manuscript', in *Studies in Late Medieval and Early Renaissance Texts in Honour of John Scattergood: The Key of All Good Remembrance*, ed. A. J. Fletcher and Anne-Marie D'Arcy (Dublin: Portland, 2005), pp. 91–99; see also Elizabeth Archibald, 'Lancelot as Lover in the English Tradition Before Malory', in *Arthurian Studies in Honour of P. J. C. Field*, ed. Bonnie Wheeler (Cambridge: D. S. Brewer, 2004), pp. 199–216.

⁵ Richard J. Moll, 'Ebrauke and the Politics of Arthurian Geography', *Arthuriana*, 15.4 (2005), 65–71 (p. 66). Moll discusses two other candidates for Lancelot's Dolorous Garde, Alnwick and Bamburgh, and the role that political concerns may have had to play in their association with the Arthurian narrative.

⁶ Zerubavel, *Time Maps*; see above at pp. 22–26.

to identify how Arthurian places were consolidated during the fifteenth century, we must first establish which Arthurian locations were up for debate. Clearly, some Arthurian places were less disputed than others, and there may be a variety of reasons – practical, political, or otherwise – for the inconsistency in claims and counterclaims.

Claims and counterclaims to Arthurian places in the fifteenth century

Tintagel: Arthur's conception

The site associated with Arthur's supposed conception – Tintagel in Cornwall – does not have any competitors. The first textual reference to the story occurs in Geoffrey of Monmouth's *Historia regum Britanniae*.[7] The story is repeated in historiographical texts derived from Geoffrey's *Historia*, such as Wace's *Roman de Brut* and Laȝamon's *Brut*, and later in the popular Prose *Bruts*; and it also appears in a limited number of romances and related texts, including Lovelich's *Merlin* and the Prose *Merlin*, and in Malory's *Morte Darthur*.[8] Arthur's conception story also makes an appearance in the French romance tradition, though another popular association for Tintagel in French romance is instead as the seat of King Mark in the Tristan stories.[9] Oliver Padel has remarked that 'a well-read

---

[7] Geoffrey of Monmouth, *History of the Kings of Britain*, 8.137–138, pp. 184–88. Tatlock has elucidated the parallels between Geoffrey's tale of Arthur's begetting with the tradition of Alexander the Great's conception; see J. S. P. Tatlock, *The Legendary History of Britain* (Berkeley, CA: University of California Press, 1950), pp. 314–19.

[8] Wace, *Wace's Roman de Brut: A history of the British*, ed. and trans. Judith Weiss (Exeter: University of Exeter Press, 2002), pp. 216–22; *The Oldest Anglo-Norman Prose Brut Chronicle*, ed. and trans. Julia Marvin (Woodbridge: Boydell, 2006), pp. 152–54. The conception story – set at 'Tyntogell' – appears in the Prose Latin *Brut*; see, for example, Cambridge, Corpus Christi College, MS 311, f. 25v. References in Laȝamon, Malory, Lovelich, and the Prose *Merlin* are all cited in Robert W. Ackerman, *An Index of the Arthurian Names in Middle English* (Stanford, CA: Stanford University Press, 1952), pp. 229–30. Arthur's Tintagel conception is also mentioned in a ballad, *Kinge Arthurs Death*, included in the manuscript known as the Percy Folio (London, British Library, Add. MS 27879) and subsequently Percy's *Reliques* by the same author, Thomas Percy (1729–1811). Despite Percy's claim that this 'curious old Poem [...] may be considered, as one of the first attempts in Epic Poetry by the English', Raluca L. Radulescu has shown this to be an early modern production based on Richard Lloyd's *Nine Worthies* (1584). See Raluca L. Radulescu, 'The Percy Folio', in *The Encyclopedia of Medieval Literature in Britain*, ed. Siân Echard and Robert Rouse, 4 vols (London: Wiley-Blackwell, 2017), pp. 1512–15 (p. 1513).

[9] G. D. West, *An Index of Proper Names in French Arthurian Prose Romances* (Toronto: University of Toronto Press, 1978), pp. 291–92; G. D. West, *An Index of Proper Names in French Arthurian Verse Romances* (Toronto: University of Toronto Press, 1969), pp. 152–53.

European' of the mid-thirteenth century 'would have heard of Tintagel as a castle of King Mark (rather than King Arthur)'.[10] This said, Tintagel has no competitors in its claim to be the site of Arthur's mythical conception, to the best of our knowledge. This may be due to the uncomfortable morality of that part of Arthur's story, which involves enchantment, adultery, and sexual violence – perhaps nowhere else *wanted* to claim this particular episode. Laura Keeler has argued that moral discomfort at this material may have led later chroniclers adapting Geoffrey's history, such as Richard of Cirencester and the author of the *Flores Historiarum*, to omit the story of Arthur's conception altogether.[11] Later, in the sixteenth century, John Leland wondered whether Bede had omitted Arthur from his list of kings because he was 'begotten in adultery'.[12] Scottish chronicler Hector Boece took Uther's depravity even further than Geoffrey, stating that Uther, 'abandoning all sense of shame and probity, raped the woman [...] and soon made her pregnant' (Sublatis pudore ac probitate [...] interceptam foeminam [...] cupide compressam, praegnantem haud multo post reddidit).[13] Whilst not strictly a counterclaim to Arthur's place of conception, it is also worth mentioning that some of Boece's fellow Scots disputed Arthur's royal claims altogether. From as early as 1301, Scottish authors such as Baldred Bisset, John Fordun, and Walter Bower were suggesting that Mordred was the rightful heir to the English throne, not Arthur, because Arthur had been begotten through adultery.[14]

Alternatively, an absence of counterclaims for the site of Arthur's conception may simply be due to the precise nature of Geoffrey's description of Tintagel – both in terms of its name and its geographical situation. Geoffrey describes the location of 'Tintagol' on the Cornish coast, standing 'completely surrounded by the sea' and only reachable 'by a narrow cliff' ('[situm est] in mari et undique circumclausum ab ipso,

---

[10] Padel, 'Cornwall and the Matter of Britain', p. 274.
[11] Laura Keeler, *Geoffrey of Monmouth and the Late Latin Chroniclers 1300–1500* (Berkeley, CA: University of California Publications in English, 1946). The *Flores Historiarum* referred to here is the version ending in 1326, thought to have been authored by Matthew Paris.
[12] John Leland, 'Notable Thinges Translatid in to Englisch by John Leylande Oute of a Booke, Caullid Scala Chronica', Appendix 1 in Thomas Gray, *Scalacronica*, ed. Joseph Stevenson (Edinburgh: The Maitland Club, 1836), pp. 259–315 (p. 260).
[13] Cited (with translation) in Elizabeth Hanna, 'A "Scottish Monmouth"? Hector Boece's Arthurian Revisions', in *The Impact of Latin Culture on Medieval and Early Modern Scottish Writing*, ed. Alessandra Petrina and Ian Johnson (Kalamazoo, MI: Medieval Institute Publications, 2018), pp. 105–26 (p. 109).
[14] Hanna, 'A "Scottish Monmouth"?', pp. 105–06.

nec est alter introitus nisi quem angusta ruper praebeat).[15] This specificity has led some scholars to believe that Geoffrey must have seen the site at first hand.[16]

Glastonbury or Gwynedd: Arthur's burial

The legitimacy of Arthur's burial site at Glastonbury is almost entirely uncontested in extant writings of the fifteenth century and earlier. Even those most sceptical of Arthur's history, such as Ranulf Higden, did not question the authenticity of Glastonbury's Arthurian associations.[17] Presumably, this is because of the apparently indisputable discovery of Arthur's grave at Glastonbury in 1191, which effectively put to bed any more fanciful rumours of Arthur's return. There is, however, one text which suggests an alternative end for Arthur in North Wales: the *Vera historia de morte Arthuri* (The True History of Arthur's Death).[18]

There is some debate as to whether the *Vera historia* dates to before or after 1191, when the disinterment took place. Berard gives a conservative dating of c. 1138–1300, Michael Lapidge and Richard Barber argue for a post-1200 dating, and Siân Echard suggests the *Vera historia* predates 1191 because there is no mention of Arthur's Glastonbury burial.[19] As Ad Putter has observed, the title of the work does seem rather pointedly to suggest that *this* version of Arthur's death is the correct one.[20] However, it is quite

---

[15] Text and translation from Geoffrey of Monmouth, *History of the Kings of Britain*, 8.137, pp. 184–88.

[16] David Rollason, 'From Tintagel to Aachen: Richard of Cornwall and the Power of Place', *Reading Medieval Studies*, 38 (2012), 1–23; Padel, 'Some South-Western Sites', p. 227.

[17] Ranulf Higden drew his readers' attention to inconsistencies in Arthur's timeline, and his absence in contemporaneous continental sources. However, he accepts without question that Arthur was buried at Glastonbury, despite being sceptical about other Glastonbury claims, such as the identity of St Patrick. Ranulf Higden, *Polychronicon Ranulphi Higden*, ed. Churchill Babington and Joseph Rawson Lumby, Rolls Series 41, 10 vols (London, 1865–85), V, p. 332. See John E. Housman, 'Higden, Trevisa, Caxton, and the Beginnings of Arthurian Criticism', *The Review of English Studies*, 23.91 (1947), 209–17.

[18] The text has been edited by Michael Lapidge, 'The *Vera historia de morte Arthuri*: A New Edition', in *Glastonbury Abbey and the Arthurian Tradition*, pp. 115–41. See also Richard Barber, 'The *Vera Historia de Morte Arthuri* and Its Place in Arthurian Tradition', in *Glastonbury Abbey and the Arthurian Tradition*, pp. 101–13; Lloyd, *The Arthurian Place Names of Wales*, pp. 29–30.

[19] Berard, *Arthurianism*, p. 103; Lapidge, 'Vera Historia: A New Edition', p. 127; Barber, 'The Vera Historia', p. 110; Ad Putter, 'Latin Historiography After Geoffrey of Monmouth', in *The Arthur of Medieval Latin Literature*, ed. Siân Echard (Cardiff: University of Wales Press, 2011), pp. 85–108.

[20] Putter, 'Latin Historiography', p. 97.

possible that the title was added at a later date: the earliest surviving witness dates to c. 1300, around 100 years later than the proposed date of composition.[21] If the *Vera historia* does indeed postdate 1191, then the text performs two actions at once, legitimising the history of Geoffrey of Monmouth and writing Gwynedd into that history whilst simultaneously rejecting the Glastonbury grave as inauthentic.

Ostensibly, the *Vera historia* does not specify the site of Arthur's burial any more closely than placing it in Gwynedd (Venedocia). The *Vera historia* describes Arthur's end in more detail than Geoffrey of Monmouth's account, and has indeed been called an 'apparent continuation' of Geoffrey's *Historia* by Siân Echard – indeed, it has actually been interpolated into the *Historia* in at least one manuscript.[22] It expands upon the brief and enigmatic description of Arthur's final journey to Avalon described in Geoffrey's text.[23] The plot is as follows: after his battle with Mordred, a recovering Arthur is stabbed by a mysterious figure holding a poisoned spear. As he is dying, Arthur requests to be taken for treatment to a chapel dedicated to the Virgin in 'Gwynedd' (Venedocia), 'since he had decided to sojourn in the delightful Isle of Avallon' ([...] ad Venedociam, quia in Auallonis insula delectabili [...] perendinari proposuerat).[24] As Arthur's condition worsens, he calls upon the archbishop of London along with two bishops (Urien of Bangor and Urbegen of Glamorgan), the archbishop of Menevia (St Davids) being indisposed with illness. However, the chapel is very small, its entrance especially so:

> for the entrance of the oft-mentioned chapel was so small and narrow that no-one could enter it unless, having wedged one shoulder in, he drew the other with a great effort of strength and ingenuity.[25]

---

[21] Lapidge, 'Vera Historia: A New Edition', pp. 116–24.
[22] Siân Echard, *Arthurian Narrative in the Latin Tradition* (Cambridge: Cambridge University Press, 1998), pp. 79–80; Berard, *Arthurianism*, p. 102.
[23] Geoffrey summarises Arthur's death as follows: 'The illustrious king Arthur too was mortally wounded; he was taken away to the island of Avallon to have his wounds tended and, in the year of Our Lord 542, handed over Britain's crown to his relative Constantinus, son of Cador duke of Cornwall.' (Sed et inclitus ille rex Arturus letaliter uulneratus est; qui illinc ad sananda uulnera sua in insulam Auallonis euectus Constantino cognato suo et filio Cadoris ducis Cornubiae diadema Britanniae concessit anno ab incarnatione Domini .dxlii.) Geoffrey of Monmouth, *History of the Kings of Britain*, 11.178, pp. 252–53.
[24] Lapidge, 'Vera Historia: A New Edition', pp. 136–37.
[25] Lapidge, 'Vera Historia: A New Edition', pp. 138–39.

> ([...] nam sepiusdicte capelle aditus ita fuit breuis et angustus ut in eam nullus intraret nisi uno latere premisso summo conamine uirium et ingenio subintroduceret alterum.)

This means that Arthur's body is too large to enter the chapel. A tomb is prepared for Arthur just outside the chapel, near its outer wall, and he is left outside while the funerary rites are performed. A terrible storm occurs, and once it is over a thick and mysterious mist sets in. After it has cleared, the mourners find that Arthur's body has vanished, and the intended tomb has miraculously sealed itself.

On the basis of certain motifs in the *Vera historia*, it is possible that the version of Arthur's end presented in the text may have its origins in narratives that circulated orally for some time before it was first committed to writing. Barber has pointed out several characteristics that appear to come from Welsh vernacular literature – the magical storm and mist, the disappearance of Arthur's body, the poisonous spearman.[26] The text also seems to feature a stone monolith connected with Arthur, a common feature of topographical lore. The miraculously sealed tomb is described as 'one single stone, whole and solid, as if fashioned with the mortar and craft of a builder, one after the other' (tota petra [...] integra et solida, quasi una cum altera cemento artificis et ingenio compacto).[27] This description is strikingly similar to John Rastell's sceptical comments about the 'stonis' of Stonehenge some centuries later:

> [t]hey [the stones] were made by craft of men as of sement and morter made of flynt stonys [...] these stonis at Stonehenge be all of one gryt without change of colour or vayne and all of one facyon therefore many grete wyse men suppose them to be made of a morter of flynt or other stonys.[28]

In altered copies of the *Vera historia* there may have been further resonances with folklore. One of the oldest extant witnesses to the text, the truncated version included in the *Hailes Chronicle*, omits the detail of the chapel's tiny entrance, and the difficulty with which normal men may fit inside.[29] This means that the Arthur of the Hailes version might be interpreted as very large in stature, another common trope in Arthurian

---

[26] Barber, 'The *Vera Historia*', p. 109; Lapidge, 'Vera Historia: A New Edition', pp. 124–25.
[27] Lapidge, 'Vera Historia: A New Edition', pp. 140–41.
[28] John Rastell, *Pastyme of People* (London: John Rastell, 1530), STC (2nd edn) 20724, sig. C2v.
[29] Lapidge, 'Vera Historia: A New Edition', pp. 138–39.

landscape folklore.³⁰ The setting described is therefore rather specific: a chapel dedicated to the Virgin in Gwynedd, apparently so tiny that a relatively large male body cannot fit through the door, and perhaps with a monolith standing nearby in the churchyard. The author may have had a particular location in mind; alternatively, the text's chapel and churchyard may represent an amalgam of different oral narratives.

The question of *where* exactly in Gwynedd the *Vera historia* is supposed to be set (if anywhere) can only invite speculative answers. The likely dating of this text to the thirteenth century lines up with an especially tumultuous time in Anglo-Welsh relations, and especially for England's relationship with Gwynedd. In the first half of the century, England's kings led a series of campaigns in an attempt to curb the rising power of the prince of Gwynedd, Llywelyn ap Iorweth.³¹ Llywelyn held his royal seat at Aberffraw, and it remained the political centre of Wales throughout the thirteenth century. Christopher Berard has therefore suggested that Arthur's Gwynedd burial in the *Vera historia* may have been especially resonant for political reasons with the Welsh princes of Aberffraw.³² In many respects, the Avalonian setting of the *Vera historia* reflects Aberffraw, not least because of its island location on Anglesey. The visibility of ancient remains at Aberffraw might well have fuelled an association with Arthur, and with ancient British history more broadly. Llywelyn's princely palace or *llys* at Aberffraw was constructed on the site of a prehistoric earthwork that may also have been inhabited in the Roman period.³³ If the *Vera historia*'s author did indeed have Aberffraw in mind as a setting, the nearby church at Llangadwalladr might readily

---

³⁰ Folklorists such as Myrddin Fardd have observed several examples of Arthur depicted as a giant; see Caitlin R. Green, *Arthuriana*, p. 95. See also Grooms, *The Giants of Wales*, pp. 113–28; Caitlin Green, *Concepts of Arthur* (Stroud: Tempus, 2008); Caitlin R. Green, 'A Gazetteer of Arthurian Onomastic and Topographic Folklore', in *Arthuriana*, www.arthuriana.co.uk/notes&queries/N&Q2_ArthFolk.pdf [accessed 14 September 2019]. On Arthurian stones, see Green, 'A Gazetteer', pp. 101–03; Padel 'The Nature of Arthur', passim.
³¹ Ifor W. Rowlands, 'King John and Wales', in *King John: New Interpretations*, ed. S. D. Church (Woodbridge: Boydell, 1999), pp. 273–87.
³² Berard, *Arthurianism*, pp. 102–05; pp. 305–06.
³³ The most recent archaeological report has suggested that the *llys* was not constructed on the site of a Roman fort, but rather a prehistoric earthwork that might have been repurposed in the Roman and medieval periods. See John Wiles, 'Aberffraw, Excavated Features, Rejected Roman Fort and Suggested Llys Site', NPRN 401126 (Royal Commission for Ancient and Historical Monuments of Wales, 2007), https://coflein.gov.uk/en/site/401126 [accessed 30 May 2022]. See also G. R. J. Jones, 'Early Territorial Organization in Gwynedd and Elmet', *Northern History*, 10.1 (1975), 3–27 (p. 9); G. R. J. Jones, 'The Site of Llys Aberffraw', *Transactions of the Anglesey Antiquarian Society* (1957), 1–4.

be identified with the chapel of the text. Llangadwalladr church seems to have functioned as a burial site for Gwynedd royalty from as early as the seventh century, for a stone measuring 1.23 metres in length and inscribed with a seventh-century epitaph to King Cadfan survives at Llangadwaladr, having been set into the wall above the door of the thirteenth-century nave that still stands today.[34] It has been suggested that the stone once stood upright in the churchyard.[35] Clearly, the decision to repurpose the stone very visibly into the fabric of the church itself, giving it pride of place above the church door, suggests that the early history of the site was a matter of importance in its design.[36] Some scholars suggest that the church's original name was 'eglwys ail', or 'wattle church', before it was renamed for Cadwaladr, the last in Geoffrey of Monmouth's line of British kings; if the church was indeed known by this name around the time the *Vera historia* was authored, this may suggest an awareness of a much earlier church on the site similar to the Old Church at Glastonbury.[37]

Although scholars have not gone so far as to identify a possible setting for the *Vera historia*, many have offered suggestions as to where the text may have been composed. Barber, Lapidge, and Putter suggest that the *Vera Historia* may have been produced at Aberconwy Abbey. This would also be a reasonable fit for the text's Avalon location. Aberconwy was founded by Llywelyn the Great in 1198 who was later buried there, making it one of the most important abbeys in North Wales.[38] It was dedicated to the Virgin Mary, and the presence of an abbreviated version

---

[34] Edward Lhwyd saw the inscribed stone over the church door, and recorded a copy of it; see Edward Lhwyd, 'An Account of Some Roman, French, and Irish Inscriptions and Antiquities', *Philosophical Transactions*, 22.269 (1700–01), 790–92; and William Camden, *Britannia: or a chorographical description of Great Britain and Ireland*, 2 vols, 2nd edn (London: Edmund Gibson, 1722), II, p. 62. See also Adam Voelcker, 'Llangadwaladr (St Cadwaladr)', in *Churches and Chapels in North-West Wales*, ed. Jonathan M. Wooding and Nigel Yates (Cardiff: University of Wales Press, 2011), pp. 102–03.

[35] Nancy Edwards, 'Welsh History Month: The Memorial Stone of King Cadfan of Gwynedd', *Wales Online*, 14 May 2013, www.walesonline.co.uk/lifestyle/nostalgia/welsh-history-month-memorial-stone-3812462 [accessed 1 April 2022].

[36] Nancy Edwards, 'Afterlives: Reinventing Early Medieval Sculpture in Wales', *Archaeologia Cambrensis*, 169 (2020), 1–29 (p. 4).

[37] See, for example, G. R. J. Jones, 'Some Donations to Bishop Wilfrid in Northern England', *Northern History*, 31.1 (1995), 22–38 (p. 25 n.); G. R. J. Jones, 'Early Customary Tenures in Wales and Open-Field Agriculture', in *The Origins of Open-Field Agriculture*, ed. Trevor Rowley (London: Routledge, 1981), pp. 202–25 (pp. 213–15); Tomos Roberts, 'Welsh Ecclesiastical Place-Names and Archaeology', in *The Early Church in Wales and the West*, ed. Nancy Edwards (Oxford: Alan Lane, 1992), pp. 41–44 (p. 42).

[38] Janet Burton and Karen Stöber, eds, *Abbeys and Priories of Medieval Wales* (Cardiff: University of Wales Press, 2015), pp. 32–35.

of the *Vera historia* in a Hailes Abbey manuscript also points to Aberconwy as a candidate, given the connections between Hailes and Aberconwy in the thirteenth century.[39] If there is indeed an Aberconwy connection, the fact that the abbey was only founded in 1198 problematises the possibility that the *Vera historia* was written before the Glastonbury discovery in 1191. However, it is worth asking why Llywelyn may have chosen to found an abbey on this site in the first place: perhaps the Marian chapel of the text was imagined to have existed at Aberconwy before the abbey's foundation, just as later chroniclers imagined the apostolic chapel at Glastonbury to have existed prior to Glastonbury Abbey's foundation by King Ine. It is uncertain what ideas the Aberconwy monks might have had about the site's history, and contemporary scholars disagree on what the abbey's early dimensions might have been.[40] However, we know that Glastonbury Abbey monks were imaginatively reconstructing the abbey's foundation church in the fourteenth century based on the evidence outlined in the previous chapter. It is quite possible that the same imaginative activities were occurring in Abernconwy. No evidence survives of stone monoliths in the vicinity of the site, but this does not mean that there have never been any; we know for example that Glastonbury Abbey cemetery contained very old engraved 'pyramids' in the Middle Ages which were gone by the early modern period.[41]

Another possible candidate for the *Vera historia*'s setting is Enlli (Bardsey Island), situated off the west coast of the Llŷn Peninsula. Its island setting is a better fit for the isle of Avalon than Aberconwy, and indeed it has been imagined to be the 'true' Avalon in more recent times by twentieth-century Arthurian questers Chris Barber and David Pykitt.[42] There are a large number of stone monoliths and ancient monuments

---

[39] Lapidge, 'Vera Historia: A New Edition', p. 128. The abbreviated Hailes version of the *Vera historia* is printed in Robert Huntington Fletcher, 'Some Arthurian Fragments from Fourteenth Century Chronicles', *PMLA*, 18.1 (1903), 84–94 (pp. 84–89). Abbreviated adaptations of legendary texts are common in *tabulae*, such as the ones which survive at York Minster.

[40] A description of the site and previous excavations is given in Burton and Stöber, *Abbeys and Priories of Medieval Wales*, pp. 32–35.

[41] The pyramids were first recorded in the twelfth century by William of Malmesbury, and were seen c. 1480 by William Worcester, and in 1542 by John Leland. By 1777, when Dr Whitaker was writing, they had gone, though Whitaker thought that this had happened within living memory. See Aelred Watkin, 'The Glastonbury "Pyramids" and St Patrick's "Companions"', *The Downside Review*, 61 (1945), 30–41; J. Whitaker, *Life of Saint Neot*, pp. 35–36.

[42] Chris Barber and David Pykitt, *Journey to Avalon: The Final Discovery of King Arthur* (York Beach, ME: Samuel Weiser, 1997). Scott Lloyd describes this particular type of Arthurian publication in his introduction to *The Arthurian Place Names of Wales*, and I mention it here not because I am agreement with Barber and Pykitt's arguments,

on the island in the vicinity of the abbey site. Enlli was famous in Wales by the early twelfth century, dubbed the Rome of Britain for its holiness and inaccessibility; it was said to be a resting place for 20,000 saints.[43] In his *Itinerary of Wales* (c. 1191), Gerald of Wales describes Enlli as home to 'extremely devout monks' called '*coelibes* or *colidei*' (probably Célí Dé) who lived to an astonishing age and were never ill.[44] This latter statement is interesting given that in the *Vera historia* Arthur intends to go to 'the Isle of Avallon [...] for easing the pain of his wounds', and that he is attended to diligently by skilled physicians on his arrival.[45] Like the chapel of the text, Enlli's Abbey was dedicated to the Virgin after its refounding in 1240 following the Augustinian takeover, though Enlli was an important pilgrimage destination well before this date.[46] It has long been associated with the Arthurian world: Dubricius, the bishop who crowned Arthur according to Geoffrey of Monmouth, was said to have retired and been buried there; Ranulf Higden's *Polychronicon*, written around 1340, attests to Merlin retiring to Enlli at the end of his life; and Trevisa's translation of *Polychronicon* states that Merlin was buried there.[47] Today the island is rumoured to be the final resting place of Arthur, though this association seems to be a modern development – Lewis Morris was the first to connect Arthur directly with Enlli in the 1740s.[48] We do not have the same manuscript evidence to support an Enlli identification as we do for Aberconwy, but it is important to acknowledge that multiple places could often accrete in folklore traditions.[49] The Isle of Avalon in the *Vera historia* may represent an elision of several different narratives and places.

---

but because Barber and Pykitt may not have been the first people to imaginatively locate Avalon on Bardsey.

[43] Kathryn Hurlock, *Medieval Welsh Pilgrimage, c.1100–1500* (Manchester: Palgrave Macmillan, 2018), p. 28; p. 22.

[44] Gerald of Wales, *A Journey Through Wales*, ed. and trans. Lewis Thorpe (London: Penguin, 1978), pp. 183–84; Lapidge, 'Vera Historia: A New Edition', pp. 136–37; Liz Herbert McAvoy, 'Anchorites in Medieval Wales', in *Anchoritic Traditions of Medieval Europe*, ed. Liz Herbert McAvoy (Woodbridge: Boydell, 2010), pp. 195–216.

[45] 'in Auallonis insula [...] (tampquam uulnerum suorum mitigandi dolorem).' Lapidge, 'Vera Historia: A New Edition', pp. 136–37.

[46] Burton and Stöber, 'Bardsey (Enlli)', in *Abbeys and Priories of Medieval Wales*, pp. 43–45 (p. 43).

[47] Hurlock, *Medieval Welsh Pilgrimage*, p. 22; Ceridwen Lloyd-Morgan, 'Narratives and Non-Narratives: Aspects of Welsh Arthurian Tradition', *Arthurian Literature*, 21 (2004), 115–36 (p. 131); Roger Waldron, 'Trevisa's Translation of Higden's *Polychronicon*, 1.38, *De Wallia*: An Edition', in *Authority and Subjugation*, ed. Kennedy and Meecham-Jones, pp. 99–136 (p. 119, ll. 297–306).

[48] Lloyd, *The Arthurian Place Names of Wales*, pp. 112-13; Lloyd-Morgan, 'Narratives and Non-Narratives', passim.

[49] Lloyd-Morgan, 'Narratives and Non-Narratives: Aspects of Welsh Arthurian Tradition', pp. 135–37.

These are just a handful of the places that might have inspired the Venedotian setting of the *Vera historia*. The question remains, however, as to what extent this Gwynedd setting was considered a counter-claim to Arthur's burial at Glastonbury in the Middle Ages. This would evidently depend on how widely known the *Vera historia* narrative was. Christopher Berard has gone so far as to suggest that the Gwynedd counterclaim was known in 1278, and was a key motivation for the translation of Arthur's remains at Glastonbury.[50] While this is impossible to prove, the *Vera historia*'s manuscript tradition suggests that its readers were weighing up its Gwynedd location alongside Arthur's purported grave at Glastonbury. Based on the surviving manuscripts, the *Vera historia* had a modest though geographically widespread circulation. Its version of Arthur's end is not mentioned at all by late medieval and early modern historiographers, although it may have been better known at an earlier date.[51] However, the surviving manuscripts of the *Vera historia* suggest that its late medieval readers and copyists considered it a counter-claim to Glastonbury. The abbreviated version of the *Vera historia* contained in the Chronicle of Hailes Abbey (c. 1300), one of the earliest extant witnesses, tweaks the text to remove some of its more controversial elements, and to situate the Gwynedd and Glastonbury place claims side-by-side. Following a description of Arthur's reign taken from varying sources, including the usual accounts of Arthur's tomb at Glastonbury as recounted by Gerald of Wales and others, the Hailes adaptor inserts the abbreviated *Vera historia*. Notably, the text's equivocation of Venedocia and Avalon is removed – Arthur asks to be taken to Venedocia (Gwynedd), but the Isle of Avalon is not named.[52] The three archbishops of the text called upon by Arthur become simply 'the bishops of the whole island' (epicopos insule tocius), and any potentially identifying information concerning the minute size

---

[50] Berard, *Arthurianism*, p. 233.
[51] In the *Gesta Regum Britanniae*, a metrical version of Geoffrey's *Historia* composed c. 1236 and perhaps by William of Rennes, Arthur's final resting place is at the 'court of the king of Avallon' (ad aulam Regis Auallonis). That this Avalon has its own king suggests a better fit with Gwynedd than with Glastonbury. There are other similarities to the *Vera historia*: Arthur crosses over to the island to be healed by a skilled medic (a 'regal maiden' in this version [*Regia virgo*], who successfully heals Arthur and keeps him there with her to this day). Alternatively, because this poem is dedicated to Bishop Cadioc of Vannes in Brittany, it may instead evidence an 'Avallon' candidate in Brittany rather than in Gwynedd. This text dates to the mid-thirteenth century, however, so it is not clear whether or not it post-dates the *Vera historia*. See William of Rennes, *The Historia Regum Britannie of Geoffrey of Monmouth V: Gesta Regum Britanniae*, ed. and trans. Neil Wright (Cambridge: D. S. Brewer, 1991), pp. 249–50.
[52] Lapidge, 'Vera Historia: A New Edition', pp. 136–37.

of the chapel where Arthur is taken are excised.[53] The biggest alteration is the text's ending. A sentence is added that does not appear in the other *Vera historia* witnesses describing the discovery of Arthur's remains at Glastonbury during the reign of King Richard I, 'so it is said' (ut dictum est).[54] The text then closes with nine lines of encomiastic verse implying that Arthur, like Elijah and Enoch, had been carried up to heaven by Christ.[55] Together, this has the effect of tempering the text, presenting two versions of Arthur's end together within the same chronicle and allowing the reader to form their own conclusion about which is the correct version.

Another manuscript that forces its reader to confront the *Vera historia* alongside Arthur's Glastonbury burial is Cotton MS Titus A.XIX, discussed in the previous chapter. This is particularly significant, as this manuscript exhibits a clear connection to Glastonbury, perhaps indicating that the Gwynedd counterclaim was known in late medieval Glastonbury. The *Vera historia* appears in the manuscript's so-called Glastonbury quire (ff. 16–31; *Vera historia* at ff. 16r–17v), and in the same hand as the Glastonbury material it accompanies. All but one of the other texts in this quire are known to have been available at Glastonbury, and some perhaps *only* at Glastonbury.[56] Both Michael Lapidge and Jean Krochalis have concluded that the quire was probably copied at York, but from material that had come directly from Glastonbury, most likely the *magna tabula* itself; as I have already pointed out, Krochalis argues for no more than a single intermediary between the Glastonbury quire and the *magna tabula*.[57] Glastonbury and York may well have established a network for textual exchange: it is worth remembering that both institutions used Arthurian pseudo-history to shore up their prestige. Both were vying with Canterbury for recognition as preeminent Christian centres in terms of their wealth and antiquity, and the author of the *Vera historia* notably identifies St Davids and London as archbishoprics – not Canterbury.[58]

---

[53] Ibid.
[54] Lapidge, 'Vera Historia: A New Edition', p. 141 n. 18.
[55] Lapidge, 'Vera Historia: A New Edition', p. 141 n. 20.
[56] Krochalis and Stones, I, pp. 131–32. The one exception is the *Pseudo-Turpin* (ff. 24–39), which spans the divide between the Glastonbury quire and the following quire in the codex.
[57] Krochalis and Stones, *The Pilgrim's Guide*, I, p. 132; Lapidge, 'Vera Historia: A New Edition', p. 119.
[58] Lapidge, 'Vera Historia: A New Edition', pp. 125–26. York's dispute with Canterbury is made clear in *Super statu Eboracensis* (see the description and translation in Purvis, 'The Tables'). Glastonbury's spat with Canterbury regarding the ownership of St Dunstan's relics is attested as late as 1508, when Archbishop Wareham insisted that St Dunstan's Canterbury tomb be re-opened. Moreover,

Given their mutual reliance on Galfridian pseudo-history, Glastonbury and York may have found it beneficial to pool their sources. For our purposes, it is immaterial whether the *Vera historia* was held at Glastonbury, at York, or somewhere else. What is important is that this scribe decided that it *should* be included alongside Glastonbury texts. Richard Barber has suggested that the *Vera historia*'s inclusion in the Glastonbury quire implies an act of 'comparison and collation' by the scribe, an effort to critically evaluate and therefore consolidate competing claims to Arthur's resting place, much like the author of the *Hailes Chronicle*.[59]

Ultimately, it is difficult to prove that the author of the *Vera historia* really intended it to represent a counterclaim to Glastonbury centred on a specific place, or perhaps a fusion of different narratives and places. However, the presence of the text directly alongside Glastonbury material in both Cotton Titus A.XIX and in the *Hailes Chronicle* suggests that it was being interpreted as a counterclaim by this point. If this is the case, it makes sense that the Glastonbury monks and vicars choral at York would be expected to know about it in order to answer any difficult questions from visitors. This may explain the *Vera historia*'s inclusion in Titus A.XIX.

Where was Arthur crowned? Competing urban places

Thanks in part to Arthur's influential refiguring during the nineteenth century, Arthur is often associated today with wild forests and craggy rocks, rough seas and isolated hermitages.[60] However, in order to try and see Arthur's geography through fifteenth-century eyes we need to imagine Arthur as a civic figure as well as a rural one. If Arthur's end on the Isle of Avalon and his conception at Tintagel were imagined as remote, the sites of his coronation and court are quite the opposite: urban centres of sparkling prestige. In the fifteenth century, various places were identified as the sites of Arthur's coronation: Silchester, Cirencester, Caerleon, Winchester, Gloucester, and Paris. Some of these identifications

---

the claim that Joseph of Arimathea founded one of the earliest churches in Europe at Glastonbury – predating Canterbury's claims to primacy – were put forward in debate by Polton at the Council of Constance in 1417; see Jean-Philippe Genet, 'English Nationalism: Thomas Polton at the Council of Constance', *Nottingham Medieval Studies*, 28 (1984), 60–78.

[59] Barber, 'Was Mordred Buried at Glastonbury?: Arthurian Tradition at Glastonbury in the Middle Ages', in *Glastonbury Abbey and the Arthurian Tradition*, pp. 145–59 (p. 146).

[60] The Victorian vision of Arthur that associates the King with remote and wild landscapes is explored in Joan Passey, *Cornish Gothic, 1830–1913* (Cardiff: University of Wales Press, 2023), pp. 130–162.

are more widely rehearsed than others – Caerleon and Silchester for example, which have their basis in Geoffrey of Monmouth's *Historia*.[61] There are various explanations for both the origins of these claims and the reasons scribes might have had for copying them: they might represent a misreading, either wilful or unintentional, of a truncated version of Geoffrey's *Historia regum Britanniae* or its derivatives. Alternatively, some of the proposed sites of Arthur's coronation may be the result of the misidentification or mistranslation of Latin place names. On the other hand, changes in the meaning and praxis of the coronation rite may also have contributed to the vast number of claims to Arthur's coronation site: festal crown wearings raised the possibility of multiple crownings, just as Arthur was said to have held his court in many places in the fifteenth century. As for the motives behind a claim to an Arthurian coronation site, episcopal and civic competition evidently had a part to play.

I: Silchester/Cirencester

In Geoffrey of Monmouth's *Historia regum Britanniae*, there seem to be at least two moments where Arthur is crowned: at Silchester (*Silcestrie*) immediately following the death of Uther Pendragon, and later at a ceremony in Caerleon (*Urbs Legionum*) described in elaborate detail.[62] It was not unusual for a king to be re-crowned in the Middle Ages at a time of urgency.[63] A temporary crowning could be performed relatively quickly after the death of a king to invest the successor with some powers prior to their official coronation at a later date, a private ritual prior to the public ceremony. Both King John and Henry the Young King were crowned twice: once alone, and later along with their queens.[64] Likewise, late fifteenth-century readers might have been familiar with Henry Tudor's stop-gap crowning on the battlefield at Bosworth followed by the official ceremony at St Paul's in London just over a week later.

A further possibility is that, in Geoffrey's *Historia*, the incident at Silchester is a coronation, whilst the subsequent ceremony at Caerleon

---

[61] Geoffrey of Monmouth, *The History of the Kings of Britain*, 9.143 pp. 192–93 (Silchester); 9.156-57 pp. 207–12 (Caerleon).

[62] On the Arthur's two crownings, see Tatlock, *The Legendary History*, pp. 49–50 (Silchester); pp. 271–74 (Caerleon).

[63] Aside from the death of a monarch, political discord could be a factor in a second coronation, as in the cases of King Stephen and Richard I; see Robert Bartlett, *England Under the Norman and Angevin Kings: 1075–1225* (Oxford: Oxford University Press, 2013), pp. 123–29.

[64] John Gillingham, 'Historians Without Hindsight: Coggeshall, Diceto and Howden on the Early Years of John's Reign', in *King John: New Interpretations*, ed. S. D. Church (Woodbridge: Boydell, 1999), pp. 1–26 (p. 13).

is a festal crown-wearing.[65] Crown-wearings, which took place on the three major feast days between c. 1066 and the early thirteenth century, were distinct from second coronations because they were intended to reinforce the king's power, rather than representing the investment of any new powers.[66] There is evidence in Geoffrey's text to support this possibility: Silchester is the site of an earlier coronation – Constantinus is also crowned there.[67] Archbishop Dubricius is called urgently to Silchester to oversee the crowning, which suggests a formal coronation.[68] In contrast, the highly public nature of the Caerleon ceremony and the fact that it falls on Pentecost – one of three major feast days – suggest a festal crown-wearing.[69]

The triannual festal crown-wearing format popularised by post-conquest kings is largely accepted to have stopped from the mid-thirteenth century.[70] Even if Geoffrey and his inheritor Wace understood festal crown-wearings as distinct from a coronation, it is quite possible that their later fifteenth-century readers may not have grasped this distinction. If this is the case, then the composers of the condensed versions of the *Historia* or the *Brut* such as those found on *tabulae*, for brevity or ease of understanding, might have only thought to include one of these crownings. Alternatively, fifteenth-century readers may have interpreted Arthur's several crownings as symbols of the acquisition of new imperial territories. Some contemporary scholars view Arthur's many crownings in this light, arguing that the ceremony at Caerleon represents a second coronation as newly conquered lands are added to his

---

[65] Tatlock, *The Legendary History*, pp. 271–72; Fletcher, *Arthurian Materials in the Chronicles*, pp. 110–11; John Gillingham, *The English in the Twelfth Century: Imperialism, National Identity, and Political Values* (Woodbridge: Boydell, 2000), pp. 35–36. For a full explanation of festal crown-wearing ceremonies, including the dates when this practice stopped and the symbolic distinction between a crown-wearing and a coronation, see Charlotte A. T. Wulf, 'The Coronation of Arthur and Guenevere in Geoffrey of Monmouth's *Historia Regum Britanniae*, Wace's *Roman de Brut*, and Lawman's *Brut*', in *Reading Laȝamon's Brut: Approaches and Explorations*, ed. Rosamund Allen, Jane Roberts, and Carole Weinberg (New York: Rodopi, 2013), pp. 229–51.

[66] David Carpenter, *The Reign of Henry III* (London: Hambledon, 1996), p. 444; Percy Ernst Schramm, *The History of the English Coronation*, trans. L. G. Wickham Legg (Oxford: Clarendon Press, 1937), p. 32; Wulf, 'The Coronation', p. 230.

[67] Geoffrey of Monmouth, *The History of the Kings of Britain*, 6.95, pp. 118–19.

[68] The act of episcopal anointing was the most important part of the coronation ceremony, representing the investment of divine power not afforded to other lords and nobles; see Christopher Daniell, *From Norman Conquest to Magna Carta: England 1066–1215* (London: Routledge, 2003), p. 78.

[69] Wulf, 'The Coronation', p. 233.

[70] According to Roger of Hoveden, Henry II put an end to repeat crown-wearings in 1158, when he vowed that neither he nor his queen should again wear the crown. See Wulf, 'The Coronation', p. 232; Carpenter, *The Reign of Henry III*, pp. 446–47.

kingdom.⁷¹ Whether or not this is what Geoffrey intended in the *Historia*, this reading may well have held more currency in the fifteenth century in light of England's wars with France. Arthurian chroniclers from the later Middle Ages who sought to emphasise Arthur's imperial conquests appear to paint Arthur's coronations in this light. For example, in John Hardyng's *Chronicle* Arthur is crowned three times: firstly in 'Circestre' (in the earlier 1457 Lancastrian version; in the shorter 1460 Yorkist version this is expanded to 'Cyrcestre than called Caercyry | And Caersegent'); with Guenevere in Paris; and at Caerleon a full nine years later.⁷² The imperial function of the Paris crowning is made explicit:

> Quene Gaynore with hiegh nobilité
> Corounde also was in that same cyté
> At that same tyme with alle servyce rialle
> That couthe be done tille estate **imperialle**.⁷³

Hardyng's multiple Arthurian coronations may have been a nod to Henry VI, described by John Rous as having been crowned twice: as king of England and later of France. These crownings took place in Winchester and Paris respectively.⁷⁴

In Geoffrey's text Arthur's first crowning takes place at Silchester immediately following the death of Uther Pendragon.⁷⁵ This section of the text is ambiguous, not least because Geoffrey expands and contracts time so dramatically (particularly during Arthur's reign); it is easy to see how the passage might be read as either a briefly described coronation taking place at Silchester, or a leap forward in time alluding to the later ceremony at Caerleon. The relevant section is reproduced below, in its

---

⁷¹ Michael Wenthe, 'Beyond British Boundaries in the Historia Regum Britanniae', in *Cultural Diversity in the British Middle Ages: Archipelago, Island, England*, ed. Jeffrey Jerome Cohen (New York: Palgrave Macmillan, 2008), pp. 95–116 (pp. 101–02).

⁷² John Hardyng, *John Hardyng's Chronicle: Edited from London British Library MS Lansdowne 204*, ed. Sarah Peverley and James Simpson, TEAMS (Kalamazoo, MI: Medieval Institute Publications, 2015), 3.2253-61 ("Cyrcestre"); 3.2688-2690 (Paris); 3.2718-2904 (Caerleon); Hardyng, *The Chronicle of John Hardyng, Together with the Continuation by Richard Grafton*, p. 121.

⁷³ Hardyng, *Chronicle*, ed. Simpson and Peverley, 3.2688-2694 (emphasis mine).

⁷⁴ John Rous describes the events in the Rous Roll in his entry for his patron Richard Beauchamp Earl of Warwick; see John Rous, *The Rous Roll*, no. 50. Rous states that 'thys lord [Richard Beauchamp] was maister to kyng here the syxt in hys tender age and with the helpe of the land crownyd hym twies at Westmystre as for kyng of England and at paris for kyng of fraunce'. This might explain why, in the *Historia regum Angliae*, Rous seems to focus more closely on the life and acts of St Dubricius (who crowned Arthur), rather than Arthur himself – particularly as Rous places Dubricius' first see at Warwick (an alteration that is apparently unique to Rous). Rous, *Historia regum Angliae*, p. 55.

⁷⁵ Geoffrey of Monmouth, *The History of the Kings of Britain*, 9.143, pp. 192–93.

entirety with no omissions, to show how it might be misunderstood if encountered in isolation (such as, for example, on a *tabula*):

> On Uther Pendragon's death, British nobles from various regions assembled in Silchester and urged Dubricius archbishop of Caerleon to crown Uther's son Arthur as his successor. They were motivated by necessity because the Saxons, when they learned of Uther's death, had invited in their countrymen from Germany and, led by Colgrinus, were aiming to expel the Britons. They had already occupied all the island from the Humber to the sea at Caithness. Moved by his country's plight, Dubricius and his bishops placed the crown of the kingdom of Arthur's head. He was a youth of fifteen, of great promise and generosity, whose innate goodness ensured that he was loved by almost everybody. As newly-crowned king, he displayed his customary open-handedness [...]
>
> (Defuncto igitur Vther Pendragon, conuenerunt ex diuersis prouinciis proceres Britonum in ciuitatem Silcestriae, Dubricio Vrbis Legionum archiepiscopo suggerentes ut Arturum filium eius in regem consecraret. Vrgebat enim eos necessitas, quia audito praedicti regis obitu Saxones conciues suos ex Germania inuitauerant et duce Colgrimo ipsos exterminare nitebantur. Subiugauerant etiam sibi totam partem insulae quae a flumine Humbri usque ad Katanesium mare extenditur. Dubricius ergo, calamitatem patriae dolens, associatis sibi episcopis Arturum regni diademate insigniuit. Erat autem Arturus quindecim annorum iuuenis inauditae uirtutis atque largitatis, in quo tantam gratiam innata bonitas praestiterat ut a cunctis fere largitati indulsit.)

(*History of the Kings of Britain*, 9.143, pp. 192–93)

Here, Arthur's crowning takes place in 'Silcestriae', where Constantinus had been crowned earlier in the text; but in one recension of Geoffrey's *Historia* Constantinus' coronation happens at 'Cirecestriam' rather than 'Silcestriam'.[76] Was this a conscious alteration? When medieval scribes did wittingly change the text during copying this was often intended as an act of correction (though of course there are many other possible reasons why a scribe might make such changes to their source).[77] These acts of correction are commonly seen when scribes copy proper names and place names that are unfamiliar or archaic within the scribes' own temporal and geographical context.[78] With this in mind, it seems possible

---

[76] Geoffrey of Monmouth, *The History of the Kings of Britain*, p. xiv.
[77] Daniel Wakelin, *Scribal Correction and Literary Craft: English Manuscripts 1375–1510* (Cambridge: Cambridge University Press, 2014), p. 58.
[78] Daniel Wakelin, 'Not Diane: The Risk of Error in Chaucerian Classicism', *Exemplaria*, 29.4 (2017), 331–48. See also Paul Broyles, '*Errare* in Romance', New

that Arthur's coronation at 'Cirecestrie' may have been corrected to make it correspond with Constantinus' own crowning at 'Silcestrie' (or vice versa), perhaps because either one of these toponyms was unfamiliar or obsolete to a particular scribe.

In other words, there may have been copies of Geoffrey's text – now either lost or unknown – which were corrected to place both Arthur *and* Constantinus' coronations at 'Cirecestrie', copies used by the authors of the *Brut* and other *Historia* derivatives that locate Arthur's crowning at some version of Cirencester. Evidently, Cirencester would have been better known to most fifteenth-century readers than Silchester. Tatlock has even suggested Geoffrey may have selected Silchester to purposely archaicise his ancient British geography: though it would have been a 'conspicuous place' in the fifth and sixth centuries it was certainly not so in Geoffrey's day.[79] It is true that Silchester's Roman ruins remained impressive and highly visible during the Middle Ages – a church was built during the twelfth century using Roman rubble, and a hall was erected in the centre of the ruined amphitheatre at around the same time. As late as the eighteenth century, William Stukeley reports having seen an amphitheatre at Silchester.[80] However, the small village settlement was completely abandoned before 1400.[81] Silchester certainly would not have been as familiar to a fifteenth-century readership as Cirencester, which was a bustling centre for the wool trade.[82] Located in Hampshire, Silchester is perhaps even less likely to be familiar to a Welsh reader than an English one as compared to the much closer Cirencester in Gloucestershire, and accordingly, Silchester is widely rejected in Welsh translations of Geoffrey's text (*Brut y Brenhinedd*). Instead, where a

---

Chaucer Society Conference (London, 13 July 2016). Wakelin gives a particular example that is pertinent here: in one cognate copy of *The Canterbury Tales* (that is, a witness known to be a direct copy of another surviving witness), a scribe has partly erased the obsolete place name 'Caunterbrigge' (i.e. Canterbury) to replace it with 'Cambrigge'. Wakelin, *Scribal Correction*, p. 68.

[79] Tatlock, *The Legendary History*, p. 49.
[80] William Stukeley, *Itinerarium Curiosum* [...] (London, 1724), p. 156.
[81] George C. Boon, *St Mary the Virgin, Silchester* (Basingstoke: Ridgeway Press, 1989); Michael Fulford, 'Calleva Atrebatum (Silchester, Hampshire, UK): An Early Medieval Extinction', in *Vrbes Extinctae: Archaeologies of Abandoned Classical Towns*, ed. Neil Christie and Andrea Augenti (Farnham: Ashgate, 2012), pp. 331–51. Silchester's medieval archaeology has been investigated in the University of Reading's 'Town Life' project; see Michael Fulford and Amanda Clarke, *Silchester Insula IX: Interim Reports 1–6* (Reading: The University of Reading, 1997–2004).
[82] David Rollison, 'A Turning Point: The Generation of 1400', in *Commune, Country and Commonwealth: The People of Cirencester, 1117–1643* (Cambridge: Cambridge University Press, 2011), pp. 60–63.

location is named at all, St Dyfrig crowns Arthur at *Kaer Vudei* (or *Budei*) in several witnesses.[83] Some scholars have suggested that this represents the Welsh name for Cirencester, with *buddei* meaning 'churn' – the name of the river which runs through the town.[84]

Although no known copies of Geoffrey's *Historia* place Arthur's coronation at 'Cirecestrie', several texts that use the *Historia* as their main source, and their derivatives in turn, state that Arthur was crowned there. Alfred of Beverley's chronicle (c. 1148–54) places Arthur's coronation at 'Cirecestriae', which likely stems from a variant of Geoffrey's *Historia* that Alfred was using.[85] Whilst most copies of Wace's *Brut* state that Arthur was crowned at 'Cilcestre', some witnesses replace this with 'Cirecestre', 'Circestre', or 'Cirencestre'.[86] The two extant manuscripts of Laȝamon's *Brut* also differ: one locates Arthur's coronation at 'Selechaestre', the other 'Cirecestres'.[87] In Robert Mannyng of Brunne's *Chronicle* (c. 1327–38), whose pre-Cadwallader material is essentially a translation of Wace's *Brut*, Arthur's coronation occurs at 'Cecestre burgh' and 'Cicestre [the noble burgh]'.[88] Later Latin continuations of Wace's *Brut* (known as the Latin Prose *Brut* chronicles) vary on the point of Arthur's coronation. The *Brut* continuations were the standard historiographical work(s) in England

---

[83] 'Kaer Vudei' appears in the story of Arthur in the Red Book of Hergest; it also appears in the following *Brut y Brenhinedd* witnesses: London, British Library, Cotton MS Cleopatra B.VI, f. 77v; Cardiff, Cardiff Central Library, Cardiff MS. 1.362 (Hafod 1), f. 75r; Oxford, Jesus College MS 111 (The Red Book of Hergest), f. 39v; NLW MS 3035 (Mostyn 116), f. 103v; British Library Add. MS 19709, f. 66r.

[84] Richard Coates, 'Rethinking Romano-British *Corinium*', *The Antiquaries Journal*, 93 (2013), 81–91 (p. 85); E. Ekwall, '24. Cirencester, Gloucestershire', in *Etymological Notes of English Place-Names*, ed. E. Ekwall (Lund: C. W. K. Gleerup, 1937), pp. 37–38; G. H. Jones, *Celtic Britain and the Pilgrim Movement* (London: The Honourable Society of Cymmrodorion, 1912), p. 280.

[85] Alfred of Beverley, *Aluredi Beverlacensis Annales, sive Historia de Gestis Regum Britanniae Libris IX*, ed. Thomas Hearne (Oxford: Sheldonian Theatre, 1716), p. 58; John Patrick Slevin, 'The Historical Writing of Alfred of Beverley' (unpublished doctoral thesis, University of Exeter, 2013), p. 126.

[86] 'Cirecestre' (British Library MS Add. 32151; Cambridge Corpus Christi College MS 50), 'Circestre' (Paris, Bibliothèque Nationale fonds fr. 1450), 'Cirencestre' (Paris, Bibliothèque Nationale nouv. Acq. Fr. 1415). See Wace, *Wace's Roman de Brut: A History of the British*, p. 226, l. 9012 (n).

[87] British Library Cotton MS Caligula A.IX, f. 116v (Selechaestre); British Library Cotton MS Otho C.XIII, edited in *Layamon's Brut*, ed. G. L. Brook and R. F. Leslie, Early English Text Society, Original Series 250, 277, 2 vols (London: Early English Text Society, 1963, 1978), II, p. 519, l. 9176 (=9177) ('Cirecestres').

[88] Robert Mannyng, *The Chronicle*, ed. Idelle Sullens (Binghamton, NY: Binghamton University, 1996), pp. 320–21, ll. 9605; 9610.

during the fifteenth and sixteenth centuries.[89] The extent of the variation among the nineteen extant witnesses of the Latin *Brut* suggests that these represent only a tiny percentage of what once existed.[90] Many omit any reference to the coronation site altogether, stating simply that Arthur was crowned by St Dubricius, archbishop of the City of Legions.[91] A further Latin *Brut* manuscript – MS Longleat 55 – states that Arthur was crowned in 'Cirrecestra'.[92] The fifteenth-century chroniclers John Hardyng and John Rous follow Geoffrey of Monmouth in stating that Silchester was its own bishopric in Arthur's day under the jurisdiction of St Maugano: John Rous claimed that 'Silchester beside Reading' (Silchestriae juxta Radingum) was itself an episcopal seat of St Mauganus (Maugannius in Geoffrey's *Historia*) in the time of Arthur.[93] Hardyng claims that St Dubricius awarded 'Mauganero, the sea pontificall | Of Chichester', which could suggest either that Hardyng's source had 'Chichester' as a variant or that Hardyng had misinterpreted the place name, perhaps from a Latin original.[94] Whilst there are no sources suggesting that St Maugano crowned Arthur, one Latin *Brut* witness erases the identity of the bishop overseeing the coronation as well as its location, perhaps a product of ecclesiastic competition.[95] What this tangle suggests is that,

---

[89] Alan Maccoll, 'The Meaning of "Britain" in Medieval and Early Modern England', *Journal of British Studies*, 45.2 (2006), 248–69 (p. 254).

[90] Scribal variation between cognates for *Brut* manuscripts is generally no more than 3 or 4 per cent; see Wakelin, *Scribal Correction*, p. 58. The most recent Prose Latin *Brut* discoveries include MS Longleat 55, identified by Erik Kooper in 2016; and Downside 78291, which I identified in 2019. Erik Kooper, 'Longleat House MS 55: An Unacknowledged Brut Manuscript?', in *The Prose Brut and Other Late Medieval Chronicles*, ed. Jaclyn Rajsic and Erik Kooper (York: York Medieval Press, 2016), pp. 75–93. Mary Bateman, 'A Newly-Discovered Latin Prose *Brut* Manuscript at Downside Abbey', *The Downside Review*, 137.4 (2019), 166–81. I am grateful to Dr Erik Kooper for kindly sharing his transcription with me.

[91] Downside 78291, f. 20v; Cambridge, Corpus Christi College MS 311, f. 26v; Oxford Bodleian Library MS Rawlinson B.169, f. 21v; Cambridge, Gonville and Caius College MS 72/39, f. 16r.

[92] Longleat MS 55, f. 41v.

[93] Cited in Leland, *Itineraries*, II, pp. 167–68. St Mauganus was said to have lived at the time of Arthur in the fifth or sixth century, and is mentioned in the *Vitae* of St Cadog and St David. The passage in Geoffrey's *Historia* reads: 'Maugannius became bishop of Silchester and Duvianus of Winchester' (Episcopatus quoque Silcestriae Maugannio et Guintoniae Duuiano decernitur). *History of the Kings of Britain*, 9.158, pp. 214–15.

[94] John Hardyng, *Chronicle*, ed. Ellis, p. 131.

[95] British Library MS Lansdowne 212, f. 50r. On quarrels between bishops regarding the right to inaugurate a king, see Johanna Dale, *Inauguration and Liturgical Kingship in the Long Twelfth Century* (York: York Medieval Press, 2019), pp. 105–29; R. M. Haines, 'Canterbury versus York: Fluctuating Fortunes in a Perennial Conflict',

originally, there must have been more copies of Geoffrey's *Historia* (or close derivatives) which placed Arthur's coronation at 'Cirencester' or 'Cirecestre' or something similar, rather than Silchester.

The town of Cirencester itself also appears to have had a localised Arthurian tradition, perhaps informed by the Arthurian texts discussed above. It is possible that this tradition was a long one: in his twelfth-century *Lai du cor*, Robert Biket claims that the drinking horn central to the lai's plot was on display at Cirencester at his time of writing.[96] By the fifteenth century, Cirencester was advertising its Arthurian credentials to visitors. We know this thanks to William Worcester, an itinerant traveller who took extensive notes during his travels around England. It is often possible to work out roughly where Worcester might have written a particular entry. During a stay in Cirencester, perhaps as a guest of the abbey, Worcester took down details about Arthurian Cirencester that are not found in any known witnesses of Geoffrey's *Historia* or its derivatives, and perhaps represent localised pseudo-history known only in the vicinity of Cirencester itself.[97] Beneath a heading reading 'Cirencester town in the county of Gloucestershire' (Siscetyr villa in comitatu Gloucestrie), Worcester notes that '*Grosmond* tower by the Chapel of St Cecilia, where Arthur was crowned, lies west of Cirencester town, which anciently was called the City of Sparrows' (Turris Grosmond iuxta capellam Sancte Cesilie vbi Rex Arthurus fuit coronatus iacet in occidentali parte ville Cirencestrie que ab antiquo vocatur Ciuitas Passerum).[98] Earlier in the notebook, Worcester also notes a 'memorandum of one Potsawe of Cirencester':

---

in *Ecclesia Anglicana: Studies in the English Church of the Later Middle Ages*, ed. R. M. Haines (Toronto: University of Toronto Press, 1989), pp. 69–105.

[96] See 'Cirenchester', in Christopher W. Bruce, *The Arthurian Name Dictionary* (New York: Garland, 1999), p. 119.

[97] Timothy Darvill, 'Grismond's Tower, Cirencester, and the Rise of Springhead Super-Mounds in the Cotswolds and Beyond', *Transactions of the Bristol and Gloucestershire Archaeological Society*, 132 (2014), 11–27 (p. 13); Irvine Gray, *Antiquaries of Gloucestershire and Bristol* (Gloucester: Alan Sutton, 1981), p. 31.

[98] Worcester, *Itineraries*, pp. 272–73. I have followed Harvey's translation except for the translation of 'grosmond' as the personal name 'Grismond'. Several scholars have argued persuasively that *grosmond* is probably a corrupted form of *grosmont*, a Norman term for a 'great hill' or 'great mound'. See K. J. Beecham, *History of Cirencester and the Roman City of Corinium*, ed. David Verey, 2nd edn (Dursley: A. Sutton, 1978 [1886]), p. 5; Welbore St Clair Baddeley, *A History of Cirencester* (Cirencester: Cirencester Newspaper co., 1924), pp. 4–7; and A. H. Smith, *The Place-Names of Gloucestershire*, 4 vols (Cambridge: Cambridge University Press, 1964–65), I (1964) p. 66; IV (1965) p. 45.

Torre Castle on the east side of Cirencester Abbey. Castle *Grosmond* is another, where King Arthur was crowned, near the Chapel of St Cecilia's the Virgin, on the opposite, west, side of the town of Cirencester. Cirencester was called the city of sparrows because a certain Africanus, who came from Africa, destroyed the city after a siege by sending birds flying over the city with wildfire tied to their tails.

(Memorandum de quodam Potsawe de Cirencestre: Castrum Torre in orientali parte de abbathia Cirencestrie. Castrum Grosmond est aliud vbi Arthurus Rex coronabatur prope capellam Sancte Cecilie virginis in altera parte occidentali ville Ciren/Cirencestre. Cirencestria vocabatur Ciuitas passerum eo quod per quondam Affricanum venientem de Aufrica destruxit per obcidionem ciuitatem per passceres cum wyldfyre ad eorum caudas ligatas volando ad ciuitatem.)[99]

This is the earliest reference to Castle Grosmond or Grosmond Tower, which in Worcester's day was a prominent landscape feature; John Leland, who visited some fifty years after Worcester, described it as 'a steepe rownd biry like a windmyl hill extramuros' where bones, graves, and artefacts had been discovered.[100] Worcester's account of Grosmond Tower's history may have onomastic explanations: perhaps the tower's name brought to mind the figure of Gormundus, the so-called 'African' from Ireland who wages fiery war on Cirencester in Geoffrey of Monmouth's *Historia*, which would explain the account given in the passage above.[101] Worcester appears to have been told this story orally during his visit to the abbey, perhaps by Potsawe himself, who may have been an abbey guide. This material can be localised to the abbey site itself: Worcester's notes are corroborated by the notes of another visitor, the aforementioned John Leland. In Worcester's *Itineraries* the *Grosmond* comment follows a detailed description of Cirencester Abbey's dimensions on the same folio, and a brief excerpt that resembles an entry from an annal (possibly from a *tabula* or a guide) about Henry I's coronation in 1100.[102] John Leland recorded the same details about Henry I's crowning when he visited, which suggests that both men encountered this material, either written or in oral form, at the abbey. Worcester follows his note on Castle Grosmond with a description of

---

[99] Corpus Christi College MS 210, p. 206; Worcester, *Itineraries*, pp. 284–85.
[100] Leland, *Itineraries*, III, pp. 101–02; cited in Darvill, 'Grismond's Tower', p. 14.
[101] Geoffrey of Monmouth, *History of the Kings of Britain*, 11.184–86, pp. 256–57.
[102] The dimensions which Worcester describes closely echo the information recorded on his visit to Glastonbury (the dimensions of the church and chapels, and details about the window glazing). *Itineraries*, ed. Harvey, pp. 284–85.

the tomb of 'Lord St Amand' (Dominus Seynt Amond) who was buried in the abbey, and a comment about Alexander Neckham, connected with Cirencester but not buried there.[103] John Leland recorded exactly the same sequence of information in his later *Itineraries*: a translation of the Henry I annal entry ('Henry the first made this college an abbay of chanon regulares [...] and buried in the body of the chirch, as it apperith by the epitaph on his tumbe'); a brief description of the antiquity of the abbey's different parts; the tombs of '2. Noble men of S. Amandes' in the presbyterie; some extra information on tombs and suchlike in the abbey not included by Worcester; then the description of Alexander Neckham's burial at Winchester and his association with Cirencester.[104] Although the manuscript of Worcester's *Itineraries* was re-bound in the early modern period, the extracts from Cirencester Abbey appear on the same folio – there is no question that they followed each other. Because Leland recorded almost all this material in his own words and in the same order as Worcester when he visited, we can be fairly certain that Worcester's notes were also taken down *in situ* during his visit. That the Arthurian tales related by this Potsawe are sandwiched in the middle of this information in Worcester's *Itinerary* suggests that Worcester was told about Arthur's coronation at Castle Grosmond in person during his tour of Cirencester Abbey (though Worcester seems to have already known the story, as he mentions Arthur's coronation at Cirencester earlier in his notebook). It is worth noting, however, that Worcester also records the tradition of Arthur's Pentecostal crowning at the City of Legions elsewhere in his *Itineraries*, and does not appear to be concerned about these duplicate claims.[105]

In sum, it is easy to see how 'Cirecestre' might easily be a mistranslation or attempted correction of the unfamiliar 'Silchester' in Geoffrey's *Historia*. In surveys of Latin place names, 'Cirecestria' or 'Cicestria' are glossed as Chester, Cirencester, 'Urbs Legionum', Chichester, and (appropriately) 'Corinium' – which, in turn, is glossed as Wantage (Berkshire), Cirencester, and Gloucester.[106] There are other

[103] We know that Lord St Amand's tomb was at Cirencester Abbey (even though Worcester does not say this explicitly) because Leland tells us this. See John Leland, *Itineraries*, I, p. 129.
[104] Leland, *Itineraries*, I, pp. 128–30.
[105] Worcester, *Itineraries*, ed. Harvey, pp. 212–13.
[106] Charles Trice Martin, *The Record Interpreter: A Collection of Abbreviations, Latin Words and Named Used in English Historical Manuscripts and Records*, ed. David Iredale, 3rd edn (Plymouth: Phillimore, 1982 [1892]), p. 363; J. G. Graesse, *Orbis Latinus: Lexikon lateinischer geographischer Namen des Mittelalters und der Neuzeit*, ed. Helmut Plechl and Sophie-Charlotte Plechl, 3 vols (Brunswick: Klinkhardt und Biermann, 1972), I, p. 520, p. 521, p. 572. It should be noted, however, that a review of Graesse's *Orbis*

outliers, too. The Burgundian chronicler Jean de Wavrin, who visited England, describes Arthur's coronation in a passage that closely echoes the *Brut* chronicles, although in this version Arthur is crowned 'en la cite de Clocestre' (in the city of Gloucester).[107] Thomas Gray, in the *Scalacronica* (c. 1363) has Arthur crowned twice: initially at *Carlioun* (Caerleon); and later in a more formal ceremony at *Winchestre* (Winchester).[108] Both Gray and Jean were noble laymen and knights writing in French. They may therefore have used different vernacular sources to the other chroniclers mentioned above, which could explain this disparity. Moreover, Winchester and Gloucester were two of the three major abbeys at which post-conquest kings would have traditionally held their festal crown-wearings, and this may have influenced Wavrin and Gray; Henry III was crowned at Gloucester, and Richard I was crowned at Winchester for a second time in 1194.[109] Winchester is also a coronation site in Geoffrey's *Historia* for Uther, Arthur's father.[110] Finally, there is a more prosaic explanation: 'Clocestre' seems like a reasonable scribal correction for the unfamiliar 'Cilcestre' (particularly if abbreviated), especially if kings were known to have been crowned there.

II: The City of Legions: Caerleon/Chester/Warwick

For the towns and cities of the later Middle Ages, the possibility of claiming rights to Arthur's coronation site conferred both episcopal and civic pre-eminence. Rivalries between the bishoprics and archbishoprics in the period are well documented.[111] Civic competition even occurred

---

Latinus found complaint that some identifications, including Wantage/Corinium, were 'positively wrong': see H. W. C. D., 'Short Notices', *English Historical Review*, 25.100 (1910), 804–34 (p. 804). An alternative to 'Corinium' is 'Cironium', which is given in the Ravenna Cosmography; see Richard Coates, 'Rethinking Romano-British *Corinium*'.

[107] Jean de Wavrin, *Recueil des chroniques et anchiennes istories de la Grant Bretaigne, à present nommé Engleterre*, ed. William Hardy, 2nd edn, 3 vols (Cambridge: Cambridge University Press, 2012 [1864]), I, 3.12 (p. 353). On Wavrin's visits to England, see Livia Visser-Fuchs, *History as Pastime: Jean de Wavrin and His Collection of Chronicles of England* (Donington: Shaun Tyas, 2018).

[108] Leland was interested in Gray's Winchester identification, and copied it from *Scalacronica* when he consulted it, later working it into his defence of Arthur, *Assertio inclytissimi Arturii*. See John Leland in Thomas Gray, *Scalacronica*, p. 260; Leland, *Assertio*, sig. B2v.

[109] Henry Gerald Richardson, 'The Coronation in Medieval England: The Evolution of the Office and the Oath', *Traditio*, 16 (1960), 111–202 (p. 127).

[110] Geoffrey of Monmouth, *History of the Kings of Britain*, 8.134–135, pp. 179–81.

[111] For an overview, see C. Wordsworth, *The Precedence of English Bishops and the Provincial Chapter* (Cambridge: Cambridge University Press, 1906). On the issue of the St David's archbishopric claim and Gerald of Wales' own ambitions

within dioceses where multiple settlements presented different options for the location of a see. When Bishop Thomas Bekynton was deciding on the best location for his episcopal seat in the fifteenth century he was presented with a 'Little book' (libellus) by Thomas Chaundler weighing up the pros and cons of the cities of Bath and Wells respectively.[112] In the twelfth century, a bishop would have to place the crown on the king's head whenever he wore it in public, so coronations could also fire up these rivalries.[113] Henry the Young King's coronation was postponed on account of a dispute between York and Canterbury regarding which archbishopric held the right to officiate.[114] There was also civic bickering over the right to host coronation ceremonies: H. G. Richardson reports the dispute between Winchester and London over which should act as the official site of royal coronations.[115] Thus, there were underlying motives for competing claims to the site of Arthur's crowning: any space left by ambiguous or omitted toponyms allowed those who abridged or translated the *Historia* to adapt the text to suit their own allegiances.

This is particularly true of Urbs legionum (the City of Legions). As well as the location of Arthur's second crowning, it is also the site of Arthur's court in Geoffrey's *Historia*, and constitutes one of the Arthurian

---

regarding it, see Christopher Brooke, 'The Archbishops of St David's, Llandaff and Caerleon-on-Usk', in *Studies in the Early British Church*, ed. Nora K. Chadwick and others (Cambridge: Cambridge University Press, 1958), pp. 201–42; Putter, 'Latin Historiography', pp. 85–91; Huw Pryce, 'Gerald of Wales and the Welsh Past', in *Gerald of Wales: New Perspectives on a Medieval Writer and Critic*, ed. Georgia Henley and A. Joseph McMullen (Cardiff: University of Wales Press, 2018), pp. 19–45; Robert Rouse, 'Reading Ruins: Arthurian Caerleon and the Untimely Architecture of History', *Arthuriana*, 23.1 (2013), 40–51 (p. 49). On the London versus Canterbury rivalry, see D. P. Johnson, 'Bishops and Deans: London and the Province of Canterbury in the Twelfth Century', *Historical Research*, 86.234 (2013), 551–78; and on York versus Canterbury see Haines, 'Canterbury versus York'.

[112] Thomas Chaundler's *Libellus de laudibus duarum civitatum* (Little book on the merits of two cities) presents, for the benefit of Bishop Thomas Bekynton of Bath and Wells, a satirical debate weighing up the pros and cons of Wells and Bath, in order to assist Bekynton in deciding which city would be the best location for his see. See David Rundle, 'Humanist Eloquence among the Barbarians in Fifteenth-Century England', in *Britannia Latina: Latin in the Culture of Great Britain from the Middle Ages to the Twentieth Century*, ed. Charles Burnett and Nicholas Mann (London: Warburg Institute, 2005), pp. 68–85 (pp. 70–71); Daniel Wakelin, *Humanism, Reading, and English Literature, 1430–1530* (Oxford: Oxford University Press, 2007), pp. 163–65; Thomas Meacham, 'Exchanging Performative Words: Epistolary Performance and University Drama in Late Medieval England', *Medieval English Theatre*, 22 (2010), 12–25.

[113] Schramm, *The History of the English Coronation*, p. 32.

[114] Matthew Strickland, *Henry the Young King, 1155–1183* (New Haven, CT: Yale University Press, 2016), pp. 50–51.

[115] Richardson, 'The Coronation', pp. 134, 39n.

battle sites originally listed in the *Historia Brittonum*, one of Geoffrey's key sources.[116] It therefore has a triple significance which may explain how it came to spawn so many different place claims despite Geoffrey's specificity regarding its location. Geoffrey's 'City of Legions' is Caerleon-on-Uske, which he locates precisely by describing its surrounding geography and religious houses dedicated to St Julius and St Aaron.[117] Yet despite Geoffrey's clarity regarding the City's location – and its uniqueness – Urbs Legionum has nevertheless been associated with many different places between the twelfth and twenty-first centuries. This may be due to more than simply its Arthurian associations: according to Geoffrey of Monmouth, it was one of Britain's three pre-Christian religious centres or *archiflamines*, along with York and London, before being made an archbishopric when Britain was converted to Christianity. Several scholars have questioned Geoffrey's motives for placing Wales' archbishopric at Caerleon, rather than St Davids: whilst some believe this can be attributed to local pride, others have argued that Geoffrey was thumbing his nose at St Davids' claim to episcopal precedence.[118] The episcopal rivalries between Caerleon and St Davids may explain why some versions of Arthur's story omit the Caerleon ceremony, and sometimes even the identity of the Caerleon archbishop – Dubricius – who crowns Arthur, as in the *Brut* contained in MS Lansdowne 212. Clearly, the identity of Urbs legionum is closely bound up with disputes about episcopal anteriority and prestige.

By the fifteenth century there were several sites which were claimed to be the City of Legions. It is unclear where or when this splitting originated, but there is a clue in the writings of the fifteenth-century antiquary John Rous. Rous claims that there were three cities of the legion:

> previously, many armies would frequently gather in the middle of the kingdom. This being considered, I learn that there were formerly three cities of the legions: the first in South Wales; the second on the border of England and North Wales, which is now called Chester;

---

[116] See [Pseudo]-Nennius' battle list in Chambers, *Arthur of Britain*, pp. 238–40 (p. 239).

[117] Geoffrey of Monmouth, *The History of the Kings of Britain*, 3.44, pp. 58–59; 9.156, pp. 208–09. Whilst Andrew Breeze argues that the cults of St Julius and St Aaron were instead located at Leicester, A. Seaman has suggested that a church dedicated to both saints existed in the vicinity of Caerleon until the late fifteenth century: see A. Seaman, 'The Church of Julius, Aaron, and Alban at Caerleon', *The Monmouthshire Antiquary*, 34 (2018), 3–16.

[118] Brooke, 'The Archbishops', pp. 210–11; Valerie I. J. Flint, 'The Historia Regum Britanniae of Geoffrey of Monmouth: Parody and Its Purpose. A Suggestion', *Speculum*, 54.3 (1979), 447–68.

the third in England, which at one time was called Caerleon, and now is called Warwick.

(Saepius ante hoc medio regni adunatae sunt tales excercituum congregationes. Istis consideratis, reperio quod erant antiquitus tres urbes legionum: prima in Suthwallia; secunda in confinibus Loegriae & Northwalliae, quae nunc Cestria dicitur; tercia in Loegria, quae nunc Caerleon, quae nunc Warwyk appellatur.)[119]

There is precedence for the Chester identification: Chester is called the City of Legions in the *Annales Cambriae* and also in the writings of Bede.[120] However, Rous does not claim Bede as his source, despite erroneously citing Bede elsewhere instead of Geoffrey of Monmouth.[121] Instead, Rous mentions three authorities, emphasised below:

> [Guthelinus] a monge many othere as ys schewed in the abbey of Evysham in **dan Thomas Wynchombys warkys** he made thys borow abowte the byrthe of kyng Alysaunder the grete conqueror on of the ix worthy and named hyt Caerleon [...] In Walys and Albany were ij Cyteys called Carleon as wrytys **mayster Gerald Barre in hys cronycle**. Of thes Cyteys hit that is in Sowthe Walys yete holdys the name to thys day. The second ys in the Egge of Northe Walys and Albany Wyche now ys called Chestur and the water of dee that hyt stondythe on partes hyt from Northe Walis. The thyrde as wrytys **mayster Gyldas** is thys borow wycche aftyr was called Cairumbre, and aftyr Cayr Gwayr and now Warwyk and stondythe in the logyr that ys [...] the Cheffe parte of Englond better than Walys.[122]

Here, Rous cites Gerald of Wales [Barry], Gildas, and Thomas Wynchcombe, an Oxford scholar and precentor of Evesham Abbey.[123] We

---

[119] Rous, *Historia regum Angliae*, p. 27, translation mine.
[120] Higham, *Myth-Making*, p. 147; Jane Beal, 'Mapping Identity in John Trevisa's English Polychronicon: Chester, Cornwall and the Translation of English National History', in *Fourteenth Century England*, III, ed. W. M. Ormrod (Woodbridge: Boydell, 2004), pp. 67–82 (p. 69). Bede gives *Carlegion* as the previous name for Chester; see Bede, *Ecclesiastical History of the English People*, ed. Bertram Colgrave and R. A. B. Mynors (Oxford: Clarendon Press, 1969), pp. 140–41; Keith J. Fitzpatrick-Matthews, 'The Xxuiii Ciuitates Brittannię of the Historia Brittonum: Antiquarian Speculation in Early Medieval Wales', *Journal of Literary Onomastics*, 4.1 (2015), 1–19 (p. 6); K. H. Jackson, 'Nennius and the Twenty-Eight Cities of Britain', *Antiquity*, 12 (1938), 44–55.
[121] Rous, *Historia regum Angliae*, p. 48, cited in Gransden, p. 25.
[122] Rous, *The Rous Roll*, no. 1. Emphasis mine.
[123] Martin Camargo, 'Tria Sunt: The Long and the Short of Geoffrey of Vinsauf's Documentum de Modo et Arte Dictandi et Versificandi', *Speculum*, 74.4 (1999), 935–55 (p. 953).

might indeed expect Gerald to refer to a City of the Legions other than Caerleon somewhere in his writings, given that he spent much of his life struggling to gain the bishopric of St Davids and elevate the see to an archbishopric. Indeed, Gerald went so far as to claim that St Dubricius transferred the archbishopric to St Davids following Arthur's coronation, an elaboration on the prophetic statement ascribed to Merlin in Geoffrey's *Historia* that St Davids would one day 'wear the pallium of Caerleon'.[124] However, there are no references to the three Cities of the Legion in any of these authors' surviving writings.[125] It was not unusual for manuscripts to be misattributed to Gildas, and Rous may have witnessed such a work, particularly as he makes a point of attributing the Warwick identification to Gildas.[126] Indeed, John Leland reports a 'little booke entituled *Gilde*' owned by Rous, which Leland gathered from Rous's description to be a copy of pseudo-Nennius' *Historia Brittonum*.[127]

Regarding the statement that there are three legionary cities, however, Rous may have taken his sources second-hand from another text: Ranulf Higden's *Polychronicon*, a wildly popular work of historiography which

---

[124] Ad Putter, 'Gerald of Wales and the Prophet Merlin', *Anglo-Norman Studies*, 31 (2012), 90–103; Robert Rouse, 'Reading Ruins', p. 49.

[125] According to some early modern antiquarians Wynchcombe composed a work on the antiquities of Evesham Abbey; either this is now lost, or they were using Rous as their source. Although a chronicle written for Evesham Abbey survives, the extant copies do not contain material on Guthelinus nor the legendary foundation of Warwick. Dugdale records notes taken on Thomas Wynchcombe in the *collectanea* of the antiquary Thomas Allen; see John Stevens, *The History of the Antient Abbeys, Monasteries, Hospitals, Cathedral and Collegiate Churches* […], 2 vols, (London: Thomas Taylor, 1722), I, p. 215, no. 248. Wynchcombe is also mentioned in Anthony à Wood, *The Life and Times of Anthony Wood: Antiquary, of Oxford, 1632–1695, described by himself*, ed. Andrew Clark, 5 vols (Oxford: Clarendon Press, 1891–1900), IV, p. 94.

[126] Rous, *Historia Regum Angliae*, pp. 68–69. This tradition may have begun with Geoffrey of Monmouth himself; see Sjoerd Levelt, 'Citation and Misappropriation', passim. William Worcester saw a manuscript of the *Historia Brittonum* of pseudo-Nennius in Oxford, which he attributed to Gildas (Worcester, *Itineraries*, pp. 278–79). The sixteenth-century antiquarians John Leland and John Prise, discussed later in this book, disagreed over which works were really authored by Gildas. Prise held a copy of pseudo-Nennius' *Historia Brittonum* that was attributed to Gildas, and Prise disagreed with Leland over whether or not Gildas could have been the author. Both Leland and Prise suspected that Gildas's *De excidio et conquestu Britanniae*, published by Polydore Vergil in 1525, was a fake. See N. R. Ker, 'Sir John Prise', *The Library*, 10.1 (1955), 1–24 (pp. 6–9); Mary Bateman, 'Foreignness and Nativity', *Arthurian Literature*, 35 (2020), 152–72.

[127] 'John Rous […] hath a little booke entituled *Gilde*, which booke (so farre as I gather by his speech) had not to Authour *Gildas*, but *Nennius*)' (Joannes Rhesus […] habet libellum Gilde titulo inscriptum, qui quantum ego, ex eius oratione colligo, non Gildam, sed Nennium parentem habuit). Leland, *Learned*, sig. C3v; Leland, *Assertio*, sig. B3v.

survives in at least 147 witnesses.[128] In the following section of the *Polychronicon*, Higden cites Gerald of Wales in support of two pieces of information: 1) that there was more than one city of the legion; and 2) that one of the legionary cities, 'Caerusc', was located in South Wales. Higden then indicates a return to his own original material with the rubric '*Ranulfus*' (in Trevisa's translation this is replaced with 'Trevisa'). At this point, Higden claims that his native Chester was the second city of the legion. The crucial element in Rous's misunderstanding of Higden's text lies in the fact that the two earliest versions of the *Polychronicon* omit the *Ranulf* rubric that separates Gerald's material from Higden's own. In the following extract, the base text is the fuller version, with bold text indicating rubrics; struck through text indicates material excluded in the earlier *Polychronicon* witnesses:

> **Giraldus in his Itinerary.** The City of Legions, which, in Welsh, is named Caerlegion or Caerleon, is twofold. The one in Demetia in South Wales is called Caerusc, since it is situated where the river Usk falls into the Severn Sea near Glamorgan [...] **Ranulf.** And there is another City of Legions of the same name, ~~where the present chronicle was produced, as is exposed by the letterforms of the capitals of the first book~~ [...] the city situated on the marches of England in sight of Wales, between two arms of the sea, the Dee and the Mersey. In the time of the Britons, it was the metropolitan city of Venedotia in North Wales [...] Now its name is Chester, or City of Legions.
>
> (**Giraldus in Itinerario.** Urbs Legionum duplex est, quae Britannice vocatur Caerlegion vel Caerleon; una est in Demetia, id est, Southwallia, quae dicitur Caerusc, ubi Usca flumen cadit in Sabrinum mare juxta Glamorgantiam [...] **Ranulfus.** Est et alia Urbs Legionum ejusdem nominis, ~~ubi et praesens chronica fuit elaborata, sicut per capitales hujus primi libri apices clarius patet~~. Urbs quidem in confinio Angliae ad prospectum Cambriae, inter duo marina brachia, Dee et Mercee, situata; quae tempore Britonum caput fuit et metropolis Venedotiae, id est, Northwalliae [...] nunc autem dicta est Cestria, sive Urbs Legionum.)[129]

---

[128] John Taylor, *The Universal Chronicle of Ranulf Higden* (Oxford: Clarendon Press, 1966), pp. 152–58; A. S. G. Edwards, 'Notes on the *Polychronicon*', *Notes and Queries*, 25 (1978), 2–3; A. S. G Edwards and James Freeman, 'Further Manuscripts of Higden's Polychronicon', *Notes and Queries*, 63.4 (2016), 521–22. I thank Trevor Russell Smith for sharing with me his extensive expertise on the manuscript tradition of this extraordinary text; his study of the *Polychronicon* is forthcoming.

[129] Text from Ranulf Higden, *Polychronicon*, ed. Babington and Lumby, II, pp. 74–78. Translation mine. Babington points out the textual alterations at I, pp. xvi–xvii. Babington did not use all 147 extant witnesses in his critical edition, but the omissions occur in the shorter form of the oldest *Polychronicon* ending in 1327; see John Taylor, 'The Development of the Polychronicon Continuation', *The English*

In this passage, the omission of the 'Ranulfus' rubric would lead the reader to assume that this information regarding Chester originated with Gerald of Wales. This may, then, be a case of simple misreading similar to the example proposed in the previous chapter with regards to John Hardyng. Although the later versions of the *Polychronicon* rectify this elision by clarifying Higden as the source for the Chester association, this evidently came too late to prevent the attribution from gaining purchase among late medieval historiographers. Whether or not Higden had seen a further witness attributed to Gerald of Wales arguing the existence of two Cities of the Legion is another matter, and a question that surviving evidence does not allow us to answer.

Whilst Caerleon and Chester are named as legionary cities in other sources, the claim to Warwick as a City of the Legions is unique to Rous. Given that Rous dedicated his life's work to glorifying his patrons, the earls of Warwick, and the city to which they were attached, this is hardly surprising.[130] Personal local pride may be a factor here too: after all, Rous was born in Warwick. Whilst this does not quite equate to a counterclaim to Caerleon-on-Uske *per se* as the site of Arthur's crowning, it certainly muddies the waters, elevating Warwick to equal status with its splendid Welsh equivalent. As a result of Rous's tweaks, other events from Britain's legendary past said to have occurred in the City of Legions, such as Arthur's battle in the *Historia Brittonum*, might reasonably have taken place in Warwick or Chester instead, especially given that Rous also makes Warwick the first See of St Dubricius (rather than Caerleon-upon-Uske) prior to his promotion from bishop to archbishop.[131] Rous's historiography and *collectanea* were important sources for subsequent

---

Historical Review, 76.298 (1961), 20–36 (p. 22). A continuation to 1340 written by Higden himself exists as San Marino, CA, Huntington Library, MS Huntington 132. I have not been able to examine this manuscript to see whether Higden added the rubric himself in order to correct his dubious referencing. See V. H. Galbraith, 'An Autograph MS of Ranulph Higden's "Polychronicon"', *Huntington Library Quarterly*, 23.1 (1959), 1–18.

[130] Martha W. Driver, 'Inventing Visual History: Re-Presenting the Legends of Warwickshire', in *Essays in Manuscript Geography: Vernacular Manuscripts of the English West Midlands from the Conquest to the Sixteenth Century*, ed. Wendy Scase (Turnhout, Belgium: Brepols, 2007), pp. 161–202; Yin Liu, 'Building History in the English Rous Roll', *Viator – Medieval and Renaissance Studies*, 42.2 (2011), 307–20, https://doi.org/10.1484/J.VIATOR.1.102253>.

[131] Rous, *The Rous Roll*, no. 6. Rous gives more detail in his lost work, *De antiquitate academiarum*, an extract of which was copied out by Leland: 'All of the saints in Warwick Castle were also translated to the church of Llandaff, of whom the foremost was the bishop [i.e. Dubricius] who was eventually made archbishop of the City of Legions, and whom David succeeded, who transferred the See to Menevia [St Davids]' (Omnium Sanctorum in castro Warwicensi, idem translatus ad ecclesiam Landavensem, cujus primus erat episcopus, demum factus fuit

major antiquarians such as John Leland and William Camden, and perhaps we have Rous's splitting of the City of Legions to thank for the many theories that persist today about the possible location of the various City (or Cities) of the Legion: in other words, the ways in which Arthur was localised in the fifteenth century continue to influence how Arthur's places are contested today.[132]

Arthur's court and the Round Table

The City of the Legion is significant to Arthur's geography for more than just his coronation, or as a battle site; it is one of the three locations in which Arthur is said to have held court, according to Geoffrey of Monmouth.[133] At this stage there was no 'Camelot', nor was there a 'Round Table' until Wace's *Brut* (c. 1150).[134] Quite quickly, Arthur's court came to be represented as something portable mirroring 'the peripatetic style of kingship of the earlier Middle Ages'.[135] The first mention of Arthur's court at Camelot appears in Chrétien de Troyes' *Le chevalier de la charrette* in the 1170s, but this is by no means the only place where Arthur holds court in Chrétien's romances. Chrétien's Arthurian heroes also set out on their quest from courts at Cardigan (*Erec*), Winchester (*Cligès*), Camelot (*Charette*), and Carduel (*Yvain, Perceval*); and Chrétien's Arthur also holds court at the unknown 'Quarrois', Caerleon, the 'city' of Orkney, Nantes, and 'Disnadaron', a possible corruption of *Dinas d'Aron* or the city of Aaron (perhaps originally Caerleon).[136]

---

archiepiscopus civitatis Legionum, cui successit David, qui sedem transtulit Meneviam.) Leland, *Itineraries*, II, p. 168.

[132] Alongside the three candidates put forward by Rous we can now include York: see P. J. C. Field, 'Gildas and the City of Legions', *The Heroic Age*, 1 (1999), www.heroicage.org/issues/1/hagcl.htm [accessed 25 October 2019]. In his assessment of the cult of St Julius and St Aaron, said by Gildas, Geoffrey, and their inheritors to have centred on Caerleon, Andrew Breeze has also suggested that Gildas had instead meant Leicester: see Andrew Breeze, 'Legionum Urbs and the British Martyrs Aaron and Julius', *Voprosy Onomastiki*, 13.1 (2016), 30–42, https://doi.org/10.15826/vopr.

[133] Geoffrey of Monmouth, *The History of the Kings of Britain*, 9.155, pp. 207–08 (Paris); 9.156–157, pp. 207–12 (Caerleon). Geoffrey's Arthur also appears to hold court in London (9.144, pp. 193–94).

[134] Wace, *Wace's Roman de Brut: A History of the British*, ed. and trans. Judith Weiss (Exeter: University of Exeter Press, 1999); see also Beate Schmolke-Hasselmann, 'The Round Table: Ideal, Fiction, Reality', *Arthurian Literature*, 2 (1982), 41–75; Norris J. Lacy, 'The Arthurian Legend Before Chrétien', in *A Companion to Chrétien de Troyes*, ed. Norris J. Lacy and Joan Tasker Grimbert (Cambridge: D. S. Brewer, 2005), pp. 43–51 (p. 49).

[135] Field, 'Searching for Camelot', p. 1.

[136] Field, 'Searching for Camelot', pp. 3–4.

P. J. C. Field argues that Chrétien intended his readers to interpret these courts as real-world locations, anchor points distinct from the ambiguous spaces Chrétien's knights passed through on their quests.[137] Of course, this does not necessarily mean that Chrétien or his readers would have actually been familiar with these toponyms as real-world places.[138] In the Arthurian French prose tradition that exploded in the three centuries after Chrétien, Camelot came to dominate almost exclusively as the site of Arthur's court, singular but geographically non-specific.[139] In contrast, Middle English romance privileged real-world places such as Carlisle and Caerleon as the locations of Arthur's court; Carlisle appears especially frequently as an Arthurian court setting in the popular English Gawain romances.[140]

I: Caerleon and Winchester

Although there was a clear tendency towards a more pluralistic vision of Arthur's court by the fifteenth century, there were nevertheless several real-world places that became established in the cultural imagination as sites of King Arthur's principal court. Even those who suggested Arthur's Round Table was peripatetic nevertheless believed Arthur to have preferred certain locations: the sixteenth-century antiquarian John Stow believed that Arthur kept his Round Table 'in diuers places, but especially at Cairleon, Winchester, and Camalet in Somerset-shire'.[141] 'Camalet' in Somerset has its origins with Stow's contemporary, the antiquarian John Leland, and is discussed in subsequent chapters of this book. The other two places Stow mentions, Caerleon and Winchester, are both identified with Camelot in the Caxton edition of Malory's *Morte Darthur*: Caerleon by Caxton in his preface, and Winchester by Malory in the main text. Unlike the multiple sites of Arthur's crowning or the many legionary cities, this is clearly a contradiction in terms: Winchester and Caerleon are not merely places where Arthur was said to have held court, but

---

[137] Field, 'Searching for Camelot', pp. 3–4. Field suggests that Chrétien 'saw geographical anonymity as a positive factor' when it came to questing locations (p. 3).

[138] Field points out that Chrétien seems far more familiar with the South and South-East of England than the rest of the island. Field, 'Searching for Camelot', p. 3.

[139] Field, 'Searching for Camelot', p. 6.

[140] Rouse and Rushton, 'Arthurian Geography', p. 220. On Arthur's court at Carlisle in insular romance, see Hahn's introduction in *Sir Gawain: Eleven Romances and Tales*, ed. Thomas Hahn, TEAMS (Kalamazoo, MI: Medieval Institute Publications, 1995), at pp. 29–31.

[141] John Stow, *The Chronicles of England from Brute vnto this present yeare of Christ* (London: Ralph Newberry, 1580), sig. F3r, p. 81.

are instead identified as *Camelot*, a specific if ambiguous location from the realm of Arthurian romance. While Malory took pains throughout the *Morte* to carefully map the settings of his romance sources onto a believable real-world geography, it may be that Caxton had different goals in mind when writing his preface.

Caxton, citing the arguments of an anonymous gentleman, suggests that his readers might find 'the toune of Camelot' in Wales, 'the grete stones & meruayllous werkys of yron lyeng vnder the grounde, & ryal vautes, which dyuers now lyuyng hath seen'.[142] Caxton may have had Caerleon in mind, or possibly nearby Caerwent.[143] Both would have had visible Roman remains in Malory's time much as they do today: Caerleon's Roman past was visible through the Middle Ages and in the sixteenth and seventeenth centuries;[144] and Roman rubble from Caerwent seems to have been consciously and decoratively used as a 'special' or 'precious material' in the construction of the eleventh-century Great Tower at nearby Chepstow Castle.[145] Caerleon is perhaps the more likely candidate. Given the prominence of Caerleon as a site of Arthur's court and coronation in the historical and literary traditions predating the publication of Malory's *Morte*, from Geoffrey of Monmouth's *Historia* and its derivatives to Arthurian romance in French, Welsh, and English, it would hardly be surprising that Caxton should point to it as the site of Arthur's most famous court.

Malory, on the other hand, places Camelot at Winchester in the main text of the *Morte Darthur*.[146] At the same time, Malory strengthens the impression of Winchester as the real-world Camelot through geographic accretion, placing other romance locations in a logical way onto the surrounding map. For example, Malory suggests that Guildford represents Astolat, home to the ill-fated Elaine who travels upriver by boat after her death to an Arthurian court at Westminster; indeed, Arthur spends a night at Astolat on his way from Westminster

---

[142] Malory, *Works*, p. xiv.
[143] Lloyd, *The Arthurian Place Names of Wales*, p. 51.
[144] On the visibility of Caerleon's ancient past during the Middle Ages, see Rouse, 'Reading Ruins', passim; Ray Howell, 'Roman Past and Medieval Present: Caerleon as a Focus for Continuity and Conflict in the Middle Ages', *Studia Celtica*, 46.1 (2012), 11–21; and, for early modern interest in Caerleon's ancient material past, see Jeremy Knight, 'Welsh Stones and Oxford Scholars: Three Rediscoveries', *Bulletin of the Institute of Classical Studies*, 44.S75 (2000), 91–101.
[145] Abigail Wheatley, *The Idea of the Castle in Medieval England* (York: York Medieval Press, 2004), pp. 128–29.
[146] Malory, *Works*, 2.19, p. 58; 12.10, p. 505; 18.8, p. 621; 18.10, p. 624.

to Camelot (Winchester), which makes perfect geographical sense as a real-world stop-off point.[147]

Why might Malory have chosen to locate Camelot at Winchester, in contradiction to his editor Caxton? An obvious reason is Winchester's historical significance. Winchester had functioned as the symbolic heart of English political power since the pre-Conquest period.[148] Moreover, Winchester was already an established Arthurian location in textual and popular tradition. The scholarly consensus, summarised succinctly by Robert Rouse and Cory Rushton, is that Malory's association of Winchester with Camelot can probably be traced back through a series of texts, objects, and events.[149] Winchester already had significant Arthurian connotations well before this stage, and especially in the francophone Arthurian tradition: some of these associations have already been discussed in this chapter, such as Thomas Gray's identification of Winchester as a site of Arthur's crowning in his *Scalacronica*, and Winchester's appearance as a site of Arthur's court in romances such as *Cligès*.[150] Winchester is also the setting of a major tournament in the *Mort Artu* (c. 1225) that forms the set piece of the first half of the romance, and subsequently too in the Middle English Stanzaic *Morte* based upon it.[151] In 1290, King Edward I held an Arthurian-themed tournament at Winchester, perhaps inspired by romances like the *Mort Artu* that are known to have been popular with the king and his immediate family.[152] It is thought that Edward I ordered the construction of a replica wooden Round Table for this very occasion, an artefact that hangs on display to this day in Winchester Castle. Martin Biddle suggests that 'the making of a Round Table' at Winchester 'was the making of Arthurian Winchester', transforming the city from an Arthurian location into Arthur's 'own city'.[153]

---

[147] Armstrong and Hodges, *Mapping Malory*, p. 2; p. 4; pp. 112–13; Barry Gaines, 'Malory's Castles in Text and Illustration', in *The Medieval Castle: Romance and Reality*, ed. Kathryn Louise Reyerson and Faye Powe (Dubuque, IA: Kendell Hunt, 1984), pp. 215–28 (pp. 215–16); J. D. Parry, 'Following Malory Out of Arthur's World', *Modern Philology*, 95.2 (1997), 147–69 (p. 151).

[148] Robert Allen Rouse, *The Idea of Anglo-Saxon England in Middle English Romance* (Cambridge: D. S. Brewer, 2012), p. 62; Molly Martin, *Castles and Space in Malory's Morte Darthur* (Cambridge: D. S. Brewer, 2019), pp. 47–48.

[149] Rouse and Rushton, *The Medieval Quest for Arthur*, pp. 21–48.

[150] See above at pp. 122–26.

[151] Martin Biddle, 'The Making of the Round Table', in *King Arthur's Round Table: An Archaeological Investigation*, pp. 337–92 (p. 354); *Stanzaic Morte Arthur*, ed. Larry D. Benson, rev. Edward E. Foster (Kalamazoo, MI: Medieval Institute Publications, 1994), p. 42, l. 93.

[152] Biddle, 'The Making of the Round Table', p. 357; Rouse, *The Idea of Anglo-Saxon England*, pp. 150–51.

[153] Ibid.

Might the Winchester Table have directly inspired Malory's identification of Winchester with Camelot? Perhaps, although scholars disagree on how personally familiar Malory actually was with Winchester itself and the surrounding area.[154] Another possibility is that Malory was influenced by the later version of John Hardyng's *Chronicle*, which he used as a key source for the *Morte Darthur*.[155] Hardyng's *Chronicle* is the earliest known text to describe the physical Round Table hanging at Winchester, stating that Winchester was the place where the Round Table 'beganne, | And there it ended, and there it hangeth yet'.[156] It is impossible to know exactly when the Table was hung on display – Hardyng seems to think it had done so since the disintegration of Arthur's Round Table brotherhood. Perhaps the Table was hung up in 1348–49, when Winchester Castle's great hall was remodelled and the Order of the Garter established.[157] Gray's *Scalacronica*, the earliest known text to place Arthur's coronation at Winchester, was written within two decades of this event, and records both the Order's foundation and Edward III's 'great fest at Wyndesore at Christemes, where he renewed the Round Table and the name of Arture'.[158] Whether Malory first learned of the Winchester Round Table through Hardyng, through seeing it personally, or simply via popular tradition, his association of Winchester with Camelot clearly represents a triangulation of Winchester's political significance, the material reality of the Round Table, and the influence upon Malory of

---

[154] P. J. C. Field and Susan Holbrook suggest Malory was not intimately familiar with Winchester, while Earl R. Anderson suggests a degree of familiarity with the city and its surrounds. See Field, 'Searching for Camelot', p. 8; Sue Ellen Holbrook, 'Malory's Identification of Camelot as Winchester', in *Studies in Malory*, ed. James W. Spisak (Kalamazoo, MI: Western Michigan University Press, 1985), pp. 13–27 (pp. 21–22); Earl R. Anderson, 'Malory's Camelot, Winchester, and "the Chirche of Seynte Stevins"', *Neuphilologische Mitteilungen*, 92.2 (1991), 211–13.

[155] Hardyng's influence on Malory has been discussed at length. See E. D. Kennedy, 'Malory's Use of Hardyng's *Chronicle*'; Ralph C. Norris, *Malory's Library: The Sources of the Morte Darthur* (Cambridge: D. S. Brewer, 2008), passim; E. D. Kennedy, 'Malory's Use of Hardyng's Chronicle: A Reconsideration'; Roland, 'The Rudderless Boat'. It has even been argued that Malory was influenced by the page design of Hardyng's manuscripts; see K. S. Whetter, 'Malory, Hardyng and the Winchester Manuscript: Some Preliminary Conclusions', *Arthuriana*, 22.4 (2012), 167–89; K. S. Whetter, *The Manuscript and Meaning of Malory's Morte Darthur: Rubrication, Commemoration, Memorialization* (Cambridge: D. S. Brewer, 2017), pp. 23–53.

[156] Hardyng, *Chronicle*, ed. Ellis, p. 146.

[157] Jon Whitman, 'National Icon: The Winchester Round Table and the Revelation of Authority', *Arthuriana*, 18.4 (2008), 33–65 (p. 35); Biddle, 'The Hanging of the Table', in *King Arthur's Round Table: An Archaeological Investigation*, pp. 393–424.

[158] This part of the *Scalacronica* is missing from surviving witnesses but was paraphrased by John Leland; cited in Moll, *Before Malory*, p. 34.

Hardyng's English Arthurian geographies.[159] Caxton on the other hand (or his nameless gentleman) appears to have been influenced primarily by the establishment of Caerleon in the chronicle tradition, and by the physicality of the ruins that he claims himself to have seen.

II: Arthur's multiplying courts

Although Malory's inspiration for locating Camelot is probably Hardyng, Hardyng does not explicitly state that Winchester *is* Camelot; only that the Round Table was founded and disbanded there, which some have taken as a suggestion that Arthur held his main court at Camelot.[160] In fact, Hardyng's *Chronicle* exemplifies the extreme multiplicity seen in models of Arthur's court from the fifteenth century. With the exception of authors such as Malory who attempted to reconcile romance and real-world geographies, by this stage most of Arthur's defenders were looking to purge Arthurian history of its romance elements by returning to the plural, real-world models for Arthur's court put forward in historical chronicles derived from Geoffrey, such as the *Brut*. This meant that those looking to emphasise the reach of Arthur's dominion could locate Arthur's strongholds in any number of places, and indeed there were so many candidates by the later Middle Ages that it would be impossible to catalogue them all here.[161] Instead, I will attempt to make some observations about the kinds of places claimed to be the sites of Arthur's court or Arthur's Round Table and the reasons why they may have acquired these associations if they did not already exist in earlier works.

In addition to Winchester, Hardyng sets forth an impressive list which emphasises Arthur's supremacy 'thurghout alle Bretayne grounde'.[162] Unexpectedly, given the condensed nature of Hardyng's revised 1460 chronicle, the list is even longer in the later version (twenty sites instead of seventeen), and with an increased number of locations in Scotland:

[1457 version]
Whar Kynge Arthure helde moste usually his housholde in Bretayne[163]

---

[159] Roland, 'The Rudderless Boat', passim.
[160] P. J. C. Field, 'Searching for Camelot', pp. 6–7.
[161] Gazetteers are useful for this purpose, although sometimes locations are missed that are not widely attested (Dunnideer, for example, which is attested by John Hardyng, is not included in these lists). See Geoffrey Ashe, *Guide to Arthurian Britain*; Caitlin R. Green, *Arthuriana*, pp. 89–116; Lloyd, *Arthurian Place Names of Wales*.
[162] John Hardyng, *Chronicle*, ed. Simpson and Peverley, 3.2579.
[163] Bold indicates rubricated text.

> [...]
> Whiche tyme so than the kynge Arthure rialle
> Hys housholde helde thurghoute Grete Bretayn alle
> At Edynburgh, Stryvelyn,[164] and Dunbretayne,[165]
> At Cumbyrnalde,[166] Dundonalde,[167] and at Perte,
> At Bamburgh[168] als, at Yorke the sothe to sayne,
> And at Carlele with knyghtes manly and perte.
> And open house he kepte ay in aperte
> The Table Rounde abowte he dyd remewe
> In every place whare that he remewed newe.
> At Londoun, als Carnarvan, and Cardyfe,
> At Herforde, als Wynchestere, and Carlyoun,
> In Cornewayle ofte, and Dovere als ful ryfe,
> And ofte within the Ile of Avaloun
> That Glasenbyry now is of religioun
> Thise were his places and his habitacions
> In whiche he had his hertes consolacions.
>
> (*Chronicle*, ed. Simpson and Peverley, 3.2581–3.2596)

> [1460 version]
> He held his household and the rounde table,
> Some tyme at Edenburgh, some tyme at Striveline,
> Of [kynges renomed] and moost honourable
> At Carleile sumwhile, at Alclud[169] his cite fine
> [Emong all his knightes and ladies full feminine];
> At Bamburgh also, and Ebrauk cite,[170]
> At London, at Wynchester, with greate royalte.
> At Carlion, Cardif, and Aualyne;[171]
> In Cornewaile also, Douer, and Cairlegion;
> And in Scotlande, at Perthe, and Dunbrytain,
> [At Dunbar, Dumfrise, and saint Johns towne,[172]
> All of worthy knightes moo then a legion,

[164] Stirling.
[165] Dumbarton.
[166] Cumberland.
[167] Dundonald Castle, Ayrshire.
[168] Bamburgh Castle, Northumberland. Referred to elsewhere by Hardyng as 'Mounte Dolorouse', the castle containing the Dolorous Garde (Hardyng, *Chronicle*, ed. Simpson and Peverley, 2.1033–44). On this association, see Richard J. Moll, 'Ebrauke and the Politics of Arthurian Geography', *Arthuriana*, 15.4 (2005), 65–71.
[169] Loomis identifies this as Dumbarton, although Hardyng already includes 'Dunbrytain' here. R. S. Loomis, 'Scotland and the Arthurian Legend', *Proceedings of the Society of Antiquaries of Scotland*, 89 (1955), 1–21 (p. 7).
[170] York.
[171] Avalon.
[172] Also known as Dalry in Dumfries, Galloway.

At Donydoure[173] also, in Murith[174] region,
And in many other places bothe cite and towne]

(*Chronicle*, ed. Ellis, pp. 126–27)

Hardyng likely visited several of these places himself. Aside from his knowledge of Winchester suggesting the possibility of a personal visit, a number of the castles, cities, and towns in Hardyng's list – 'Dunbretayn', 'Dony Dowre', 'Stryvelyn', 'Carlele', 'Dunbar', 'Seynt Jonstoun', 'Edenburgh'– find themselves represented in his maps of Scotland.[175] James Simpson and Sarah Peverley rightly point out Hardyng's obvious Scottish agenda in this passage and elsewhere: suzerainty over Scotland was a life-long fixation for Hardyng, so staking claim to Arthurian strongholds in Scotland gave support to his rhetoric in favour of a re-invasion. However, Hardyng's list of Arthur's courts does not exclusively represent his own invention. Some are well attested in Arthurian textual traditions: Winchester, Caerleon, Carlisle, and also Dover and Cardiff are the locations of Arthur's court in several romances, and the links with Cornwall, London, and Glastonbury are also well attested (though Hardyng is unusual in claiming that Arthur held court in Cornwall or Glastonbury).[176] Moray (Hardyng's 'Murith') appears in Geoffrey's *Historia* as 'Murreif', the location of Arthur's battle against the Scots and the Picts.[177] Carnarvon appears in Malory's *Morte Darthur* (though not as King Arthur's court).[178] Dumbarton (alias 'Alclud') is referred to in a 1367 parliamentary record as 'Arthur's Castle', and it is also a key location in Geoffrey's *Historia*.[179]

---

[173] Dunnideer castle in Aberdeenshire.

[174] Moray.

[175] London, British Library, Harley MS 661, ff. 187v–188r; British Library, Lansdowne MS 204, f. 226v.

[176] See Ackerman, *An Index of Arthurian Names*, p. 52 and West, *An Index of Proper Names in French Arthurian Prose Romances*, p. 56 (Cardiff); Ackerman, p. 244, West, p. 83, and West, p. 305 (Winchester); Ackerman, p. 75 (Dover). Arthur does hold his court in Glastonbury in a limited number of insular romances, such as *Lybeaus desconnus*, which we know that Hardyng had read: see Hardyng, *Chronicle*, ed. Simpson and Peverley, 3.2567.

[177] Geoffrey of Monmouth, *History of the Kings of Britain*, 9.149, pp. 200–01. See also Ackerman, *An Index*, p. 171.

[178] Malory, *Works*, 19.15, p. 666. See also Richard R. Griffith, 'The Authorship Question Reconsidered', in *Aspects of Malory*, ed. Toshiyuki Takamiya and Derek Brewer (Cambridge: D. S. Brewer and Rowman & Littlefield, 1981), pp. 159–78 (p. 163).

[179] In Geoffrey's *Historia* Dumbarton is won from the Picts and Scots by Uther Pendragon, fought over during Arthur's lifetime, and the place where Hoel of Brittany is left to convalesce during his illness. See Geoffrey of Monmouth, *The History of the Kings of Britain*, 8.137, pp. 182–85; Katie Stevenson, 'Chivalry, British Sovereignty and Dynastic Politics: Undercurrents of Antagonism in Tudor–Stewart Relations, c.1490–c.1513', *Historical Research*, 86.234 (2013), 601–18.

Hardyng seems a little confused on Alclud's location, concluding that he believes it to be 'at ende of the Peghte Walle', 'a litil fro Carlele'.[180] In the thirteenth century, Laȝamon's *Brut* associated Edinburgh with the Castle of Maidens of Arthurian romance, and by the late fifteenth century Edinburgh was touted as 'Arthur's Seat' by James IV.[181]

Other candidates in Hardyng's list are more ambiguous: they may be Hardyng's own embellishments, or they may have been connected to Arthur in late medieval oral traditions that cannot be traced. Although there are several topographical features in Herefordshire with Arthurian names or stories attached, Hereford itself is not a major location in Arthurian literature or historiography in the late fifteenth century.[182] Dunbar largely does not feature in Arthur's geography, although Hector Boece identified it as the Pictish 'Horestria' in which Guenevere was held captive, so there may have been some Arthurian folklore connected with it.[183] Alternatively, two locations in Perthshire have been linked to Guenevere's end.[184]

Some candidates in Hardyng's list – such as Dumfries, St John's Town, or Dunnideer – are not known to have been connected with

---

[180] Hardyng, *Chronicle*, ed. Simpson and Peverley, 3.2946–2948 (n.).

[181] Roland Blenner-Hassett, 'Geoffrey of Monmouth's *Mons Agned* and *Castellum Puellarum*', *Speculum*, 17.2 (1942), 250–54; Loomis, 'Scotland and the Arthurian Legend', pp. 7–9; Stevenson, 'Chivalry, British Sovereignty and Dynastic Politics', p. 612. Richard Coates has also drawn attention to the strong appeal of the 'Castle of Maidens' toponym in Scotland and the very north of England, most often in reference to hillforts, earthworks, or prominent rock formations. See Richard Coates, 'Maiden Castle, Geoffrey of Monmouth and Hārūn al-Rašīd', *Nomina*, 29 (2006), 5–60 (pp. 45–46).

[182] A Neolithic burial chamber in Herefordshire has been known as 'Arthur's Stone' since at least the thirteenth century; see Dean, *Arthur of England*, p. 58. There is an 'Arthur's Cave' in the side of a Herefordshire hillfort known as 'Little Doward' and 'Ganarew'. In the fifteenth century, William Worcester identified this location as 'Genorem' on mount 'Cloart', the location where Vortigern's final battle and death take place in Geoffrey's *Historia*. A search inside the cave for 'Arthur's hall and treasure' is said to have taken place c. 1700, during which an abnormally large skeleton with a spear was purportedly discovered (possibly another manifestation of the 'Arthur as giant' folklore motif). See Worcester, *Itineraries*, pp. 212–13; Geoffrey of Monmouth, *History of the Kings of Britain*, 8.119, pp. 160–61; A. M. Apsimon, 'King Arthur's Cave, King Arthur's Hall and the Giant's Skeleton', *Proceedings of the University of Bristol Spelaeological Society*, 20.1 (1994), 75–76; F. Edmunds, 'The Skeleton Found in King Arthur's Hall', *Transactions of the Woolhope Naturalists' Field Club*, 5–6 (1874), pp. 28–31.

[183] Elizabeth Hanna, 'A "Scottish Monmouth"?', passim. Hanna identifies a passage in which Boece appears to elide Guenevere's imprisonment at Dunbar and her burial at Meigle some distance away, which may be connected with the standing stone known as the 'Vanora Stone' at Meigle (p. 118). See also Chambers, *Arthur of Britain*, pp. 155–57.

[184] Chambers, *Arthur of Britain*, p. 191.

Arthur by anyone other than Hardyng. Their Arthurianisation may be Hardyng's doing, or he may have encountered popular tradition locally that connected them to Arthur. There are several reasons why these places may have been associated with Arthur's court: their strategic location, or perhaps their visible ancient monuments. Dunnideer castle, for example, was built in the centre of an Iron Age earthwork.[185] It was not unusual for medieval castles to be constructed on top of ancient sites, which could be powerful and sometimes political reminders of an ancient past.[186] Sometimes, materials were repurposed from these ruins, materials referred to by some early antiquarians as 'Briton brykes' whether or not there were so (as at Dover Castle and Hereford, two other locations in Hardyng's list).[187] Many of Arthur's better-known court sites, such as Carlisle and Caerleon, would still have had visible ancient remains throughout the Middle Ages, which may partly explain how they came to be connected with Arthur in the first place.[188] At Cirencester, the purported site of Arthur's coronation, there is a Roman amphitheatre just outside the town walls.[189] Although Caerleon's amphitheatre is not referred to explicitly as Arthur's Round Table until the late sixteenth century, a possible earlier reference exists in the chronicle of Enguerrand de Monstrelet (c. 1444), which describes the French forces visiting 'the

---

[185] Dunnideer Castle was built inside an Iron Age vitrified hillfort. The remains of a thirteenth- or fourteenth-century medieval tower have been excavated on site. For the history of jurisdiction over the castle based on charter evidence, see W. Douglas Simpson, 'The Castles of Dunnideer and Wardhouse, in the Garioch, Aberdeenshire', *Proceedings of the Society of Antiquaries of Scotland*, 69 (1935), 460–70; for the site's archaeological history, see Murray Cook and others, 'New Light on Oblong Forts: Excavations at Dunnideer, Aberdeenshire', *Proceedings of the Society of Antiquaries of Scotland*, 140 (2010), 79–91; 'Hill of Dunnideer, Fort, Platform Settlement and Tower (SM95)', Historic Environment Scotland, 1934, amended 2003, http://portal.historicenvironment.scot/designation/SM95 [accessed 5 November 2019].

[186] Ray Howell has argued that the Roman remains at Caerleon may have been pulled down by Marcher lords in an orchestrated attempt to quell uprisings by the Welsh, to whom these ruins may have given hope. Raymond Howell, 'The Demolition of the Roman Tetrapylon in Caerleon: An Erasure of Memory', *Oxford Journal of Archaeology*, 19.4 (2000), 387–95; Ray Howell, 'Roman Past and Medieval Present: Caerleon as a Focus for Continuity and Conflict in the Middle Ages', *Studia Celtica*, 46.1 (2012), 11–21.

[187] Oliver Harris, 'John Leland and the "Briton Brykes"', *The Antiquaries Journal*, 87 (2007), 346–56.

[188] On the visibility of ancient remains at Carlisle, see Abigail Wheatley, 'King Arthur Lives in Merry Carlisle', in *Carlisle and Cumbria: Roman and Medieval Architecture, Art and Archaeology*, ed. Mike McCarthy and David Weston (Leeds: The British Archaeological Association, 2004), pp. 63–72.

[189] P. Brown, C. David, and Alan D. McWhirr, 'Cirencester, 1966', *The Antiquaries Journal*, 47.2 (1967), 185–97.

Round Table, that's to say the noble abbey', after landing in South Wales to aid the Glyndŵr rising in 1403.[190]

There are other examples in Hardyng's list where visible ruins might have had a part to play in a site's Arthuring. 'Cumbyrnalde' (Cumberland) may refer to the ancient earthwork known as King Arthur's Round Table in Penrith, Cumbria.[191] It has previously been thought that the earliest reference to the site's Arthurian connections was in John Leland's *Itineraries*, written when he visited in the 1530s.[192] However, an earlier source dating to the first half of the fifteenth century– when Hardyng himself would have visited the Cumberland area – identifies the site with Arthur. This is the copy of *Stafford's Chronicle* with its accompanying gloss contained in MS Harley 1808, the same chronicle discussed in Chapter 1 in relation to the Glastonbury sestet found in William Worcester's notes and in Cotton MS Titus A.XIX.[193] To reiterate, the glosses accompanying *Stafford's Chronicle* are unique to each witness, tailored to the locality of the copy (although they clearly share several sources). MS Harley 1808,

---

[190] Enguerrand's text reads: 'et de là entrant ou pays de Morgine [Glamorgan] allerent à la Table Ronde, c'est à savoir l'Abbaye Noble' (and from there, entering into the country of Glamorgan, they went to the Round Table, that's to say the Noble Abbey). *Chroniques d'Enguerrand de Monstrelet*, ed. Jean-Alexandre Buchon, 8 vols (Paris, 1826), I, p. 136. Translation mine. See also Hanno Wijsman, 'History in Transition: Enguerrand de Monstrelet's Chronique in Manuscript and Print (c. 1450–c. 1600)', in *The Book Triumphant: Print in Transition in the Sixteenth and Seventeenth Centuries*, ed. Malcolm Walsby and Graeme Kemp (Leiden: Brill, 2011), pp. 199–252. Thomas Churchyard, in his description of Caerleon, also appears to describe the amphitheatre, 'in Arthur's time a table round [...] and yet a plot of goodly land | Was there whereat he sate: | As yet a plot of goodly ground, | Sets forth that rare estate'. The marginal note reads: 'A deepe and large round peece of ground shewes yet where Arthur sate.' Thomas Churchyard, *The Worthines of Wales* (London, 1587), sig. D2r.

[191] Another possibility is Castle Hewin, sometimes attributed to the castle of the Grim Baron or to Yvain (though the earliest attestation dates to the eighteenth century): see Glennie, *Arthurian Localities*, p. 74; Dean, *Arthur of England*, p. 58; William Patterson, 'Oliver Castle, Upper Tweeddale', *The Journal of Scottish Name Studies*, 11 (2017), 93–102 (pp. 97–98).

[192] 'Withyn a myle of Penrith, but in Westmerland, is a ruine [...] the ruine is of sum caulled the Round Table, and of summe Arture's Castel. A myle lower m[etithe] Loder and Emot at Burgham Castel'. Leland, *Itineraries*, V, p. 48. Christopher Dean argues that the Arthurian connection must be a late development; see *Arthur of England*, pp. 58–59.

[193] See above at **p.** . The reference to Arthur's Round Table in this version of *Stafford's Chronicle* was noted by Hammer, 'Une version métrique', p. 150. However, Hammer did not attempt to identify the location. It is also observed by Rigg, *A Book of British Kings* [Stafford's Chronicle], p. 6, 14n. Rigg does not include the gloss from this manuscript (*H*) in his edition of this chronicle and its commentary. Interestingly, both MS Harley 1808 and Cotton Titus A.XIX share another text in common as well as *Stafford's Chronicle*: the pseudo-Turpin.

the manuscript in which the following statement appears, presents the most unique variants in its gloss, revealing a clear concern with Northern affairs around the Scotland/England border, just like Hardyng's *Chronicle*.[194] The following appears in the gloss accompanying the Arthur section of the *Stafford Chronicle* in the Harley manuscript:

> Arthur [...] [was] lethally wounded and buried [at] Glastonbury. He restored this city of Borowham with a pair of castles (that is, Plompton Castle and the Castle of Giants, next to the Round Table), which Hengist burned and destroyed.
>
> (Arthurus [...] in prelio cum Modredo, nepote suo, inito, letaliter vulneratur et Glastonie sepelitur. Hic civitatem de Borowham reparavit cum duobus castellis, videlicet castello de Plompton et castello Gigancium, iuxta la Roundtable, quos Hengistus combussit et destruxit.)[195]

As the quires in which this text is contained date from the first half of the fifteenth century, this constitutes the earliest known reference to Arthur's Round Table in Cumbria in Arthurian terms.[196] All the places named here would have been embedded in, or located alongside, the remains of ancient ruins in the Middle Ages. Brougham Castle was built in the early Middle Ages on the site of a Roman settlement, *Brovacum*, whose ruins are visible from the medieval castle.[197] Like other locations in Hardyng's list such as Dunnideer and Carlisle, Brougham Castle was built using Roman remains: an inscribed Roman tombstone has been used as a ceiling slab in a hallway leading to the castle keep.[198] 'Plompton' must refer to Plumpton Voreda, a nearby site where the remains of a Roman fort are still visible (this is also a likely candidate for the 'palais' at 'Plumton Land' of the *Awntyrs off Arthure*).[199] Arthur's Round Table is the name still given to

---

[194] Hammer, 'Une version métrique', p. 150; Rigg, *The Book of British Kings* [Stafford's Chronicle], pp. 14–15; pp. 5–6.

[195] British Library Harley MS 1808, ff. 35r–v.

[196] See the manuscript description in N. R. Ker, *Medieval Libraries of Great Britain: A List of Surviving Books*, 2nd edn (London: Royal Historical Society, 1964). 'Detailed record for Harley 1808', *British Library Online Catalogue of Illuminated Manuscripts*, www.bl.uk/catalogues/illuminatedmanuscripts/record.asp?MSID=6645&CollID=8&NStart=1808 [accessed 1 November 2019].

[197] E. Towry Whyte, 'Brougham Castle, Westmorland', *Archaeologia*, 58 (1903), 359–82. (p. 359).

[198] Whyte, 'Brougham Castle', p. 360; Henry Summerson et al., *Brougham Castle, Cumbria: A Survey and Documentary History* (Kendal: Cumberland and Westmorland Antiquarian and Archaeological Society, 1998), p. 10, p. 117, p. 173.

[199] 'The Awntyrs off Arthure', in *Sir Gawain: Eleven Romances and Tales*, ed. Thomas Hahn, TEAMS (Kalamazoo, MI: Medieval Institute Publications, 1995), l. 475; see also Susan Kelly, 'Place-Names in the *Awntyrs off Arthure*', *Literary Onomastic*

the circular Neolithic henge next to Eamont Bridge.²⁰⁰ The 'castle of the giants' probably refers to Brougham Castle (here 'Borowham'), although Mayburgh henge is another possibility, located immediately 'next to' (iuxta) Arthur's Round Table. It is not unusual for henges to be attributed to giants: Stonehenge is perhaps the most famous example, which according to Geoffrey of Monmouth was brought to Mount Killaurus in Ireland from Africa by giants, who used it for medicinal bathing before Merlin relocated it to Salisbury Plain.²⁰¹ One fourteenth-century *Brut* manuscript appears to show Merlin in the temporary form of a giant re-assembling Stonehenge.²⁰² Perhaps on account of Brougham Castle's proximity to the henge at Mayburgh, there is some evidence of giant folklore surrounding the castle which could explain how it came to be known as the castle of the giants to the author of the Harley manuscript gloss. When William Stukeley visited in 1725, he reported the local belief that Lancelot, who resided at Mayborough, had slain a giant named 'Turquin' who lived in Brougham Castle.²⁰³ Stukeley also noted in the churchyard at Penrith a 'monument of a giant' whom he supposed to be 'a knight of king Arthur'.²⁰⁴ The visibility of the ancient remains at Brougham, Mayburgh, and Plompton Voreda may explain why these sites became associated with giants, as well as their incorporation into Arthurian lore.

Circular earthworks were so valued as evidence of Round Table sites that at least one may have been created artificially during the later Middle Ages, perhaps for political purposes.²⁰⁵ In the fourteenth and fifteenth

---

Studies, 6 (1979), 1–38 (p. 5); Andrew R. Walkling, 'The Problem of "Rondolesette Halle" in the *Awntyrs off Arthure*', *Studies in Philology*, 100.2 (2003), 105–22 (pp. 106–08). On Plumpton Voreda, see F. Haverfield, 'Voreda, the Roman Fort at Plumpton Wall', *Transactions of the Cumberland and Westmorland Antiquarian and Archaeological Society*, 13.2 (1913), 177–99.

²⁰⁰ R. Bradley and P. Topping, 'The Penrith Henges: A Survey by the Royal Commission of the Historical Monument of England', *Proceedings of the Prehistoric Society*, 60 (1992), 285-324; Stephen Leach, 'King Arthur's Round Table Revisited: A Review of Two Rival Interpretations of a Henge Monument Near Penrith, in Cumbria', *The Antiquaries Journal*, 99 (2019), 417–34.

²⁰¹ Geoffrey of Monmouth, *The History of the Kings of Britain*, 8.128–129, pp. 171–73.

²⁰² British Library, Egerton MS 3028, f. 30r.

²⁰³ William Stukeley, *Itinerarium Curiosum* [...], 2 vols (London: Baker and Leigh, 1776), II, p. 45. This may be an echo of Lancelot's battle with Sir Tarquin in Malory's *Morte Darthur*; see Malory, *Works*, 1.262–68. The story is also preserved in ballad form, quoted in Shakespeare's Henry IV part II and printed in Thomas Percy, *Reliques of Ancient English Poetry*, 3 vols (London: J. Dodsley, 1765), I, pp. 181–86 (sigs. N3r–N5v).

²⁰⁴ Stukeley, *Itinerarium* (1776), II, p. 46.

²⁰⁵ To the example at Stirling given in this paragraph, we can also add the 'Round Table, 200 feet across' (Rotundam tabulam in circumferencis latitudinis .CC.

centuries, Stirling was touted as a castle built by Arthur and the site of the Round Table, claims which may have had their origin in David II's propaganda campaigns.[206] The King's Knot, a very distinctive earthwork in Stirling Castle's grounds, was likely constructed in the seventeenth century atop an existing circular enclosure.[207] For decades, scholars wondered whether this was a similar case to Dunnideer and Brougham, whereby the King's Knot was purposely built on top of an ancient earthwork. Whilst this remains a possibility, other scholars have argued that the earlier earthwork was not, in fact, ancient. Instead, they suggest, it may have been built under David II in the 1360s, made to resemble an ancient earthwork and perhaps used for jousting tournaments.[208] When Edward I held his Arthurian-themed tournament at Winchester in 1290, he, too, ordered the construction of an earthwork just outside the city, perhaps to serve as a tournament arena during the festivities.[209] The older earthen structure at Stirling may be the feature referred to in John Barbour's 1377 Scots poem *The Bruce* as the 'Round Table'.[210] Stirling Castle was certainly being marketed to visitors as an Arthurian site under the reign of David II, and perhaps later than this, when Hardyng himself visited during his tour of Scotland. When Jean Froissart visited Stirling on royal business in 1365 he was told by the king that Stirling was previously known as 'Sinaudon', a common toponym in Arthurian romance (a corrupted version of Snowdon), and that the Round Table was held there in Arthur's day.[211] A

---

pedem), built at Windsor Castle by Edward III c. 1343–44 as a meeting place for the Order of the Garter. The building's remnants were observed by fifteenth-century visitor William Worcester (*Itineraries*, pp. 438–39). See also Munby et al. (eds), *Edward III's Round Table at Windsor: The House of the Round Table and the Windsor Festival of 1344*.

[206] R. S. Loomis, 'From Segontium to Sinadon: The Legends of a Cité Gaste', *Speculum*, 22.4 (1947), 520–33; M. A. Penman, *David II, 1329–1327* (London: Tuckwell, 2004), pp. 340–43; Stevenson, 'Chivalry, British Sovereignty and Dynastic Politics', p. 611.

[207] Stephen Digney and Richard Jones, 'Recent Investigations at the King's Knot Stirling', *The Forth Naturalist and Historian*, 36 (2013), 129–48.

[208] Digney and Jones, 'Recent Investigations'; E. M. R. Ditmas, 'The Round Table at Stirling', *Bulletins Bibliographiques de La Société Internationale Arthurienne*, 26 (1974), 188–96; Dean, *Arthur of England*, p. 42; Katie Stevenson, *Chivalry and Knighthood in Scotland, 1424–1513* (Woodbridge: Boydell, 2006), pp. 72–75.

[209] Rouse, *The Idea of Anglo-Saxon England*, p. 151.

[210] 'And benewth the castell went thai sone, | Rycht by the Round Table away; | And fine the Park enweround thai.' John Barbour, *The Bruce*, ed. A. A. M. Duncan, revised edn (Edinburgh: Canongate, 2007), pp. 498–99, 13.378–380.

[211] Jean Froissart, *Oeuvres*, ed. Kervyn de Lettendove, 25 vols (Brussels: Devaux, 1867–1877), II, p. 313; Stevenson, *Chivalry and Knighthood in Scotland, 1424–1513*, p. 72; Loomis, 'Scotland and the Arthurian Legend', pp. 15–16; A. H. Diverres, 'Jean Froissart's Journey to Scotland', *Forum for Modern Language Studies*, 1.1 (1965), 54–63 (pp. 34–63).

Burgundian visitor in 1421 was also told that the castle had been built by Arthur;[212] and William Worcester, visiting several decades later c. 1477–78, wrote that 'King Arthur kept the Round Table in Stirling Castle, otherwise called "Snowdonwest" castle' (Rex Arthurus custodiebat le Roundtable in Castro de Styrlyng aliter Snowdonwest castell).[213]

After the late fifteenth century when William Worcester visited Stirling, itinerant antiquarians were happy to accommodate other places as the sites of Arthur's court (or the Round Table), particularly ancient monuments like many of the examples in Hardyng's list. In the Round Table section of the *Assertio*, Leland follows his peer John Stow by stating that he considers Cadbury ('Camalat'), Caerleon, and Winchester to be the sites of Arthur's courts.[214] He does not include other locations that 'sum caulle' the Round Table which appear in his *Itinerary*, such as Bwrdd Arthur in Denbighshire and Arthur's Round Table (or Castle) near Penrith.[215] Leland's observation of Arthur's Hall and Guenevere's chamber at Dover also suggest that, like Hardyng, Leland saw Dover as one of Arthur's residences.[216] Geoffrey's *Historia* and its derivatives portrayed Arthur's court as plural, and this provided a model for chroniclers and site visitors from the fifteenth century, such as John Hardyng and John Leland, to locate Arthur's courts wherever they saw fit.

What, if any, conclusions can we draw from such a multiplicity of places? Aside from Arthurian locations that were already well-attested in Geoffrey of Monmouth's *Historia*, there seem to have been an ideal set of circumstances in which an Arthurian place association could arise. Most obviously, the existence of a location in pre-existing Arthurian historiography or romance might play a role: a battle site such as Dover could readily be upgraded to an actual court of Arthur (in the case of Dover, perhaps, by the judicious custodians of the castle hoping to impress visitors). Another factor to consider is the political or strategic significance of a particular location, such as the caves below Nottingham Castle or the city of Winchester. The caves also evince a third factor which can cause a place to become associated with Arthur: the presence of visible and striking topographies or ancient remains. Such sites prompted a tangible and imaginative connection with the past in the Middle Ages

---

[212] Stevenson, 'Chivalry, British Sovereignty and Dynastic Politics', p. 611.
[213] Worcester, *Itineraries*, pp. 6–7.
[214] Leland, *Assertio*, sig. D2r–v.
[215] Leland, *Itineraries*, III, p. 99.
[216] Leland, *Itineraries*, IV, p. 55; V, p. 48.

136 LOCAL PLACE AND THE ARTHURIAN TRADITION

and into the early modern period and functioned as 'mnemonic bridges'. Arthurian enthusiasts of the fifteenth century therefore had a multiplicity of places they could choose from when cultivating a geography for Arthur. The following chapter evaluates the ways in which one Arthurian writer of the early sixteenth century – John Leland – manipulated this wealth of material in order to sculpt a particular region for Arthur in the West Country.

Map 1. Map of Arthurian locations discussed in Chapter 2.

3
The best of the west: John Leland's West Country Arthur

Although many factors could contribute to the Arthurianisation of specific places – from local pride to ancient earthworks to scribal misreading – one factor in particular encouraged the gradual emergence of Arthurian *regions*; that is, a gathering of several Arthurian localities. We might consider this factor in terms of the 'contagious' sacred geographies proposed by Laura Varnam, or else as a kind of logic of geographical association.[1] Often, this logic involved reasoning on the basis of a location's proximity to existing Arthurian places presumed to be genuine. Assuming Geoffrey's *Historia* to be reliable, how far would Arthur realistically have travelled in pursuit of Mordred from Winchester to Camlan? And might it make more sense for Gawain to buried in Dover, where he died, rather than Rhos in Wales? Arthurian settings could be more readily mapped over real-world places that were close to established Arthurian locations. One example is Pomparles bridge between Street and Glastonbury, located within walking distance of Arthur's alleged grave at Glastonbury Abbey. It is recorded by its romance name, the 'Poynt Perilous' (that is, the perilous bridge) in the Middle English romance *Lybeaus Desconus* (c. 1375–1400). The author of *Lybeaus Desconus* translates the geographies of their French romance source, moving Arthur's court from Caerleon to Glastonbury, and the nearby 'gue perilleus' (perilous ford) to the 'poynt perillous'.[2] Pomparles bridge is also recorded as 'pons periculosus' in a local charter of 1344 and a 1415 hundred court roll.[3] Later in the sixteenth century, the antiquarian and poet John Leland (c.

---

[1] See above at p. 15. Conversely, Dorsey Armstrong and Kenneth Hodges discuss the '(il)logics of space' in Malory's *Morte Darthur*, a kind of logical spectrum ranging from unambiguous names (such as Winchester and Guildford) to more dubious geographies, including journeys which seem illogical in terms of their length or direction. Armstrong and Hodges, *Mapping Malory*, pp. 1–2.

[2] *Lybeaus Deconus*, ed. Eve Salisbury and James Weldon, TEAMS (Kalamazoo, MI: Medieval Institute Publications, 2013), ll. 198–200 (Lambeth Palace MS, Naples MS); ll. 300–312 (Lambeth Palace MS); ll. 310–21 (Naples MS); Robinson, *Two Glastonbury Legends*, pp. 25–26.

[3] James P. Carley, 'Arthur, Avalon, and the Bridge Perilous', in *Glastonbury Abbey: The Holy House at the Head of the Moors Adventurous* (Woodbridge: Boydell, 1988),

1503–52), the subject of this chapter, visited the Glastonbury area, and in his notes he recorded passing by 'Pontperlus, wher men fable that Arture caste in his swerd'.[4] Perhaps because of its dubious romance associations, the bridge did not make it into Leland's later published Arthurian text, a defence of Arthur's existence titled the *Assertio inclytissimi regis Arthurii regis Britanniae* [An assertion of the most famous Arthur, King of Britain] (1544). Yet other geographically logical sites put forward by Leland, such as Cadbury Castle, would go on to be fully incorporated into Arthur's geography even to the present day. These presumptive geographies were vital to the emergence of an Arthurian West Country region by the mid-sixteenth century, accruing incrementally around the one Arthurian site which remained largely uncontested: Glastonbury.

Yet not even Glastonbury, with its impressive material remains, would remain entirely uncontested for long. Polydore Vergil's infamous history of the English, *Anglica Historia* (written 1513, published 1534), stirred up a flurry of impassioned rebuttals, of which Leland's *Assertio* was but one, for its sceptical attitude towards Geoffrey of Monmouth's British History. For Leland, and indeed for his fellow Arthurian defenders whose works are discussed later in this book, Polydore's greatest insult was his perceived scepticism surrounding native Arthurian places. In fact, these assumptions are rarely borne out in Polydore's writing. A clear example of this is Polydore's comment on Glastonbury, Arthur's grave site and the jewel in the crown of Britain's Arthurian legends. On the subject of Arthur's tomb at the Abbey, Polydore remarked:

> a few years ago a magnificent tomb for Arthur was erected in the monastery of Glastonbury, that posterity might understand that he was worthy of all ornaments, since in Arthur's day that monastery had not yet been founded.
>
> (Abhinc item paucos annos positum fuit Arthuro in Glasconiensi coenobia sepulchrum opera magnificum, quo posteri intelligerent illum omnibus ornamentis dignum fuisse, quando Arthuri tempore coenobium illud nondum erat conditum)[5]

---

pp. 155–62 (pp. 164–65); John Morland, 'Pomparles, Glastonbury', *Proceedings of the Somerset Archaeological and Natural History Society*, 58 (1912), 53–59 (p. 57).

[4] R. S. Loomis, 'Arthurian Tradition and Folklore', *Folklore*, 69 (1958), 1–25; Aelred Watkin, 'The Glastonbury Legends', in *Glastonbury Abbey and the Arthurian Tradition*, pp. 13–28 (p. 22); Carley, 'Arthur, Avalon, and the Bridge Perilous', passim.

[5] Polydore Vergil, *Anglica Historia (1555): A Hypertext Critical Edition*, ed. and trans. Dana F. Sutton, The Philological Museum (Irvine, CA: University of California, 2005), www.philological.bham.ac.uk/polverg/ [accessed 1 September 2017], 3.13.

Here, Polydore's only explicit crime is to diverge from existing histories of the abbey, claiming (correctly) that the abbey had been founded later by King Ine and did not yet exist in Arthur's day.[6] This does not mean that Polydore considered Glastonbury to be unimportant as a religious site before the abbey's foundation. He agreed with the tradition that Joseph of Arimathea 'erected a small chapel' (parvulum sacellum condidisse) at Glastonbury, and an apostolic religious house could quite easily justify Arthur's burial there.[7] However, Polydore's critics interpreted his comments as a dismissal of Arthur's having been buried at Glastonbury altogether. If Arthurian places were the most powerful means of supporting belief in Arthur, and in turn the things that Arthur could represent, then anything perceived to be undermining them was a real problem.

A key strategy for Arthur's defenders in responding to Polydore was to consolidate Arthurian place claims, separating those that they saw to have some historic basis from those that they considered fabulistic. To consolidate means to solidify or strengthen something, or to combine multiple things into a coherent whole.[8] In the context of Arthurian places, this meant sorting the real claims from the fakes, before gathering together these disparate places into a coherent and realistic Arthurian region. Whilst those doing the consolidating may have been unaware of how their biases affected where they placed Arthur, consolidation itself seems to have been a conscious process. In the preface to *Britannia*, William Camden describes his project as an attempt to 'sift out the truth'.[9] Camden explains this consolidation more fully in the preface to the 1610 edition, remarking that 'some will blame me for that I have omitted this and that towne and Castle', and that he has aimed to 'seeke, rake out, and free from darkness such places as […] antique writers have specified and Time hath overcast with mist and darknesse by extinguishing, altering, and corrupting their old true names'.[10]

Camden's predecessor, John Leland, also engaged consciously in this

---

[6] Vergil, *Anglica Historia*, 4.32.
[7] Vergil, *Anglica Historia*, 2.7, 4.32.
[8] 'Consolidation, n.', *Oxford English Dictionary*, accessed online (Oxford University Press, December 2019), https://oed.com/view/Entry/39693 [accessed 3 February 2020].
[9] Camden, *Britain* (1610), preface (n.p.).
[10] Ibid. In Ralph Brooke's invective against Camden, Camden was accused of mangling his genealogies in a 'mist of coniectures'. Ralph Brooke, *A discouerie of diuers errors published in print in the much commended Britannia, 1594* (London: J. Windet, 1599), STC (2nd edn) 3834.5, sig. C4v. Camden seems to be implicitly responding to Brooke here: the errors catalogued in *A discouerie* are organised by marginal rubrics which consist largely of noble family names, towns, and castles.

process of Arthurian place consolidation. A product of John Colet's new programme of humanistic education at St Paul's School, Leland went on to study at Christ's College Cambridge and in Paris, where he spent his time composing poetry and perusing the manuscript collections.[11] Leland later worked as chaplain to Henry VIII, and is often referred to as 'the king's antiquary' for the work he carried out surveying the holdings of monastic libraries on behalf of the crown.[12] His notes survive as his *Collectanea* and *Itinerary*, both published long after his death by Thomas Hearne (1715; 1710). His best-known Arthurian compositions were defensive in nature, written in response to Polydore. Initially, Leland's response took the form of an unpublished tract written in 1536.[13] This was eventually developed into a dedicated defence of Arthur, the aforementioned *Assertio* (1544), with an English translation by Richard Robinson following in 1582.

Leland's writings are extremely important witnesses to localised Arthurian tradition in the sixteenth century: several pieces of folklore are first attested in Leland's *Itineraries*, and his archival work in monastic and institutional libraries has preserved important Arthurian associations that would otherwise have been lost to the Reformation. Leland's written materials are also illuminating because they are preserved in various stages. Leland's *Itinerary* and *Collectanea* were not published in his lifetime, and as such the Arthurian geographies Leland observed and recorded on his journeys can be productively compared with what he decided to include in his published rebuttal to Polydore. From these materials, it is possible to piece together a sense of how Leland pruned and cultivated his sense of Arthur's geography. In his Arthurian defence, Leland laments that 'obscure and absurd reports haue crept into the historie of *Arthure*: which thing is of the curious sorte easily found faulte with' (quandoquidem manifestissime constat, obscura, & absurda inrepsisse in Arturii historiam: id quod a curiosis facile deprehenditur).[14] The implication is that some Arthurian places are genuine and some are not, and that it is the responsibility of those defending Arthur and

---

[11] Ágnes Juhász-Ormsby and James P. Carley, 'Survey of Henrician Humanism', in *The Oxford History of Classical Reception in English Literature*, ed. Rita Copeland (Oxford: Oxford University Press, 2016), I, pp. 583–605 (p. 516).

[12] John Leland, 'New Year's Gift', in John Bale, *The laboryouse journey and serche of Johan Leylande* (London: S. Mierdman, 1549), STC (2nd edn) 15445, sigs E1v–E2r. For an overview of Leland's life and achievements, see James P. Carley, 'John Leland', *The Oxford Dictionary of National Biography*, www.oxforddnb.com/view/10.1093/ref:odnb/9780198614128.001.0001/odnb-9780198614128-e-16416 [accessed 7 December 2018].

[13] Carley, 'Polydore Vergil and John Leland on King Arthur', p. 87.

[14] Leland, *Learned*, sig. D2r-v; Leland, *Assertio*, sig. C2r.

the British History to distinguish between them. For Leland, this meant pulling Arthur's geography away from North Wales and Scotland and into South-West England and the southern Welsh Marches, with Glastonbury Abbey – the least contested of Arthur's sites – at the centre. Presenting Arthur in these regional terms – that is, with a centre and periphery – meant that Leland could render Arthur's geography more logically, and therefore realistically: nobody, not even Arthur, could be in all places at once.

This need to express Arthur in terms of his central and peripheral places reflects wider changes in the political, cultural, and social fabric of late fifteenth-century and early sixteenth-century England: the move towards state centralisation, the imperial aspirations of Henry VIII, and anti-foreign popular sentiment in the years before and after England's split from Rome.[15] At the same time, innovations in cartography driven by the rediscovery of Ptolemy's geographical writings transformed the spatial imaginary from the fifteenth century, creating a sense of 'modern map consciousness' where space was previously written, read, and imagined through narrative forms such as the itinerary.[16] As a result, it became necessary for those wanting to strengthen the impression of Arthur's reality to assert a spatially believable geography for Arthur. The present chapter focuses on how John Leland, an individual well-versed in the arts of both itinerary and cartography, attempted to define an Arthurian region in the West Country.

Blurring the edges

Leland's effort to cultivate a West Country Arthur was partly an attempt to shore up the existing Arthurian geography of Geoffrey of Monmouth's *Historia regum Britanniae*. It is important to remember Leland's avowed indebtedness to Geoffrey, the original subject of Leland's defence before its rededication to Arthur.[17] Leland's Arthurian defence started life as an attempt to recentre Geoffrey's *Historia* as authentic Arthurian history in the wake of alternatives put forward by authors like Hector Boece and

---

[15] Steven G. Ellis, *Tudor Frontiers and Noble Power: The Making of the British State* (Oxford: Oxford University Press, 1995), pp. 251–71; David Michael Loades, *Power in Tudor England* (New York: Palgrave Macmillan, 1997), pp. 1–9.
[16] Rouse, 'Walking (between) the Lines', passim; Robert Allen Rouse, 'What Lies Between?: Thinking Through Medieval Narrative Spatiality', in *Literary Cartographies: Spatiality, Representation, and Narrative*, ed. Robert T. Tally Jr (New York: Palgrave Macmillan, 2014), pp. 13–30 (p. 14).
[17] Leland, 'Codrus', passim.

Polydore Vergil.[18] Geoffrey's Arthurian narrative, centred around his native Monmouthshire, formed the geographical blueprint for Leland's work, and Leland maintained many of Geoffrey's key locations. Of course, a model emperor should also be connected with other wide-reaching territories: Geoffrey's Arthur lives and holds court in Paris, battles the Scots and Picts in Moray, and conquers as far as Iceland and Scandinavia.[19] Likewise, Leland is also keen to present Arthur as an imperial model for the benefit of his Tudor patron, dedicating a chapter of his Arthurian defence to Arthur's expeditions in France (*Learned* sigs D1r–D2r; *Assertio* sigs C1r–C2r), and another to Arthur's seal (*Learned* sigs D4r–E2v; *Assertio* sigs E4v–F3r), an artefact whose inscription proclaims Arthur 'emperor of the British, French, Germans, and Danes' (Patricius Arturius Britanniae, Galliae, Germaniae, Daciae imperator).[20] Henry VIII would go on to use the seal to stake claim to his own imperial title.[21]

For Leland's purposes, though, there were obvious problems with Arthur's distant exploits in the *Historia*. Arthur's battles abroad were not corroborated in continental textual traditions, as Polydore Vergil observed; and some of the least believable events of the *Historia*, such as the defeat of the Mont St Michel giant, take place during Arthur's time away.[22] Aside from these issues, there was something else wrong with

---

[18] See Warren, *History on the Edge*, especially pp. 25–60.

[19] Geoffrey of Monmouth, *The History of the Kings of Britain*, 9.155, pp. 206–09 (Paris); 9.149, pp. 200–01 (Moray); 9.153, pp. 204–05 (Iceland); 9.154–155, pp. 204–06 (Norway and Denmark).

[20] On Leland's imperial vision, see Mottram, '"An Empire of Itself". Leland explains the title 'Patricius' as an aspect of romanitas, citing Tacitus and Livy: 'Romulus created 100 Senators, which were called Patres or Fathers, by reason of their progeny'. Leland, *Learned*, sigs F1v–F2r; Leland, *Assertio* sig. E1v. Arthur is referred to in these terms in other texts: John of London's lamentation after the death of Edward I draws comparisons between the deceased king and 'Patricius Arthur, King of the Orkneys, Norway, Aquitaine, Scotland and Ireland' (Patricius Arthurus rex Orcadas, Norwagicas, Aquitannicas, Scoticas et Hybernicas [...]). Johannis de Londonia, 'Commendatio Lamentabilis in Transitu Magni Regis Edwardi', in *Chronicles of the Reigns of Edward I and Edward II*, ed. William Stubbs, 2 vols (London: Rolls Series, 1882–83), I, pp. 1–22 (p. 15). Cited in Juliet Vale, 'Arthur in English Society', in *The Arthur of the English*, pp. 185–96 (p. 189).

[21] In a letter to Emperor Charles V, the English ambassador Eustace Chapuys reported that Thomas Howard, duke of Norfolk, avowed 'that the King [Henry VIII] had a right of empire in his kingdom, and recognised no superior; [...] [that] he had lately shown the ambassadors of France the seal or the tomb of King Arthur [...] in which there was a writing, which I would see in a bill of parchment [...] This bill contained only the words "Patricius Arcturus, Brittanniae, Galliae, Germaniae, Daciae Imperator". I said I was sorry he was not also called Emperor of Asia.' Cited in Mottram, '"An Empire of Itself"', p. 156. See also J. J. Scarisbrick, *Henry VIII* (Berkeley, CA: University of California Press, 1968), p. 272.

[22] Geoffrey of Monmouth, *History of the Kings of Britain*, 10.165, pp. 224–28.

these aspects of Geoffrey's *Historia*. Whilst Geoffrey's broad geographical spread was helpful in painting Arthur as a glorious conqueror, it was less helpful in transforming Arthur from a figure of romance and myth to a realistic historical king. Many of Arthur's battles in the *Historia* take place in locations far from home, even when we ignore Arthur's overseas conquests. A significant portion of these distant battles have their origins in Geoffrey's source texts, such as the *Historia Brittonum* attributed to Nennius, whose list of Arthurian battles paints a picture of a mythic pan-British military leader.[23] Although Leland was keen to acknowledge the reach of Arthur's dominion – particularly given the imperial ambitions of Henry VIII, his intended patron – his primary concern was to make Arthur seem more real in the wake of Polydore's attack. To achieve this, Leland would need to create a more sharply defined sense of Arthur's native places.

In other words, the issue with Geoffrey's text was not so much the breadth of Arthur's geography itself, but rather a problem of perspective. The *Historia* exhibits a kind of flatness in which there is no great intensity of focus in either time or place. Battles which take place in far-flung locations are given the same attention as domestic episodes (if not more); and distant histories from Britain's foundation are just as clear as more recent events. The reader finds themselves in all places and all times at once. These qualities in the *Historia* are perhaps a result of the text's quasi-historical epic mode. In his study of realism in Western literature, Erich Auerbach observed a similar two-dimensionality in Homer's *Odyssey*:

> One might think that the many interpolations, the frequent moving back and forth, would create a sort of perspective in time and place; but the Homeric style never gives any such impression [...] any such subjectivistic-perspectivistic procedure, creating a foreground and background, resulting in the present lying open to the depth of the past, is entirely foreign to the Homeric style; the Homeric style knows only a foreground, only a uniformly illuminated, uniformly objective present.[24]

This flatness of space and time exposes a problem for Leland and other Arthurian defenders; it disrupts not only the perception of Arthur's

---

[23] Higham, *Myth-Making and History*, p. 148. Geoffrey Ashe also views Nennius' 'far-flung geography' as a vision of Arthur as a 'national rather than a local leader'. Geoffrey Ashe, 'Origins', in *An Arthurian Handbook*, ed. Geoffrey Ashe and Norris J. Lacy, 2nd edn (New York: Garland, 1997), pp. 1–56 (p. 15).

[24] Edward Auerbach, *Mimesis: The Representation of Reality in Western Literature*, ed. Edward Said, trans. Willard R. Trask (Princeton, NJ: Princeton University Press, 2013), p. 7.

reality (space), but also any imaginative and emotional experiences of the past (time). In Geoffrey's text, Arthur's exploits abroad are given equal emphasis in terms of page space and detail to his activities closer to home. For example, Arthur's series of battles against the Emperor Lucius, which take place near Autun, take up almost the entirety of book ten, over a third of Geoffrey's Arthurian material. The clashes with Lucius are described in minute detail: their locations, the topography of the battlefields, battle strategies, death lists, and rousing speeches. In contrast, details of Arthur's home territories in the *Historia* are not full enough. These gaps were noticed and exploited by the authors of romance: Ad Putter has observed that the empty peaceful periods in which time passes in the *Historia* (nine years of peace, twelve years of peace) were filled by romance writers who set quests and activity during these intervals.[25]

Clearly, the details in Geoffrey's text were not in entirely the right place. This caused some problems for Arthur's early modern defenders. As I have already argued, familiarity was crucial to the impression of locality, and an absence of any detail regarding Arthur's domestic places in Geoffrey's text made it very difficult to encourage a sense of connection to Arthur and the locations associated with him. In the Middle Ages, geographical horizons were far closer at hand than they are today, and for many people textual encounters with places any further than their immediate locality, even the nearest market town, might have been their only access to such locations.[26] In fact, as Robert Rouse has argued within the context of romance narratives, a text could actively participate in the construction of its audience's world because 'each new story [...] adds to this accretive and palimpsestic model of geographical knowledge [...] romance not only articulates the world of its audience, but also actively participates in its construction in a vicariously experiential manner'.[27] For Arthur's defenders, then, it was essential to give more textual attention to whatever they considered to be Arthur's native places in order to resituate their readers at the heart of Arthur's world, rather than at its edges.

Leland's response to these concerns was to add definition and depth where they were lacking, bringing out details at the centre of Arthur's realm whilst blurring its distant peripheries. In doing so, Leland recovered the reader's perspective, positioning them as a direct witness to Arthur's existence in the places where he was said to have lived. The reader is

---

[25] Ad Putter, 'Finding Time for Romance: Mediaeval Arthurian Literary History', *Medium Aevum*, 63 (1994), 1–12.

[26] Robert Rouse, 'Walking (between) the Lines', pp. 136–39; Cooper, *The English Romance in Time*, p. 68, cited in Rouse, 'Walking (between) the Lines', p. 138.

[27] Rouse, 'Walking (between) the Lines', p. 139.

invited along with Leland to view Arthur's places and artefacts directly; we might think of this perspective as a kind of 'participatory or empathic realism'.[28] This is not only a recuperative and imaginative perspective, but also a realistic perspective: the reader can make out details that are close at hand, whilst those further away retreat into the background. If we compare Leland's approach with the world of painting, an art form in which Leland was unusually interested, we might consider the kinds of techniques which render a painting realistic.[29] Although Leland was working in the medium of words rather than paint, he might be compared with innovators in the visual arts from the fifteenth century. Painters such as Brunelleschi and Masaccio, and later Leonardo, Michelangelo, and Van Eyck revolutionised the use of perspective and depth of focus in painting to achieve more realistic results than the flatter productions of their predecessors, and to place their viewers directly in the middle of the painted scene. Similarly, to achieve a sense of depth in his representation of Arthur Leland employed two complementary strategies. On one hand, he drew attention away from the edges of Arthur's empire, dramatically reducing the geographic and narrative detail of Arthur's exploits in distant places. At the same time, he enhanced the granularity of Arthurian sites at home, clustered at the centre of his realm. In so doing, Leland created a realistic Arthurian perspective in place of the flatter, more scattered geographies of epic myth, or the vague landscapes of Arthurian romance. One might be forgiven for thinking that this shift in focus can be attributed to Leland's increased familiarity with Arthur's native places – he had, after all, conducted extensive itineraries across England and Wales in search of historical texts in the years preceding the *Assertio*'s composition. Leland had also spent considerable time in France, however, where he also carried out archival work, and the considerable range of foreign sources ('externi') appended to the beginning of the *Assertio* demonstrate Leland's confident grasp of continental Arthurian representation. Moreover, Leland worked to shift Arthur away from

---

[28] Alastair Fowler, 'Perspective and Realism in the Renaissance', in *A Companion to Tudor Literature*, ed. Kent Cartwright (Oxford: Blackwell, 2010), pp. 339–49.

[29] Leland composed a series of encomiastic poems in praise of the merits of contemporary painting, singling out particular works of art and artists, including Holbein. See L. Bradner, 'Some Unpublished Poems by John Leland', *Publications of the Modern Langauge Association*, 71 (1956), 827–36; Susan Foister, 'Humanism and Art in the Early Tudor Period: John Leland's Poetic Praise of Painting', in *Reassessing Tudor Humanism*, ed. Jonathan Woolfson (London: Palgrave Macmillan, 2002), pp. 129–50; David Rundle, 'Instaurations: John Leland and the Process of the Renaissance in England', Centre for Medieval and Early Modern Studies Seminar (University of Kent, 3 February 2022).

not only foreign places, but also the familiar places that did not quite fit with the West Country geography Leland had in mind for him. One such example is Caerleon, a location that Leland would have known personally as well as textually thanks to the visit he made during his 1538 itinerary through Wales.

The strategy of increasing focus on Arthur's domestic exploits is not original to Leland. Earlier texts, such as the group of chronicles known as the Prose *Brut*, also took pains to emphasise Arthur's home rule. By the fifteenth century, the Prose *Brut* had become one of the most popular forms of English historiography.[30] This popularity may be due to the Prose *Brut*'s availability in the vernacular, or perhaps because the text went further than Geoffrey's *Historia* by continuing beyond the reign of Cadwallader to include the lives of the most recent English kings, connecting the mythic past with the present in a way that Geoffrey's text did not.[31] The Prose *Brut* presents Arthur as a realistic governor, distinct from the heroic warrior of the chronicle tradition or the king of romance:

> Geoffrey celebrates Arthur's military prowess and focuses on his victories over the Saxons, his conquests on the Continent, and his campaign against the Roman Empire, and Wace follows his lead, while expanding the scenes of battle [...] The Oldest Version [of the Prose *Brut*], however, makes Arthur a governor first, a warrior second, and a lover not at all [...] distant from the romance tradition but also distinct from his chronicle antecedents[.][32]

---

[30] Tamar Drukker observes that fifteenth-century households in possession of more than one book would more than likely own a *Brut* text of some sort. Tamar Drukker, 'I Read Therefore I Write: Readers' Marginalia in Some Brut Manuscripts', in *Readers and Writers of the Prose Brut*, ed. William Marx and Raluca Radulescu (Lampeter: Trivium, 2006), pp. 97–130 (p. 97).

[31] Late medieval and early modern annotators of Prose *Brut* texts seem to have focused the bulk of their marginalia around ancient Britain, but this is not to say that they were uninterested in more recent history; indeed, it seems to be the later parts of the *Brut* (particularly the Latin *Brut*) where the most variation can be found. The sheer number of Prose *Brut* continuations speak to the importance of a sense of continuity in the mind of its copyists and their readers between distant past and immediate present. On marginalia in the Prose *Brut*, see Drukker, 'I Read Therefore I Write', passim; and for annotations in Caxton's print edition, *Cronicles of Englond* (1480), see Julia Crick, *The Historia Regum Britannie of Geoffrey of Monmouth: Dissemination and Reception in the Later Middle Ages* (Cambridge: D. S. Brewer, 1991), p. 23. On the variants in the latter parts of the Prose *Brut*, see Lister M. Matheson, *The Prose Brut: The Development of a Middle English Chronicle* (Tempe, AZ: Arizona Centre for Medieval and Renaissance Studies, 1998), pp. 79–171.

[32] Julia Marvin, *The Construction of Vernacular History in the Anglo-Norman Prose Brut Chronicle: The Manuscript Culture of Late Medieval England* (York: York Medieval Press, 2017), p. 94.

Julia Marvin has shown how Arthur is thus adapted from Wace's *Brut* for the Prose *Brut* chronicles: play-by-play details of Arthur's battles abroad are dramatically condensed, and although Arthur's status as a wide-conquering emperor is by no means revoked the focus is clearly on his domestic governance.[33] In the Prose *Brut* chronicles, Arthur's native places are sharpened by their expression through the characters who populate Arthur's domestic world. For example, the guest list at Arthur's inaugural crowning is much abridged in the Prose *Brut* as compared to Geoffrey's or Wace's texts, with a greater emphasis on native nobles rather than guests from faraway places: earls from 'Bath, Chester, Salisbury, Canterbury, Chichester, and Leicester', for example.[34] Arthur's bloody siege against the Scots in Wace is entirely removed in the Prose *Brut*, and many of Arthur's continental expeditions are drastically reduced.[35] The overall effect is of an effective domestic leader, a strong administrator capable of maintaining positive relationships with his native earls and barons. This was, of course, an ideal model for the kings of the later Middle Ages, a time characterised in England by civil unrest between the king and the gentry.[36] It may be that Leland's decision to locate Arthur's centre in the West Country was a response to contemporary political concerns. Somerset sat at a double boundary point: between Wales and England, but also between Cornwall and the rest of England. When Leland was writing his *Assertio*, the Cornish Rebellion had taken place within living memory, and Cornwall was still continuing to cause serious problems for the Tudors in the period between 1537 and 1549.[37] At the same time, the relationship between England and Wales remained under negotiation; Leland was drafting the *Assertio* in the uncertain period after the passing of the first Act of Union (1536) but before the second (1542), when much still remained to be finalised regarding Wales' annexation.[38] Leland was working, we must remember, as the king's agent in terms of his antiquarian endeavours, and by situating Arthur's heartland in South-West England Leland could construct a fantasy of control over these difficult crown territories.

---

[33] Marvin, *The Construction*, p. 99.
[34] Marvin, *The Construction*, pp. 99–100.
[35] Marvin, *The Construction*, p. 53.
[36] Raluca Radulescu, '"Talkyng of cronycles of kinges and of other polycyez': Fifteenth-Century Miscellanies, the Brut and the Readership of Le Morte Darthur', *Arthurian Literature*, 18 (2001), 125–42 (pp. 136–38).
[37] Anthony Fletcher and Diarmaid MacCulloch, *Tudor Rebellions*, 5th edn (London: Routledge, 2014), p. 23.
[38] Williams, *Renewal and Reformation*, p. 269.

Much like the Prose *Brut*, Leland's *Assertio* is focused more on Arthur as a domestic ruler than an international conqueror. Even in the chapter titled 'King Arthur's expedition towards the French' (Arturij in Gallos expeditio), Leland is more concerned with Arthur's merciful acts and peaceful governance than recounting the minute details of the French battles themselves.[39] In contrast, once Arthur reaches the shores of Kent to pursue Mordred Leland reverts to more detailed battle descriptions.[40] Despite the chapter title, Leland cannot help but allow Arthur's home affairs (and places) to creep in: he lists the seven home provinces that Mordred treacherously gifts to Cerdic (Sussex, Surrey, Berkshire, Wiltshire, Dorset, Devon, and Cornwall), although his source Geoffrey of Monmouth instead states that Mordred gifted Cheldric lands between the River Humber and Scotland, and in Kent.[41] Arthur's nine years of rule in France are compressed into less than a sentence, and should the reader wish to learn more about Arthur's French wars Leland coyly refers them to two obscure continental sources (the chronicles of St Bénigne of Dijon and Valerius Anselmus Ryd, respectively).[42] Similarly, specifics of place

---

[39] Leland, *Assertio*, sigs C1r–2r; Leland, *Learned*, sigs D1r–2r. The French expeditions chapter is structured as follows: a description of Arthur's impending betrayal by Mordred and Guenevere; an extremely brief reference to Arthur subduing the governors of France ('debellatis regulis', *Assertio* sig. C1r; *Learned* sig. D1r); the story of Arthur's quest to Mont St Michel to rescue Hoel's niece from a bloody giant ('greate and horrible Monster' [monstrum ingens horrendumque], *Learned* sig. D1r; *Assertio* sig. C1r); a brief reference to other texts where readers might read more about Arthur's wars in France (discussed below); acknowledgement of Arthur's peaceful nine-year reign in France; Mordred's invitation of Cedric and betrayal of Arthur; and an abrupt conclusion alluding to Arthur's seal and its imperial description, with the statement that 'there are (besides these) many things, which I with a certaine zeale doe omit altogether' (multa praeterea sunt, quae ego studio plane quodam omitto) (*Learned* sig. D2r; *Assertio* sig. C2r). At this point Leland refers the reader to Valerius Anselmus Ryd for more information on Arthur's vanquishment of thirty kingdoms.

[40] The description of the battle at Richborough is extensive, taking up several folios. It gives details of the battle action itself. Arthur even delivers a speech which Leland includes word-for-word. Leland, *Learned*, sigs F4r–v (folio missing in the original edition; see 'Learned Assertion', in *The Famous Historie of Chinon of England*, pp. 45–47); Leland, *Assertio*, sigs E3r–E4r.

[41] Leland, *Assertio*, sig. C1v; Leland, *Learned*, sig. D1v; Geoffrey of Monmouth, *The History of the Kings of Britain*, 11.177, pp. 248–51.

[42] Leland cites 'Valerius' as his source for two pieces of information: (1) That Arthur lived at the same time as the Byzantine emperor 'Zenonis' (Leland, *Assertio*, sig. I4r; Leland, *Learned*, sig. L1r); and (2) that Arthur conquered thirty kingdoms (Leland, *Assertio*, sig. C2r; Leland, *Learned*, sig. D2r). In Ussher's *Britannicarum Ecclesiarum* 'Valerius Anselmus Ryd' is cited for the same information concerning Arthur (see James Ussher, 'Britannicarum Ecclesiarum', in *The Whole Works*, V, p. 233; p. 534). Valerius Anselmus Ryd (or Valerius Anshelm, 1475–1546/47) was a Swiss chronicler and author of a Latin world chronicle, written c. 1510 and printed

as well as time are removed from Arthur's period spent in France. No French Arthurian locations are named at all; regarding the abduction of Hoel's niece, the singular reference to the contemporary toponym 'Mont St Michel' in the earlier 'Codrus' text is removed in the later *Assertio*.[43]

There is another chapter in the *Assertio* in which Leland refers to Arthur's extensive imperial reach: the discussion of Arthur's seal ('Sigillum Arturij').[44] The seal hung at St Edward the Confessor's shrine in Westminster Abbey during the fifteenth and sixteenth centuries, but it no longer survives.[45] As well as Leland's detailed description of the artefact, John Rastell reports having seen it (though he argues that it

---

in 1540 as *Catalogus annorum et principum geminus ab homine condito* (Bern, 1550). This text must be Leland's 'Valerius' source: Ryd describes Arthur as living at the same time as 'Zenonis imperium' and also describes Arthur's thirty battles ('triginta bello'); Valerius Anselmus Ryd, *Catalogus annorum et principum geminus* [...] (Bern, 1550), sig. M4r. Leland has entered 'Valerius' into his list of foreign sources (Externi) in the material preceding the *Assertio*. On Valerius, see Friedrich Wilhelm Bautz, 'Anshelm, Valerius', in *Biographisch-Bibliographisches Kirchenlexikon*, ed. Friedrich Wilhelm Bautz (Hamm: Bautz, 1975), I, col. 188. The 'Dijon chronicle' ('cronica divionensis') may refer to the chronicle of St Bénigne, Dijon. How Leland encountered this chronicle is a mystery. The only extant witness which Leland could have seen is an eleventh-century manuscript (thirteen later copies exist, the earliest of which was made by Claude-Énoch Virey in the late 1500s, after Leland had died). However, the monks of St Bénigne probably showed the chronicle to erudite abbey visitors, including Jean de Gagny, who pursued a nationwide search for patristic texts in France's libraries almost two decades before Leland undertook a similar project in England. Leland may have met Jean during his time at the University of Paris in the 1520s, and indeed Jean might have told Leland about the St Bénigne chronicle: Jean describes manuscripts that he had collected from St Bénigne, and also a work credited to 'Claudius Marius Victor' found at l'Ile Barbe, Lyons: this may be the identity of Leland's 'Claudius, a Frenchman' (see below at pp. 196–97; and also James P. Carley, '"Many Good Autors": Two of John Leland's Manuscripts and the Cambridge Connexion', *Transactions of the Cambridge Bibliographical Society*, 15.3 [2014], 27–56). The St Bénigne chronicle as we receive it makes no mention of Arthur, so it is possible that Leland saw an interpolated version, misread a source citing the chronicle, heard a garbled or exaggerated story about it from Jean or someone else, or perhaps meant a different Dijon chronicle altogether. See *Chronique de l'abbaye de Saint-Bénigne de Dijon*, ed. Joseph Garnier and Louis-Émile Bougad (Dijon: Darantiere, 1875), pp. vii–viii; R. W. Hunt, 'The Need for a Guide to the Editors of Patristic Texts in the Sixteenth Century', *Studia Patristica*, 17.1 (1982), 365–71 (p. 368); James P. Carley and Pierre Petitmengin, 'Pre-Conquest Manuscripts From Malmesbury Abbey and John Leland's Letter to Beatus Rhenanus Concerning a Lost Copy of Tertullian's Works', *Anglo-Saxon England*, 33.1978 (2004), 195–223, https://doi.org/10.1017/S0263675104000079; Juhász-Ormsby and Carley, 'Survey of Henrician Humanism', pp. 516–17.

[43] Leland, 'Codrus', p. 7.
[44] Leland, *Assertio*, sigs D4r–E2v; Leland, *Learned*, sigs E4v–F3v.
[45] For further discussion of Arthur's seal, see E. M. R. Ditmas, 'The Cult of Arthurian Relics', pp. 29–30; Rouse and Rushton, *The Medieval Quest for Arthur*, pp. 98–100.

is inauthentic).[46] The earliest known mention of the seal is in Caxton's preface to the *Morte Darthur*, which prompted Leland's visit.[47] In the early seventeenth century Brian Twyne pointed to the different imperial claims listed on the seal as evidence to dispute the authenticity of a charter attributed to Arthur held at the University of Cambridge.[48] The seal's inscription proclaims Arthur emperor of the Britons, French, Germans, and Dacians [Danes], and we might expect the seal chapter of Leland's *Assertio* to discuss Arthur's conquests in these distant places. But aside from a brief explanation of the obsolete toponym 'Dacia' Leland does not dwell on these conquered lands, nor on any details about Arthur's battles in these places. This is partly due to an absence of such details in Leland's prized ancient textual sources (a gap which, unusually, Leland freely acknowledges).[49] Instead, Leland uses the same strategies here as he does in his French expeditions chapter, responding to his (imagined) reader's questions about these foreign conquests by pointing them to two foreign sources: 'Volteranus in his 3. booke of *Geography* affirmeth, that part of Fraunce, of Norway, and of Dacia was conquered by Arthure. Also Tritemius writeth on this manner' (Volateranus libro 3, Geographiae adfirmat Arturium partem Galliae Noruuegiae, & Daciae ab Arturio deuictam fuisse. Trittemius quoque haec scribit).[50] 'Volteranus' refers to Raphael Maffei's *Geographia* (1506); and 'Tritemius' indicates Johannes Trithemius' abridged chronicle of the Franks.[51] Both 'Volateranus' and

---

[46] Rastell, *The Pastyme of the People*, sig. C3r.
[47] Malory, *Works*, p. xiv.
[48] Rouse and Rushton, *The Medieval Quest for Arthur*, p. 87, pp. 98–100.
[49] 'It now remaineth (that being put in minde of the inscription of his seale) concerning Germanie & Denmarcke I should speake somewhat. But here the authoritie of auncient historiographers (while I would proceede to so honest a purpose) doth not minister vnto me (according as my desire is to write) sufficient matter in this poynte.' (Superest vt inscription sigilli admonitus de Germania, & Dacia aliquid loquar. Sed hic expeditum me ad tam honestum munus historiographorum veterum autoritas non satis ex voto scripturienti mihi materiam subministrat.) Leland, *Assertio*, sig. E2r; Leland, *Learned*, sig. F3r.
[50] Leland, *Learned*, sig. F2v; Leland, *Assertio*, sig. E2v.
[51] Maffei often published under some version of the name 'Volateranus'. Leland cites extracts from Maffei's *Geographia* directly in the chapter on Arthur's Round Table (Leland, *Assertio*, sig. D2v; Leland, *Learned*, sig. E2v); the information Leland cites corresponds with Raphael Maffei, *Commentariorum urbanorum XXXXIII libri* [...] (Lyon: Sebastianus Gryphius, 1552), 3.73. As for Johannes Trithemius, Leland specifies elsewhere in the *Assertio* that he is using Trithemius' 'abridgement of Cronicles' (in Compendio annalium) as his source (Leland, *Learned*, sig. M2r; Leland, *Assertio*, sig. K4v). This must be Trithemius' abridged history of the Franks (1515), in which Arthur's victories over the 'Scots, Irish, and Orcadians' (Scotos Hibernicos & Orchadas) and his subjugation of the kings of 'Dacia and

'Tritemius' are listed in the 'foreign' (externi) section of Leland's source table, omitted in error in the first edition of the *Assertio* but added subsequently in the printer's errata, which demonstrates how important these foreign sources were to Leland's defence.[52] By making only vague references to Arthur's distant exploits, and by referring his reader to foreign-authored texts, Leland renders the distant edges of Arthur's world less distinct, allowing them to act as a foil to Arthur's more emphatically articulated home places.

Sharpening the centre

In contrast, Leland articulates the sites at the centre of his imagined Arthurian realm through the physicality of the seal itself. Rather than elaborating on the distant places implied in the seal's description, Leland instead describes his visit to Westminster and his eyewitness experience there of the seal and its environment around Edward's tomb.[53] At this point, Leland proceeds to speculate on the earlier history that he imagines for the seal at Glastonbury. He envisions that the Glastonbury monks, on witnessing the crumbling of their archival holdings all around them, may have sought to preserve the seal for posterity by transferring it to Westminster where it could be better protected:

> Surely if a man might lawefully by any coniectures gather and set downe the trueth in writing, I would not thinke[54] that such a seale had beene translated from Glastenburie [...] By meanes whereof also it might come to passe, that the parchment being eaten out with little wormes, and meathes[55] by long tract of time, so famous a monument of antiquitie being founde [at Glastonbury], he deliuered the same to the Monasterie of first fame, there to be kept safe, and to be seene for euer of the nobylitie in all posterities.[56]

> (Certe si fas esset coniecturis vllis collineare verum, tantum non crederem, sigillum a Glessoburgo translatum fuisse [...] Vnde & fieri quidem potuit, vt ex esa membrana a blattis, & tineis longo temporis cursu, repertum tam illustre antiquitatis monumentum,

---

Norway' (reges Daciae, Norwegiaeque) are mentioned: see Johannes Trithemius, *Compendium sive Breviarum* (Mainz: Schöffer, 1515), sigs G1v–G2r.

[52] The errata are printed in John Leland, 'Assertio inclytissimi', in *The Famous Historie of Chinon of England*, p. 151.
[53] Leland, *Learned*, sigs E4v–F1r; Leland, *Assertio*, sigs D4r–E1r.
[54] Robinson's translation here renders the sense unclear – we might instead translate this as a rhetorical 'would he not think?'
[55] Moths.
[56] Leland, *Learned*, sig. F2r.

monasterio primi nominis conseruandum, & a nobilitate perpetuo videndum tradiderit).⁵⁷

Thus, Leland provides detail for Arthur's home territories and their associated artefacts even while discussing Arthur's distant imperial conquests, reinforcing the sense of "here at home" and "over there" and shoring up a realistic perspective of Arthur's realm. Although the seal was housed at Westminster, and there is no evidence of it having ever been at Glastonbury, Leland creates the impression that this must have been its origin. The seal is therefore used in support of Leland's project to create a realistic West Country geography for Arthur.

Elsewhere in the *Assertio* Leland describes Arthur's court, the centre of Arthur's world. He also shifts this centre. In perhaps the biggest departure from Geoffrey's *Historia*, Leland moves Arthur's court from Caerleon to Cadbury Castle in Somerset, identifying it as Camelot. Although Geoffrey's Arthur holds court at several other places (including Paris and perhaps London), Caerleon stands out in the *Historia* for both the quantity and detail of its Arthurian episodes. Geoffrey sets Arthur's festal crowning and plenary court in Caerleon, and it is also the place where key discussions between Arthur and his counsellors take place. In the *Historia*, then, Caerleon is unquestionably the heart of Arthur's realm. In Leland's writings, however, Caerleon's representation is dramatically different, though not completely altered: this would undermine Leland's secondary aim to defend Geoffrey's work from attack. Surprisingly, Leland does not record anything about Caerleon's Arthurian associations in his *Itineraries*.⁵⁸ In the earliest draft of his response to Polydore, Leland mentions Caerleon (briefly) as the place where Arthur lived and to which the archbishopric was transferred from Llandaff, information that he may have taken from the *Life* of St Dubricius.⁵⁹ In the *Assertio*, however, Leland downplays Caerleon's connections to Arthur. Caerleon is mentioned in the list of Arthur's battles but is not described in detail.⁶⁰ The *Assertio*'s

---

⁵⁷ Leland, *Assertio*, sig. E1r.
⁵⁸ Leland, *Itineraries*, III, pp. 13–14, p. 44.
⁵⁹ John Leland, 'Codrus', pp. 6–7. Llandaff was claimed to have been founded by St Dubricius, archbishop of Caerleon according to Geoffrey (see Brooke, 'The Archbishops', pp. 202–03). This claim does not appear in Geoffrey's *Historia*, but it does feature in the *Life of St Dubricius*, contained in the Book of Llandaff. Leland refers to the *Life* in the *Assertio* (Leland, *Learned*, sig. C3v; Leland, *Assertio*, sig. B3r), and in *De uiris illustribus* Leland states that he learned of Dubricius' Bardsey death in 'the annals of the church of Llandaff' (ex annalibus Tauanae ecclesiae). Leland, *De uiris illustribus*, I, pp. 82–83. Presumably, Leland learned about this text from his friend John Prise; see below at pp. 181–82.
⁶⁰ Leland, *Learned*, sig. C3v; Leland, *Assertio*, sig. B3r.

most sustained description of Caerleon does not describe it as Arthur's court at all, but as a centre of learning, a 'Learned Quier of Ecclesiastical persons' (mystarum chorum eruditum) founded by Arthur, which Leland compares to his alma mater, Cambridge.[61] Instead of Arthur, this passage connects Caerleon with other people – St Amphibalus and the martyrs Julius and Aaron.[62] Leland describes Arthur's coronation by Dubricius at Caerleon; but he also refers, immediately afterward, to an alternative crowning location, Winchester, put forward by Thomas Gray in his *Scalacronica* (c. 1363).[63] In the chapter describing Arthur's piety, Leland reports claims made by those living in Menevia (St Davids) that St Dubricius' Episcopal See was translated there from Caerleon at Arthur's behest, a claim which first appears in the writings of Gerald of Wales.[64]

It should be noted, at this point, that Leland's translator Richard Robinson took Leland's de-Arthurianisation of Caerleon even further by mistranslating certain places in Wales and placing them in South-West England. In chapters 5 and 17 of *A Learned Assertion*, the text refers to the city of the legions at 'Isca [...] the most noble Cytie of Deuonia', but this is a mistranslation by Robinson. Leland's original Latin in fact reads 'Isca Demetarum': Isca in the land of the *Demetia* – that is, in South Wales.[65] If we were to take Robinson's translation at face value, we might assume that Leland erases the Welsh Caerleon altogether by locating the city of the legions at Exeter in Devon, when in fact such errors are Robinson's own doing (perhaps intentionally).

In the Round Table chapter, the shifting of Arthur's headquarters from Caerleon to Cadbury is made most explicit. Leland cannot help but mention that Arthur especially held his Round Table in Caerleon 'which place he notably esteemed of' (quem locum insigniter coluit); but this Caerleon court is not described in detail, and instead Leland progresses

---

[61] Leland, *Learned*, sig. D4v–E1r; Leland, *Assertio*, sig. C4v. Leland claims to have taken this information from John Rous, who is known to have composed a now-lost text on the history of Britain's academic institutions (including 'Caerlleon'), extracts of which were copied by Leland (*Itineraries*, II, pp. 167–68). This reflects a wider tradition of an Arthurian foundation myth at Cambridge, on which see Alfred Hiatt, 'Forgery at the University of Cambridge', *New Medieval Literatures*, 3 (1999), 95–118; Ad Putter, 'King Arthur at Oxbridge: Nicholas Cantelupe, Geoffrey of Monmouth, and Cambridge's Arthurian Foundation Myth', *Medium Aevum*, 72.1 (2003), 63–81.

[62] Leland, *Learned*, sig. D4v–E1r; Leland, *Assertio*, sig. C4v.

[63] Leland, *Learned*, sig. C2v; Leland, *Assertio*, sig. B2v. See above at p. 114.

[64] Leland, *Learned*, sig. E3r; Leland, *Assertio*, sig. D3r. See Putter, 'Gerald of Wales', pp. 101–02.

[65] Leland, *Learned*, sig. D4v–E1r; Leland, *Assertio*, sig. C4v (chapter 5); Leland, *Learned*, sig. M1v; Leland, *Assertio*, sig. K4r (chapter 17). In fact, Leland expands on the Caerleon/Isca etymology in Leland, *De uiris illustribus*, I, pp. 36–37.

immediately to his vivid account of 'Camalet', which he places at Cadbury hillfort in Somerset.[66] This description is an expansion of material first recorded in Leland's *Itinerary*, and a comparison of the two passages reveals Leland's rhetorical efforts to reposition Cadbury as the symbolic heart of Arthur's empire. In the *Itinerary*, Leland renames Cadbury 'Camallate', 'sumtyme a famose toun or castelle, apon a very torre or hille'.[67] Even in these unpublished notes Leland centres Cadbury's status as an ancient monument:

> in the upper parte of the coppe of the hille be 4. diches or trenches [...] in the very toppe of the hille above al the trenchis is *magna area* or *campus* [...] where yn diverse places men may se fundations and *rudera* of walles. There was much dusky blew stone that people of the villages thereby hath caryid away. [...] Much gold, sylver and coper of the Romaine coynes hath be found ther yn plouing: and likewise in the feldes in the rootes of this hille, with many other antique thinges, and especial by este. Ther was found *in hominum memoria* a horse shoe of sylver at Camallate. The people can telle nothing ther but that they have hard say that Arture much resortid to Camalat.[68]

While this original version is rich in archaeological detail, the tone is detached, the focus factual. Moreover, information regarding local Arthurian lore seems comparatively undeveloped (although, as I will explain in due course, the silver horseshoe may be significant). Leland claims that the local people 'can telle nothing' except for the assertion that 'Arture much resortid to Camalat', which, if the Camelot toponym was indeed current prior to Leland's visit, would hardly be surprising.[69] This bathetic statement is entirely altered in the later *Assertio*, in which Leland employs all his rhetorical skill to transport his reader to Cadbury and convince them of its Arthurian authenticity. As we will be dealing with this passage in some detail, I reproduce it in its entirety here, along with my own translation (Robinson's is unreliable at this point):

---

[66] Leland, *Learned*, sig. E2r; Leland, *Assertio*, sig. D2r.
[67] Leland, *Itineraries*, I, p. 151.
[68] Leland, *Itineraries*, I, p. 151.
[69] If this is the case then the 'Camelot' name was apparently not an official one. Leland claims that villages in the vicinity of the hillfort were known as 'Quene-Camallat' when there is no evidence of Queen Camel and West Camel, the villages in question, being referred to as 'Camelot', 'Camalat', or anything similar in any records pre-dating Leland. See Leslie Alcock, *'By South Cadbury is that Camelot...'*: *The Excavation of Cadbury Castle 1966–1970* (Aylesbury: Thames and Hudson, 1972), p. 12.

The [oral] tradition of the *Murotriges* living at the bottom of the Camelot hill proclaims, exalts, and sings the name of Arthur who once lived in the castle. It was once most magnificent and most strongly fortified, and it is situated at a most elevated prospect, where the hill rises up. Good lord, so many deep ditches are there here; so many ramparts emerge from the ground, singularly steep; and to end with few words, it seems to me to be a wonder of both craft and of nature.

'But cornfields stand where Troy once was, stabling in the city,

And flocks in the deep ditches; and in the turgid ramparts,

The badger and the cunning foxes set up their beds'

Such is the vicissitude of the human condition. On the one side Ilchester, the ancient city, and on the other Sherborne, the busy market town, gaze upon the loss here with sorrowful eyes brought to tears. Meanwhile, the inhabitants need only plough its surface after first sowing, and every single year they turn up golden, silver, and bronze Roman coins, the embossed faces [seeming] almost alive. The locals go looking for these coins, and I even received a few from them as a gift. Francis Lord Hastings Earl of Huntingdon, heir to the Piperells, Boterells and Hungerfords, an excellent ornament among all the noble youths of Britain and once one of my previous pupils, possesses the remains of Camelot together with its neighbouring estates.[70]

(Fama publica Murotrigum radices Camaletici montis incolentium praedicat, attollit, cantitat nomen Arturij incolae aliquando castri, quod idem olim, & magnificentissimum, & munitissimum, atque in aeditissima specula, vbi mons consurgit, situm est. Dij boni quantum hic profundissimarum fossarum; Quot hic egestae terrae valla; Quae demum praecipitia; Atque vt paucis finiam, videtur mihi quidem esse & artis & naturae miraculum.

'At seges est vbi Troia fuit stabula[n]tur in vrbe

Et fossis pecudes altis, valloque tumenti

Taxus, & astutae posuere cubilia Vulpes.'

Hanc calamitatem hinc Iscalis vrbs antiqua; hinc Clarus [F]ons frequens emporium moestis inspiciunt oculis, lachrimisque indulgent. Incolae interealoci solum aratro vertunt, & annis singulis numismata aurea, argentea, aerea Romanorum imagines tantum non viuas exprimentia, quaerentes inuenient, ex quibus & ego pauca

---

[70] Leland, *Learned*, E2r–E2v.

dono ab eis accepi. Franciscus Hastingius Comes Venantodunensis nobelium iuuenum regiae Britannicae ornamentum egregium, & alumnus olim in bonis literis meus Camaleti rudera una cum latifundiis viciniis, vtpote haeres Piperellorum, Botellorum, & Hungrefordorum possidet.)[71]

Unlike the blissfully unaware inhabitants indicated in the *Itineraries*, here a fully-fledged local Arthurian tradition is implied ('fama publica'), perhaps with sung or spoken components ('praedicat, attollit, cantitat'), though this may be a rhetorical flourish on Leland's part. Leland's broader project to add definition and depth to Arthur's geography is replicated here on a microscale. Everything in Leland's description is three-dimensional and hyperreal: the Roman visages push forth from the coins ('exprimentia'); the camp itself surges forth from the landscape ('consurgit'); and the wrinkled topography of the camp is exaggerated. Moreover, Leland makes archaeological embellishments that exaggerate his role as both eyewitness and "handwitness", much like the description of his handling of the seal at Westminster. No longer has he merely *heard* that archaeological fragments have been excavated at Cadbury; he now claims that he himself has personally been *given* such remains by the local inhabitants. There is a strong sense of the physical location at Cadbury itself – the deep ditches, the valleys – over which the vision of a lost Troy is projected. Leland focuses on the fragility of physical remains, and the tragedy of loss. Thus, when we compare this description with Leland's depiction of Arthur's mouldering seal transferred (imaginatively) from Glastonbury, a recurring approach begins to emerge, one which Leland applies most keenly to the places at the heart of his imagined Arthurian West Country.

Leland's decision here to amplify not only Cadbury's physical traces but also its Arthurian folklore may seem strange given his wider aim to rescue Arthur from fable and restore his status as a historic king. An absence of a textual tradition for Cadbury perhaps requires Leland to turn to oral tradition as a counterpart to the site's more impressive physical remains. Echoing the Virgilian tenor of the poetic excerpt, Leland collocates Cadbury's current residents with the fragments of its past, describing the 'remains of Camelot, together with its neighbouring estates' still held by the Hungerfords (Camaleti rudera una cum latifundijs vicinis). Leland may even be implying the presence of more recent properties built using ancient rubble, like the 'Briton brykes' of

[71] Leland, *Assertio*, sigs D2r–D2v.

Dover, Hereford, and Brougham.[72] Such a reading is borne out by the following lines in his *Itineraries*: 'In the very toppe of the hille [...] yn diverse places men may se fundations and *rudera* of walles. There was much dusky blew stone that people of the villages thereby hath caryid away.'[73] The people who live at the base of the camp are referred to by Leland as 'Murotriges', a nod to the ancient British tribe that was believed to have inhabited the area in Arthur's day.[74] The implication is that Cadbury's local people are literally living among Arthur's material history, and perhaps are even themselves a living remnant of Cadbury's ancient past, figured rhetorically as living witnesses. They represent what Pierre Nora has termed 'peasant culture, that quintessential repository of collective memory', and are – like the hillfort itself – *lieux de mémoire*.[75] By positioning the local people and Cadbury's archaeology as not just side-by-side but inextricably linked, Leland presents the site's Arthurian tradition as a fragment of authentic history that has become corrupted, much like the moth-eaten seal, the ploughed and overgrown hillfort, or the scribal transmission of Geoffrey's *Historia*.[76]

Before moving on to some other examples of south-western locations in Leland's work, it is perhaps worth considering *why* Leland might have opted for Cadbury as the centrepiece of his Arthurian world, and whether or not it is possible to draw any conclusions regarding the extent of the pre-existing Arthurian tradition at Cadbury. Leland's references to Arthurian Cadbury lore are the earliest known. Leslie Alcock assesses the evidence for an Arthurian tradition at Cadbury before Leland's day, concluding that there must have been such a tradition, though Alcock believes the Camelot attribution to be Leland's own invention.[77] Thomas

---

[72] See Harris, 'John Leland and the "Briton Brykes"', passim. Disingenuously, Robinson translates this as 'the ruined old cotages of Camelet, together with the large grounds adiacent', implying the remains of ancient cottages (rather than, as Leland suggests, newer constructions using old materials). Leland, *Learned*, sig. E2v.

[73] Leland, *Itineraries*, I, p. 151.

[74] Leland uses 'Murotriges', here and elsewhere, to refer to one of the two people groups native to Somerset: 'The Murotriges who with the Somurotriges were commonly called Somerset men' (Murotriges, qui & Somurotriges vulgo Somersetshire menne). Cited in Dai Morgan Evans, '"King Arthur" and Cadbury Castle, Somerset', *The Antiquaries Journal*, 86 (2006), 227–53 (pp. 235–36).

[75] Nora, 'Between Memory and History', p. 7; discussed above at pp. 24–25.

[76] Blaire Zeiders, 'Conjuring History: The Premodern Origins and Post-Truth Legacy of John Dee's Brytanici Imperii Limites', *Journal of Medieval and Early Modern Studies*, 49.2 (2019), 377–401 (pp. 383–84).

[77] Leslie Alcock argues that the Cadbury/Camelot identification was likely Leland's own invention, and has 'no confidence that he had received the identification from local informants'. Alcock, '*By South Cadbury*', pp. 12–13; and Alcock, 'Cadbury-

Jones has observed a reference made in 1552 by Elis Gruffydd to a legend of a sleeping Arthur 'under a hill near Glastonbury' (mewn googoff dan vryn garllaw Glasynbri). Jones argues that this is not Glastonbury Tor, as might be expected, but Cadbury camp (Alcock agrees).[78] Jones reaches this conclusion on the basis that there is no evidence of there ever having been a 'cave story at Glastonbury or anywhere in the immediate neighbourhood – unless we accept as such evidence the reference in Elis Gruffydd's comment'.[79]

Let us first consider the counterarguments to Jones' conclusion. In many respects, Glastonbury Tor is the more plausible candidate. The most obvious point is that, at twelve miles distant from Glastonbury, Cadbury Castle can hardly be said to be right next to ('garllaw') Glastonbury, though this error could be explained by Gruffydd's unfamiliarity with the area.[80] One of Jones' key reasons for dismissing the Tor is his claim that there is no Arthurian cave legend there.[81] Whilst there is no definitive evidence of a sleeping Arthur legend at Glastonbury Tor in Leland's day, neither is there any explicit iteration of a sleeping Arthur at Cadbury until at least the nineteenth century.[82] Jones uses the subject of his discussion (Gruffydd's statement) as his key evidence for a pre-existing Cadbury tradition, and there is thus a circularity to his argument. The truth is that folklorists are often forced to work with circumstantial scraps and shades of possibility: the earliest written record of an oral tradition is often produced long after it has been circulating in oral form (or forms). Jones' assertion that there has *never* been a sleeping Arthur tradition at Glastonbury Tor is not entirely true. In more recent times the notion of Arthur sleeping beneath the Tor is commonplace, particularly in the Glastonbury area; this is perhaps a result of nineteenth- and twentieth-century research concerning the Tor's associations with Avalon, Yniswitrin, and narratives about entrances to the underworld, along with the apex of New Age culture in Glastonbury that peaked within the

---

Camelot: A Fifteen-Year Perspective', *Proceedings of the British Academy*, 68 (1983), 355–88.

[78] NLW, MS 5276Dii, f. 342r; edited and translated in Thomas Jones, 'A Sixteenth Century Version of the Arthurian Cave Legend', in *Studies in Language and Literature in Honour of Margaret Schlauch*, ed. Mieczyslaw Brahmer, Stanislaw Helsztynski, and Julian Krzyzanowski (Warsaw: PWN, 1966), pp. 175–85 (p. 179); Alcock, '*By South Cadbury*', pp. 13–14. Jones' argument is disputed by Morgan Evans, '"King Arthur"', passim.

[79] Thomas Jones, 'A Sixteenth Century Version', p. 180.

[80] Morgan Evans, '"King Arthur"', p. 229.

[81] Jones, 'A Sixteenth Century Version', p. 180.

[82] Caitlin Green, *Arthuriana*, p. 246.

same time frame.[83] Moreover, whilst we cannot trace an early Arthurian cave legend at Glastonbury Tor, we can say with some certainty that the Tor has been associated with an entry to the otherworld for some time. As Jones himself acknowledges, the Welsh Life of St Collen, *Buchedd Collen* (c. 1536), describes '[f]ynydd Glassymbyri' (the mountain of Glastonbury – that is, the Tor) as a gateway to the otherworld, where the saint meets with the fairy king Gwyn ap Nudd.[84] Ceridwen Lloyd-Morgan suggests that the tradition represented in the *Buchedd Collen* may be what Gruffydd is referring to in his dismissive comments about the hill next to Glastonbury.[85] The references to Arthur dreaming in 'Morgan's chamber' atop the Tor in the fourteenth-century *Quedam narracio*, discussed in my first chapter, seem to indicate that the Tor has been identified with the Isle of Avalon since at least the early fourteenth century: Avalon was, after all, where Arthur was reportedly taken by Morgan to heal before making his return, and is frequently figured as an otherworld in its literary depictions.[86]

If there was a sleeping king/hollow hill legend at Glastonbury Tor it would not be in Leland's interest to draw attention to it, because this would not support the impression of a realistic historical Arthur; perhaps we see Leland downplay Pomparles Bridge in the *Assertio* for the same reason.[87] The Glastonbury Abbey grave site and the abbey's various holdings are the star witnesses around which Leland chose to build his evidence. So instead of Glastonbury Tor, Leland looked for something else: a realistic court for Arthur in the vicinity of his other West Country geographies, ideally one with a Glastonbury connection of some sort (imagined or otherwise). Cadbury may have proven useful for these purposes, both as an ancient hillfort but also perhaps as somewhere

---

[83] Marion Bowman, 'Procession and Possession', pp. 274–75; and 'Going with the Flow', p. 256. See also Stout, *Glastonbury Holy Thorn*, pp. 94–126.

[84] *Rhyddiaith Gymraeg, gyfrol I: detholion o lawysgrifau, 1488–1609*, ed. T. H. Parry-Williams (Cardiff: University of Wales Press, 1954), pp. 36–41 (p. 39). Jones, 'A Sixteenth Century Version', p. 180. See also Aelred Watkin, 'Last Glimpses of Glastonbury', *The Downside Review*, 67 (1949), 83–86, and 'The Glastonbury Legends', passim. The earliest textual witness of *Buchedd Collen* dates to 1536, though it might have been circulating orally for longer than this; see Xiezhen Zhao, 'Dreams in Medieval Welsh Literature' (unpublished doctoral thesis, University of Cardiff, 2021), p. 170; Ronald Hutton, 'The Making of the Early Modern British Fairy Tradition', *The Historical Journal*, 57.4 (2014), 1135–56 (p. 1145); Ceridwen Lloyd-Morgan, 'Glastonbury in Welsh Vernacular Tradition', in *Glastonbury Abbey and the Arthurian Tradition*, pp. 161–78 (p. 176).

[85] Lloyd-Morgan, 'Glastonbury in Welsh Vernacular Tradition', p. 174.

[86] See above at pp. 51–52. On Avalon as an otherworld, or portal to the otherworld, see Wade, *Fairies in Medieval Romance*, pp. 39–71; Byrne, *Otherworlds*, pp. 119–29.

[87] See above at pp. 137–38.

with a pre-existing Arthurian tradition that simply had not been recorded in writing yet.

Whilst we cannot really know whether or not Gruffydd's statement about Arthur sleeping under a hill refers to Cadbury, there is certainly some suggestive evidence in favour of a pre-existing Cadbury tradition that has come to light since Jones' time of writing (albeit circumstantial, but often this is all we have to work with when it comes to oral traditions). In 1278 and 1331, both Edward I and Edward III appear to have taken detours to Cadbury, staying for several nights at the site during an itinerary to visit Glastonbury Abbey.[88] No good reason can be found to account for these Cadbury visits, and Caroline Shenton suggests that they may indicate an Arthurian itinerary planned by both Edwards. If this is the case, it may be significant that Edward III's visit occurred over the Christmas period. Eventful Christmas feasts at Arthur's court are a staple in insular romance and historiography alike.[89] More intriguing still is the Cadbury legend, first recorded in the late nineteenth century but perhaps much older, of King Arthur's festive hunt, a ghostly ride from Cadbury Castle to Glastonbury on Christmas Eve, during which only the silver shoes of Arthur's horse are visible.[90] The Arthurian wild hunt is a widespread iteration of Arthurian folklore across Britain, recorded as early as 1211 by Gervase of Tilbury.[91] The route that the Cadbury riders were said to have taken – from Cadbury to Glastonbury – would have been the same route traced by Edward III on his visit in December 1331, and may represent the 'K. Arthur's hunting causey' recorded by Stukeley in the eighteenth century.[92] The detail of the horseshoes is strikingly reminiscent of the silver horseshoe Leland claims had been discovered at Cadbury in his *Itineraries* (although at least one of the nineteenth-century antiquarians who recorded the fuller version of the legend was familiar with Leland's Cadbury description, and the horseshoes may thus have been worked in later).[93] Moreover, the exchange of coins features in

---

[88] Caroline Shenton, 'Royal Interest in Glastonbury and Cadbury: Two Arthurian Itineraries, 1278–1331', *The English Historical Review*, 114.459 (1999), 1249–55.

[89] Some examples are given in Kenneth Hodges, 'How King Arthur Invented Christmas: Reimagining Arthur and Rome in Early Modern Scotland and England', *Arthuriana*, 29.3 (2019), 25–42 (pp. 28–29).

[90] H. H. Winwood, 'Summary of Proceedings for the Year 1889–99', *Proceedings of the Bath Natural History and Antiquarian Field Club*, 7 (1893), 67–95 (p. 82); Arthur J. Evans, 'The Rollright Stones and their Folklore', *Folklore*, 6.1 (1895), 6-51 (p. 25); Chambers, *Arthur of Britain*, pp. 184–85; Kingsley Palmer, *The Folklore of Somerset* (London: B. T. Batsford, 1976), p. 83.

[91] Chambers, *Arthur of Britain*, p. 228; cited in Green, *Arthuriana*, p. 248.

[92] Stukeley, *Itinerarium* (1724), p. 142.

[93] Winwood, 'Summary of Proceedings', p. 83.

some versions of the Arthur cave legend, such as a separate Arthurian cave story from Gloucestershire reported by Elis Gruffydd.[94] These coins are given to the witness by Arthur's servant in exchange for a horse, or recovered from the treasure trove that Arthur is guarding. In Gruffydd's Gloucestershire cave legend, the coins are described as 'coins of such a stamp that there was no one in that land who was able to read any of the legend' (kyuriw vath ar vwnai ac nad oedd neb ynn y wlad hono a vedrai ddarllain dim o'r ysgriven).[95] Ancient impressed coins also feature in Leland's description of Cadbury, and although this may be simple coincidence (ancient coins might well be expected to turn up at a hillfort, and Leland describes similar coins found at Camlan), it may represent an attempt by Leland to subtly draw together the threads of oral tradition and material history, maintaining the glamour of folklore traditions while grounding Arthur firmly in the realm of the historic and the material.

In sum, Leland's claim that an Arthurian tradition already existed at Cadbury when he visited could well be genuine. Nevertheless, it is clear, based on the differences between the *Itinerary* and the *Assertio*, that Leland sought to exaggerate Cadbury's Arthurian significance. The fact that Leland chose to not only record the tradition but to amplify it, placing it at the heart of his Arthurian defence, demonstrates the site's twofold strategic value: to draw out a realistic Arthurian geography in Somerset; but also to show that local lore that has remained rooted to a place, however fabulistic or defective, can sometimes be supported by some kind of physical evidence. By invoking the site's archaeology and elevating it with poetry, Leland raised Cadbury from obscurity to create a new Arthurian monument: Cadbury would go on to dominate as the location of Camelot in the writing of Leland's contemporaries and inheritors, from John Stow to William Camden.

Selective scepticism

Camlan

Further evidence for Leland's preferential treatment of Cadbury (and other West Country places) lies in the inconsistency of his critical approach. Leland is often criticised for his credulity, particularly when it comes to Arthurian place names; but there is evidence in his work of a critical, even a sceptical, attitude towards such matters. However, Leland does not treat all his sources equally. Authors and places that undermine

---

[94] Jones, 'A Sixteenth Century Version', pp. 182–84.
[95] Text and translation from Jones, 'A Sixteenth Century Version', pp. 182–83.

his West Country vision of Arthur are met with increased scepticism, sometimes even hostility. When it comes to the South West, however, Leland's critical faculties are jettisoned. For example, there is no evidence of the Camelot toponym in the vicinity of Cadbury in any records predating Leland; yet he uses these toponyms without qualification.[96] Leland may have obtained these place names from the same local people that he claims had told him about Cadbury's Arthurian legends, and he does not appear to question their authenticity.

In comparison, Leland treats the Arthurian onomastics of the Scottish historiographer Hector Boece with the utmost disdain. Boece's *Historia gentis Scotorum* (1527), a reworking of Geoffrey's *Historia*, refigures aspects of Arthur's story in order to 'reshape' Arthurian narrative 'with a shift in the focus of the action north of the Humber River' and a diminishment of Galfridian Arthurian events from elsewhere.[97] Unlike Hardyng, Boece is not concerned with emphasising Arthur's control over Scotland, but rather with portraying the Scots and Picts in a more significant and powerful light than does Geoffrey of Monmouth. Controversially, Boece places Arthur's final battle with Mordred at Camlan on the banks of the Humber.[98] Though not named in the *Historia Brittonum*'s famous battle list, Camlan appears in the *Annales Cambriae* and other early texts.[99] Like the named battles in the *Historia Brittonum* list it does not represent a toponym that remained in use later in the Middle Ages. However, Geoffrey's *Historia* – which provides the template for Leland's Arthurian geography – specifies that Mordred fled to the River Camlan from Winchester.[100] Assuming Geoffrey of Monmouth's narrative to be correct, which Leland does, there would be no logic in Mordred fleeing from Winchester to Scotland.[101] Boece's Scottish Camlan is thus not only a major challenge to Leland's project to root Arthur firmly in a realistic West Country geography, but also to the Arthurian narrative established by Geoffrey. Unsurprisingly, Leland responds to Boece

---

[96] Alcock, '*By South Cadbury*', p. 12.
[97] Hanna, 'A "Scottish Monmouth"?', p. 107.
[98] Hanna, 'A "Scottish Monmouth"?', p. 115.
[99] Andrew Breeze, ''The Historical Arthur and Sixth-Century Scotland', *Northern History*, 52.2 (2015), 158–81 (p. 160).
[100] '[Modred] hurriedly took ship and fled to Cornwall. Arthur, greatly disheartened because Modred had escaped so often, pursued him there to the river Camblan, where his nephew was waiting.' ([Modred] remige fugae euectus uersus Cornubiam iter arripuit. Arturus autem, interna anxietate cruciatus quoniam tociens euasisset, confestim prosecutus est eum in praedictam patriam usque ad fluuiam Camblan, ubi ille aduentum eius expectabat.) Geoffrey of Monmouth, *History of the Kings of Britain*, 11.178, pp. 250–51.
[101] Leland, *Learned*, sig. G1r; Leland, *Assertio*, sigs E4v–F1r.

angrily, employing the same line of attack that he uses against Polydore Vergil, another individual that Leland deems guilty of uprooting Arthur from his authentic places. Leland accuses Boece of glorifying his 'owne country' ('patrios [...] agros', literally 'father land'):

> Hector Boethius the Scot, which (as his maner is) applieth all most famous facts of antiquity in Brittaine to the commendation of his owne country, beyond all meane & measure [...]
>
> (Hectore Boethio Scotto, qui pro more suo illustrissima quaeque in Britannia antiquitus facta praeter modum, & mensuram omnem in patrios deducit agros [...])[102]

Leland also derides Boece for his speculation regarding place names: '[Boece] boldly affirmeth that Arthure (with his last ensignes) fought it out not far from the great flowing riuer of Seuerne, which he barbarously calleth Humbar not knowing the circumstance of the phrase' (hic audacter pronunciat extremis Arturium depugnasse signis non procul ab Abro aestuario maximo, quod ille Humbrum barbare, ignota vocabuli notatione, appellat).[103]

In contrast, Leland does not apply the same scepticism to the Cornish location that he envisions for Camlan. He even admits his conjecture, stating:

> This is my coniecture, both by reason of the situation of the place, & also for the name of the riuer Alaune, running hard by, yet not far dissonant (if a man behold it more thoroughly) from Camblan.
>
> (Haec mea est coniectura, tum propter loci situm, tum Alauni fluminis vicini nomen, non admodum, si quis penitius inspiciat, a Camblan dissonum)[104]

Leland only allows himself this conjecture after he has put forward some evidence regarding his proposed location for Camlan. As Camlan fits into Geoffrey's existing Arthurian narrative, unlike Cadbury/Camelot, Leland's description of Camlan is slotted into a narrative section describing Arthur's return from France, and his pursuit of Mordred to 'the mountayny soiles of Cornwale' (per montana Coriniae).[105] Camlan's south-western location is foregrounded: Leland traces Mordred's journey from 'the hauen of Tammeroth on the Sea coaste of Cornwaile' (Tamarinum [...] portum limitem Coriniae) to Camlan, 'by way that

---

[102] Leland, *Learned*, sig. G1r; Leland, *Assertio*, sig. E4v.
[103] Leland, *Learned*, sig. G1r; Leland, *Assertio*, sigs E4v–F1r.
[104] Leland, *Learned*, sig. G1r–v; Leland, *Assertio*, sig. E4v–F1r.
[105] Leland, *Learned*, sig. G1r; Leland, *Assertio*, sig. E4v.

leadeth to the banckes of Seuerne' (qua spectat littora Sabrinaica non longe dissita).[106] Leland also suggests a contemporary place with which Camlan might be associated, 'a fewe Myles aboue the Towne Athelstowe otherwise Padstowe' (paucis passuum millibus supra Athestouam alias Padestow).[107] Much like the description of Cadbury, Leland's material on Camlan emphasises the site's local geography and its archaeological discoveries, though the coins purportedly found here do not show 'Roman' faces, like those found at Cadbury, but rather 'ancient' ones:

> Many things no doubt euen in this our age are founde out of the same place by ploughmen & those that delue at the Riuer: such as are these quoynes which shewe the gouernments of auncient personages, ringes, fragments of harnesse & brazen ornaments for Bridles vnguilte, for trappers & also Saddles for Horses.
>
> (Multa quidem vel hac nostra aetate ibidem ab aratoribus, & fossoribus ad ripam eruuntur: qualia sunt numismata antiquorum imperium ostentatia, annuli, fragmenta armorum, & aenea ornamenta inaurata ex frenis, phalerisque, & ephippijs equorum.)[108]

This archaeological information is placed side-by-side with a description of the oral reports of the local Camlan inhabitants 'so many ages preserued' (tot saeculis [...] conseruata) proclaiming the area the site of a major battle.[109] Here, as with the Cadbury *Murotriges*, Leland rhetorically frames the Camlan inhabitants as timeless living witnesses. Whereas Leland faced an absence of textual witnesses in support of Cadbury, forcing him to rely on the site's material history and local oral tradition, Leland has recourse to textual sources in support of Camlan (Geoffrey's *Historia*). In this case, Leland can argue that the locals' ignorance of the Galfridian tradition makes them impartial witnesses, and therefore all the more believable:

> [The inhabitants] declareth that of olde time, there was made a notable garboile by fighting in that place, but in meante time the truth of the historie is vnknowne vnto the common sorte.
>
> ([...] praedicat hoc loco insignem olim pugnando stragem fuisse factam, sed historiae veritas interim ignota vulgo)[110]

Finally, Leland closes the chapter with a poetic extract, which echoes the descriptions of both the seal and of Cadbury by invoking a poignant sense

---

[106] Leland, *Learned*, sig. F4v; Leland, *Assertio*, sig. E4r.
[107] Leland, *Learned*, sig. G1v; Leland, *Assertio*, sig. F1r.
[108] Leland, *Learned*, sig. G1v; Leland, *Assertio*, sig. F1r.
[109] Leland, *Learned*, sig. G1v; Leland, *Assertio*, sig. F1r.
[110] Leland, *Learned*, sig. G1v; Leland, *Assertio*, sig. F1r.

of loss, this time of stories rather than physical monuments or objects: 'Who shall that bloodie broyle expresse or the dead corpses name? | Or who can iustly tell the toyles, with iust teares for the same?' (Quis cladem illius pugnae, quis funera fando | Explicet; aut possit lachrymis aequare labores).[111] This all feels very familiar. In this description of Camlan, Leland follows the same methodology that he employs for his descriptions of the seal and Cadbury, planting all three firmly in the West Country and encouraging his reader to imaginatively reconstruct them there.

Gawain's burial site

A further example of Leland's partiality occurs when he is faced with the predicament of two contradictory places claiming to be Gawain's burial site – Dover Castle and 'Rossia' (Rhos) in Pembrokeshire, Wales.[112] Though there are many examples where Leland favours a particular place over another throughout the *Assertio*, this one is worth mentioning because it shows how even Arthurian sites located elsewhere can still be pertinent to Leland's project to centre Arthur in the West Country. Although Dover is not in the West Country, Arthur's battle is said to have taken place there after his return from France according to Geoffrey's *Historia*, and it does not behove Leland to disagree with the key source for his Arthurian geography. Moreover, Dover falls along the route taken by Arthur from the continent to his final battle with Mordred in the West Country (Dover – Winchester – Cornwall), and therefore supports Leland's project. To back up his assertion that Gawain is buried in the chapel at Dover, Leland invokes local tradition, supplementing it with an appeal to textual authorities such as Thomas Gray's *Scalacronica*:

> And also the history of the celebrated Arthur, by which I mean the [versions] composed in the vernacular tongue and passed around, asserts that Gawain was buried in some chapel at Dover. Regardless of the quality of the book in question, this is not so entirely incorrect, as the book titled the *Scalacronicon* clearly refers to the same [information]: and the inhabitants of the Castle exhibit his almost Giant-like bones in that place as a wonder.

> (Historia quoque Arturij fabulosa quidem illa, quae vulgo vernacula lingua scripta cirumfertur, adfirmat Gallouinum Dori in sacello quodam sepultum fuisse. Qua parte qualiscunque liber, adeo non omnino fallit, vt idem Scalaechronicon aperte referat: & castella ni eius ossa pene Gigantea etiam nunc miraculi ostentent loco).[113]

---

[111] Leland, *Learned*, sig. G1v; Leland, *Assertio*, sig. F1r.
[112] Leland, *Learned*, sigs D2v–D4r; Leland, *Assertio*, sigs C2v–C4r.
[113] Leland, *Assertio*, sig. C3r; translation mine.

Here, Leland concludes that oral traditions such as those he had encountered at Dover do not always 'misseth [...] the marke altogether.'[114] This implication that local lore functions blindly – yet still meets its target somehow – further reinforces the idea that it represents a kind of ignorant honesty, and is somehow impartial and therefore believable (much like local reports at Camlan). Leland also pairs local oral tradition with local textual tradition, identifying a local work called the Dover *Annales* as an authority on Dover's ancient history, including its Arthurian connections.[115] Interestingly, Leland neglects to mention the discussion of Dover's Arthuriana in a more widely read text, William Caxton's preface to Malory's *Morte Darthur*.[116] This may be a symptom of Leland's efforts to de-romanticise Arthur's historical geography.

The other location mentioned by Leland as claiming to be Gawain's grave site – Rossia (Rhos) – first appears in William of Malmesbury's *Gesta regum Anglorum*.[117] William's other work, *De antiquitate*, was a key source for Leland's discussions about Glastonbury. William states that Gawain's grave was found in Rhos, Wales, 'on the sea-shore, fourteen feet long' (super oram maris, quattuordecim pedes longum).[118] However, Leland dismisses this discovery as the burial site of one of Britain's native giants, stating that there were no such giants in Gawain's day – presumably, following Geoffrey's *Historia*, because Britain's native giants had been eliminated following the arrival of Brutus and Corineus.[119] Notably, Leland does not mention this problem with regards to Gawain's 'gyantlike' (Gigantea) bones found at Dover, which Leland himself had

---

[114] Robinson's translation in Leland, *Learned*, sig. D4r.
[115] Leland describes the Dover *Annales* again later in the same chapter: 'the cronicles of the porte of Dorcester [sic], a worke sauouring of antiquitie [which] makes mention of Caradocus' (Annales Durensis portus opus antiquitatem redolens meminere Carodoci) (Leland, *Learned*, sig. E1v; Leland, *Assertio*, sig. D1r). In the earlier 'Codrus' draft, Leland seems to imply *two* Dover books, material found 'in the book of the Civil History [of Dover]' (in libro de Civili historia) and in a 'newly found little book on the antiquities of Dover' (nuper inveni historiolam de antiquitate Dovarensi) (Leland, 'Codrus', p. 7). Leland also describes these two books, along with his experience of being shown round Dover Castle by the castellans, in *De uiris illustribus*, I, pp. 316–17.
[116] Caxton, 'Preface' in Malory, *Works*, pp. xiii–xv.
[117] For a discussion of this early textual appearance of Gawain, see Rachel Bromwich, 'Gwalchmei m. Gwyar', in *Gawain: A Casebook*, ed. Keith Busby and Raymond H. Thompson (London: Routledge, 2006), pp. 95–102 (p. 97); and Raymond H. Thompson and Keith Busby, 'Introduction', in *Gawain: A Casebook*, pp. 2–3.
[118] William of Malmesbury, *Gesta Regum Anglorum*, ed. R. M. Thomson and M. Winterbottom, Oxford Medieval Texts (Oxford: Oxford University Press, 1999), I, 3.287, p. 521; and II, p. 261 n.
[119] Geoffrey of Monmouth, *History of the Kings of Britain*, 1.21, pp. 26–29. On the persistent belief in Britain's aboriginal giants in the sixteenth century, see Ferguson, *Utter Antiquity*, pp. 106–13.

seen.[120] Here too, as with Boece, Leland is exceedingly sceptical about place names. During his exposition on the alternative grave site for Gawain in Wales, Leland refers to a nearby 'Castle called Galouine' that was 'in times past [...] on the sea shoare', and whose traces, for Leland, were 'yet apparent'.[121] Scott Lloyd identifies this as Walwyn's Castle in Rhos, Pembrokeshire, an eleventh-century castle built within an Iron Age hillfort next to the Cleddau estuary.[122] When discussing this location, Leland employs a sceptical approach, remarking that it 'was not the habitation of the Gyant, as neyther perhappes of that *Galouine* of *Arthure*, but of some latter vycegerent bearing the same name' (Sed illud non fuit sedes gigantis, vt neque forsan Gallouini Arturiani, sed recentioris alicuius subreguli eiusdem nominis).[123] This recognition that Arthurian place names (and personal names) could be applied retrospectively to ancient sites is a principle that remains central to contemporary Arthurian onomastic studies. However, Leland is reluctant to practise the same scepticism regarding places within his south-western golden circle. Given his desire to create a realistic impression of Arthur's West Country territories, it seems odd that Leland would include the Rhos claim at all. Leland justifies a side-by-side comparison 'so the discreet Reader might even fully try as it were at a tutchstone the sincere brightnesse of true gold from that which is counterfeite' ([...] vt hinc prudens lector, veluti ad Lydium lapidem verifulgorem genuinum ab adulterino curiose excutiat).[124] Leland also sees fit to include the Rhos claim as told by William of Malmesbury so that it does not 'eyther weare out of memory or vtterly perish' (aut intercidat, aut emoriatur), suggesting a value

---

[120] Leland, *Learned*, sig. D3r; Leland, *Assertio*, sig. C3r.
[121] 'Neyther am I ignorant that in times past there was on the sea shoare a Castle called Galouine, touching which the Authour Meildunensis as aboue hath written: whose footesteppes are as yet apparent' (Nec me fugit castellum olim fuisse nomine Gallouinum in littore, de quo supra Meildunensis, cuius vel ad huc vestigia comparent). Robinson translates 'vestigia' as 'footsteps', but this might feasibly refer to the castle's foundations. Leland also describes the location in the *Itineraries*, III, pp. 62–63, in which he also refers to the 'vestigia of Martine Castel' (probably Castlemartin motte and bailey castle). Leland, *Learned*, sig. D4r; Leland, *Assertio*, sig. C4r.
[122] Lloyd, *Arthurian Place Names of Wales*, p. 24.
[123] Leland, *Learned*, sig. D4r; Leland, *Assertio*, sig. C4r. Lauran Toorians has suggested that Walwyn's Castle could be 'the place where the Welsh personal name Gwalchmai was equated with the Continental name Walewain, thus laying the foundation for the Gawain of Arthurian romance'. Lauran Toorians, 'Flemish in Wales', in *Languages in Britain and Ireland*, ed. Glanville Price (Oxford: Blackwell, 2000), pp. 184–86 (p. 185); L. Toorians, 'Wizo Flandrensis and the Flemish Settlement in Pembrokeshire', *Cambridge Medieval Celtic Studies*, 20 (1990), 99–118 (pp. 99–103).
[124] Leland, *Learned*, sig. D3v; Leland, *Assertio*, sig. C3v.

placed in Arthurian topographical stories as heritage objects (even if they are deemed to be inauthentic).[125]

By observing Leland's treatment of Arthurian places in the West Country (and the counter-claims that unseat them), a pattern of uneven treatment begins to emerge that exposes Leland's biases when it comes to locating Arthur. By focusing his rhetorical efforts on supporting Arthurian places in the West Country, Leland effectively maps out a space for Arthur in the South West that seems realistic and logical, a far cry from the breadth and flatness of Geoffrey's of Monmouth's epic geographies. Leland's strategy for reviving Arthur as a believable figure in the mind of his reader is to sharpen the definition of Arthur's home territories whilst defocusing the distant parts of Arthur's empire, and this has the effect of placing the reader's perspective at the heart of Arthur's realm. Although Leland's Arthuriana clearly leans into south-western England, some of the West Country locations that appear in the English translation of the *Assertio* – such as Somerton (for *Murotriges*) and Dorchester (for Dover) – can be attributed to the mistranslations of Leland's translator, Richard Robinson.[126] However, this is perhaps a testament to the effectiveness of Leland's Arthurian regionalisation: given the clustering of West Country Arthurian places in the *Assertio*, it would make sense for Robinson to continue in Leland's footsteps, seeking out south-western candidates for any uncertain toponyms that he found in Leland's Latin original. In terms of the broader arc of Arthur's localisation, Leland's Arthurianisation of Cadbury provided a major contribution to the gradual shifting of Arthur into the West Country. Arthurian Cadbury appears again in the works of Leland's inheritors, many of whom made extensive use of Leland's notes, and these south-western Arthurian places continued to gain prominence well into the seventeenth, eighteenth, and nineteenth centuries.

More importantly, for the purposes of this book's enquiry into Arthur's localisation, it is not just the locations of Leland's Arthurian places that had a lasting legacy, but also his strategy in describing them. The stylistic influence of Leland's Cadbury description can be clearly seen in descriptions of comparable places by later writers. A particularly clear example is Humphrey Llwyd's description of his experience at another impressive earthwork, 'Caradoc's city' (Caer Caradoc in Shropshire), which Llwyd describes in a passage remarkably similar to Leland's description of Cadbury:

---

[125] Leland, *Learned*, sig. D3v; Leland, *Assertio*, sig. C3r.
[126] Leland, *Learned*, sig. E2r; Leland, *Assertio*, sig. D3r.

And I remember very well that a few yeres agoe, when I was in the frontirs of Shropshyre [...] I chaunced to fall into the view of a place, exceedingly well fortified both by nature and art. The situation whereof was upon the toppe of an high hill, environed with a triple ditche of greate depth. [...] These thinges when I beheld, I understood by the inhabitants that this place was called *Caer Caradoc*, that is to say the cittie Caradoc, and that there have bin many fierce battayles fought there against a certaine kyng called Caradoc, who at last was vanquished and taken of his enemies. For our countrymen cal not only walled cities and townes, but also al maner places which are entrenched and walled up by the name *Caer* [...] Wherfore when I perceived that this place was within the confines of the Siluri and the Ordovici [...] and that it so agreed in al points with the description of Tacitus that nothing could be wanting, I dare boldly affirme that this is the very selfe same place in which Ostorius contended with Caractacus in bataile and vanquished him, from whence fliyng and puttyng himself in trust to the faith and credite of Cartimandua the queen of Brigantes, was betrayed.[127]

(Et ego in memoriam revoco me ante paucos annos [...] in Salopiae finibus [...] agerem, incidisse in locum quendam et natura et arte munitum. Situs eius erat in aediti montis plano, triplici vallo et fossis profundissimis circundatus. [...] Haec cum viderim, ab incolis accepi hunc locum *Caer Carador* nuncupari, id est urbem Caradocam, et illic maxima bella gesta fuisse adversus quendam regem Caradocum, qui tandem ab inimicis captus et victus erit. Nam nostrates non solum urbes muro circundatas, sed omnia loca vallo et fossis munita [...] hoc nomine appellitant. Cum igitur hunc locum in confinibus et Silurum et Ordovicum esse prospicerem [...], et etiam cum Taciti descriptione adamussim quadrare, ut nihil desiderari potuit, audacter affirmare ausim hunc esse ipsum locum in quo Ostorius praelio cum Carataco certavit et eum vicit, unde fugiens et in Cartimanduae Brigantum reginae fidem sese cedens deceptus est).

We know that Llwyd knew and respected Leland's work. Llwyd referred to him as 'our [friend] Leland' (nostro Lelando) throughout his writings, so it is perhaps unsurprising that he should have been influenced by Leland's approach.[128] Nor was Leland's impact restricted to the works of those writers willing to refer to him in such affectionate terms. As the

---

[127] Text and translation from Humphrey Llwyd, *Commentarioli Britannicae Descriptionis Fragmentum: A Hypertext Edition*, ed. Dana F. Sutton, The Philological Museum (Irvine, CA: University of California, 2005), www.philological.bham.ac.uk/llwyd/, §§39–40.

[128] Llwyd, *Commentarioli*, ed. Dana F. Sutton, §11, §28, §36, §113.

170 LOCAL PLACE AND THE ARTHURIAN TRADITION

final chapter of this book will make clear, William Camden's detailed descriptions of Arthurian places are also indebted, in both their content and their methodology, to Leland. Evidently, Leland's geographical choices, and his strategy in presenting them, had important ramifications for the broader development of Arthur's localisation.

Map 2. John Leland's Arthurian places.

4
Locating Arthur in England and Wales: John Leland, John Prise, and Elis Gruffydd

While Leland was busy centring Arthur in South-West England, his contemporaries were carving out their own Arthurian regions elsewhere.¹ This chapter examines the use of physical places as historical evidence in a series of texts written to defend the integrity of Arthur's history, especially as it appeared in Geoffrey of Monmouth's *Historia regum Britanniae*. For Arthur's defenders, Arthur's native places indicated a historical king that existed beneath the noise and disinformation of romance and fable, disinformation that was often framed as foreign interference.² However, Arthur's defenders located his native sites differently, often in relation to their own sense of identity.

In order to shed light on how Arthur's emplacement could differ depending on the perspectives of his defenders, three Arthurian writers and their works provide excellent case studies. These figures include John Leland, whose geographical machinations were discussed in the previous chapter; Leland's contemporary and friend John Prise; and the Welsh chronicler Elis Gruffydd. These texts were composed between c. 1540 and 1568, shortly after the passing of the first Act of Union and Britain's split from Rome. Each writer's sense of Arthur's geography, and also of the source of the attack on Arthur's credibility, was coloured by their own sense of selfhood. Leland and Prise saw themselves as British, and identified the hostile attack on Arthur as Italian and Roman in origin, personified in the controversial figure of the historian Polydore Vergil. Leland and Prise's rebuttals to Polydore formed a coordinated effort, for it is evident that the pair worked together to rebut Polydore. In contrast – and despite a 2018 press release dubbing him a 'British Tommy' – Elis

---

¹ An earlier version of this chapter was published as '"The Native Place of That Great Arthur": Foreignness and Nativity in Sixteenth-Century Defences of Arthur', *Arthurian Literature*, 35 (2020), 152–72.
² Barbara N. Sargent-Baur, 'Veraces Historiae aut Fallaces Fabulae?', in *Text and Intertext in Medieval Arthurian Literature*, ed. Norris J. Lacy (New York: Routledge, 1996), pp. 2–39; Julia Marvin, 'Arthur Authorized: The Prophecies of the Prose Brut Chronicle', *Arthurian Literature*, 22 (2005), 84–99 (p. 96).

Gruffydd clearly identified as Welsh, not British.[3] For him, the British were a discrete historic people group ending with Llywelyn. Gruffydd's ideas about foreign attacks on the British History are quite different to his contemporaries: he presents the English as the hostile party. As such, the majority of Gruffydd's references to Arthurian sites concern places in his native North Wales, and he often rejects English Arthurian places as unreliable.

The context: Arthur and the nation in the sixteenth century

This chapter's broad aim is to show how Leland, Prise, and Gruffydd each held a different sense of Arthurian geography depending on their own senses of native identity. The century in which these authors were writing was an especially tumultuous period in the British archipelago when it came to how different kinds of identity were imagined, and indeed there was a new sense of national identity on the rise by the end of the century that we might think of as neo-British (or proto-British, depending on perspective). The relevance of this context to our discussion about Arthurian places is clear: as N. J. Higham puts it, 'to be interested in Arthur is to be interested in how "Britishness", "Englishness", "Welshness", "Cornishness", "Scottishness" and so on, have been constructed and successively revalued, both in the present and in many pasts'.[4] The negotiation of such identities was at a critical point in the sixteenth-century British archipelago. In particular, the century saw a tumultuous shift in Anglo-Welsh relations. Henry Tudor had ascended the English throne in 1485. This was considered a great victory by Henry's supporters in Wales, some of whom saw him as the *Mab Darogan*, the 'son of prophecy' who would restore the whole of Britain to the Britons.[5] Henry was framed as not only the king to unite the houses of Lancaster and York, but also the states of Wales and England, claiming to descend from the royalty of both. John Prise wrote that:

---

[3] 'Chronicle written by a "British Tommy" awarded UN recognition', National Library of Wales, 9 June 2018, www.library.wales/information-for-press-and-media/press-releases/2018-press-releases/chronicle-written-by-a-british-tommy-awarded-united-nations-recognition/ [accessed 15 July 2019].

[4] Higham, *Myth-Making and History*, p. 6.

[5] Glanmor Williams, *Harri Tudur a Chymru* (Cardiff: University of Wales Press, 1985); Williams, *Renewal and Reformation*, pp. 212–30; David Rees, *The Son of Prophecy* (London: Black Raven Press, 1985), pp. 100–09; Philip Schwyzer, *Literature, Nationalism and Memory in Early Modern England and Wales* (Cambridge: Cambridge University Press, 2004), pp. 15–18.

Henry the Seventh [...] was indubitably descended from the royal stock of their [the Welsh's] own princes. Then they began to give their allegiance to a prince who was shared by both nations, and did so willingly, not from fear but from love.

(Henricum Septimum, qui ex eorum regali principum progenie haud dubie prognatus est. Atque inde non tam metu quam amore libenter communi vtriusque gentis principi parere coeperunt.)[6]

Henry's relationship with his Welsh supporters was, to some extent, mutually beneficial: after he took the throne many of the Welsh gentry flocked to London in the hope of taking offices close to the king, positions from which they had been barred since 1401 following the Glyndŵr uprising.[7] In the next century, the unification of England and Wales was realised in the Acts of Union of 1536 and 1542. The Acts 'incorporated, united and annexed' Wales to England, and on paper this meant extending to the literate Welsh gentry the same rights that their English counterparts enjoyed. Of course, in real terms this meant serious restrictions: any administrative and judicial proceedings had to be carried out in English, and any elected officials were required to 'use the English speech or language'.[8]

These political changes were supported by cultural developments as all eyes turned to the matter of Britain. Though the contemporary usage of the toponym Britain would not be brought into common parlance until the publication of William Camden's *Britannia* (1586), this evidently reflects gradual changes in how Britain was imagined over the course of the sixteenth century. Under the support of Henry VIII, John Leland sought to create an enormous topographical tabletop map of Britain, along with a 'Liber de Topographia Britanniae' (Book of British Topography), a British history titled 'De Antiquitate Britannica' (On British Antiquity), and three separate books on Britain's noble lineage,

---

[6] John Prise, *Historiae Britannicae Defensio / A Defence of the British History*, ed. and trans. Ceri Davies (Toronto: PIMS, 2015), pp. 160–61. Subsequent citations are from Davies' edition.

[7] *Calendar of Close Rolls: Henry IV, 1399–1402*, ed. A. E. Stamp (London: His Majesty's Stationery Office, 1927), I, March 1401, p. 328. See also Williams, *Renewal and Reformation*, p. 264. Amongst other restrictions, these laws prevented Welshmen from acquiring land, property, or office within English border boroughs, or in English towns in Wales.

[8] Williams, *Renewal and Reformation*, pp. 268–69. This unification was not a straightforward or uncontested process, and followed a long history of imposed English subjugation over Wales; see *Authority and Subjugation in Writing of Medieval Wales*, ed. Ruth Kennedy and Simon Meecham-Jones (London: Palgrave Macmillan, 2008), passim.

'De Nobilitate Britannica'.[9] These endeavours were probably intended to support King Henry's political machinations: revivifying the classical unit of Britain or Britannia helped to present a unified vision of England and Wales. Looking beyond the bounds of the archipelago itself, the revival of Britannia also functioned as an aspect of *romanitas*, situating Britain as an imperial centre to rival the classical world. The notion of Britain as an empire state was emerging, both in terms of territorial expansion and independence following its separation from Rome.[10] By the end of the century, the restoration of Britain in the public's consciousness had been successfully realised. The British Empire is described as a contemporary reality rather than a historic one in Humphrey Llwyd's *Commentarioli* (1567), Richard Prise's preface to his father John Prise's *Defensio* (published 1573), and most famously in John Dee's *The Perfecte Arte of Navigation* (1576).[11] Thus, in the intervening years the Anglo-Welsh state had come to be understood as British, a historic unit renewed for contemporary political purposes. When Leland and Prise conceive of themselves as British they are therefore acknowledging not only their own self-fashioned identities, but their acceptance of the Anglo-Welsh state and the pseudo-historic justifications for its unification.

This was the background against which Polydore Vergil composed his highly critical *Anglica Historia* (1534).[12] The timing could not have been worse for Polydore: in the same year that his *Historia* was published the Act of Supremacy was passed, cementing England's split from Rome. Anti-Italian sentiment was running high, and to Arthur's patriotic defenders Polydore represented a 'Romish' foreigner meddling in the affairs of an increasingly independent Britain. This is reflected in the backlash against the *Anglica Historia*, which is sometimes openly xenophobic. John Bale, the ardent protestant polemicist and friend to John Leland, accused Polydore of 'polluting our English Chronicles most shamefully with his Romish lies and other Italish beggarys'.[13] Others accused Polydore of burning British books which evidenced Arthur, or squirreling them away to Rome.[14] These accusations represent an interesting and perhaps accidental refiguring of the *Ysgolan* of Welsh legend (*Scolan* in Brittany), a shadowy figure responsible for the destruction of a number

---

[9] Carley, 'John Leland', *The Oxford Dictionary of National Biography*.
[10] Humphrey Llwyd appears to have been the originator of the term 'British Empire' in an Early Modern context; see Bruce Ward Henry, 'John Dee, Humphrey Llwyd, and the Name "British Empire"', *Huntington Library Quarterly*, 35.2 (1972), 189–90.
[11] On Dee, see Ward Henry, 'John Dee', passim.
[12] Discussed above at pp. 38–39.
[13] Cited in Hay, *Polydore Vergil*, p. 158.
[14] Hay, *Polydore Vergil*, p. 159.

of ancient British-language books.[15] Many of Polydore's contemporaries took the *Anglica Historia* as an outright rejection of Arthur's existence, an assumption that has been echoed much more recently in the scholarship of the past century. However, this has since been persuasively disputed by James P. Carley. Polydore never actually rejects Arthur outright, but instead seems more concerned with wresting him back from the domains of fable and myth, an aim that Polydore shares with his greatest critics.[16] The *Anglica Historia* has therefore been misrepresented as a foreign attack on native soil, a result of both Polydore's Italian identity and a perceived uprooting of Arthur from the native places with which he was associated.[17]

Defending Arthur: Leland, Prise, Gruffydd

John Leland was one of the first to respond to Polydore in an unpublished rebuttal written in 1536, followed by his *Assertio inclytissimi Arturii regis Britannia* in 1544.[18] Leland was English, but apparently identified more with "Britishness", and disparages the English vernacular on occasion in his work. Leland took great pleasure in what he saw as Anglo-Welsh political union, and he exploited the borderless nature of an imagined Arthurian Britain in his antiquarian work. Stewart Mottram has argued that Leland's imperial vision was anglocentric in nature, and whilst this is certainly true it bears repeating that some of the most brazen acts of anglicisation attributed to Leland were actually the work of his translator, Richard Robinson. For example, Mottram points out that Leland anglicises Caerleon-upon-Uske as 'Caerlegion, or Chester vpo[n] Vske'; but there is no mention of Chester in Leland's original Latin.[19] Mottram also states

---

[15] Schwyzer, *Literature, Nationalism and Memory*, pp. 81–84. For a thorough discussion of the Ysgolan tradition, see A. O. H. Jarman, 'Cerdd Ysgolan', *Ysgrifau beirniadol*, 10 (1977), 51–78.

[16] Carley, 'Arthur and the Antiquaries', p. 156.

[17] Although Italy did not exist as a discrete political unit at this stage, Polydore is still referred to frequently by his critics as 'Polydore the Italian'. It is not within the scope of this book to explore Polydore's perception of his own native identity at length; however, the concept of a united Italy was posited as early as 1517 in Niccolo Machiavelli's *Discourses on Livy*. Some scholars also identify a 'proto-national [...] pan-Italian' sentiment in the works of Petrarch, and particularly in terms of his reception in the early sixteenth century. See for example William J. Kennedy, *The Site of Petrarchism: Early Modern National Sentiment in Italy, France, and England* (Baltimore, MD: Johns Hopkins University Press, 2003), pp. 1–2, pp. 23–24; John R. Hale, *England and the Italian Renaissance: The Growth of Interest in its History and Art*, 4th edn (London: Blackwell, 2005), pp. 2–3.

[18] Carley, 'Polydore Vergil and John Leland on King Arthur', p. 87.

[19] Stewart Mottram, '"An Empire of Itself"', p. 170. Robinson mentions the 'citie of Caerlegion vpon Uske' (Leland, *Learned*, sigs C2v–C3r); 'the saide cittie of Chester

that Leland relocates Camelot 'via Geoffrey of Monmouth' from Caerleon to Cadbury; but there is no mention of Camelot anywhere in Geoffrey's *Historia*.[20] Geoffrey's Arthur does hold court in Caerleon, but he also holds court in Paris and, perhaps, in London.[21] Like Geoffrey, Leland acknowledges a multiplicity of Arthurian court places in the Round Table chapter of the *Assertio*. My own view is that Leland sought to identify himself as British in order to support his vision of Anglo-Welsh unity, and I think it is worth comparing his defence with that of Prise, whose political visions were similar.

At the same time that Leland was composing the *Assertio*, the Brecon-born antiquarian Sir John Prise, then in communication with Leland, was writing his own rebuttal in the form of the *Historia Britannicae Defensio*, published posthumously by Prise's son Richard at his father's request in 1573. Prise's defence prioritised ancient Welsh manuscripts as evidence, and Prise encountered many of these sources in religious houses during work carried out on behalf of the crown. He was eventually appointed as justice of the peace for all of Wales, as well as the English marcher counties of Herefordshire, Shropshire, Worcestershire and Gloucestershire.[22] This appointment came in 1543, the same year the second Act of Union was passed. Like Leland, Prise saw himself as British. He was delighted to see a king on the throne of England and Wales stemming (apparently) from the royal families of both nations, and was fully supportive of the unification project. He refers to Hereford, where he settled, as his 'adopted home place' (mihi adoptiua est patria).[23] Though he places his knowledge of the Welsh language and landscapes at the heart of his defence, Prise nevertheless refers to them consistently as British: 'I have been versed from boyhood in the old language of the Britons and in their antiquities', he tells us ([...] in Britannorum ipse lingua prisca et antiquitatibus iam inde a puero exercitatus materiam saltem aliquam).[24] This might be assumed to refer to the Britons as a historic people group, but Prise uses the same terms to refer to the Welsh in his own day: 'the old Britons long for a king descended from their ancient princes, and in

---

vpon Uske' (Leland, *Learned*, sig. D4r); and 'the citie of Caerlegion or Chester vpon Huske' (p. 87). At these same junctures, however, Leland refers to Caerleon exclusively as 'vrbe Legionis' (the City of Legions) (Leland, *Assertio*, sigs B2v–B3r; Leland, *Learned*, C4v; K4r; M1r).

[20] Mottram, '"An Empire of Itself"', p. 170.

[21] Geoffrey of Monmouth, *The History of the Kings of Britain*, 9.155, pp. 207–08 (Paris); 9.156–7, pp. 207–12 (Caerleon). Geoffrey's Arthur also appears to hold court in London (9.144, pp. 193–94).

[22] John Prise, *Historiae Britannicae Defensio*, p. xxi.

[23] John Prise, *Historiae Britannicae Defensio*, pp. 236–37.

[24] John Prise, *Historiae Britannicae Defensio*, pp. 32–33.

you [that is, King Henry] they find that very person' (veteres Britanni regem expectant e suis antiquis principibus ortum).[25] Prise sees himself as part of the same group, referring to his 'fellow-Britons' (Britanni nostri).[26] In a sense, then, Prise figures himself as another kind of living witness to Arthur on account of his possession of the 'old language of the Britons', and this is an aspect of Prise's self-fashioned British identity to which his fellow defender, Leland, does not have access.[27]

Prise and Leland both considered themselves British as well as English or Welsh respectively. However, the third writer discussed in this chapter, Elis Gruffydd, does not appear to have envisioned his own identity in the same way. In the premodern period, and indeed today, the construction of identity was a matter of perception, inflected by not only a sense of self but also of the Other, and prone to change depending on various emotional and practical circumstances affected by both internal self-fashioning and external forces. Andrea Ruddick has demonstrated the ambivalent qualities of late medieval identities in her study of Welshmen seeking English denization in the later Middle Ages.[28] Similarly, Elis Gruffydd, through the many writings he has left behind, figures himself variously as proud Welshman and English soldier, as well as identifying as Prise does with the historic Britons. Gruffydd served in the English army in Calais from 1518.[29] After eighteen years there, he wrote his Welsh language universal chronicle, *Cronicl o wech oesoedd* (Chronicle of The Six Ages), completing it in 1552 before sending it home to his native Flintshire.[30] Welsh language and culture were clearly at the

---

[25] John Prise, *Historiae Britannicae Defensio*, pp. 28–29.
[26] John Prise, *Historiae Britannicae Defensio*, pp. 30–31.
[27] John Prise, *Historiae Britannicae Defensio*, pp. 32–33 (cited above).
[28] Ruddick, '"Becoming English"', passim.
[29] Ceridwen Lloyd-Morgan, 'Welsh Tradition in Calais: Elis Gruffydd and his Biography of King Arthur', in *The Fortunes of King Arthur*, ed. Norris J. Lacy (Cambridge: D. S. Brewer, 2005), pp. 77–91 (p. 77).
[30] The chronicle survives in manuscript form as National Library of Wales MS 5276Di–ii and MS 3054Di–ii. Perhaps on account of its enormity, the *Cronicl* has never been edited in its entirety, though several scholars have published editions and translations of parts of the work, and this chapter is indebted to their efforts. These include Prys Morgan, 'Elis Gruffudd of Gronant: Tudor Chronicler Extraordinary', *Journal of the Flintshire Historical Society*, 25 (1971–72), 9–20; Thomas Gerald Hunter, 'The Chronicle of Elis Gruffydd' (unpublished doctoral thesis, Harvard University, 1995); Ceridwen Lloyd-Morgan, 'Welsh Tradition in Calais'; and, most recently, the excerpts published in Elis Gruffydd, *Tales of Merlin, Arthur, and the Magic Arts, From the Welsh Chronicle of the Six Ages of the World*, ed. Jerry Hunter, trans. Patrick K. Ford (Oakland, CA: University of California Press, 2023). Ceridwen Lloyd-Morgan is currently working on a translation and edition of the Arthurian portions of Gruffydd's chronicle, which is forthcoming. Where material has not yet been edited or translated, I provide my own diplomatic edition and translation.

forefront of Gruffydd's mind during his years abroad, for he composed a number of texts in Welsh, including a compilation of Welsh folklore and poetry.[31] When the first Act of Union was passed in 1536, it explicitly condemned the use of any languages other than English in Ireland and Calais.[32] This would clearly have had an impact on Gruffydd, whose use of Welsh sources in his *Cronicl* and references to book borrowing suggest he enjoyed participating in a rich network of learned Welshmen in Calais who shared their libraries with each other.[33] Moreover, Gruffydd was in the process of converting to Protestantism during his Calais years, and read the works of Tyndale, whose vernacular translation of the Bible would lead to his execution in 1536.[34] This may also have been a factor in compelling Gruffydd to compose works in his native Welsh.

Gruffydd's attitude towards England and the English is complicated: he begins his chronicle by explaining that 'after I settled down in Calais, I began to record the way of the world, especially that of the realm of England' (ac ynnol J mi breseddu ynGhalais, myui a ddechreuais nodi kwrs y byd ac ynn vnwedig tyrnas Loegyr).[35] Gruffydd's writing evinces the bilingualism of his environment, for his Welsh sometimes slips into anglicisms. Despite this, Gruffydd evidently identifies as Welsh, framing the British as a historic, indigenous group of people rather than a present reality. Gruffydd's *Cronicl* draws a clear distinction between the Welsh and the English on the subject of the British History, and rather than taking issue with the Italians and Romans for meddling with the Matter of Britain, as his contemporaries do, Gruffydd frames the English as those responsible for foreign interference.

Place and language

For Leland and Prise, Polydore's greatest insult was his perceived scepticism surrounding native Arthurian places. Leland's sarcastic response to Polydore's comments about Glastonbury Abbey demonstrate

---

[31] Cardiff, Cardiff Central Library MS 3.4 (previously MS Cardiff 5), described in J. Gwenogvryn Evans, *Reports on Manuscripts in the Welsh Language* (London: Historical Manuscripts Commission, 1898–1910), I (1898), p. 99.

[32] Amy C. Mulligan, 'Moses, Taliesin, and the Welsh Chosen People: Elis Gruffydd's Construction of a Biblical, British Past for Reformation Wales', *Studies in Philology*, 113.4 (2016), 765–96. (p. 773); P. R. Roberts, 'The Union with England and the Identity of "Anglican" Wales', *Transactions of the Royal Historical Society*, 22 (2007), 49–70 (p. 61). For the act and its Calais provision, see 'Calais, 1536: 27 Henry VIII, c. 63', in *The Statutes of the Realm III: 1509–1545*, ed. Alexander Luders et al. (London: The Record Commission, 1817), III, p. 648.

[33] Lloyd-Morgan, 'Welsh Tradition in Calais', p. 83.

[34] Prys Morgan, 'Elis Gruffudd of Gronant', p. 15.

[35] Text and translation from Gruffydd, *Tales of Merlin*, p. 9.

the sensitivity surrounding the issue. Leland brings Polydore's knowledge of British antiquity into question:

> Polidorus (according to his equitie and iudgment, and so farre as his aucthoritie serueth him) declareth there was no Monasterie at Glastenbury in Arthures time: so exquisite a iudge is he of Antiquitie and specially concerning Brittaine.
>
> (Polidorus pro suo iure, atque adeo autoritate pronunciat non fuisse monasterium Aualoniae tempore Arturii: tam exquisitus censor est antiquitatis & maxime Britannicae)[36]

The implication here is clear: how can Polydore, an Italian, possibly have any authority when it comes to Arthur's native places? Polydore must be ignorant about such matters simply because he is foreign. There is a circular logic to Leland's endeavour: to support belief in Arthur meant fomenting the impression of locality or familiarity with his places, and a foreign-born agent, on account of his foreignness, could never truly be familiar with them. To form identity through opposition is to create a mirror image of selfhood, and given that Leland is so concerned with places and their objects in his defence of Arthur, it is telling that his dismissal of Polydore prioritises physical place as a marker of difference. Leland refers to him as 'Polydore the Italian' throughout the *Assertio*, and once as 'the doctor from the city of Urbino' (Vrbinatem medicum).[37] Leland's insistent repetition of Polydore's Italian identity may hint at an underlying anxiety regarding Polydore's denizened status, which Polydore had held since 1510.[38] That Polydore had been commissioned by the king himself to compose a history of the English must have been especially painful for Leland. Even Polydore's harshest critics seem to have been confused by his nationality: a note referring to Polydore scribbled in the margin of John Bale's *Scriptorum illustrium* reads: 'that most rascall dogge knave in the worlde, an Englyshman by byrth, but he had Italian parents [...]'.[39] These responses to Polydore underscore the insecurity and complexity of national identity in late medieval and early modern England, if it existed at all: as Robert Bartlett and others have pointed out, factors such as shared language, ethnicity, customs, laws, land, and monarch could, in different combinations, produce

---

[36] Leland, *Learned*, sig. E3v; Leland, *Assertio*, sig. D3v.
[37] Leland, *Assertio*, sig. K3v.
[38] 'Henry VIII: October 1510', in *Letters and Papers, Foreign and Domestic, of the Reign of Henry VIII*, ed. J. S. Brewer (London, 1920), I, no. 1283. British History Online, www.british-history.ac.uk/letters-papers-hen8/vol1/pp338-347 [accessed 20 November 2018]
[39] Cited in Hay, *Polydore Vergil*, p. 159.

various kinds of national feeling.⁴⁰ For Leland, then, reinforcing Polydore's connection with Italy in his critiques was not only a matter of undermining Polydore's authority, but also of entrenching Leland's own identification with Arthur's British places, and therefore Leland's construction of his own British identity.

John Prise was also quick to present Polydore as an ignorant foreigner, but where Leland's line of defence centred around physical Arthurian places and artefacts, Prise's approach was to prioritise textual sources, mostly from his native Wales. Prise argued that Polydore lacked sufficient knowledge of either the Arthurian landscape or the native textual tradition to qualify him as an authority on Arthur. The textual sources Prise centred in his defence are also physical, however, for he places heavy emphasis on the manuscripts themselves in which these texts appear, many of which Prise had discovered during his work in religious houses across Wales. As such, although much of Prise's Arthurian geography overlaps with the places set forward by Leland on account of their collaboration, most of his Arthurian emplacement is subtly filtered through the manuscripts he had encountered, and the various locations where he had encountered them. In his *Defensio* Prise describes his strategic approach in countering Polydore, stating that although other respondents past and present had dealt with the arguments of Polydore and his fellow Arthurian naysayers already,

> Even so I have decided to augment their writings by quoting some things which I have gathered concerning Arthur from the annals and antiquities of the Britons. I shall also add some proofs relating to this matter which I put together a long time ago. Leland also mentions these things, but I have thought it not inappropriate to repeat them afresh here. I do this, partly because the oftener they are transcribed the less likely they are to be forgotten, and partly because the original manuscripts (from which Leland himself took the material, when he and I met and comprehensively discussed the whole topic over several days) are, most of them in my possession: the accuracy of my copy of them can therefore be trusted.
>
> ([p]auca tamen quae ex Britannorum tum annalibus tum antiquitatibus de Arthuro acceperim, hiis adiicienda statui; atque nonnulla quae in hoc a me iamdudum parata sunt argumenta, etsi ab eodem Leylando memorata, partim quo saepius transcripta minus obliuioni obnoxia sint, partim quia prothotypa ipsa vnde ea et ipse accepit, dum hac de re vltro citroque dies aliquot sermonem

---

⁴⁰ Bartlett, *The Making of Europe*, p. 53. The issue of premodern national thinking is discussed above at pp. 10–12.

vna conferremus, penes me pleraque sunt, vnde fides certior hiis facienda sit, hic denuo repetere non ab re fore putaui.)[41]

For Prise, the Arthurian monuments that lie at the heart of his defence are therefore also muniments, ancient manuscripts he had collected during his visitation of monasteries across Wales on behalf of the English crown.[42] The age of these manuscripts is crucial to the strength of Prise's defence, and he purposely avoids citing evidence he believes to postdate Geoffrey's *Historia* to avoid the accusation that 'what is produced by these writers [...] was in fact derived from him' (quisquam ab eodem acceptum fuisse quod in hanc rem astruendam protulerint).[43] Frequently, Prise centres the locations where he had found these ancient manuscripts as much as their contents, and as such the texts are figured as emplaced monuments performing a rhetorical function, reminiscent in some respects of the *tabulae* described in this book's opening chapter.

The cathedral church at Llandaff provided Prise with such a codex, a charter on the church's early foundations that recorded a gift of land 'called Pen Alun and also of Llandeilo Fawr, on the river Tywi' ([terra] vocata Penalynn, necnon Landeiliaw Vawr, super ripam Teyuii fluminis), apparently granted to the church by 'Noe, son of Arthur' (Noe quodam filio Arthuri) during 'the time of Archbishop Dubricius' (tempore Dubricii Archiepiscopi facta).[44] The same manuscript apparently contained a copy of St Dubricius' *Life* which also described the deeds of Arthur.[45] This piece of textual evidence is doubly associated with place, for Prise not only names the specific territories granted to Llandaff by Arthur's immediate kin, but also imagines a distinct context for the manuscript as a spatio-temporal mnemonic used by the priests at Llandaff to connect with the Arthurian past: 'it is evident that, long before Geoffrey's times, priests at the cathedral in Llandaff rehearsed this *Life* of Dubricius every year, on the day dedicated to Saint Dubricius' memory' (quam quidem vitam longe ante Gaufredi tempora in Ecclesia Landauensi, die D. Dubricii memoriae dicato, quotannis ab ipsius ecclesiae cultribus repetitam fuisse liquet).[46] Just as John Leland imagined Glastonbury's monks recovering Arthur's seal from oblivion, so too does Prise envision the contents

---

[41] John Prise, *Historiae Britannicae Defensio*, pp. 192–93.
[42] On Prise's manuscripts, and their importance to Prise's defence of Arthur and the British History, see Helen Fulton, 'Sir John Prise and His Books: Manuscript Culture in the March of Wales', *The Welsh History Review*, 31.1 (2022), 55–78.
[43] John Prise, *Historiae Britannicae Defensio*, pp. 192–93.
[44] John Prise, *Historiae Britannicae Defensio*, pp. 221–22.
[45] John Prise, *Historiae Britannicae Defensio*, pp. 221–22.
[46] John Prise, *Historiae Britannicae Defensio*, pp. 221–22.

of the Llandaff manuscript being preserved, physically and orally, by the cathedral's priests. In this sense, Prise figures both manuscript and priests as witnesses to Llandaff's Arthurian connections.

When it comes to Prise's emplacement of his manuscripts as a strategy for defending Arthur, the Llandaff codex is far from a standalone example. In fact, using institutional histories collectively, as well as independently, meant that Prise could present them as impartial witnesses to Arthur's history. Prise cites an entry on Arthur's rule, his defeat by Mordred, and his final journey to Avalon in the annals of the Cathedral Church of Mynyw (that is, St Davids).[47] Despite claiming to have not remembered having read of such things elsewhere, Prise immediately states that the same information can be found in chronicles from Carmarthen Priory and from Canterbury's Metropolitan Church.[48] He asserts that documents such as these and other 'very old annals' (praeterea annales peruetusti) of the realm's churches and abbeys are especially trustworthy because they were written by people 'who were separated from each other' (a diuresis seorsim positis) but are nevertheless consistent in the histories they present.[49] Whilst it is clear from manuscripts like Cotton MS Titus A.XIX and Cotton MS Cleopatra C.IV that there was probably some sharing of materials between institutions like Glastonbury Abbey and York Minster for the purposes of narrating their origin stories, Prise is quick to interpret the historic practices of distant religious institutions as operating in a kind of vacuum. In this sense, it was not only the contents of the institutions' histories that Prise turned to as evidence, but also their physical locations. Plotted widely across England and Wales – St Davids, Carmarthen, Canterbury – the histories of these places, when gathered together and consolidated by Prise, work to support the impression of Arthur's reality because of their separation. Unlike the geographical logic of Leland's West Country geography, it was their distance rather than their proximity that made them effective in support of Arthur's existence.

Prise's Llandaff codex was written in Welsh, and within the context of the Polydore controversy Prise was therefore positioning himself as an essential mediator of the evidence on account of being a native Welsh speaker. Unlike Leland, whose Arthurian defence was grounded primarily in places and their related objects, Prise's sense of his own Britishness, and therefore his rebuttal to Polydore, was shaped by his native language. Prise pointedly states that he has written his defence in

---

[47] John Prise, *Historiae Britannicae Defensio*, pp. 223–24.
[48] John Prise, *Historiae Britannicae Defensio*, pp. 223–26.
[49] John Prise, *Historiae Britannicae Defensio*, pp. 222–23.

Latin because it would be wrong 'to publish a response to a writer and speaker of Latin in a language which is foreign to him' (neque Latine scribenti loqentiue responsum peregrino sermone aedere conueniret).[50] Prise later questions whether Polydore's errors are due to his 'ignorance of the ancient languages of this island' (ex inscitia linguarum vetustarum huius insulae) or to his being 'too lazy to analyse of material of this kind with due thoroughness' (siue ex nimia oscitanti in rebus huiusmodi discutiendis), rather than because of bias or ill will.[51] Leland and Prise's treatment of Polydore is echoed by their fellow Arthurian defender and self-professed 'Cambro-Briton', Humphrey Llwyd, who finds Polydore an inappropriate writer of British history on account of his foreignness and his assumed ignorance: 'but to make an ende I saye that he beinge firste a stranger borne, and aswell ignorante in the histories of this realme as of the diverse tonges and languages used therin, colde never set furth the true and perfecte cronicle of the same'.[52] Llwyd's recourse to the 'diverse tonges and languages' of Britain and its 'histories' – notably expressed in plural terms – supports the argument that difference and variety, rather than uniformity, was crucial to supporting the construction of nascent British identity; but within this dynamic, according to Leland and Llwyd at least, there was no room for the voices of those born beyond the bounds of the British archipelago.[53]

Language was also a point of concern for John Leland. Throughout his Arthurian defence, Leland is quick to disparage Arthurian texts written in Europe's various vernacular languages. Yet whilst written sources in Welsh and insular Latin form the crux of Prise's rebuttal, Leland is far quicker to turn to physical places instead as his first line of defence, combining them with native textual sources. This difference may simply be due to both writers' areas of expertise: Leland's grand itinerary had given him a confident grasp of Arthurian places, whilst Prise's key area of competency was his knowledge of the Welsh language and manuscripts. Leland and Prise's diversity of approach may also be symptomatic of the different ways in which they imagined their own British identity. As scholars such as Thorlac Turville-Petre and Robert Bartlett have established, a shared language could be a powerful force for constructing a sense of national unity, and for Prise this was clearly true even across

---

[50] John Prise, *Historiae Britannicae Defensio*, pp. 18–19.
[51] John Prise, *Historiae Britannicae Defensio*, pp. 144–45.
[52] Humphrey Llwyd, *The Breviary of Britain*, ed. Philip Schwyzer (London: MHRA, 2013), p. 4; Humphrey Llwyd, *Cronica Walliae*, ed. Ieuan M. Williams (Cardiff: Cardiff University Press, 2016), p. 65.
[53] On diversity as a marker of premodern English nationhood, see above at pp. 10–12.

time: a connection could be drawn between the historic Britons on the one hand, and Prise and his fellow Welshmen's sense of their own Britishness on the other.[54] The English-born Leland could not even pretend to lay claim to a shared first language with either Arthur or contemporaries like Prise and Llwyd. While Latin-inscribed Arthurian objects such as the seal at Westminster might have encouraged the humanistically educated Leland to imagine a shared Latinity between himself and the Arthurian past, this was not as exclusive as Prise's British tongue, and could not therefore work to construct identity in opposition to Polydore (who, of course, had a better grasp of Latin than Leland himself). Instead, Leland turned primarily to physical places, to the idea of shared land, to foment his sense of his own Britishness, his connection to Welsh contemporaries, and his connection to Arthur, whom Leland refers to as 'his countryman' (conterraneum meum).[55] Eviatar Zerubavel frames constancy of place as a mnemonic, a means of remembering the past; but in this case shared land could also be a potent amnesiac, erasing various kinds of difference – ethnic, linguistic – to create the illusion of a shared national identity, an impression that cut vertically across time but also horizontally by uniting Leland with contemporaries such as Prise.[56]

To illustrate Leland's double weaponisation of native texts and native places, we might consider how Leland introduces his list of Arthur's knights in the *Assertio*. If establishing a sense of connection to Arthurian places – a sense of locality – relied upon those places becoming familiar, as I have suggested it does, it is noteworthy that Leland introduces Arthur's companions thus:

> Therefore, because it is a worke of greater importaunce, than wee presentlie are in hande with, exquisitely, curiously and perfectlie to displaye all the deedes of Arthure, let us for this reason omitte the *Romaines*, and let us advance with penne his famylier friendes.

> (Ergo quia maioris operis est, quam in praesentia agimus, exquisite, curiose, & ad unguem facta Arturii omnia excutere, omittamus tantisper Romanos, & familiares illius calamo illustremus.)[57]

In compiling this list, Leland is highly selective with his sources, explicitly rejecting the rather-too-continental *Romaines* ('Romanos' in Leland's Latin original) in favour of natively authored texts: foreign texts

---

[54] Cited above at pp. 10–12.
[55] Leland, *Learned*, sig. C1r; Leland, *Assertio*, sig. B1r.
[56] Cited above at pp. 22–26. Laura Ashe has illustrated the ways in which a sense of shared land worked to construct an emergent English national identity after the conquest; see Laura Ashe, *Fiction and History in England*, passim.
[57] Leland, *Learned*, sig. D2v; Leland, *Assertio*, sig. C2v.

are not suitably serious for Leland's grave undertaking. Native places are also crucial to Leland's list, and he connects many of the knights who follow with specific real-world places across the island of Britain. Leland's sequence of knights is curious, and deserves further scholarly attention. He ranks Arthur's knights in order, and the list is similar in this respect to the Welsh text *Pedwar marchog ar hugain llys Arthur* (The Twenty-Four Knights of Arthur's Court), though Leland's list is different to that in *Pedwar marchog*.[58] Leland includes only seven knights from *Pedwar Marchog* (eight including Mordred, whom Leland declines to discuss).[59] There was a wider tradition of knight lists in the medieval Welsh Arthurian tradition, borne out in texts such as *Llyma enwav y Milwyr waithian* (Here now are the names of the warriors) and *Marchogion y Vort Geon* (The Knights of the Round Table).[60] Arthurian knight lists may have been known in anglophone oral or written tradition, too: the seventeenth-century balladeer Martin Parker seems to have sent up the genre to humorous effect, including worthies like 'Syr Friske', 'Syr Doguery', and 'Syr Freake' alongside more recognisable names in his own Arthurian knight list.[61]

In his more serious list Leland prioritises knights who are well-documented in the insular Latin and Welsh traditions that predate continental Arthurian romance. He privileges knights who were reported to have fought in Arthur's foreign campaigns, or who governed states within the borders of his empire, though Leland is careful to refer to them as governors (regulus) rather than kings. Hoel of Brittany appears at the very top of the list 'by a certaine righte of his' (iure quodam suo poscit).[62] Hoel is the son of Arthur's sister in the *Historia regum Britanniae*, but neither Leland nor Geoffrey of Monmouth give any indication as to what this 'ancient right' might be. In *Les Grandes Chroniques de Bretaigne* (1514), the Breton publisher Alain Bouchard insists that Hoel was *not* Arthur's subject, despite being a Round Table member; and Hywel is named as one of Arthur's three royal knights ('tri brenhinawl varchoc') in *Pedwar*

---

[58] Elis Gruffydd copied an extract of this text at some point between 1524 and 1529 during his time in London; see Lloyd, *The Arthurian Place Names of Wales*, p. 94.
[59] Rachel Bromwich, 'Pedwar Marchog Ar Hugain Llys Arthur (The Twenty-Four Knights of Arthur's Court)', *Transactions of the Honourable Society of Cymmrodorion*, 1956, 126–32.
[60] Ceridwen Lloyd-Morgan, 'Later Hybrid Narrative Texts', pp. 207–08.
[61] Parker may have had Leland's *Assertio* in mind. Whilst it is unclear whether Parker knew of Leland's defence, the *Most admirable historie* seems to echo the *Assertio* in term of its tone, page design, and structure. Martin Parker, *The most admirable historie of that most renowned Christian worthy Arthur King of the Britains* (1660), STC (2nd edn) R181453, pp. 14–15, sigs C1v–C2r.
[62] Leland, *Learned*, sig. D2v; Leland, *Assertio*, sig. C2v.

marchog.⁶³ It may be that Leland knew some similar version of Hoel's narrative that emphasised his position as an independent ruler in his own right. Augusellus, 'a beneficiall Gouernour ouer the Scottes' (Scottis regulus beneficiarius praefectus sit), comes in at third place.⁶⁴ Both of these men, we are told, fought abroad in Arthur's French expeditions, and both are important figures in Geoffrey of Monmouth's *Historia*. If Leland's knight list is a manifestation of how he imagined Arthur's geography, the positioning of Hoel and Auguselus towards its beginning mark the outer bounds of Arthur's realm.

In second place, ahead of Augusellus, we find Arthur's blood relative Gawain, to whom Leland dedicates a large amount of page space.⁶⁵ Yder appears in fourth place, a figure also common to Welsh and Anglo-Latin sources predating continental Arthurian romance. In contrast to the preceding men, Lancelot, the darling of the French romance tradition, comes rather further down the list. He is only discussed very briefly, and commended chiefly for his faithful friendship with Arthur.⁶⁶ This may be a reflection of existing insular tastes, rather than Leland's personal aversion to Lancelot. Hardyng is similarly uninterested in the knight;⁶⁷ and, as Helen Cooper suggests,

> English interest in Lancelot [...] is barely traceable in England before 1400 [...] we need to consider very seriously a late-medieval population for the vast majority of whom Arthur was a great king supported by Gawain as his leading knight [...] for whom Lancelot, if they had heard of him at all, was merely one of the minor knights.⁶⁸

Lancelot is followed only by Caradoc and Cador respectively, and he is the only figure in Leland's list of greats who does not appear in the insular tradition prior to the golden age of continental French Arthurian romance. This again seems to suggest that Leland is prioritising the figures

---

⁶³ Jane H. M. Taylor, *Rewriting Arthurian Romance in Renaissance France* (Cambridge: D. S. Brewer, 2014), p. 3; Bromwich, 'Pedwar Marchog', p. 122.

⁶⁴ Leland, *Learned*, sig. D4v; Leland, *Assertio*, sig. D4r–v. Augusellus comes from Geoffrey of Monmouth's *Historia regum Britanniae*, where he is also sometimes referred to as Angusellus.

⁶⁵ Leland, *Learned*, sig. D2v; Leland, *Assertio*, sig. C2v.

⁶⁶ Leland, *Learned*, sig. E1r; Leland, *Assertio*, sig. D1r.

⁶⁷ Elizabeth Archibald, 'Malory and the Post-Vulgate Cycle', in *Romance Rewritten: The Evolution of Middle English Romance: A Tribute to Helen Cooper*, ed. Elizabeth Archibald, Megan G. Leitch and Corinne Saunders (Cambridge: D. S. Brewer, 2018), pp. 115–32 (p. 119).

⁶⁸ Helen Cooper, 'The *Lancelot-Grail Cycle* in England: Malory and His Predecessors', in *A Companion to the Lancelot-Grail Cycle*, ed. Carol Dover (Cambridge: D. S. Brewer, 2003), pp. 147–62 (p. 153).

of native sources above foreign texts, perhaps in order to separateArthur from continental romance traditions and cultivate his image as a figure of the native historical tradition instead.

Most significantly for the purposes of this book, the 'native sources' that Leland prioritises are physical as well as textual, for the figures whom he lists are tied to insular places. According to Leland, Gawain fought bravely in the battle at Dover and is buried there. Leland witnessed Gawain's so-called tomb in Dover, and both Malory's *Morte Darthur* and its preface by Caxton also attest to Dover's Arthurian credentials even if Leland chose not to focus on them in his Arthurian defences.[69] Of course, Glastonbury is another important site for Leland, and he connects it with several of the knights in his list. Leland tells us that Yder organised Arthur's burial at Avalon, that he is named as a benefactor of Glastonbury Abbey on a *tabula* hanging in the Abbey church (evidently the *magna tabula*), and that there was a text about Yder's exploits held in Glastonbury Abbey's library.[70] From the 1300s, Yder's remains were displayed atop a tomb in the abbey choir nearby to the tomb of Arthur and Guinevere, so it is also possible that Leland would have seen these remains when he visited.[71] Lancelot, too, is connected with Glastonbury by Leland, who states that Lancelot had carried Guenevere's body from Amesbury, where Leland believes Lancelot to be buried, to Glastonbury to be interred alongside Arthur.[72] Elsewhere, Leland states that 'writers make mention' (scriptores referunt) of Guenevere taking the veil at Amesbury and being buried there before Lancelot took her remains to 'Aualonia'.[73]

---

[69] John Leland, *Itineraries*, IV, p. 55; Malory, *Works*, p. xiii; 12.2, p. 710. See also above at pp. 68–69.

[70] There are extracts about Yder in John of Glastonbury's *Cronica*, the *magna tabula*, and in the interpolations made to William of Malmesbury's *De antiquitate* which supports Leland's claim to have consulted a text about Yder in the abbey library. The episode that appears in these sources seems to originate from a romance with Glastonbury connections, although no such romance survives. See John of Glastonbury, *Cronica*, pp. 76–77, p. 284, n. 116; Nitze and Jenkins, eds, *Le Haut livre du Graal*, II, pp. 303–06, as well as the discussion above at pp. 61–62.

[71] Luxford, *Art and Architecture*, p. 170.

[72] See Mary Bateman, 'A Grave Discovery?: Guinevere's Death and Burial at Amesbury in Medieval and Early Modern Tradition', in *The Arthurian World*, ed. Victoria Coldham-Fussell, Miriam Edlich-Muth, and Renée Ward (London: Routledge, 2022), pp. 413–28. Richard Robinson mistranslates Leland's statement here, and assumes that Lancelot brought Arthur's body from Amesbury to Glastonbury. Leland, *Learned*, sig. E1v; Leland, *Assertio*, sig. D1r.

[73] Leland, *Learned*, sig. I1r; Leland, *Assertio*, sig. G4v; Bateman, 'A Grave Discovery?', pp. 414–17. This curious statement about Guinevere's burial at Amesbury had an interesting afterlife when a noblewoman's tomb was discovered at Amesbury in

Elsewhere in the *Assertio*, Leland makes the value that he identifies in Arthur's native places explicitly clear. In the following passage, he presents foreign vernacular texts as foils for Arthurian places, and reinforces the believable qualities of Britain's physical sites:

> When books about his [Arthur's] great prowess, and also his victories are printed, as I have learned, in the Italian tongue, and also the Spanish and French tongues, and from which the English collection, by the author Thomas Malory has come forth [...] I know the adversary will say that many lies have crept into them. [...] As I scorn fables, so I do embrace and cherish true histories. I escape from the ungrateful, and at the rocks and engraved witnesses of Arthur's fame and his majesty I take refuge. [My translation.][74]

> When books printed of [Arthur's] prowess, & victories (as I haue learned) are read in the Italian tongue yea in the Spanish, and also in the French tongue: whereupon also the English collection of Thomas Mailerius his trauaile, is published abroad [...] the aduersarie I know will say, that many lyes haue crept into those old books. [...] As I contemne fables, so I reuerence & imbrace the truth of the history [...] Unthankfull persons I vtterly eschew and I betake me vnto those Rockes & monuments, the true witnesses of Arthures renounce and maiestie. (Leland, *Learned*, sig. G4r)

> (quando libri de eius cum fortitudine, tum victoriis, impressi, vt ego didici, Italice legantur, Hispanice etiam, & Gallice. Vnde & collectio Anglica, autore Thoma Mailerio, prodiit. Dixerit aduersarius in illos mendacia irrepsisse multa Pernoui. Quare hoc aliud nihil quam edoctum docere. Vt fabulas contemno, nisi cum vita, a me unquam distrahi amicam. Ingratos refugio, & ad rupes. & saxa testes nominis, & maiestatis Arturianae confugio.) (Leland, *Assertio*, sig. F3v)

Leland dismisses books printed in the 'Italian', 'Spanish', and 'French' tongues. He also mentions the works of 'the author Thomas Malory' (autore Thoma Mailerio).[75] Despite treating Malory as an 'author', Leland nevertheless frames Malory's *Morte* as a collection or compilation ('collectio') that has 'come forth' from the aforementioned foreign works, which may explain Leland's reluctance to explicitly name Malory or Caxton as evidence in support of his Arthurian defence. This framing of

---

the early seventeenth century and attributed to Guinevere; see below at pp. 257–58 and also Bateman, 'A Grave Discovery?', passim.

[74] I provide my own translation here to supplement Robinson's.

[75] *Assertio*, sig. F3v. On the changing attitudes regarding Malory's status as an 'author' (rather than a translator, compiler, or redactor), see Roberta Davidson, 'The "Freynshe booke" and the English Translator: Malory's "Originality" Revisited', *Translation and Literature*, 17.2 (2008), 133–49.

Malory's Arthurian works as a translated collation of other texts is picked up and amplified by Leland's fellow antiquary John Bale.[76] Conversely, Leland turns to native histories and sites in his search for historical truth concerning Arthur. The native places of Arthur – the 'rocks and engraved witnesses' (rupes & [...] saxa testes) – are treated as vital pieces of evidence that also provide an emotional connection to the past. Leland makes these values explicit in the final chapter of his defence, stating that 'the infinite force of thinges worthie of memory, and of noble effect consisteth rather of eye witnesses at home resident and inhabiting, then of the vncertaine relation made by forraine writers' (infinita vis rerum memorabilium, & nobilitatis pendet potius ab incolis oculatis domi testibus, quam ex incerta exterorum relatione).[77] In other words, natively authored British histories are more reliable because of their authors' physical proximity to their subject matter; but native places are the only means of witnessing traces of Britain's history in person, first-hand. The 'eye witnesses at home resident and inhabiting' that Leland had in mind may represent the people living their daily lives around Camlan and Cadbury Castle, and it is perhaps telling that Leland frames the honest and inanimate 'rocks and engraved witnesses' in the same terms as his living witnesses.

Leland's passionate speech in defense of Arthur's 'rocks and engraved witnesses' had an impact, even among Leland's more sceptical readership. Raphael Holinshed, whose *Historie of England* (1586) is a 'near verbatim' translation of Polydore's *Historia*, diverges from his source on the subject of two Arthurian sites: Badon and Glastonbury.[78] Unlike Polydore, Holinshed insists that Arthur led the Britons himself in the Battle at Badon.[79] Holinshed also disagrees (so he thinks) with Polydore on the authenticity of Arthur's grave at Glastonbury, arguing that its discovery quelled the 'vaine' fable of his return:

---

[76] 'Once thoroughly versed in [historical and literary] texts, [Malory] collated the many materials written in both Latin and French and painstakingly translated them into our own tongue' (Vnde in earum lectione diutissime versatus, ex multis authoribus, & libris Latine ac Gallice scriptis magno labore collegit, atque in linguam nostrum uertit). Translation from *Sir Thomas Malory: The Critical Heritage*, ed. and trans. Marylyn Parins (London: Routledge, 1987), pp. 54–55; Latin original in John Bale, *Scriptorum illustrium maioris Brytannie* (Basel: Ioannem Oporinum, 1557–59), STC (2nd edn) 1296, pp. 628–29.

[77] Leland, *Learned*, sig. L3v; Leland, *Assertio*, sig. K2r.

[78] See Laura Ashe, 'Holinshed and Mythical History', in *The Oxford Handbook of Holinshed's Chronicles*, ed. Felicity Heal, Ian W. Archer, and Paulina Kewes (Oxford: Oxford University Press, 2012), pp. 153–70.

[79] James P. Stapleton, 'King Arthur, Badon Hill, and Iconoclasm in Milton's *History of Britain*', *Renaissance Papers*, 18 (2013), pp. 147–59 (p. 149).

> But others there be of a constant beleefe, who hold it for a grounded truth, that such a prince there was; and among all other a late writer, who falling into necessarie mention of prince Arthur, frameth a speech apologeticall in his and their behalf that were princes of the British bloud, discharging a short but yet a sharpe inuectiue against William Paruus, Polydor Virgil, and their complices, whom he accuseth of lieng toongs, enuious detraction, malicious slander, reprochfull and venemous language, wilfull ignorance, dogged enuie, and cankerd minds; for that they speake vnreuerentlie and contrarie to the knowne truth concerning those thrisenoble princes. Which defensitiue he would not haue deposed, but that he takes the monuments of their memories for vndoubted verities.[80]

This 'late writer' is Leland, and the 'speech apologeticall' is clearly the *Assertio*. The above quotation does not appear in the *Historie*'s earlier 1577 edition. In the first edition, Holinshed simply acknowledges with some awkwardness that there are some who 'haue doubted of the truthe of the whole historie whyche of hym is written' before changing the subject.[81] By 1587, the English translation of Leland's *Assertio* had been in circulation for five years, and its wider dissemination emboldened writers like Holinshed to invoke it in their own work. In the quotation above, the emphasis is on physical places as evidence of Arthur's 'grounded truth', and the 'defensitiue' of Leland's *Assertio* is justified because Leland 'takes the monuments of [Arthur's] memories for vndoubted verities'. Holinshed understands Leland's motivations, and acknowledges that such angry responses to Polydore stem from a need to defend Arthurian sites. Holinshed's comments evince the power of Arthur's places to suspend disbelief, even in more sceptical minds.

Like Leland, Prise was captivated by Arthur's places in the Welsh landscape. For Prise as for Leland, Arthurian places were surviving remnants of a lived past, proofs which could stand in defence of Arthur where human-authored texts failed to do so: 'even if human beings were to be silent about [Arthur]', writes Prise, 'the mountains and rocks and crags of this part of the world will for ever proclaim his name, so inseparable a companion of every virtue is glory' (Denique vt homines ipsi de Arthuro sileant, inclamabunt saltem montes, saxa et rupes huius regionis ipsius perpetuo nomen, adeo virtutis omnis omes tam indiuulsa

---

[80] Raphael Holinshed, *Chronicles*, The Holinshed Project, http://english.nsms.ox.ac.uk/holinshed/ [accessed 13 October 2017], 1587, II, p. 92.

[81] Raphael Holinshed, *Chronicles*, The Holinshed Project, http://english.nsms.ox.ac.uk/holinshed/ [accessed 13 October 2017], 1577, I, p. 131.

est gloria).[82] For Prise and his fellow Welshman Elis Gruffydd, the natural landscape itself proved more appealing for situating Arthur than it did for Leland, whose *Assertio* focuses more on man-made sites and objects.[83] Leland's key Arthurian sites in his defence were Glastonbury Abbey, Dover Castle, and Cadbury Castle in Somerset, with Caerleon, Tintagel, and Winchester playing a more minor role. Leland does mention two Welsh Arthurian sites in quick succession at the end of his chapter on 'Arthur's Commendation' (Laus Arturii) after proclaiming his trust in those 'rocks and engraved witnesses': Cair Arthur in Brecknockshire, which Leland translates as 'Arthur's castle' ('castrum Arturii'); and Arthur's gate in Montgomeryshire ('Portam Arturianam'). However, Leland uses these sites to evince the Welsh people's affection for Arthur, rather than to defend Arthur's existence. Cair Arthur is also mentioned by Gerald of Wales, one of Leland's sources; other than this example, Leland does not seem interested in using examples from the Welsh landscape in his defence.[84] During his itinerary in Wales he noted two further examples of Arthurian topography, but neither of these would make it into the *Assertio*.[85]

John Prise, on the other hand, figures such landscapes as long-lasting proofs, and although the natural implication of Prise's comments is that these sites are enduring memorials because of the Arthurian narratives or names that people – *Welsh* people – have attached to them, it is the rocks themselves, rather than the people telling the stories, who are framed as the witnesses to Arthur. Of the 'sites and rocks' (loca et rupes) in Wales with Arthurian associations, Prise says that 'thanks to their very substance they are more inured against being worn down, and they will preserve the name of Arthur for a longer time than other memorials made by hand' (quae vt duratiora sunt ipsa materia, sic et diuturnius caeteris manufactis monumentis nomen Arthuri conseruabunt).[86] For Prise, the landscape complete with its Arthurian place names can operate as a witness even if Arthur becomes forgotten by its human counterparts, though this does raise the question of whom Prise imagines to be

---

[82] John Prise, *Historiae Britannicae Defensio*, pp. 234–35.
[83] This is not to say that Arthurian objects do not feature at all in Prise's defence; he mentions the reported discovery of Arthur's crown in Caernarfon by Edward I, King Arthur's Seal at Westminster, and Arthur's inscribed cross reportedly found at the Glastonbury grave site. John Prise, *Historiae Britannicae Defensio*, pp. 225–26.
[84] Leland, *Assertio*, sig. F4r; Leland, *Learned*, sig. G4v.
[85] These include Bwrdd Arthur in Denbighshire ('sum calle it the Round Table') and a burial mound in Ceredigion ascribed to a giant apparently killed by Arthur. See Lloyd, *The Arthurian Place Names of Wales*, pp. 91–92.
[86] John Prise, *Historiae Britannicae Defensio*, pp. 236–37.

experiencing the landscape's Arthurian mnemonics in an imagined future in which Arthur is no longer remembered. In this sense, Prise's powerful rhetorical manoeuvring of these 'sites and rocks' transforms them into *lieux de mémoire*, 'moments of history torn away from the movement of history, then returned; no longer quite life, not yet death, like shells on the shore when the sea of living memory has receded'.[87]

Prise puts such trust in the landscape as evidence that he even calls forth Wales' natural geography to the proverbial witness stand for Arthur's existence:

> Consider also what men of learning tell us about the great contribution made by climate and regional characteristics to the furnishing of mental power and the safeguarding of physical health. This island is second to none for the quality of both its climate and its soil. I cannot, therefore, adequately express my astonishment at the unfair views of those who [...] still refuse to believe that distinguished and remarkable heroes [...] did once flourish in this island.
>
> (Quandoquidem et coeli temperiem et locorum naturas multum ad parandam animi virtutem corporisque valetudinem tuendam conferre a doctis memoratum est, qua quidem in re haec insula tam coeli quam soli temperie nulli cedit. Quare eorum iniqua iudicia satis admirari non possum, qui [...] tam praeclaros et excellentes viros in hac insula floruisse non credant.)[88]

Though this seems rather a leap in logic, Prise is following his sources here: 'men of learning' probably refers to Gerald of Wales. Owain Nash has demonstrated the humoral understanding of climate and its effects on national characteristics in Gerald's writings, which were a major source for Prise.[89] Nevertheless, Prise's certainty at this point is strangely at odds with the final chapter of his work, where he states that Wales' rugged and undivided terrain naturally lends itself to criminal activity.[90] By placing physical sites and landscape at the centre of their defences, Prise and his fellow defenders took advantage of the qualities of honesty and truth that these places seemed to hold, using them as foils for foreign sources deemed to be untrustworthy.

---

[87] Nora, 'Between Memory and History', p. 12. *Lieux de mémoire* are discussed above at pp. 24–25.
[88] John Prise, *Historiae Britannicae Defensio*, pp. 34–35.
[89] Owain Nash, 'Elements of Identity: Gerald, the Humours and National Characteristics', in *Gerald of Wales: New Perspectives on a Medieval Writer and Critic*, ed. A. Joseph McMullen and Georgia Henley (Cardiff: University of Wales Press, 2018), pp. 203–20.
[90] John Prise, *Historiae Britannicae Defensio*, pp. 262–63.

Polydore and the Romans: Ignorant foreigners or cunning adversaries?

Of the foreign authorities that Arthur's self-proclaimed British defenders cite, the most resentment is reserved for those perceived to be Roman. This is perhaps unsurprising in the context of post-Reformation England; Rome symbolised attempts to dominate Britain in both the ancient and not-so-distant pasts. After all, the tale of the Roman Emperor Lucius' failed attempts to bring Arthur's realm under his jurisdiction, first outlined by Geoffrey of Monmouth, was still largely accepted as part of Britain's history at this time.[91] In Geoffrey's original telling, Arthur defeats the Romans in Gaul but fails to take Rome. From the fifteenth century this was developed further: in the later version of John Hardyng's Chronicle (c. 1464), and subsequently in Thomas Malory's *Morte Darthur* (1485), Arthur is actually crowned Roman emperor himself.[92] By the late sixteenth century England had split from Rome, and for some writers Arthur's Roman exploits seemed more immediately relevant than ever. In Thomas Churchyard's *Worthines of Wales* (1587), for example, a chorographical description of Wales' landscape and history, Churchyard lifts material on Arthur's challenge to Rome directly from Geoffrey's *Historia* – including the speeches of Arthur, King Hoel, Cador, and Emperor Lucius – and inserts it incongruously into the middle of his text.[93]

The defences of Leland and Prise reflect this context of suspicion and resentment towards Rome. Despite using Roman sources when it suits their defensive purposes, both writers present the Romans as cunning manipulators. At times, their anti-Roman tirades read as barely concealed attacks on Polydore himself, and it is sometimes unclear whether the object of attack is Polydore the (straw)man or the Romans that he is seen to represent. As such, Polydore is paradoxically presented as both calculating and ignorant. John Prise accuses him of fabricating his 1525 edition of Gildas' *De excidio*, which inconveniently makes no mention of Arthur despite having been written around the same time Arthur

---

[91] An important exception is Ranulf Higden's *Polychronicon*, which points out that Arthur cannot have lived at the same time as Emperor Lucius. This discrepancy is also noted by the Glastonbury monk, Dom. Murelege. Murelege shared the Abbey's Arthurian holdings with William Worcester, holdings which perhaps included Higden's extremely popular and widespread work. See Housman, 'Higden, Trevisa, Caxton', p. 211; Worcester, *Itineraries*, pp. 260–61.
[92] John Hardyng, *Chronicle*, ed. Ellis, pp. 144–45; E. D. Kennedy, 'Sir Thomas Malory's (French) Romance and (English) Chronicle', in *Arthurian Studies in Honour of P. J. C. Field*, pp. 223–34.
[93] Thomas Churchyard, *The Worthines of Wales*, sig. D2r-H1r.

was said to have lived.⁹⁴ John Prise also identifies Polydore with the Romans, claiming that Polydore is biased in their favour and is therefore an unreliable writer of ancient British history: Polydore 'is, of course, himself an Italian by birth, and therefore more favourably disposed towards the Romans' (ipse quidem Italus genere, et ideo in Romanos propensior).⁹⁵ At the same time, however, Prise accuses Polydore of disingenuously abusing his Roman sources: 'Polydore has tampered with what Tacitus says [...] in the way he treats authors, he leaves no kind of trick untried' ([...] detractum a Polydoro ex Taciti loco iam citato [...] vt nullum genus artificii praetermittere videatur in tractandis authoribus).⁹⁶ Prise levels similar accusations of tricky wordplay and source manipulation at the Romans more generally, as this remark about Caesar's duplicity makes clear:

> All the Romans have always been greedy for glory [...] All those situations that turned out adversely for [Caesar] he covered over with wonderful artifice, subtly modifying his choice of words
>
> ([...] Romanis, qui omnes semper laudis auidi fuere [...] Sed ille omnia, quae sibi contigere aduersa, verbis immutatis miro artificio obtexit)⁹⁷

John Leland also employs this stereotype, characterising the Romans as eloquent and dishonest. His descriptions are similar to Prise's in terms of vocabulary, implying decoration, artifice, and duplicity:

> For the matter [of Britain] was so handled by them [the Romans], that they woulde elegantly and not truly pleade their cause. They painted out such thinges in writings [...]
>
> (Agebatur enim vt elegantissimi, non autem verissime causam dicerent. Talia pingebant in chartis [...])⁹⁸

Thus, Leland and Prise present Polydore – and his classical sources – as articulate but artificial, beautiful but unreliable, perhaps intentionally so. Polydore's refined modern style was apparently in vogue when Prise was writing, as Prise's dedicatory letter to William Herbert Earl of Pembroke prefacing the *Historia* makes clear:

---

[94] Gildas, *De calamitate excidio, & conquest Britanniae*, ed. Polydore Vergil (Antwerp, 1525).
[95] John Prise, *Historiae Britannicae Defensio*, pp. 144–45.
[96] John Prise, *Historiae Britannicae Defensio*, pp. 148–49.
[97] John Prise, *Historiae Britannicae Defensio*, pp. 82–83.
[98] Leland, *Learned*, sig. L3v; Leland, *Assertio*, sig. K2r.

What is at issue here, however, is a debate not about words but about facts, a situation in which truth, not eloquence, is called for. At the same time, I am well aware how fastidious men's ears are these days: nothing pleases them unless it is eloquent and polished and refined in every way possible, and they are almost more concerned about the effort which is put into embellishment of expression than they are about the examination of actual facts. I cannot approve of the view held by such people (I regard it, indeed, as preposterous) [...]

(At non hic agitur de verborum sed de rerum controuersia, qua in re veritas non eloquentia requiritur. Porro non sum nescius quam delicatae hac tempestate sint hominum aures, vt nihil arrideat nisi quod eloquio vsque quaque politum et nitidum sit, plusque fere laborent in sermonis ornatu quam in rerum ipsarum consideratione; quorum vt iudicium ceu praeposterum non probo)[99]

The sense of conservatism here implies a distrust of the new aesthetics of continental humanism and a yearning for a past imagined to have been plainer and more honest. Prise sets 'words' against 'facts', 'eloquence' against 'truth', and seems to provide support for the repurposing of native texts and physical sites as proofs to combat foreign texts. When framing the opposition as artificial, elaborate, and untrustworthy, Arthur's defenders again find that native sites and their artefacts provide very useful foils that seem clumsy and inelegant but honest by contrast, perhaps even on account of their clumsiness or inelegance. This implication of simplicity and honesty echoes Leland's treatment of the inhabitants of Cadbury and the site he proposes for Camlan. Leland likewise describes the inscription contained on Arthur's cross as comprising 'not so greate Romane letters, but indifferent cunningly grauen' (literis Romanis maiusculis illis, sed parum dextere insculptis) (*Learned* sig. H3v; *Assertio* sig. G2v). Just as Leland's focus is on artefacts and places, Prise uses his own area of expertise – language – to similar rhetorical effect, stating at the end of his opening address to the earl of Pembroke: 'our subject matter now is not Roman history and a Latin realm, but rather a realm which is British. Romans do not understand this realm, nor do they respect it in the same way as do the indigenous people of this land, even if the latter are barbarian in their speech' ([...] non de Romanis rebus regnoque Latino, sed de Britannico, nunc agitur, quod non aeque a Romanis atque ab huius terrae indigenis, etsi sermone barbaris, tenetur atque recolitur).[100]

---

[99] John Prise, *Historiae Britannicae Defensio*, pp. 16–19.
[100] John Prise, *Historiae Britannicae Defensio*, pp. 22–23.

Collaboration and contestation

Despite the obvious hostility that Leland and Prise show towards Polydore, their responses to foreign sources are not exclusively negative, and it is worth saying something here about how both writers used foreign sources to supplement their rhetorical use of native Arthurian places. Foreign sources clearly had their uses as counterparts to native evidence – particularly native places, or native texts writing about native places such as Glastonbury. Foreign sources were useful for various reasons: to give an impression of objectivity, to subsidise gaps in native material, or to evince Arthur's fame abroad. For example, John Leland prefaces the *Assertio* with a list of authorities used, divided into two columns: 'foreign' authorities (externi) and 'British' authorities (Britannici).[101] Leland's native sources originate exclusively from England and Wales, whilst his 'foreign' sources are all continental writers. The list was important enough to be maintained in Robinson's 1582 English translation, though Robinson further subdivides the foreign authorities into 'Poets' and 'Historiographers' (*Learned* sig. B2v). This may reflect contemporaneous debates on the values and role of poetry in historiographical practice as epitomised in Sir Philip Sidney's *Defence of Poesy*.[102]

Although the array of native writers among Leland's two lists is considerably larger, he does not treat all his foreign authorities with hostility. Some of the writers mentioned in Leland's list of foreign sources are well-known and were also consulted by Polydore, authorities such as Tacitus, Lucan, and Juvenal. Others are more enigmatic, and Leland must have selected them to defend Arthur for his own particular reasons, though they are especially important to Leland for shoring up the reality of native Arthurian places. When defending Arthur's tomb, for example, John Leland invokes the testimony of 'Claudius, a Frenchman', 'to the end the reader may understand that the credible report of Arthures Tombe found hapned euen vnto straungers vpright and perfect' (Claudius homo Gallus, vt lector intelligat fidem inuenti sepulchri vel ad

---

[101] *Assertio*, sig. A4v.
[102] Discussed below, pp. 243–44. Sidney identifies poetry as a useful tool for building engagement with history and learning, and for 'draw[ing] with [...] charming sweetness the wild untamed wits to an admiration of knowledge'. See Philip Sidney, *An Apology for Poetry (Or the Defence of Poesy)*, ed. R. W. Maslen, 3rd edn (Manchester: Manchester University Press, 2002), p. 82. On Sidney's treatment of history and poetry, see F. J. Levy, 'Sir Philip Sidney and the Idea of History', *Bibliothèque d'Humanisme et Renaissance*, 26:3 (1964), 608–17; Elizabeth Story Donno, 'Old Mouse-eaten Records: History in Sidney's *Apology*', in *Sir Philip Sidney: An Anthology of Modern Criticism*, ed. Dennis Kay (Oxford: Oxford University Press, 1987), pp. 147–67.

extero integram peruenisse).¹⁰³ Leland uses this unknown 'Claudius' as a valuable foreign witness to the story of Arthur's exhumation, providing support to the better-known testimony of native sources that he wishes to authenticate (Gerald of Wales, John Bever, the chronicler of Pershore Abbey, Matthew Paris, and Ranulf Higden).¹⁰⁴ In addition to 'Claudius', Leland also cites 'Ponticus Verunnius, an Italian but yet one that loued the Brittaines well' (Ponticus Virunius homo Italus, philobritannus tamen).¹⁰⁵ Ponticus Virunius was the earliest printer to publish his own abridgement of Geoffrey of Monmouth's *Historia* in 1508, which would be republished again in 1534 and eventually in 1585 by the Welsh printer David Powel.¹⁰⁶ As such, he provided Leland with a useful counterpart to Polydore: a learned Italian humanist who, unlike Polydore, looked favourably upon the Galfridian history and upon Arthur. Amusingly, Leland falls foul of the same crime of which Polydore is accused: source manipulation. Leland claims that Virunius had written to rebut Polydore Vergil. In fact, there is no mention of Polydore in Virunius' 1508 *History*, because it was first published five years before the earliest extant draft of Polydore's *Anglica Historia* was written.¹⁰⁷ In any case, Virunius died around 1520, fourteen years before the earliest publication of Polydore's *Anglica Historia* in Basel in 1534. As with Leland's treatment of Gawain's burial sites and the location of Camlan, Leland's critical approach is inconsistent: Leland makes no attempts made to undermine or even question Virunius' knowledge. Ironically, Leland himself appears to be either ignorant or manipulative of the foreign sources that he is using.

Prise is more willing to turn to non-native sources in his defence than Leland. For Prise, foreign sources are vital in order to avoid accusations of bias, to support his native sources, or to show Arthur's universal fame. There is, he claims,

> no more reliable evidence than that of one's opponents. [...] But what answer is to be made to Roman authors? They too, here and there in their books, had occasion to discuss British affairs. The events which they recount are almost identical with those contained in the history translated by Geoffrey.

---

[103] *Learned*, sig. K2v; *Assertio*, sig. I1v.
[104] *Learned*, sigs K2v–K3v; *Assertio*, sigs I1v–I2v.
[105] *Learned*, sig. L3r; *Assertio*, sig. K1v.
[106] P. Virunii, *Historiae Britannicae Libri VI* (Reggio, 1508), Cambridge, CUL, Norton d. 170. In the same year, Ivo Cavellatus also published an edition of the *Historia* in Paris. See *The Historia Regum Britannie of Geoffrey of Monmouth*, ed. Neil Wright (Woodbridge: Boydell, 1985), I, pp. xlvi–xlvii.
[107] Vatican MS Codices Urbinates Latini 497/498, which dates to 1513.

(Ad aduersariuorum testimonio nihil locupletius [...] quid authoribus Romanis respondebitur? Qui, dum sparsim suis libris de rebus Britannicis agere se infert occasio, eadem fere rerum euenta commemorant quae in historia a Gaufredo traducta habentur)[108]

Prise thus advocates for the synthesis of native and foreign sources, and chastises Polydore for failing to do the same. Polydore's aim, he says, should have been to 'reconcile' Roman and British historiography to one another (conciliare), so that 'the points of agreement between them' are made manifest (vt [...] rebus conuenire viderentur).[109] Prise, deeming Polydore's approach to be insufficient in this regard, points to Henry of Huntingdon as an exemplar. Demonstrating both Henry's collegiality and his acceptance of Galfridian history, Prise asserts that Henry had written his own history of Britain before discovering Geoffrey's *Historia*, after which he appended a summary of Geoffrey's text to the end of his own work.[110]

As well as describing Henry of Huntingdon's treatment of Geoffrey of Monmouth, Prise also implies a somewhat unlikely collaborative relationship between Henry and Gerald of Wales. Although Prise admits that Henry is 'ignorant of the British tongue' (ob Britannicae linguae imperitiam), he argues that Henry probably consulted with contemporaries such as Gerald of Wales, 'learned men' who were 'equally versed in Latin and in the British tongue' (viri eruditi qui latinam iuxta ac britannicam callerent).[111] Of course, Henry of Huntingdon died in 1160 when Gerald was a mere teenager, and it is therefore most unlikely that they collaborated as historians.[112] Nevertheless, Prise followed this imagined example of collegiality, pooling his expertise with others in his own antiquarian practice. He spoke fondly of his collaborative meetings

---

[108] John Prise, *Historiae Britannicae Defensio*, pp. 72–73.
[109] John Prise, *Historiae Britannicae Defensio*, pp. 154–57.
[110] John Prise, *Historiae Britannicae Defensio*, pp. 70–71. Henry of Huntingdon was gifted a copy of Geoffrey of Monmouth's text from the library at Bec Abbey, probably by Robert de Torigni. See Benjamin Pohl, 'When did Robert of Torigni first receive Henry of Huntingdon's *Historia Anglorum*, and Why Does It Matter?', *Haskins Society Journal*, 26 (2015), 143–67. See also Jaakko Tahkokallio, *The Anglo-Norman Historical Canon: Publishing and Manuscript Culture* (Cambridge: Cambridge University Press, 2019), pp. 38–46.
[111] John Prise, *Historiae Britannicae Defensio*, pp. 70–71.
[112] Robert Bartlett, 'Gerald of Wales [Giraldus Cambrensis, Gerald de Barry] (c. 1146–1220x23)', *Oxford Dictionary of National Biography*, www.oxforddnb.com/view/10.1093/ref:odnb/9780198614128.001.0001/odnb-9780198614128-e-10769 [accessed 7 December 2018]; D. E. Greenway, 'Henry [Henry of Huntingdon] (c. 1088–c. 1157), *Oxford Dictionary of National Biography*, www.oxforddnb.com/view/10.1093/ref:odnb/9780198614128.001.0001/odnb-9780198614128-e-12970 [accessed 7 December 2018].

with his 'friend Leland' (a Leylando nostro) in which the pair studied old British manuscripts together.[113] Yet Prise also understood Leland's linguistic limitations, admitting Leland to be 'ignorant' (ignari) of the British tongue.[114] This seems to suggest that Prise saw his relationship with Leland as a collaborative one in which expertise was to be shared.

There is also evidence of a cooperative relationship between Prise and another Arthurian defender, Humphrey Llwyd: Llwyd must have known about Prise's *Historia* before its 1573 publication, as he refers to Prise's 'apologie of the British historie' in the *Cronica Walliae* (1559).[115] This raises an interesting possibility, for Llwyd also refers to Leland as 'nostro Lelando' (my freende M. Leland) in the *Commentarioli Britannicae*.[116] Here, Llwyd repeats Prise's words almost verbatim, and whilst it is unlikely that Llwyd collaborated with Leland it is possible that he did work with Prise. If Llwyd or his publisher lifted this phrase directly from Prise, this implies a kind of performed collaboration, the presentation of a united front against a perceived foreign attack from Polydore.[117] In contrast, Prise indicates that Polydore had not been so collegial. In his prefatory letter to the earl of Pembroke, Prise claims that Polydore has failed to address any of the issues that his Welsh-speaking contemporaries had drawn to his attention:

> For a long time I was encouraged by the great hope that Polydore Vergil would be honourable enough to put right some matters in the history which he has published, a history of the English people (as he puts it in his title). I refer to matters, in that publication of his, which – thanks to what men of learning have made known, either in speech or in writing – he discovers were not at all as he reported them in his history. Now, however, that Polydore has made it clear in so many ways that he has not the least intention of correcting his work [...]
>
> (Etsi diu quidem ingens me spes fouebat (Vir ornatissime) Polydorum Vergilium ab aedita historia sua quam gentis Anglorum inscribit nonnulla, quae ab eiusdem aeditione, doctorum virorum partim sermonibus, partim scriptis aeditis, aliter se habere quam ipse in historia huiusmodi prodidisset comperit, ingenue correcturum:

---

[113] John Prise, *Historiae Britannicae Defensio*, pp. 192–93.
[114] John Prise, *Historiae Britannicae Defensio*, pp. 232–33.
[115] Llwyd, *Cronica Walliae*, pp. 13–14.
[116] Llwyd, *Commentarioli*, ed. Sutton, §11.
[117] Llwyd, *Breviary of Britain*, ed. Schwyzer, p. 59 n. Schwyzer points out that Llwyd probably did not work with Leland, as Leland was severely mentally ill by the time that Llwyd was in his late teens.

nunc vero, postquam id se quam minime facturum esse multis argumentis ostendit [...])[118]

Thus, objectivity and the sharing of both native and foreign knowledge are qualities that Prise values in historiographical practice. Unlike Leland, Prise does not take such issue with foreign attempts to write Britain's history – provided that such attempts take pains to listen to the voices of native men such as himself who claim a superior knowledge of Britain's languages, manuscripts, and landscapes.

A different perspective: Elis Gruffydd

As I have already suggested, Prise and Leland saw themselves as British, writing their defences in Latin, a *lingua franca* for a learned Latinate audience that stretched well beyond the bounds of the British archipelago. Sympathetic to the union of England and Wales, Prise and Leland were keen to present a united front against the hostile foreign agent that they imagined to be Italian or Roman: a source from outside of Britain. Thus, performing a shared British identity was vital to the effectiveness of their defences against Polydore. In contrast, Elis Gruffydd wrote his chronicle in Welsh, and specifically for his fellow Welshmen at home in his native Flintshire. Gruffydd sent his chronicle home to Llanasa after he had written it, stating at the end of the *Cronicl*'s preface that 'this I caused to write down that the matter be not forgotten in Llanasa' (Hyn a ddaruu J mi Isgriuenv hrag mynned y matter dros gof ynn Llanhassaph).[119] Whereas Leland and Prise point to the Italians and Romans as the anti-British foreign agents, Elis Gruffydd identifies the attack on the British History as English in origin. Thus, the identity of the imagined hostile foreign agent was prone to change across Arthurian defences depending on the native identity that the authors constructed for themselves. As these writers' concepts of foreignness are rooted in a sense of difference, they are articulated in relation to the authors' own native identities and their perceptions of who, or what, is foreign.

Consequently, the native places that these writers envision for Arthur also differ. In contrast to Leland and Prise, the places that Gruffydd uses to shore up his impression of Arthur are overwhelmingly located in Wales.[120] Some of these are mapped straight out of the romance

---

[118] John Prise, *Historiae Britannicae Defensio*, pp. 16–17.
[119] NLW MS 5276Di, f. 2v. Translation from Morgan, 'Elis Gruffydd of Gronant', p. 9.
[120] Gruffydd's Arthurian material is largely concentrated to NLW MS 5276Dii, ff. 320v–342v. The manuscript is imperfect, with a leaf missing between folios 340 and 341; however, a faithful copy of the original manuscript was made by Dafydd

tradition, often onto Gruffydd's native North Wales. Sorelois, the land originally belonging to King Loholt in the French Lancelot–Grail cycle, becomes Surloes in 'Bon y Don' (Moel y Don) in 'Vwnai' (Menai).[121] Scott Lloyd has suggested that Gruffydd, in changing Pont Norgalois to 'Moel y Don', may have had in mind the bridge of boats that English forces constructed to aid their invasion of Bangor in 1282.[122] If this is the case, then Gruffydd is centring not only the real-world site of the Moel y Don crossing, but the history of Anglo-Welsh conflict. Welsh sources are crucial to Gruffydd's sense of Arthur's native places; Arthur is raised in the household of Cynydd Cain Farfog, lord of Penllyn, next to 'Llyn Tegid' (Lake Bala) in North Wales.[123] Gruffydd appears to have based his account of Arthur's childhood on at least two Welsh sources, although as Ceridwen Lloyd-Morgan has pointed out at least one of these sources, the fourteenth-century *Birth of Arthur*, attests to a rich comingling of Welsh and francophone literary culture in late medieval Wales.[124] Gruffydd also includes a number of sites in his Arthurian geography that are more widely attested. Arthur battles Colgrim in York and Gwilmor in Ireland; he brings Gawain's body to Dover Castle; Guinevere retires to a nunnery in Caerleon; and Arthur pulls the sword from a stone sitting in a churchyard in London, though Gruffydd also includes the alternative location of Winchester.[125] Gruffydd also refigures some of Arthur's best-known places in surprising ways; for example, Arthur's final battle with Mordred takes place not in Cornwall but in a field beside Glastonbury Abbey.[126]

Gruffydd pulls his Arthurian place associations from a variety of traditions, including chronicle and romance, and makes use of sources in multiple languages, including French, English, Welsh, and Latin.[127] Gruffydd would have had ready access to such a multilingual collection during the periods he spent in London and Calais, but his contemporaries

---

Parry around 1700, and survives as NLW MS 6209 E. See Lloyd-Morgan, 'The Welsh Tradition in Calais', p. 78.

[121] This section has been edited and studied in Thomas Jones, 'Chwedl Huail ap Caw ac Arthur', in *Astudiaethau Amrywiol a Gyflwynir i Syr Thomas Parry-Williams* (Cardiff: University of Wales Press, 1968), pp. 48–66 (pp. 55–56); translation from Lloyd, *The Arthurian Place Names of Wales*, p. 95.

[122] Lloyd, *Arthurian Place Name of Wales*, p. 95.

[123] NLW MS 5276Dii, f. 322r.

[124] Lloyd-Morgan, 'The Welsh Tradition in Calais', p. 79; Ceridwen Lloyd-Morgan, 'Crossing the Borders: Literary Borrowing in Medieval Wales and England', in *Authority and Subjugation in the Writing of Medieval Wales*, pp. 159–74 (p. 163).

[125] NLW MS 5276Dii, f. 327r; f. 322v; ff. 339v–340r; ff. 325r–v.

[126] NLW MS 5276Dii, f. 340r.

[127] On Gruffydd's sources for this Arthurian material, see Ceridwen Lloyd-Morgan, 'Welsh Tradition in Calais', passim.

writing at home in Wales were also drawing on sources in French, English, and Latin as well as Welsh, and had been for centuries. This was especially true in Gruffydd's native Flintshire, situated on the border between Welsh- and English-speaking areas.[128] Gruffydd's recourse to francophone sources, and particularly to romance texts, indicates that he was not as squeamish as Leland and Prise when it came to the types of sources he used when deciding where to locate Arthur. This more relaxed approach is partly because, as a Welshman serving the English army in Calais, Gruffydd's own sense of selfhood was particularly complicated, but also because Gruffydd's text is not explicitly framed as an Arthurian defence in the same way as Prise's *Defensio* and Leland's *Assertio*. Indeed, Gruffydd's Arthur is not always presented in an entirely positive light, although this is because Gruffydd tends to follow his sources: his English and Anglo-Latin sources present Arthur positively, whilst French and Welsh sources are more critical.[129] Where he is critical of Arthur, Gruffydd describes him as a murderous, cross-dressing philanderer, an echo of the less positive portrayal of Arthur that we see in many of the Welsh saints' lives, such as those of St Gildas, St Carannog, and St Cadog.[130] Following the reference to Surloes, Gruffydd begins a section on Arthur's relationship with, and eventual murder of, Gildas' brother, Huail ap Caw. This tale takes places in Edeirnion, an ancient commote of Wales that was located not far from Gruffydd's birthplace in Flintshire.[131] The topographical set piece of this section is Huail's stone, a site which is also mentioned by John Prise, though without the detailed back story that Gruffydd provides.[132] The story of Arthur killing Gildas' brother, Huail, existed before Gruffydd's *Cronicl* and is first attested as early as the 1120s or 1130s.[133] However, whilst Gruffydd's Arthurian material is taken from a rich variety of textual sources in English, French, Latin, and Welsh, his

---

[128] Lloyd-Morgan, 'Crossing the Borders', pp. 167–68.
[129] Ceridwen Lloyd-Morgan, 'The Welsh Tradition in Calais', p. 87.
[130] See Ceridwen Lloyd-Morgan, '*Breuddwyd Rhonabwy* and Later Arthurian Literature', in *The Arthur of the Welsh*, ed. Rachel Bromwich and Brynley F. Roberts (Cardiff: University of Wales Press, 1991), pp. 183–209 (p. 192); Elissa R. Henken, 'Folklore and Popular Tradition', in *Arthur in the Celtic Languages*, pp. 214–30 (pp. 216–18).
[131] NLW MS 5276Dii, ff. 329v.
[132] NLW MS 5276Dii, ff. 334v–5r.
[133] Arthur and Huail's enmity is described in twelfth-century texts such as *Culhwch ac Olwen*, Caradoc of Llancarfan's *Vita Gildae*, and Gerald of Wales' *Descriptio Kambriae*, and later in John of Glastonbury's *Cronica*. See Gerald of Wales, *Journey Through Wales and Description of Wales*, ed. and trans. Lewis Thorpe (London: Harmondsworth, 1978), p. 259; Caradoc of Llancarfan, 'Vita Gildae', in Chambers, *Arthur of Britain*, pp. 262–64; John of Glastonbury, *Cronica*, pp. 73–75; Tatlock, *The Legendary History*, p. 189.

account of the murder of Huail is different to any earlier sources that exist on the subject.[134] Whilst it is technically possible that Gruffydd's version is original to Gruffydd himself, there is evidence of an extant Welsh tradition about the grave of Huail, so Gruffydd's account likely has its origins in oral tradition.[135] In Gruffydd's account, Huail steals one of Arthur's mistresses (we never hear of Arthur having mistresses in other Arthurian narratives); and at one point Arthur dresses in women's clothing in order to seduce a woman.[136] When Huail offends Arthur by breaking an oath whereby he had promised to not mention an injury previously given to the king in combat, mocking Arthur's lopsided dancing, Arthur flies into a rage, beheading Huail against a stone in the town of Ruthin. 'Because of this', Gruffydd tells us, 'to remember this deed the stone was called from then to today, Maen Huail [the Stone of Huail]' (ac o'r achos yma, j ddwyn koof o'r weithred hon j gelwir y maen hwn jr hyny hyd heddiw Maen Huail).[137] This episode is hardly a positive portrayal of Arthur: he is shown here as lustful, depraved, wrathful, and violent. However, Gruffydd nevertheless presents Arthur's historic existence as a reality. As Gruffydd tends to follow his sources, whether positive or negative on the subject of Arthur, this is consistent with his historiographical practice. It also demonstrates that Gruffydd places his faith in the authenticity of Arthurian topography that he is familiar with from his native North Wales. Physical monuments like Maen Huail, which still stands even today, function for Gruffydd as enduring and honest reminders of the past, echoing Prise's own sentiments about rocks and monuments that 'preserve the name of Arthur for a longer time' because they are more 'inured against being worn down'.[138]

In fact, John Prise also mentions Huail's Stone in his defence; however, Prise frames the stone and its story very differently. After agonising over the absence of Arthur in Polydore's edition of Gildas' *De excidio*, Prise weighs up the manuscript evidence in painstaking codicological detail,

[134] On Gruffydd's sources, see Morfydd E. Owen, 'The Prose of the *Cywydd* Period', in *A Guide to Welsh Literature 1282–c.1550*, ed. A. O. H. Jarman and Gwilym Rees Hughes (Cardiff: University of Wales Press, 1997), II, pp. 319–29.
[135] The fifteenth-century poet Lewis Glyn Gothi compares the grave of 'Master Watkin, lord of Herast' to the grave of 'Huail e hun' (Huail himself); see Lloyd, *The Arthurian Place Names of Wales*, p. 96. Lloyd-Morgan argues that the tale of Huail ap Caw must have its origins in oral tradition; see Lloyd-Morgan, 'Welsh Tradition in Calais', pp. 80–81; Ceridwen Lloyd-Morgan, 'Oral et Écrit Dans La Chronique d'Elis Gruffydd', *Kreiz 5: Études Sur La Bretagne et Les Pays Celtiques*, 49.165 (1996), 179–86.
[136] Lloyd-Morgan, 'Welsh Tradition in Calais', pp. 80–81.
[137] Jones, p. 57; translation from Lloyd, *Arthurian Places Names of Wales*, pp. 96–97.
[138] Cited above at pp. 191–92.

examining different Gildas manuscripts side-by-side and commenting on palaeographical dating, differences in computation, changes of ink, interpolation, and palimpsesting or erasure.[139] Prise does this in order to determine whether Gildas, angry at his brother's death, had purposefully destroyed books evincing Arthur's history and replaced them with other material, a prospect which has a strong emotional effect on Prise: 'I confess that I found welling up inside me a huge longing to see for myself at least some of Gildas' own writings' (ingenti fateor studio aestuabam Gildae ipsius aliqua saltem scripta videre).[140] Ultimately, Prise will not definitively state whether or not he believes Polydore's edition of Gildas to be genuine and seems somewhat confused on this point: despite setting out at some length to disprove the authenticity of Polydore's text, Prise also mentions the enmity between Arthur and Huail, the murder, and Huail's stone, information that he says he has read in the works of Gerald of Wales, 'ancient genealogies', 'ancient accounts of Gildas' life' in both 'the British tongue' and in Latin, and the Chronicles of Glastonbury.[141] Whilst this seems contradictory, it exposes a problem for Prise: to demonstrate that Gildas may have tampered with Arthurian history helps to explain unwanted gaps in the textual tradition; but to concede that Polydore's edition of *De excidio* might be genuine undermines Prise's attempts to present his opponent as ignorant and manipulative. This explains why Prise – selectively and carefully – has chosen to include the example of Huail's Stone in his list of Arthurian places. The stone testifies not only to Arthur's existence, but also to Huail's bloody murder, an event sufficiently appalling to explain the enmity between Arthur and Gildas, and therefore Gildas' destruction of Arthurian historiography.

Gruffydd's treatment of native Arthurian places suggests a similar attitude towards foreignness to Leland and Prise. For Gruffydd, as for his contemporaries, foreign sources are presented as ignorant, and foreign authors the sources of the fabulistic elements in Arthur's history. Here, however, the ignorant adversary and the source of untruths surrounding Arthur is English rather than continental. This is particularly clear in

[139] John Prise, *Historiae Britannicae Defensio*, pp. 200–05.
[140] John Prise, *Historiae Britannicae Defensio*, pp. 200–07.
[141] 'And ancient genealogies of the Britons bear witness that Howel or Huail was indeed Gildas' brother, and that Arthur killed the aforenamed Howel or Huail. Ancient accounts of Gildas' life which are written in the British tongue, and also some others in Latin, confirm this.' (Hoelum siue Huelinum ipsum fuisse Gildae fratrem antiquissimae apud eos genealogiae attestantur, quodque Arthurus iam dictum Hoelum siue Huelinum occiderit et antiquissima Britannice scripta monumenta et Latine nonnulla alia, videlicet quae de vita ipsius Gildae habentur, comprobant.) John Prise, *Historiae Britannicae Defensio*, pp. 246–49.

Gruffydd's inconsistent treatment of Arthurian sites in England and Wales with their basis in oral folklore. As in many other Arthurian texts, Gruffydd maintains several of Arthur's key strongholds from Geoffrey of Monmouth, such as Caerleon (or 'Caerllion-ar-Wysg').[142] Gruffydd also proposes Caerleon as an alternative setting for the story of Merlin's birth, though he also includes the better-attested Carmarthen, perhaps indicating he was more familiar with North Wales than South Wales.[143] However, Gruffydd's *Cronicl* is the earliest text to mention Arthurian courts at Nannerch (probably Moel Arthur) and Caerwys, locations in Gruffydd's native Flintshire:

> [Arthur's court] was in a town which the story of the Sangreall calls Caerhass, that which the story professes is today called Caerwys [...][144]

> ([Y llys Arthur] a [o]edd mewn tref yr hon j mae ysdori y Sang Real yn i hennwi Kaerhass, yr hon wrth broses yr ysdori a elwir heddiw Kaerwys)[145]

> at that time, according to some of the stories, Arthur made a court in that place now called Nannerch. And even now the spot is called Llys Arthur. And it is said that the church was his chapel and was for long afterwards called Capel Gwial [the wicker chapel].[146]

> (ynn yr amser yma ynn ol hrai o'r ysdoriae j gwnnaeth Arthur lys yn y lle heddiw a elwir Nannerch. An etto j gelwir y man Llys Arthur. Ac yvo a ddywedir mae j gappel ef hen bobylydoedd yr eglwys, yr hwnn a alwyd ynn hir o amser ynn ol y Kappel Gwial)[147]

As neither of these places are attested in any sources earlier than Gruffydd, and assuming Gruffydd himself was not their originator, they must have been obtained either from a now-lost source or through oral tradition in Gruffydd's native Flintshire. Gruffydd explicitly states his reliance on oral history several times during his *Cronicl*, and does not exhibit any misgivings about this. He readily attests to material he has gathered from 'yr hen bobyl' (the old people), or 'gwr krededun' (credible men).[148]

Gruffydd does not explicitly state why he finds certain people more credible as oral witnesses than others, but he is openly dismissive of

---

[142] Lloyd-Morgan, 'The Welsh Tradition in Calais', p. 82.
[143] NLW MS 5276Dii, f. 298v.
[144] Lloyd, *The Arthurian Place Names of Wales*, p. 96.
[145] Jones, 'Chwedl Huail', p. 56.
[146] Lloyd, *The Arthurian Place Names of Wales*, p. 96.
[147] Jones, 'Chwedl Huail', p. 57.
[148] NLW MS 5276Dii, ff. 322v–324r, translation mine.

English folklore surrounding Arthurian places. When complaining that the English accuse the Welsh of gullibly believing in Arthur's return, Gruffydd retorts that in his view the English 'talk much more about him than we do' (mae yn vwy j son wyntt amdano eg no nnyni).[149] He gives specific examples that he finds particularly risible, such as those who believe Arthur to be sleeping in 'a cave under a hill near Glastonbury' (mewn googof dan vryn garllaw Glasynbri) from whence he is said to have emerged and 'conversed with many people in many strange ways' (ymddiuanodd a lawer o bobyl mewn llawer modd hryuedd).[150] At another point, Gruffydd speaks of 'many strange tales circulated among the common people of the kingdom' (j bu lawer o chwedl e hryuedd ymhlith kyffredin y dyrnas), including a report from Gloucestershire of a woman who met one of Arthur's servants whilst riding home, who brought her to the cave where he was sleeping in an attempt to sell her one of Arthur's horses.[151] Gruffydd is again derisive, stating that this is as likely to be true as 'stones are to speak or the sea to burn' (wrth fy nhyb a'm hamkann, jr ydoedd y chwedyl hwn kynn wiried a bod y kereig yn dywedud ne'r moor yn llogsi).[152] Gruffydd associates Gloucestershire with the more fantastical locations of Arthurian romance, such as the glassy isle where Merlin meets his end ('Ynnys Wydrin'), though even here Gruffydd is quick to offer an alternative location for the episode in Brittany.[153] There is no mention of Ynys Wydrin's association with Glastonbury. When contrasted with Gruffydd's allusions to Arthurian landscape folklore in Wales, this clearly demonstrates that Gruffydd places more belief in places in his native Wales than in English sites.

There are other moments when Gruffydd seems to present the English within the same ignorance/manipulation dichotomy as Leland and Prise present's presentation of Polydore and the Romans. Sometimes, the two archetypes appear at the same time. When addressing the controversy surrounding the British History, Gruffydd cites Arthurian sceptic John Rastell. Rastell is best known for his 1530 chronicle *The Pastyme of People*, one of the earliest chronicles to be printed in English. Rastell's work was a popular source for Gruffydd and his contemporaries, largely on account

---

[149] NLW MS 5276Dii, f. 342r. Translation from Lloyd-Morgan, 'The Welsh Tradition in Calais', p. 91.

[150] Translation and text from Lloyd-Morgan, 'The Welsh Tradition in Calais', p. 91. For a discussion of whether this 'cave under a hill' was more likely to represent Cadbury or Glastonbury Tor, see above at pp. 157–61.

[151] Text and translation from Ceridwen Lloyd-Morgan, 'Later Hybrid Narrative Texts', p. 210.

[152] Ibid.

[153] NLW MS 5276Dii, f. 352r.

of its ready availability in print, a technology that Gruffydd lauded.¹⁵⁴ Rastell's approach to historiography was extremely critical – indeed, to a fault, for he was convinced that Stonehenge was too large to be made out of real stones and must have been made from cement using large moulds.¹⁵⁵ Rastell's commentary on Arthurian history was no different, and was as critical as Polydore's, if not more so. Rastell openly questioned the authenticity of Arthur's material history, including Arthur's seal at Westminster.¹⁵⁶ He also pointed out inconsistencies between English and continental histories of Arthur, as the following passage demonstrates. Gruffydd quotes this excerpt from Rastell almost verbatim, but he makes subtle yet significant changes that drastically alter its tone. Below, I include Gruffydd's version side-by-side with Rastell's original. Gruffydd's alterations are shown in bold:

[Rastell]

Therefore some men at this day therbe, which, what for these reasons and dyuers other, take that story of Galfridus but for a feyned fable; supposing that because this Galfridus was a welchman born, that he should fayn that story himself for the only pryes of his countremen; because we rede of no writer of storis before his dais that euer wrot therof, or spekith of this Brutus, nor makith therof no mencion [...]¹⁵⁷

[Gruffydd]

Ac ynn unwedic am i vod ef yn Gymro i mae **y Ssaesson a nashiwn eraill mae jr klod a** moliantt yw genhedleth jr ysgriuenodd ef yr ysdori yma oi ben ac oi awdurdod j hun **oherwydd na uedrant weled** llyvyr or ysdori yma yn ysgrivenedig o wa ith neb or awdurion ymlaen Gallfreidws [...]

(Because he [Geoffrey] is a Welshman, **the English and other nations think that** it was to honour and glorify his people that he wrote this history, out of his head and on his own authority, **because they could not find** a book with this story written by any of the authors before Geoffrey [...])¹⁵⁸

These changes transform the passage from damning evidence against Arthur to an attack on the integrity and knowledge of Arthur's foreign naysayers. For Rastell, no histories exist before Geoffrey which mention the same material; but for Gruffydd, the 'English and other nations'

---

¹⁵⁴ Gruffydd, *Tales of Merlin*, p. 12.
¹⁵⁵ Rastell, *Pastyme of People*, sig. C2v.
¹⁵⁶ Lloyd-Morgan, 'The Welsh Tradition in Calais', p. 95.
¹⁵⁷ Rastell, *Pastyme of People*, p. 7.
¹⁵⁸ NLW MS 5276Dii, f. 83r; translation from Gruffydd, *Tales of Merlin*, p. 48.

simply 'could not find' these histories. Here, '[g]weled' is translated as 'find', but it can also mean 'understand', or 'comprehend'. We know that Gruffydd had a rich seam of Welsh textual and oral sources available to him. Just as Gruffydd's contemporaries were quick to attack Polydore's ignorance of the Welsh textual tradition, Gruffydd is employing the same tactics here against the English. By mentioning them explicitly, rather than simply referring to 'other nations' as a collective, Gruffydd places blame firmly on the English, rather than the Italians, as the corrupters of native British history. It is unclear here whether Gruffydd also has Polydore in mind, as an English denizen, or whether he is more interested in attacking Rastell. Either way, he employs the same tactics as Prise and Leland to demonstrate how anti-Welsh bias has affected the reception of British history. It is Geoffrey's Welshness, Gruffydd suggests, that has prevented him from being believed.

Elsewhere, Gruffydd employs the foreign manipulator trope in a far more obvious way. In the following passage, remarkably similar to the anti-Italian material in Leland and Prise's texts, Gruffydd accuses the English of 'soffistri', one of the earliest known examples of the anglicism in the Welsh language:

> And yet despite these peculiarities and objections within the stories, Geoffrey's work may yet be true. The English, however, in their sophistry bring these objections before us like dust to blind our trust and acceptance and to get us to believe, as most of them do, that neither the women mentioned here [Albina and her sisters] nor Brutus were ever in this realm.

> (Onid etto er hyn oll o ymrauaelion ac o wrthnebion mewn ysdoriae, yvo allai j waith Galffreidws vod yn wir, namyn bod y bobyl Seissnig drwy j souesdri yn hroddi yr achoshion hyn gar yn bron ni megis bryche j ddalu yn koel an meuerdod ni ac j geisshio genym ni gredu a choelio megis ac j mae y hran vwia [sic] o honaunt twy yn koelio ac yn kredu nab u na'r marched a dreithir ynn y blaen na'r Bruttus a dreithir vchod jrmoed o vewn y dyrnas hon.)[159]

At this point, the imagery and tone seem almost religious: Gruffydd relies on the strength of his belief where sources and evidence fail him. Immediately after this point in the text, Gruffydd dutifully provides the various arguments put forward by his contemporaries for the unreliability of Geoffrey's *Historia*; but he nevertheless closes the discussion with his doctored quotation from Rastell. By ending the passage on this note, Gruffydd leaves open the possibility that doubts surrounding the British

[159] NLW MS 5276Dii, f. 81r; translation from Gruffydd, *Tales of Merlin*, p. 46.

History can be dismissed if they are expressed by people who are unable to understand sources on Britain's early history in the Welsh language, be they textual or oral. Gruffydd handles his material skilfully enough to retain the ambiguity of this passage; but the alterations that he makes to Rastell betray his attempts to present his English adversaries as ignorant and manipulative.

Despite the clear anger in the previous extracts, Gruffydd sees value in the synthesis of foreign and native sources, just like his contemporary John Prise. This is particularly noticeable when Gruffydd describes the grave of the Welsh hero, Llywelyn ap Gruffydd, whom tradition claims to have been laid to rest in Cwmhir Abbey. Aside from evincing the use of poetry on tombs – and the fluidity of it – in the sixteenth century, providing a useful comparison to Arthur's sepulchral poetry at Glastonbury Abbey, this example also appears, at first glance, to illustrate Gruffydd's even-handed philosophy when it came to using foreign and native sources. Gruffydd tells us that on Llywelyn's grave, a Welsh poet had written the following lines in metrical verse:

> The brave and powerful defender,
> Llywelyn the prince and the highly praised ruler,
> And guardian of virtues with the strength of his sword,
> And of all manner of men
> And the flower of lords,
> To death, without favour,
> Truly paid his dues.
> Mirror of all princes and lords
> Who ever were and who will be in our nation,
> Of all dukes, princes,
> And noble men –
> To uphold the law for good men,
> He was the most righteous.
> In this grave, I say,
> Lies a prince, the brightest of the bright.
>
> (Yr ymddiffynwr gwrol grymus
> Llywelyn y tywysog ar hriolwr molianvs
> Ac o nerth j gledde keidwad hrinwedde
> Ac o bob kyuriw ddyn ac o arglwyddi y blodeun
> Yr hwn j angau heb geed
> A dalawdd j wir ddled
> Drych tywysogion ac arglwyddi
> Araun ac aravydd on kennedlaeth ni
> O dduwk o dywysog Ac o wyr dyledog
> j gadw y gyraith ar wyrda

> Y vo a vu y kyuiowna
> Ynn y Bedd hwnn meddaf j
> i gorwedd tywysog Eglurdeb y goleuni).[160]

At some point, Gruffydd tells us, an English poet or versifier came to the grave site at a later date and added the following words to extend the poem on the grave, which are rather less laudatory:

> Here leith of Erwr the pryns yf ye wyl ken
> Thif and Rober & trayttur to Englishmen
> A dym Bronde a Sectte of dyvers Evyl
> God of Welshmen euyr w[ith]out ysgil
> Ynn slaing the good and leader of the bad
> lastly Rewardid as he deseruyd had
> Of Troians blwde the drostes and nott the sid
> a Rwtt of ffalssed and kaws of menney yll did[161]

Gruffydd concludes by stating that 'no one should place too much faith in any of the two [inscriptions], neither in the honour and praise of kinsmen, nor in the defamation and dishonour of enemies' (ddyly neb Roddi gormod kreduniaeth Jr un o'r ddau Nac J glod a moliant y kredigion nag J ogan ac anglod y gelynnion).[162] This echoes John Prise's statement that 'there is no more reliable evidence than that of one's opponents'.[163] The epitaph anecdote seems at first glance a slightly *too* fortuitous example for Gruffydd: it is placed directly after his harrowing description of Llywelyn's murder, and the Middle English of the offensive verse is suspiciously Welsh-looking: doubled F ('ffalssed'); the use of W as a vowel ('yw', 'rwtt') or I for a long E sound [i:] ('thif', 'sid', 'did'); and other assorted Welsh orthographies ('ysgil', 'kaws').[164] In fact, as the traces of Gruffydd's errors in copying make clear, Gruffydd has taken the anecdote from elsewhere, though his Welsh orthography remains a puzzle. The epitaph appears in one of Gruffydd's sources, Fabyan's *Chronicle*, but Fabyan provides both halves in Latin alongside English translations, and although the latter half's English translation is a close textual match for Gruffydd's version the orthography is not.[165] Fabyan's source for the two

---

[160] NLW MS 3054Di, f. 111r. Translation mine.
[161] NLW MS 3054Di, f. 111r.
[162] Ibid. Translation mine.
[163] Cited above at pp. 197–98.
[164] Similar orthography can be found in the *Hymn to the Virgin*, a text probably copied by a Welshman in English. See E. J. Dobson, 'The Hymn to the Virgin', *Transactions of the Honourable Society of Cymmrodorion*, 70 (1955), 70–124.
[165] Robert Fabyan, *Prima par cronecarum / Newe cronycles of Englande and of Fraunce* (London: Richard Pynson, 1516), STC (2nd edn) 10659, sigs Gg7v–Gg8r.

halves of the epitaph seems to be Higden's *Polychronicon*, where they are both given in Latin. At least one other translation into English was attempted, an interpolation added to a Prose *Brut* manuscript (c. 1460) that, by the sixteenth century, was in Ruthin some twenty miles from Gruffydd's native Llanasa; but this is not a match for Gruffydd's version, and instead appears to represent an independent English translation from Higden's *Polychronicon*.[166] As far as can be established, Gruffydd's rendering of the epitaph is unique in presenting the first half of the epitaph in Welsh.

Gruffydd's shrewd placement of this excerpt at this point in his *Cronicl* may represent an attempt to stoke an emotional response against the English from his readers under the veil of translingual collegiality. Considering the level of patriotic fervour that Arthur's Glastonbury epitaph was able to stir up, it is perhaps unsurprising that Gruffydd opts for a similar approach by turning to the example attributed to the grave of Llywelyn. This said, there is evidence elsewhere in Gruffydd's *Cronicl* of a less cynical approach to collaboration across linguistic boundaries. The following quotation is taken from the *Cronicl*'s preface. Employing an extended metaphor that echoes Gruffydd's description of a dying Arthur taken away on a lakeside by a group of otherworldly women, the author suggests that his polyglottal skills have enabled him to bring hidden histories to light:[167]

> I do not consider myself to be anything more than a simple man [...] who has taken it upon himself to be chief mariner to steer and help on their way a shipload of men of splendour and prestige across a wide stretch of sea, to a land where none of them has even been before.
>
> (nid wyf i ynn kymerud arnnaf amgennach no gwr sympyl [...] vai ynn kymerud arno vod yn benn llongwr i lywio ac i gyurwyddo

---

[166] Aberystwyth, National Library of Wales MS 21068D, f. 88v. This manuscript is edited, along with the corresponding Latin from Higden's *Polychronicon*, in *An English Chronicle 1377–1461: Edited from Aberystwyth, National Library of Wales MS 21608, and Oxford, Bodleian Library MS Lyell 34*, ed. William Marx (Woodbridge: Boydell, 2003), pp. 16–17. Ceridwen Lloyd-Morgan points to this manuscript as an early example of Welsh ownership of English-language manuscripts in the early sixteenth century; see Ceridwen Lloyd-Morgan, 'Writing Without Borders: Multilingual Content in Welsh Miscellanies from Wales, the Marches, and Beyond', in *Insular Books: Vernacular Manuscript Miscellanies in Late Medieval Britain*, ed. Margaret Connolly and Raluca Radulescu (London: The British Academy, 2015), pp. 175–92 (p. 176).

[167] Cited in Lloyd-Morgan, 'Later Hybrid Narrative Texts', p. 209.

llongiaad o wyr o vliant ac annrhyddedd dros vor llydann i wlad ynn yr h[o]n ni biasai neb o honnunt twy irmoed ynn y blaen)[168]

What is the destination here, and what the point of origin? Gruffydd composed his chronicle in English-occupied Calais, in Welsh, before sending it home, so this metaphor also reflects the journey of Gruffydd's chronicle over the sea to Llanasa. Elsewhere, Gruffydd states that he intends to 'convey many remarkable things from excellent, noble stories from the eastern parts, ones which have never before been recounted in Wales amongst the common people' (dwynn llawer o bethav nodedig o ysdoriay ardderchion, dyledog, o barth'r dwyrain, o'r hrain nib u gyswyn amdanaunt o vewn Kymru ymysg y kyffredin Jrmoed ynn y blaen).[169] Moreover, Gruffydd chose to write his work in the form of a universal chronicle. This perhaps suggests that he saw his overarching goal as one of a global citizen bringing foreign knowledge home to his native Wales, echoing the cosmopolitan multilingual Welshmen of the past that Gruffydd holds up as ideals in his *Cronicl*.[170] However, in the first quote above, as elsewhere, Gruffydd writes enigmatically, leaving just enough space for interpretation. Is Gruffydd only bringing tales of European heroes over the sea to his fellow Welsh people? Is he introducing Wales' oral traditions into the written record? Or is he transporting the figures of the past, some of them virtually forgotten, across the seas of time and into the present, and hopefully the future? However we are to interpret this metaphor, Gruffydd clearly positions himself throughout his chronicle as a mediator between native and foreign, past and present.

By studying these authors comparatively, it is possible to gain an insight into their complex and often contradictory sense of native identity, manifested in their expression of Arthur's places and also in opposition to who or what they deemed to be foreign. Criticisms of Arthurian history were grounded in inconsistencies early modern historians noticed when comparing insular and continental histories, but Gruffydd's chronicle reveals a different perspective in Welsh-authored, Welsh-language texts. It is therefore unsurprising that such histories – and their foreign

---

[168] Translation from Morgan, 'Elis Gruffudd of Gronant', p. 18.
[169] Text and translation from Lloyd-Morgan, 'The Welsh Tradition in Calais', p. 91.
[170] Gruffydd points to figures of the past such as Maelgwyn who were able to read and write in 'various languages like Latin, French, Welsh and English' (ymrauaelion Jeithau megis Lading, Ffrangeg, Kymraeg, a Saesonaeg) – just like Gruffydd himself. Cited (text and translation) in Mulligan, 'Moses, Taliesin, and the Welsh Chosen People', p. 771.

authors – would be placed under such scrutiny by Arthur's defenders. A key problem lay in the need to demonstrate Arthur's popularity abroad. Foreign authors may have been assumed to have had other agendas, or to have been too remote from the places and sources of British history. They may have been seen to lack the language skills necessary to consult Welsh textual sources effectively, sources which Prise figured rhetorically through the lens of native places. However, foreign sources were also the most important evidence of Arthur's universal fame. As such, Arthurian defences often show a tension between secrecy and celebrity, claiming to be uncovering historic truths that had previously been shrouded in darkness while also arguing for Arthur's universal fame. At the same time, the personal identities of Arthur's defenders also affected how they perceived foreignness, and in turn where they chose to locate Arthur. Leland and Prise found a collective scapegoat in Polydore, a symbol of imperial Rome and contemporary Italy: both framed as opponents to an imagined past and present Britain. For Gruffydd, however, living in a time and place which saw his native language heavily suppressed, the damage to the British History, and to Arthurian history, came from a decidedly different source.

Map 3. John Prise's Arthurian places.

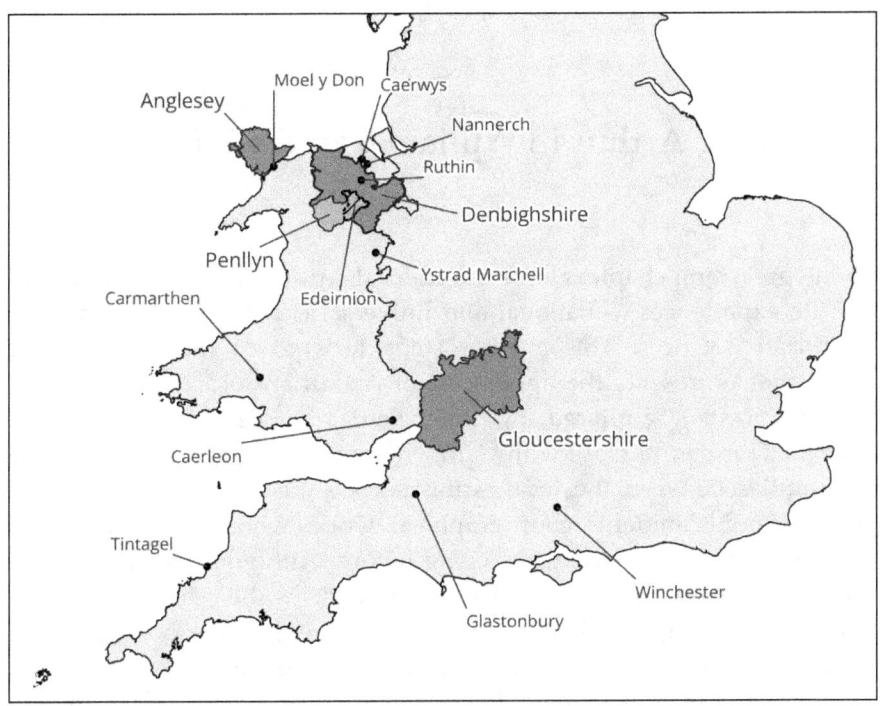

Map 4. Elis Gruffydd's Arthurian places.

5
Placing Arthur in William Camden's *Britannia*

The preceding chapters have traced local Arthurian histories from on-site experiences to national and universal chronicles and dedicated Arthurian defences. This chapter steps forward in time to consider a text that represents the apotheosis of Arthurian local representation: *Britannia* (1586), authored by the celebrated Elizabethan antiquary William Camden.[1] I close with Camden because I want to draw out the continuities between the local Arthurian site histories of the fifteenth century and Camden's chorographical work, which is often treated as a departure from what has come before. Although Camden was a founding member of the Society of Antiquaries, he was not the first antiquarian, and Camden's antiquarian forbears have been touched upon in previous chapters. Some of these figures, such as John Leland, John Prise, and Humphrey Llwyd, were direct sources for Camden. Others, such as John Rous and John Hardyng, had an indirect impact on Camden's work because their writings were in turn vital sources for Leland, Prise, and Llwyd.

Arguably, these earlier antiquarians' attempts to defend Arthur's native places also paved the way for Camden. There is little scholarship on Camden's attitude towards Arthur, but that which does exist claims that Camden was indifferent to or perhaps even ashamed of him. This is contradicted by Camden's presentation of Arthur throughout *Britannia*, by the text's editorial history and Camden's control over it, and by his selective use of poetic and historical sources. As a result, Camden was perhaps the first Arthurian defender to truly succeed in reviving Arthur's native locations in the public consciousness. This success was due to a number of related factors. First, the institutionalisation of antiquarianism

[1] William Camden, *Britannia* (London: 1586), STC (2nd edn) 4503. Several of the *Britannia* editions are referenced in this book; subsequent references to the various editions will be indicated by their date of publication. Where English translations of the Latin can be supplied from the 1610 English edition they have been; otherwise I provide my own translation. The Latin cited will always be taken from the earliest edition to include a particular quotation. Willliam Camden, *Remaines of a greater worke, concerning Britaine, the inhabitants thereof, their languages, names, surnames, empreses, wise speeches, poësies, and epitaphes* (London: Simon Waterson, 1605), STC (2nd edn) 4521.

during the reign of Elizabeth I made Camden and his work seem more authoritative than those who had come before. A second factor in Camden's success was his use of visual imagery in the form of woodcuts and engravings, which replicated the eyewitness experience of Arthur's places and relics more effectively than earlier Arthurian defences such as Leland's *Assertio*. These visual renderings were combined with poetic fragments that served the purpose of glorifying their subject matter by acting as textual memorials. By presenting these physical and textual artefacts within a chorographical structure, Camden succeeded in historicising Arthur where his antiquarian forbears had failed. Camden framed Arthur's places in their geographical (rather than narrative) context, and in so doing harnessed the mnemonic properties that Eviatar Zerubavel attributes to 'constancy of place', enabling his readers to suspend their disbelief (or to 'make believe') more effectively.[2] Or, to return to Mikhail Bakhtin's idea of the chronotope, Camden succeeded because he framed Arthur in the museum-like context of 'castle time' because of the geographically organised structure of the *Britannia*, which superimposed disparate points of history in place on top of each other.[3]

The chimera of the new antiquarian

Camden is best known for founding the Elizabethan Society of Antiquaries. Arnaldo Momogliano's oft-repeated definition distinguishes the antiquary (or antiquarian) as 'a student of the past who is not quite a historian because [...] historians write in a chronological order; antiquaries write in a systematic order'; antiquaries 'collect all the items that are connected with a certain subject'.[4] Camden took this systematic approach in his work; both *Britannia* (1586) and *Remaines Concerning Britain* (1605) catalogued the textual and physical remains of Britain, gathered by

---

[2] Zerubavel, *Time Maps*, p. 41.
[3] See above at pp. 23–24.
[4] Arnaldo Momogliano, 'Ancient History and the Antiquarian', *Journal of the Warburg and Courtauld Institutes*, 13 (1950), 285–315 (pp. 286–87). Momigliano's thesis has since been re-examined by other scholars: Ingo Herklotz countered that early antiquarians' work was characterised by miscellaneity rather than systematism. Ingo Herklotz, 'Arnaldo Momigliano's "Ancient History and the Antiquarian": A Critical Review', in *Momogliano and Antiquarianism: Foundations of the Modern Cultural Sciences*, ed. Peter Miller (Toronto: University of Toronto Press, 2007), pp. 127–53. Angus Vine has attempted to reconcile these seemingly opposing positions by demonstrating that Camden's *Britannia* exhibits both systematism and also the qualities of a miscellany. See Angus Vine, *In Defiance of Time*, pp. 11–16; Angus Vine, *Miscellaneous Order: Manuscript Culture and the Early Modern Organization of Knowledge* (Oxford: Oxford University Press, 2019), pp. 98–100.

Camden during his perambulations or crowd-sourced from others, and recorded meticulously in numerous notebooks.[5] In contrast, Leland's *Assertio* sits somewhere between a chronological and systematic ordering: a gathering of all the information pertinent to a defence of Arthur, yet also arranged in a chronology of sorts. The *Assertio* is structured as follows: Arthur's coronation; his twelve battles; his journeys to and from France; his final mortal battle; after his death, the development of Glastonbury Abbey; the 1191 discovery of his grave; the translation of his bones; and the bitter Arthurian disputes of Leland's present day.

Both Camden and Leland exhibit another important element of antiquarianism in their writings: imagination. In the late medieval and early modern periods, Angus Vine identifies a more imaginative form of antiquarianism blooming, a 'dynamic, recuperative, resurrective response to the past' that is 'essentially imaginative'.[6] According to his biographers, Camden was driven by this recuperative impulse from an early point in his career. Thomas Smith reports that 'even when he was a schoolboy, he could neither hear nor see anything of an antique appearance, without more than ordinary attention and notice'.[7] As a teenager at Oxford it was reportedly 'not in his power to keep within doors: the bent of his own Genius was always pulling him out [...] [to] stately Camps and ruinous Castles, those venerable Monuments of our Fore-fathers'.[8] This imaginative approach to antiquarianism stretches back far earlier than the careers of William Camden and John Leland. Vine locates its origins in the Italian humanist tradition, which was already influencing a burgeoning English humanism from as early as the fifteenth century.[9] Whilst Momogliano's systematism is visible wholly in

---

[5] It bears repeating that here, and elsewhere, I do not use the term Britain as it is understood today, but rather as my fifteenth- and sixteenth-century sources would have understood it in their own terms: for Camden, Britain was a freshly emerging Roman *Britannia* revived for a new age, which encompassed the whole of the largest island in the British Archipelago. For a discussion of the shifting nature of Britain and my approach to this contentious toponym, see the introduction of this book at pp. 17–19.

[6] Vine, *In Defiance of Time*, p. 3.

[7] Thomas Smith, 'Life of Camden', in *Camden's Britannia*, ed. and trans. Edmund Gibson (London: F. Collins, 1695), sig. B1v, cited in Graham Parry, *The Trophies of Time: English Antiquarians of the Seventeenth Century* (Oxford: Oxford University Press, 1995), p. 22.

[8] Ibid.

[9] Vine, *In Defiance of Time*, pp. 3–4. Even as early as the fifteenth century, the writings and classical translations of Italian humanists were beginning to circulate in England thanks to figures like Humphrey Duke of Gloucester, who commissioned new humanist literary works and collected an impressive library of classical texts. See G. L. Harris, 'Humphrey, Duke of Gloucester (1390–1447), *Oxford Dictionary of*

Camden's work and partly in Leland's, the imaginative antiquarianism identified by Vine is also clear in the work of much earlier writers such as William Worcester and John Hardyng. Indeed, the site apparatus described in the first chapter of this book – the brass plaque and *magna tabula* at Glastonbury, the tablets and glazing scheme at York, the 'pore men' guides of Guy's Cliffe dressed to embody Guy as a hermit – also reflect this approach to the past, encouraging site visitors to engage in imaginative reconstruction. Antonia Gransden has drawn out the continuities between these earlier and later forms of mental recuperation, arguing that localised pseudo-histories such as those at Glastonbury and elsewhere spurred the work of antiquarians: '[antiquarianism] developed despite the concurrent elaboration of the legends of British history – of Brutus and King Arthur [...] [T]he British History, by firing enthusiasm for the past in general and for any place or relic particularly associated with the legends, stimulated [the antiquaries'] researches.'[10]

A further distinction that is often made between the historian and the antiquarian relates to their methodologies: a reliance on narrative texts (the historian) versus the study of fragments (the antiquarian). This is perhaps most readily comparable to the modern distinction between historians and archaeologists, although this is rather a blunt comparison: archaeologists draw out narratives from the fragments with which they work, and for the earliest antiquarians fragments could readily be textual as well as physical.[11] Sweet suggests that these two methodological approaches remained separate until the seventeenth century, when the advancement of Pyrrhonian scepticism started to bring up new concerns about the forgeability of literary texts.[12] However, there is evidence in the writings of earlier antiquarians of both a combined approach and a suspicion about the authenticity and reliability of textual witnesses. A case in point, as we have already discussed, is the flood of accusations levelled at Polydore Vergil for tampering with texts, and particularly the accusation that Polydore had fabricated his publication of Gildas' *De excidio* (1525). In his *Historia*, John Prise describes in detail his painstaking codicological enquiry within the context of this debate, weighing up the textual

---

National Biography (Oxford: Oxford University Press, 2004), www.oxforddnb.com/view/article/14155 [accessed 15 August 2017]; Daniel Wakelin, *Humanism, Reading, and English Literature 1430–1530* (Oxford: Oxford University Press, 2007), passim.

[10] Gransden, *Historical Writing in England*, II, p. 309.

[11] Rosemary Sweet, *Antiquaries: The Discovery of the Past in Eighteenth-Century Britain* (London: Hambledon, 2004), p. 1. On the two kinds of fragmentary study – physical and textual – see Daniel Woolf, *The Social Circulation of the Past: English Historical Culture 1500–1730* (Oxford: Oxford University Press, 2003), pp. 141–50.

[12] Sweet, *Antiquaries*, p. 2.

and material qualities of various manuscripts attributed to Gildas and drawing comparisons about their usefulness and reliability in much the same way that a contemporary codicologist might.[13] Aside from evincing textual distrust, Prise's approach also collapses the distinction between the historian's textual approach and the antiquarian's fragmentary one. Likewise, John Leland segues historical and antiquarian methods in his work. On the one hand, Leland draws on the works of chroniclers and classical historians such as those listed in the table of authorities prefacing the *Assertio*. On the other hand, he invokes physical fragments to support his work: Arthur's seal, the archaeological discoveries and oral traditions at Cadbury and Camlan, and the inscriptions of purportedly ancient *tabulae* in Wales and elsewhere.[14] It is evident from these writers' works that seventeenth-century antiquarianism should be seen as a continuation of past practices, rather than a departure from them.

Nevertheless, between Leland's composition of the *Assertio* (1544) and Camden's composition of *Britannia* (1586) the perceived role of the antiquary underwent a change. For example, Leland has often been dubbed 'the king's antiquary' on account of the work that he did on behalf of Henry VIII. Leland did refer to himself as 'antiquarius', apparently the first early modern antiquarian to do so. Yet despite enjoying royal patronage, there is no evidence that the epithet 'King's antiquary' was an official title. It was probably an embellishment made by William Camden's biographer, Thomas Smith.[15] Smith wrote this in 1691, by which point antiquarianism had become a veritable institution following the foundation of the Society of Antiquaries in 1586 before its disbanding by King James in 1614.[16] Despite the society's ultimate failure to achieve formal royal recognition, this is nevertheless something that its members attempted to secure – twice.[17] W. H. Herendeen has remarked that the Elizabethan antiquarians' initiative to self-organise in this way 'presumes recognition of the value of the enterprise itself' – in other words, the value of antiquarian methodologies.[18] Although earlier antiquarians did work collaboratively, as the previous chapter's discussion of Leland

---

[13] John Prise, *Historiae Britannicae Defensio*, pp. 200–05, discussed above at pp. 203–04.
[14] See above at p. 38
[15] Leland, *De uiris illustribus*, I, p. xxv; James P. Carley, 'The Manuscript Remains of John Leland, "The King's Antiquary"', *Text*, 2 (1985), 111–20 (p. 117).
[16] T. D. Kendrick, *British Antiquity* (London: Methuen, 1950), pp. 114–15.
[17] Richard Helgerson, 'The Land Speaks: Cartography, Chorography, and Subversion in Renaissance England', *Representations*, 16 (1986), 50–85 (p. 68). The society's various proposals to Elizabeth (pp. 320–28) and James (pp. 328–33) are discussed in W. H. Herendeen, *William Camden: A Life in Context* (Woodbridge: Boydell, 2007).
[18] Herendeen, *William Camden*, p. 320.

and Prise's work shows, an antiquarian group had not been formally coordinated in this way before. Though the society was not an official royal institution, as is often assumed, it does demonstrate a move towards the professionalisation of the antiquarian, just as Camden's *Britannia* represents a commodification of the antiquarian's work.[19] Between Leland's self-declaration as an 'antiquarius' and the formation of a dedicated antiquarian society, antiquarianism became codified and understood as a recognisable and valid practice.

Despite the increasingly coordinated approach to antiquarianism, however, the change in actual antiquarian practices has been overstated. This seems to be due to the imagined divide between the medieval and the early modern which has governed the way that historic approaches to the past have been interpreted.[20] Scholarship of the nineteenth and early twentieth centuries (and sometimes even later) has tended to venerate the concepts of humanism and the Renaissance uncritically, setting them in opposition to a medieval past rather than drawing out continuities between the two periods.[21] Such disparagement of the medieval and reverence for the modern may be due to the importance of ideals associated with the Renaissance – reason, rationality, and so forth – to the academic identities of nineteenth- and twentieth-century scholars. A significant example is Jacob Burckhardt's influential *Civilization of the Renaissance in Italy* (1860).[22] Regarding changes in antiquarian practice, T. D. Kendrick described the founders of the Society of Antiquaries as representing 'the modern antiquary', a figure interested in the 'practical past' who was 'too busy to bother with Brutus and his problems'.[23] Kendrick proclaims that:

> the British antiquary was changing into a new kind of person with much more important things to do than bother about unverifiable

---

[19] Herendeen, *William Camden*, p. 249.
[20] The issue of periodisation has been discussed previously: see Jacques Heers, *Le Moyen Age: Une Imposture* (Paris: Perrin, 1992); Brian Stock, 'The Middle Ages as Subject and Object: Romantic Attitudes and Academic Medievalism', *New Literary History*, 5 (1974), 527–48; Utz, 'Hic iacet', pp. 33–34; Cooper, 'The Origins of the Early Modern', passim; Margreta de Grazia, 'The Modern Divide: From Either Side', *Journal of Medieval and Early Modern Studies*, 37.3 (2007), 453–67.
[21] Wakelin, *Humanism, Reading, and English Literature, 1430–1530*, p. 6; de Grazia, 'The Modern Divide: From Either Side', passim.
[22] Jacob Burckhardt, *The Civilization of the Renaissance in Italy: An Essay*, ed. and trans. L. Goldscheider, 4th edn (London: Phaidon, 1951); Stephen Bowd, 'Introduction', in *Renaissance? Perceptions of Continuity and Discontinuity in Europe, c. 1300–c. 1550*, ed. Alexander Lee, Pierre Péporté, and Harry Schnitker (Leiden: Brill, 2010), pp. 1–16 (pp. 1–2).
[23] Kendrick, *British Antiquity*, p. 104; p. 114.

> legends [...] [the Society] was not a company of tender-skinned patriots puffing themselves up with pride in Brutus and King Arthur, but a group of sober-minded gentlemen interested in [...] the 'practical' past, the past that was immediately important in their own lives and thoughts.[24]

This assertion is overly simplistic if not straightforwardly incorrect, and speaks to the efficacy of the re-branding of antiquarianism enacted in the foundation of the Society and in its subsequent re-founding in 1707.[25] When we consider its members, their interests and their approaches, we find a group of people not too dissimilar to John Leland, John Rous, and William Worcester. The distinction that Kendrick draws between 'old' antiquarianism characterised as 'tender-skinned' and interested in 'unverifiable' Brutus legends and a more 'sober-minded' 'new' antiquarianism is a fallacy. For example, Kendrick distinguishes the 'new' antiquaries by their study of 'subjects of portentous antiquarian solemnity, such as ancient law, the origin of institutions, offices, customs, privileges, and the like'.[26] These research interests were already popular with 'old' antiquarians; moreover, the work of these earlier figures often informed the writings of the 'new' antiquarians of the Elizabethan age. Earlier examples of such antiquarian work include John Rous's history of British academic institutions, *De antiquitate academiarum*, a work that is now lost but was consulted by John Leland. Leland copied sections of *De antiquitate academiarum* in his notebooks, and these notes were used extensively by subsequent antiquarians including Camden and his contemporaries.[27] Though much of *De antiquitate academiarum* seems to have consisted of legendary pseudo-history, this did not prevent Camden from citing Rous as an authority on the history of divinity lectures at Oxford, material that probably came from *De antiquitate academiarum*.[28] Indeed, the College of Antiquaries in its arcane secrecy mirrored the institutions of luminaries that Rous and Leland imagined to have populated Arthur's Britain. According to Herendeen, the Elizabethan Society of Antiquaries was run as kind of hierophantic learned secret society: members would rarely know who was in and who was out, and

---

[24] Kendrick, *British Antiquity*, p. 114.
[25] Sweet, *Antiquaries*, p. 84.
[26] Kendrick, *British Antiquity*, p. 114.
[27] On Camden's reliance on Leland's notes, see Oliver Harris, '"Motheaten, Mouldye, and Rotten": The Early Custodial History and Dissemination of John Leland's Manuscript Remains', *Bodleian Library Record*, 18.5 (2005), 460–501; Oliver D. Harris, '"Which I Have Beholden with Most Curiouse Eyes": The Lead Cross from Glastonbury Abbey', *Arthurian Literature*, 34 (2018), 88–129.
[28] Camden, *Britain* (1610), p. 379, sig. Ii2r.

an air of secrecy governed much of the college's activities.[29] Likewise, John Leland, when describing the learned college at Caerleon which Geoffrey of Monmouth labels a 'gymnasium' (a public school or college of sorts), refers to the institution as a 'Learned Quier of Ecclesiastical persons' (mystarum chorum eruditum), with 'mystarum' suggesting the same numinous, arcane quality evinced in the behaviours of the early College of Antiquaries.[30]

Other examples in Kendrick's list of 'sober' pursuits, such as the 'study of ancient law', were not only continuities of 'old' antiquarianism, but also frequently bound up with the very Brutus legends from which Kendrick was so keen to separate them. In the sixteenth century, William Lambarde, a contemporary to Camden and fellow founder of the Society of Antiquaries, printed a manuscript in his possession titled the *Leges Edwardi Confessoris* (The Laws of Edward the Confessor).[31] This text constitutes a section of a twelfth-century compilation of English customary law, sometimes referred to as the London Collection, that claimed (falsely) to have originated during the reign of Edward the Confessor.[32] However, Lambarde's manuscript contained a curious claim concerning Arthur's conquest of distant northern territories as far as Iceland (Islandiam), Greenland (Grenelandiam), and even Lapland (Lappam).[33] Lambarde did not elect to omit this information when he printed the text in his *Archaionomia* (indeed, he highlighted it with the aid of a manicule and editorial note).[34] Lambarde's fellow antiquarian John Dee, also a 'new' antiquarian and member of the Society of Antiquaries, used these fabricated laws to form the basis of his claims to Queen Elizabeth's imperial entitlement over the far north.[35]

These examples demonstrate that the demarcation often drawn between the old antiquarianism of Rous and Leland and the new antiquarianism of Camden and his contemporaries is not as clear-cut as has previously been assumed. The antiquarian's approach did not change dramatically, but in the publication of *Britannia* Camden managed to

---

[29] Herendeen, *William Camden*, pp. 316–20.
[30] Leland, *Learned*, sigs D4v–E1r; Leland, *Assertio*, sig. C4v.
[31] See Lynette Muir, 'King Arthur's Northern Conquests in the Leges Anglorum Londoniis Collectae', *Medium Aevum*, 37 (1968), 253–63; Caitlin Green, 'John Dee, King Arthur, and the Conquest of the Arctic', *The Heroic Age: A Journal of Early Medieval Northwestern Europe*, 15 (2012).
[32] This collection of legal texts is discussed in detail in Berard, *Arthurianism*, pp. 162–72.
[33] Text printed in Muir, 'King Arthur's Northern Conquests', pp. 253–54.
[34] William Lambarde, *Archaionomia sive de Priscis Anglorum Legibus libri* (London: John Day, 1568), STC (2nd edn) 15142, sigs Oo4v; Pp2v–Pp3r.
[35] Caitlin Green, 'John Dee, King Arthur, and the Conquest of the Arctic', §17.

sell antiquarianism to his readers as something relevant, timely, and important. As Herendeen observes,

> when characterizing the readers of the *Britannia* as humanists, Camden [...] implicates them in the antiquarian enterprise, legitimises it, and reinforces the political merits of its study. Camden's antiquities [...] are a commodification of the past in an age when such values were clearly ready to be made current.[36]

This marketing of the antiquarian method, and the invitation to readers to participate side-by-side in the antiquarian endeavour, is as much a factor of Camden's successful portrayal of Arthur as any innovations to the antiquarian method itself. The structural innovations of *Britannia*, however, had an even more important part to play.

William Camden: An Arthurian defender?

Given the continuities of methodology and interest between the old and new antiquarians, it is perhaps time to reconsider William Camden's approach to Arthur. We have learned that defending Arthur was a serious issue for Camden's antiquarian forbears: regarding Polydore's perceived rejection of Arthur's Glastonbury grave, Leland said with some urgency that 'it is reasonable, therefore, to deal with this matter in a little more depth, for the benefit of antiquaries' (Lubet itaque, in gratiam antiquariorum, subtilius hanc rem tractare).[37] As well as evincing the collegial spirit of antiquarianism, Leland seems to implore his antiquarian inheritors to avoid neglecting Arthur in their research. This appeal did not go unnoticed: as well as appearing in William Lambarde and John Dee's works, Arthur would also feature in other new antiquarian writings, such as Richard Carew's *Survey of Cornwall* (1602).[38]

Camden's *Britannia* was also part of this tradition. First published in 1586, it comprised a detailed description of Britain encompassing England, Wales, and Scotland, organised into chapters for each county, with information on Ireland (Hibernia) also included. F. J. Levy described the 1586 edition of *Britannia*, rather uncharitably, as 'a modest book', 'a small and rather ugly octavo of around 550 pages, unillustrated, and with the type closely packed on the pages'; 'emphatically not one

---

[36] Herendeen, *William Camden*, p. 249.
[37] Text and translation from Leland, *De uiris illustribus*, I, p. 313.
[38] Richard Carew, *The Survey of Cornwall*, ed. F. E. Halliday, 2nd edn (London: Adams & Dart, 1969).

of the triumphs of Elizabethan book-making'.³⁹ Yet even in its original form *Britannia* was an impressive work, and it made an impact. Levy's assertion that *Britannia* was 'too little impassioned for great popularity' cannot be entirely correct. We know from the sheer number of extant copies of *Britannia*, its continual stream of new editions, its English translation, and its literary and historical legacy that it was in fact hugely popular.⁴⁰ It would have been a costly text to produce and buy, especially the expanded editions with custom-produced maps; indeed, Camden acknowledges this cost in the preface to the 1607 folio edition.⁴¹ Clearly *Britannia* promised enough of a financial return to pique the interest of several partners its development, as the cost of its expansion was split between six publishers, much to the chagrin of Camden's greatest critic, Ralph Brooke.⁴² That so many were willing to purchase or invest in *Britannia*, despite the high cost, is a testament to its popularity. This meant that local Arthurian histories suddenly became far more widely known as copies of the *Britannia* were printed and purchased by an eager public, particularly after the publication of the English edition in 1610. Although *Britannia* is a systematic work on the subject of Britain and cannot therefore be treated as an Arthurian work *per se*, it should not be dismissed as a work in which Arthur was unimportant, not least because the publication of the English edition arguably elevated Arthur's visibility and therefore his import. Although Camden's ostensible aim was to glorify Britain and restore its antiquity by representing it in intricate regional and local detail, the upshot of this was increased legitimacy and importance being placed on its major historical figures, such as Arthur, and the reinforcement of these figures' local connections across Britain.

Extant scholarship tends to consider Camden as, at best, apathetic to Arthur. N. J. Higham argues that Camden 'damn[ed] the Arthurian tradition with faint praise and the criticisms – which he but feebly

---

³⁹ F. J. Levy, 'The Making of Camden's Britannia', *Bibliothèque d'Humanisme et Renaissance*, 26.1 (1964), 70–97 (p. 70).

⁴⁰ The English Short Title Catalogue counts 331 extant copies of *Britannia* (up to and including the 1610 English edition) published from the first edition of 1586 to the 1610 English translation.

⁴¹ Oliver D. Harris, 'William Camden, Philemon Holland and the 1610 Translation of Britannia', *The Antiquaries Journal*, 95 (2015), 279–303.

⁴² *A Transcript of the Registers of the Company of Stationers of London; 1554–1640 AD*, ed. Edward Arber, 5 vols (London, 1875–94), III, p. 435; Helgerson, 'The Land Speaks', pp. 66–67. Brooke claimed that the publication of his invective written in response to Camden had been delayed by Camden's 'friendes the Stationers, (who heretofore haue made no small gaine of your foure former Impressions)'. Brooke, *A discoverie of diuers errors*, sig. L4r.

protested – of other men'.⁴³ Blaire Zeiders reads Camden's Arthurian approach as one which 'qualified or replaced those that had given voice to passion', positing Camden in opposition to the more heated defences of Leland and Prise.⁴⁴ In contrast to these views, Siân Echard considers Camden's outlook on Arthur to be more positive, arguing that he 'pulls' the Trojan and Arthurian traditions 'apart', 'separating them from each other'.⁴⁵ I am inclined to agree with Echard on this point. As I will go on to discuss, Camden's manipulation of poetic sources in particular drives a wedge between Arthur and Geoffrey's narrative. In fact, Camden openly acknowledges the criticisms of Geoffrey of Monmouth's *Historia*, which might explain why he is so often interpreted as an Arthurian sceptic. We have seen the same kind of assumptions made regarding Polydore Vergil, characterised as an Arthurian non-believer despite levelling his criticisms at Geoffrey's text rather than Arthur himself.⁴⁶ In order to appreciate Camden's approach to Arthur, it is important to acknowledge that Camden's acceptance of Arthur's historicity did not mean blind acceptance of the Arthurian historical canon. Camden expresses doubts over certain elements in Geoffrey's history as tactfully and politely as possible when speaking in his own words: 'I haue impaired no man's reputation, I haue impeached no mans credit, no not Geffray of Monmouth whose history (which I would gladly support) is held suspected amongst the iudicious' (Gentem nullam in calumniam rapui, nullius famam laesi, nullius in nomen lusi, nullius fidem dimminui, ne Galfredi quidem Monumethensis, cuius historia, (quam magnopere confirmare velim) inter omnes eruditos habetur sane suspectior).⁴⁷ At times, his criticisms are razor-sharp, though he is careful to frame outright criticism of Geoffrey in the mouths of others. On the Brutus legend, Camden asserts that 'the fable, (as the Criticks of our age doe thinke) could not hang well together, vnlesse he the said Geffrey had devised three sonnes of Brutus [...] Neither make they doubt, but he would have found out more children of Brutus, if there had beene more nations distinct at the same time in Britaine' (Fabula enim, ut Critici nostri seculi existimant, constare non poterat, nisi ille e Bruto tres filios [...] Nec dubitant quin plures ille

---

⁴³ Higham, *Myth-Making and History*, p. 238.
⁴⁴ Blaire Zeiders, 'The Arthurian Book in Print: Reading the Debts and Desires of the Early Modern English Nation' (unpublished doctoral thesis, University of Wisconsin-Madison, 2013), pp. 40–41.
⁴⁵ Siân Echard, '"Whyche Thynge Semeth Not to Agree With Other Histories...": Rome in Geoffrey of Monmouth and His Early Modern Readers', *Arthurian Literature*, 26 (2009), 109–30.
⁴⁶ See above at pp. 138–39.
⁴⁷ *Britannia* 1610, 'To the Reader', n.p.; Camden, *Britannia* (1586), 'Ad Lectorem', n.p.

liberos e Bruto procreasset, si plures diuersae gentes tempore in Britannia extitissent).[48] Elsewhere, Camden rebukes Geoffrey's naysayers, such as 'William of Newborough [...] who too sharply charged Geffrey the Compiler of the British history of his untruth' (Galfredus Guilielmus Nubrigensis asperius illum his verbis conuellit).[49]

In sum, Camden's scepticism is focused on the Brutus foundation myth rather than the history of Arthur, subjects that are often elided by both Polydore's early respondents and contemporary scholars.[50] Although Camden admits that Arthur's histories are fraught with fables and exaggerations, he maintains that Arthur existed and that he was most worthy of praise. In fact, barring his criticisms of Geoffrey's *Historia*, Camden's distinction between fact and fable aligns with Leland's, coloured by a distrust of continental vernacular sources. If we turn to the list of first names entered in Camden's *Remaines concerning Britaine*, for example, Arthur, Lancelot, and Gawain are presented quite differently. Camden claims 'Arthur' to be 'a Latine name in Juvenal drawn from the goodly fixed star Arcturus, and that from Arctus is the Bear, as Ursicinus amongst the Romans. The famous Arthur made this name first famous amongst the Britains.'[51] On the other hand, Lancelot 'seemeth a Spanish name [...] some think it to be no ancient name, but forged by the writer of King Arthur's history for one of his doughty Knights'.[52] 'Gawen' is likewise glossed as 'a name devised by the author of King Arthur's table, if it be not Walwin. See Walwin.'[53] And under Walwin: 'if Walwin was a Britain, and King Arthur's Nephew, as W. Malmesbury noteth, where he speaketh of his Gyant-like bones found in Wales, I refer the signification to the Britains'.[54] Camden therefore presents Arthur as a real historic figure, albeit one that is grown over with 'the leaves of fable', as Cuming Walters would put it several centuries later.[55]

Chorography and region

To understand why Camden was so successful in historicising Arthur, the *Britannia*'s depictions of individual Arthurian locations need to be appreciated within the work's geographical structure. The effectiveness

---

[48] *Britain* (1610), sig. N4r, p. 155; *Britannia* (1586), sig. E2v, p. 52.
[49] *Britain* (1610), sig. A4v, p. 8; William Camden, *Britannia* (London: George Bishop, 1600), STC (2nd edn) 4507, sig. B4v, p. 8.
[50] See Kendrick, *British Antiquity*, pp. 13–14.
[51] *Remaines*, sig. G2v.
[52] *Remaines*, sig. I3r.
[53] *Remaines*, sig. H3v.
[54] *Remaines*, sig. L1r.
[55] Cuming Walters, *The Lost Land of King Arthur*, p. 1.

(and affectiveness) of Camden's presentation of Arthur relates to how Arthur is situated in the structural context of *Britannia*. *Britannia*, as we have established, is a catalogic work: more specifically it is a chorography, a systematic overview of a place.[56] Camden makes it clear that he intended the work as a chorography in both its original title ('Britannia [...] ex intima antiquitate chorographica descriptio') and its English title ('Britain, or A chorographicall description [...]').[57] Camden's *Britannia* is the best known early modern chorography, and is unusually broad in its parameters compared to the chorographies of Camden's contemporaries and predecessors, although William Harrison's *Description of England* (1577), published together with Raphael Holinshed's *Chronicles*, bucks this trend.[58] Other prominent early modern examples, narrower in their outlook, include William Lambarde's *A Perambulation of Kent* (1576), John Stow's *Survey of London* (1598), and Richard Carew's *Survey of Cornwall* (1602).[59] The models for Camden's chorographical project were both continental, such as Flavio Biondo's *Italia illustrata* (1474), and insular – Lambarde's finished and Leland's unfinished works, for example.[60]

At this point, the definition of chorography requires unpacking, as it is the geographical organisation of this type of text that is crucial to the regional and local presentation of Arthur in *Britannia*. Chorography is a classical genre that was revived in late medieval and

[56] On Camden as a chorographer, and on chorography more broadly, see Stuart Piggott, 'William Camden and the *Britannia*'; Andrew McRae, *God Speed the Plough: The Representation of Agrarian England, 1500–1660* (Cambridge: Cambridge University Press, 2002), pp. 231–61; Marjorie Swann, *Curiosities and Texts: The Culture of Collecting in Early Modern England* (Philadelphia, PA: University of Pennsylvania Press, 2010), pp. 97–148; John M. Adrian, *Local Negotiations of English Nationhood, 1570–1680* (New York: Palgrave Macmillan, 2011), pp. 25–28; Rouse, 'What Lies Between', pp. 16–18.

[57] *Britannia* (1586); *Britannia* (1610).

[58] Harrison's work has been interpreted by some as chorographical in nature. See, for example, Helgerson, 'The Land Speaks', p. 71; Kinga Földváry, 'On the Shoulders of Giants: Texts and Contexts behind William Harrison's Description of England', in *Early Modern Communi(cati)ons: Studies in Early Modern English Literature and Culture*, ed. Kinga Földváry and Erzsébet Stróbl (Cambridge: Cambridge University Press, 2012), pp. 32–52.

[59] William Lambarde, *A Perambulation of Kent* (London: Ralph Newberry, 1576), STC (2nd edn) 15175.5; John Stow, *A Survey of London* (London: John Windet, 1598), STC (2nd edn) 23341; Richard Carew, *The Survey of Cornwall* (London: S. Stafford, 1602), STC (2nd edn) 4615. The early modern chorographers and their works are discussed in Stan Mendyk, 'Early British Chorography', *The Sixteenth Century Journal*, 17 (1986), 459–81.

[60] Mendyk, 'Early British Chorography', passim; William Rockett, 'The Structural Plan of Camden's *Britannia*', *Sixteenth Century Journal*, 26.4 (1995), 829–41 (p. 833).

early modern humanist Europe as writers like Ptolemy and Strabo were rediscovered.[61] *Chorographia* was originally conceived by Ptolemy (second century CE) as something distinct from *geographia*: *geographia* represents 'an imitation through drawing of the entire known part of the world', whereas *chorographia* 'sets out the individual localities, each one independently and by itself, registering practically everything down to the least thing therein'.[62] Where Ptolemy identified *geographia* and *chorographia* as forms of visual representation, his contemporary Strabo argued that a chorography could be a textual as well as a visual depiction of a geographical area.[63] This view is also supported in the writings of Pomponius Mela, who is referenced frequently by Camden in the *Britannia*: 'in Greek technical literature *khôrographia* typically designates a written description (*graphê*) covering a district or region (*khôros*), perhaps a country, but in any case more than one individual place. A *topographia*, in contrast, was a description limited to a single place (*topos*).'[64] Chorography is therefore by its very nature and in its very name regional. Early modern chorographies tended to be textual rather than visual representations of place. Many early modern readers of Strabo and Ptolemy repurposed the chorography, authoring texts that predominantly operated at the smaller scale of towns and districts.[65] As well as the rediscovery of classical texts, the chorographic revival was partly the result of (and indeed the motivator for) rapid advancements in cartography: maps could be scaled more accurately, produced in larger quantities through printing, and were used increasingly as tools for

---

[61] Mark Gillings identifies early modern chorography as the ancestor of contemporary landscape phenomenology, rather than the later antiquarians of the seventeenth and eighteenth centuries; Mark Gillings, 'Chorography, Phenomenology and the Antiquarian Tradition', *Cambridge Archaeological Journal*, 21.1 (2011), 53–64.

[62] Ptolemy, *Ptolemy's Geography: An Annotated Translation of the Theoretical Chapters*, ed. and trans. A. L. Berggren and Alexander Jones (Princeton, NJ: Princeton University Press, 2000). Berggren and Jones opt to translate *geographia* as 'world cartography' and *chorographia* as 'regional cartography'.

[63] Jesse Simon, 'Chorography Reconsidered: An Alternative Approach to the Ptolemaic Definition', in *Mapping Medieval Geographies: Geographical Encounters in the Latin West and Beyond, 300–1600*, ed. Keith D. Lilley (Cambridge: Cambridge University Press, 2013), pp. 23–44.

[64] *Pomponius Mela's Description of the World*, ed. and trans. Frank E. Romer (Ann Arbor, MI: University of Michigan Press, 1998), p. 4.

[65] Lucia Nuti, 'Mapping Places: Chorography and Vision in the Renaissance', in *Mappings*, ed. Denis Cosgrave (London: Reaktion Books, 1999), pp. 90–108 (p. 91).

governance.⁶⁶ The production of Camden's *Britannia* was spurred by the same motivations that guided the work of these cartographers.

Camden was the first of the chorographic revivalists to create a work that was at once a *geographia* and a *chorographia*. *Britannia* creates an impression of Britannia as a whole, but also the composite parts within it. There is clear evidence that both Strabo and Ptolemy had a considerable influence on Camden; he mentions them both repeatedly, pointing out just before the opening of his first chapter on Cornwall that his approach to writing his chorography from west to east is modelled directly on Strabo and Ptolemy's methodologies: 'And begin I will at the farthest parts in the West, that is to say, at Cornwall, and so passe over the other countries in order, imitating herein Strabo, Ptolomee and the most ancient Geographers, who always begin their description in the Western countries, as being first from the first Meridian' (Ab vltimo autem Occidente, id est, a Cornwallia auspicabor, & inde reliquas prouincias suo ordine perlustrabo, imitatus in hoc Strabonem, Ptolomaeum, & vetustissimos Geographos, qui ab Occiduis regionibus descriptiones suas semper exordiuntur).⁶⁷ This structure means that Arthur appears from the very beginning of *Britannia*'s 'Description'; to a reader more accustomed to standard narratological structures, this might create the impression that Arthur is bound up with the very earliest beginnings of Britain. In the English edition, the marginal entry alongside this paragraph refers to it as 'the order or Method of the worke ensuing'.⁶⁸ By signposting his methodological approach in this way, Camden makes it clear to the reader that *Britannia* is a chorography, and that its structure is defined by geographical places.

The geographical organisation of *Britannia* becomes especially pronounced in the second half of the work, while the first half is chronologically ordered. Part one opens with a preface addressed to

---

⁶⁶ Peter Barber, 'England II: Monarchs, Ministers, and Maps, 1550–1625', in *Monarchs, Ministers, and Maps: The Emergence of Cartography as a Tool of Government in Early Modern Europe*, The Kenneth Nebenzahl Jr Lectures in the History of Cartography (Chicago, IL: University of Chicago Press, 1992), pp. 57–98; P. D. A. Harvey, *The History of Topographical Maps: Symbols, Pictures and Surveys* (London: Thames and Hudson, 1980); Paul Regan, 'Cartography, Chorography and Patriotic Sentiment in the Sixteenth-Century Low Countries', in *Public Opinion and Changing Identities in the Early Modern Netherlands: Essays in Honour of Alastair Duke*, ed. A. C. Duke, J. Pollmann, and A. P. Spicer (Leiden: Brill, 2007), pp. 49–68 (pp. 30–31). On the printing press and geographical works, see Elizabeth L. Eisenstein, *The Printing Revolution in Early Modern Europe*, 2nd edn (Cambridge: Cambridge University Press, 2012).

⁶⁷ *Britain* (1610), sig. Yyy1v, p. 182; *Britannia* (1586), sigs. F1r-F1v, pp. 65-66.

⁶⁸ Ibid. In the first edition of 1586 this simply reads *ordo* (meaning methodology, organisation, arrangement, order). *Britannia* (1586), sig. F1v, p. 66.

the reader ('Ad Lectorem') in which Camden introduces the aims of the work pressed upon him by Ortelius: 'that I would illustrate this Ile of Britaine, or (as he said) that I would restore antiquity to Britaine, and Britaine to his antiquity' ([...] ut Britanniam nostrum, antiquam illam illustrararem: hoc est, ut Britanniae antiquitatem et suae antiquitati Britanniam restituerum).[69] A methodical taxonomy of Britain follows the preface, covering the following subjects chapter-by-chapter: Britain's first inhabitants (*Britannia* [1586] sigs B3r–C1v, pp. 5–18); the etymology of the name Britain itself (*Britannia* [1586] sigs C2r–C4v, pp. 19–24); the Romans in Britain (*Britannia* [1586] sigs C5r–C7r, pp. 25–29); the Picts (*Britannia* [1586] sigs C7v–D1r, pp. 30–33); the Scots (*Britannia* [1586] sigs D1v–D5v, pp. 34–42); the Anglo-Saxons (*Britannia* [1586] sigs D6r–D8v, pp. 43–48); the Danes and Normans (*Britannia* [1586] sigs E1r–E1v, pp. 49–50); the Normans (*Britannia* [1586] sig. E2r, p. 51); the division of Britain, including its division through history into kingdoms, counties, and hides (*Britannia* [1586] sigs E2v–E5v, pp. 52–58); the Orders and Degrees of England (*Britannia* [1586] sigs E6r–E7v, pp. 59–62); and finally, the Law Courts of England (*Britannia* [1586] sigs E8r–F1v, pp. 63–66). The remaining pages form the work's second half and comprise the bulk of the text: a thorough description of Britain arranged geographically by county on a chapter-by-chapter basis, beginning with Cornwall in imitation of Strabo and Ptolemy (*Britannia* [1586] sigs F2r–Nn6v, pp. 67–556).[70] The predominant focus is on England and Wales (*Britannia* [1586] sigs F2r–Hh6v, pp. 65–476), with less than a hundred pages covering the entirety of Scotland and Ireland (*Britannia* [1586] sigs Hh6v–Nn6v, pp. 476–556). Whereas the English and Welsh sections of *Britannia* seek to glorify their subjects, Camden's Irish material presents the Irish as ignorant and lazy barbarians to be improved through colonisation, replicating the derogatory depiction of the Irish put forward by Gerald of Wales which Camden himself was responsible for publishing.[71] England and Wales, viewed together, are therefore crucial to Camden's idea of Britain, which may explain why the West Country vision of Arthur cultivated by John Leland seems to have shaped Camden's Arthurian geography to such a degree.

---

[69] *Britain* [1610] 'To the Reader', n.p.; *Britannia* (1586), 'Ad Lectorem', n.p.
[70] *Britannia* (1586), sig. F1v, p. 66; *Britain* (1610), sig. P5v, p. 182.
[71] Gerald's anti-Irish *Topographia Hibernica* was published for the first time by Camden in 1602, to the anger of Camden's Irish contemporaries. See Sarah E. McKibben, 'In Their "Owne Countre": Deriding and Defending the Early Modern Irish Nation after Gerald of Wales', *Eolas: The Journal of the American Society of Irish Medieval Studies*, 8 (2015), 39–70 (p. 49; p. 59); Rudolf B. Gottfried, 'The Early Development of the Section on Ireland in Camden's Britannia', *ELH [English Literary History]*, 10.2 (1943), 117–30.

Camden's organisation by county illustrates a craze that was particular to English chorographies, and prefigures the county histories of the nineteenth century.[72] According to Rosemary Sweet, the county unit continued to hold administrative, political and imaginative significance into the seventeenth and eighteenth centuries, perhaps due to the influence of Camden's *Britannia*.[73] Other antiquarians opted for a county-by-county structure, too; John Speed and Michael Drayton organised their works by county, and William Lambarde had originally intended his *Perambulation of Kent* (1576) to be developed into a chorography of the entire realm organised by county.[74] The county chorography was likely inspired by the county maps produced by early English cartographers such as Laurence Nowell in the 1560s and his better-known inheritor Christopher Saxon in the 1570s.[75] Saxon produced the first county atlas, 'a distinctive cartographic form' that was nonpareil in Europe.[76] County cartography was not a sombre interest restricted to 'sober-minded gentlemen', as Kendrick suggests.[77] John Speed's map of Somerset, produced to furnish his atlas of the British Isles *Theatre of the Empire of Great Britaine* (1611/12), includes some distinctly Arthurian toponyms in the vicinity of Glastonbury, including 'Aueland Island' and 'Pomparles Bridge'.[78] Even more playful is the set of county playing cards held by the British Library; dating to c. 1590, these constitute the earliest known playing cards to have been produced from scratch in England.[79] The cards are not divided into traditional suits, but four geographical regions (North, South, East, West) and counties (numbered I–XIII in each region,

---

[72] Sweet, *Antiquaries*, pp. 42–43; M. W. Greenslade, 'Introduction: County History', in *English County Histories: A Guide*, ed. C. R. J. Currie and C. P. Lewis (Stroud: Sutton, 1994), pp. 9–25.

[73] Sweet, *Antiquaries*, p. 37.

[74] Adrian, *Local Negotiations of English Nationhood*, pp. 25–26; Mendyk, 'Early British Chorography', p. 473; Richardson, 'William Camden and the Re-Discovery of England', *Transactions of the Leicestershire Archaeological and Historical Society*, 78.1586 (2004), 108–23 (p. 118).

[75] Greenslade, 'Introduction', p. 10.

[76] Victor Morgan, 'The Cartographic Image of "The Country" in Early Modern England', *Transactions of the Royal Historical Society*, fifth series, 29 (1979), 129–54 (p. 133).

[77] Kendrick, *British Antiquity*, p. 114.

[78] Cambridge University Library, Atlas.2.61.1, 'Somerset'.

[79] 'A set of 53 playing cards containing maps of the counties of England and Wales', (London: William Bowes(?), 1590), London, British Library, Maps C.44.d.90. See Arthur Mayger Hind, 'A historical pack of playing cards', *British Museum Quarterly*, 13 (1938–39), 2–4. The cards, which seem to have been published by William Bowes, were likely copied from Christopher Saxon's map of England and Wales. See Sylvia Mann and David Kingsley, 'Playing Cards Depicting Maps of the British Isles, and of the English and Welsh Counties', *Map Collectors' Series*, 87 (1972), 3–35.

in order from smallest to largest). They feature engravings of county maps, which – significantly – are accompanied by very brief descriptive excerpts taken from Camden's *Britannia*, paraphrased and translated to English well before the publication of the 1610 English edition. This evinces the playful reception of Camden's *Britannia*, and the key role it had to play in the emergence of the county in the public imagination.

The Bowes playing cards demonstrate another peculiarity of Camden's chorographic structure: it is organised not only by county, but also by larger areas that extend beyond county bounds. We might refer to these areas as regions (keeping in mind, of course, that regions can be produced differently by diverse individuals based on their own particular requirements). While the Bowes cards divide Britain according to the four compass points, Camden takes a different approach to region in *Britannia*. Although the *Britannia*'s chapter titles correspond with contemporary county boundaries, alternative section titles are given on facing pages which divide Britain up differently, according to the 'people indigenous or associated with the area' following Ptolemy.[80] These people groups often encompass several counties; 'Danmonii' includes parts of Cornwall and Devonshire, for example, whilst the 'Iceni' includes Suffolk, Norfolk, Cambridgeshire, and Huntingdonshire.[81] *Britannia* therefore exhibits two parallel chapter structures that run alongside each other. Camden indicates county boundaries whilst also stepping over them, tracing historic divisions on top of his contemporary county map. By breaking down county lines in this way, Camden highlights the historical, cultural, and geographical similarities that link adjacent counties, creating a distinct sense of regionality. In this way, Camden 'appropriated the pluralism [...] emerging' during his lifetime, '[redirecting] it toward a popular nationalism that could also find expression in regional identity'.[82] At the same time, this regionalising also had the effect of blurring the historic boundary between England and Wales that sat beneath the surface of the *Britannia* map.

Thus, Camden's regional structure upheld his broader effort to call Britannia into being. Camden makes the unifying aim of *Britannia* clear after his discussion of Gildas' *De excidio*, when he states the following: 'since [...] we are all now by a certain engraffing or commixtion become

---

[80] Marisa R. Cull, '"Prince of Wales by Cambria's Full Consent"?: The Princedom of Wales and the Early Modern Stage', in *Writing Wales from the Renaissance to Romanticism*, ed. Stewart Mottram and Sarah Prescott (Farnham: Ashgate, 2012), pp. 75–90 (p. 88).
[81] Herendeen, *William Camden*, p. 265.
[82] Herendeen, *William Camden*, , p. 208.

one nation, mollified and civilised with Religion, and good Arts, let us meditate and consider, both what they [our ancestors] were, and also what we ought to be' ([...] cum insitione vel commixtione [...] iam cuncti gens una simus, religione bonisque artibus emolliti, cogitemus quale et illi fuerint, et quales nos esse debeamus).[83] This is reflected in Camden's structural choices: he makes the unsurprising decision to absorb Wales into England, interpolating his Welsh chapters into the middle of his description of England. Wales is sandwiched between *Cornavii* (Warwickshire, Worcestershire, Staffordshire, Shropshire, and Cheshire) and *Brigantes* (Yorkshire, East and North Riding, Richmondshire, Durham, Lancashire, Westmoreland, Cumberland, and The Picts Wall). *Silures* encompasses both Welsh counties (Radnorshire, Brecknockshire, Glamorgan) and counties which, in Camden's day, were in England (Herefordshire and Monmouthshire).[84] The Bowes county playing cards shuffle Wales into England in the same manner, with most of the Welsh counties absorbed into the 'Western' counties. The earliest editions of *Britannia* do not focus attention on the historic absorption by England of its neighbouring territories, because the purpose of the work is to reinforce the sense of *Britannia* as a discrete, eternal, and complete whole. Only in the 1610 English edition does Camden explain the historic establishment of the princedom of Wales and the dukedom of Cornwall, and this is perhaps because the Welsh princedom 'resurfaced as an instrument of the monarchy' at this stage.[85]

The *Britannia* also presents its regionality visually. Levy's assertion that the 1586 edition was 'unillustrated' is not entirely true; even the earliest edition contained two woodcut images. By the time the fully illustrated 1607 edition was published with accompanying county maps, and subsequently its English translation in 1610, *Britannia* had been expanded considerably to over a thousand pages in length. It also boasted a much-improved title page consisting of an intricately engraved frontispiece, coloured by hand in later editions. Beneath a map of Britain labelled with the names of the ancient people groups that form Camden's parallel chapter structure, a smaller pane reveals several medieval or early modern buildings, the Roman baths at Bath, Stonehenge, and what appear to be a pair of burial mounds (see Figure 6).[86] They share the same

---

[83] *Britain* (1610), sig. I5v, p. 110; *Britannia* (1607), sig. G4r, p. 79.
[84] *Britain* (1610), sigs Eee6v–Hhh3v, pp. 615–40; *Britannia* (1586), sigs Z6r–Bb1r, pp. 347–69.
[85] Cull, '"Prince of Wales"', p. 88.
[86] It is virtually impossible to ascertain the specific portion of the baths represented in this pane due to its small size, and the uncertainty surrounding the illustrator's

Figure 6. Detail from the frontispiece of Camden's *Britannia* (1610). Image courtesy of the University of Bristol Special Collections.

landscape and jostle alongside each other for space within the frame. This collocation is especially intriguing given that Stonehenge, located near Amesbury, is over thirty miles distant from the Roman baths, and in a different county; yet they are depicted here as virtually on top of one another. Camden's reimagining of their placement pre-empts his regional approach to history and topography in the *Britannia*. While the places featured in the pane appear at first glance to be a random conglomeration of Britain's remains, they are still united in terms of their locality in the

knowledge of the baths or even the finer details of Camden's text. However, the image bears some resemblance to 'the Crosse bath' and the 'Hote Bath', and the adjoining Hospital of St John, described by Camden in *Britannia*: 'The Crosse bath [...] hath twelve seats of stone about the brink or border thereof, and is closed within a wall. The second, distant from this not fully 200. Foot is much hoter: whereupon it is termed *Hote Bath*: Adjoining to these, is a Spittle or Lazar house, built by *Reginald* Bishop of Bath.' *Britain* (1610), sig. V2r, p. 233. The baths are depicted from a bird's-eye perspective in John Speed's map of Somerset (cited above at p. 232); and a detailed image showing how these places would have appeared in the early seventeenth century can be found in Thomas Guidott's *A discourse of Bathe, and the hot waters there* (London: Henry Brome, 1676).

West Country. Of course, this also mimics the perambulations Camden carried out during his research in preparing the work. Camden probably visited both Bath and Stonehenge on a single tour of South-West England made in 1596, which also covered Oxford, Salisbury, and Wells.[87]

There may be further layers of meaning at play, too: in Geoffrey's *Historia*, Stonehenge is described as having been used for medicinal bathing by its gigantic originators.[88] Geoffrey also tells us that the stones were transported to their Salisbury location by Merlin and re-erected to serve as a memorial monument to the Britons who had been slain and buried there.[89] This could explain the visible burial mounds in the top of the frame, although of course such mounds are very visible in the vicinity of Stonehenge, even today. In any case, this pane anticipates the historical layering present throughout *Britannia*, and Camden's dedication to drawing out his vision of Britain according to Bakhtinian 'castle time'. The image depicts the ancient (Stonehenge and the burial mounds), the classical (the baths), and perhaps the contemporary (the architecture in the bottom half of the frame). There are several chains of association at play in this small pane that cut across time and space. In their proximity, these images are almost superimposed, much like John Leland's projection of a ruined Troy atop the Cadbury hillfort.

Camden's Arthuriana

Place and object

References to Arthurian sites appear frequently in *Britannia*, particularly across the South-West and Wales chapters; often, this is a result of Camden's reliance on Leland's notes. This makes it possible to map Arthur's narrative across the places with which he is identified. Cornwall is linked with Arthur's birth (at Tintagel) and death (at Camelford);[90] Camden points to Arthur's victories at Cadbury and Bath (Badon Hill) in Somerset, referencing Nennius and Gildas respectively in support of this;[91] he locates 'King Arthure's Palace' at Cadbury Castle and Arthur's 'famous Court' at Caerleon.[92] The 1610 edition even mentions Arthur's Round

---

[87] Richard L. DeMolen, 'The Library of William Camden', *Proceedings of the American Philosophical Society*, 128.4 (1984), 326–409 (p. 328).
[88] Geoffrey of Monmouth, *The History of the Kings of Britain*, 8.18, pp. 172–73.
[89] Geoffrey of Monmouth, *The History of the Kings of Britain*, 9.127–130, pp. 170–74.
[90] *Britain* (1610), sigs Q5v–Q6r, pp. 194–95; *Britannia* (1586), sigs F6v–F7r, pp. 76–77.
[91] *Britain* (1610), sig. T2r, p. 221, *Britannia* (1586) sig. H2r, p. 99; *Britain* (1610), sig. V2v, p. 234; *Britannia* (1586), sigs H6r–v, pp. 107–08.
[92] *Britain* (1610), sig. T2r, p. 221, *Britannia* (1586), sig. H2r, p. 99; *Britain* (1610), sigs Ggg4v–Ggg5r, pp. 636–37; *Britannia* (1586), sigs Aa5v–Aa6r, pp. 362–63.

Table at Winchester, albeit with a degree of scepticism: 'As concerning that Round Table there, hanging up against the wall which the common sort useth to gaze upon with great admiration, as if it had beene King Arthurs table, I have nothing to say but this, That, as any man which vieweth it well may easily perceive, it is nothing so antient as King Arthur.'[93] In the later editions of *Britannia*, following new information-gathering trips by Camden, there are also references to Arthurian topographies in the northernmost parts of England, and in Scotland and Wales. These include Arthur's Oven in Scotland and Arthur's Table in Cumberland.[94] Beneath an entry for 'Brecknockshire', Camden's commonplace book describes an Arthurian legend from Builth concerning the footprint of Arthur's dog on top of a pile of stones, supplemented with textual fragments from the *Historia Brittonum*.[95] Many of these references to local Arthurian lore are not crucial to a vision of a historic West Country Arthur, and seem to stand alone as readily as they fit into pre-existing Arthurian corpora. Prior to their collation and publication in *Britannia*, they were likely of more significance to those who lived in the respective locations they describe than to the Arthurian canon more widely. This is evident in the case of Castle Rous in Shropshire whose 'neighbor inhabitants […] report that it was a most famous place in King Arthurs daies', another addition made for the 1610 edition.[96] These smaller pieces of landscape folklore do not undermine Camden's vision of a historic Arthur in the West Country and Wales, but rather underscore the impression of Arthur's fame and popularity across the entire island of Britain. This tactic strengthens the impression of a united Britain that Camden was so keen to foster.

The *Britannia*'s longest Arthurian passage is the description of Glastonbury.[97] Camden plays a crucial role in the historic discussions of Arthurian Glastonbury, acting as a key witness to the long narrative of the town's Arthurian legends. The *Britannia* filled the gap between Camden's medieval sources – particularly the accounts of the grave discovery by writers like Gerald of Wales – and the intricate developments of the Glastonbury myths from the seventeenth century to the present day. In *Britannia*, a description of Arthur's grave site and an image of his epitaph are accompanied by extracts from poetry and historiography on the

---

[93] *Britain* (1610), sig. Y6r, p. 265.
[94] *Britain* (1610), sig. C2v, p. 28; sig. Ttt2v p. 776. There are brief mentions of these Arthurian places in the chapters on Hereford, Radnor, Brecon, Monmouth, and Glamorgan, though not in the other Welsh chapters, nor in any Scottish chapters north of the Antonine Wall.
[95] London, British Library Cotton MS Cleopatra A.IV, f. 15v.
[96] *Britain* (1610), sig. Ddd1r, p. 593.
[97] *Britain* (1610), sigs T4r–T5v, pp. 225–28; *Britannia* (1586), sigs H2r–H4v, pp. 101–04.

subject of Arthur, as well as a survey of other mysterious inscriptions Camden recorded in the vicinity of the grave site attributed to important figures of Britain's shadowy past. 'To reckon up here the Kings of the West-Saxons, that were buried in this place, would be but needlesse', Camden states.[98] Here, Camden contextualises Arthur's grave site, spatially and in history, by referring to other fragmentary monuments of forgotten kings in the vicinity, providing a context for Arthur at Glastonbury whilst suggesting that truths are often lost to history.

These details about the surroundings of the grave site were added to later editions of *Britannia*. The direct involvement that Camden had in creating new material for these subsequent editions and in overseeing their production suggests that his interest in Arthur, and especially the physical evidence tying Arthur to specific places, was growing. Arthur was given increasing attention and page space as newer editions of *Britannia* were published from 1587 onwards. These developments suggest that Camden and his printers were becoming aware of Arthur's increasing appeal following the publication of the Arthurian defences of John Prise and Humphrey Llwyd during the 1570s and 1580s.[99] The new edition of John Leland's *Assertio* had, moreover, been published in English translation in 1582, making it accessible to a broader audience of non-Latinate readers within England itself.

The most noticeable expansion in the Glastonbury section relates to its illustration. We know that Camden had a hand in the development of the *Britannia*'s illustrations, so this is a good place to look for evidence of Camden's increasing interest in Arthur.[100] The first edition of *Britannia* contained just two woodcuts, both facsimiles of epitaphs. The first appears in the Sussex chapter: an inscription found in a church at Lewes announcing 'one Magnus descended from the bloud roiall of the Danes, who embraced a solitarie life' and 'was there buried' (Qui innuunt Magnum quendam e Danorum regio sanguine oriundum ibi conditum).[101] The second is a careful copy of the letterforms inscribed

---

[98] *Britain* (1610), sig. T6v, p. 230.
[99] Discussed above in Chapter 4.
[100] Camden tells us as much just before the full-page engraving of Stonehenge in the post-1600 editions of *Britannia*: 'the description or draught whereof such as it is, because it not so fitly be expressed in words, I have caused by the gravers helpe to be portraied here underneath' (Gigantum Chorea a magnitudine. Eius vero qualemcumque delineationem cum verbis satis commode exprimi non potest, hic opera sculptoris subiungendam curavi). *Britain* (1610), sig. X5r, p. 251; *Britannia* (1600), sig. P5v, p. 218.
[101] *Britain* [1610], sig. Cc5v, p. 314; *Britannia* (1586), sigs L7v–L8r, pp. 158–59.

on the lead cross found at Arthur's grave in Glastonbury, an artefact which does not survive.[102] Alongside the image, Camden provides a brief descriptive analysis which makes constant reference to the roughness and barbarity of the letterforms themselves, as well as lamenting:

> the barbarism of that age, when ignorance (as it were) by fatall destinie bare such sway, that there was none to be found, by whose writings the renowme of Arthur might be blazed, and commended to posteritie.
>
> ([...] & eius aetatis barbariem plane loquuntur, quae adeo fatalibus tenebris inuoluta erat, vt nemo fuerit, cuius scriptis Arthurij nomen celebraretur.)[103]

Here, Camden expresses regret that there were no living witnesses to Arthur who could preserve the truth of his actions in eloquent writing as they had in carving the physical proof of the epitaph, a lament about the impermanence of history that is a recurring theme in the *Britannia*.[104] This melancholy echoes John Leland's descriptions of Arthurian traces, such as Arthur's seal, and John Prise's comments about the enduring nature of landscape features named after Arthur.[105] The effect is all the more powerful here because Camden, beyond his preface, rarely interrupts *Britannia* with his own opinion. When he does so at this point, he immediately follows his sad exclamation with a request to the reader to 'behold the said Crosse and Epitaph therein' (Sed ecce inscriptionem).[106] This calls to mind the ways in which Leland attempts to include his reader as eyewitness in his descriptions of Cadbury and Camlan.

---

[102] The woodcut appears at *Britannia* (1586), sig. H4v, p. 104; *Britain* (1610), sig. T5v, p. 228. The cross was reportedly last owned by William Hughes, Chancellor of Wells, in the eighteenth century, though this appears at best to be speculation. In Sharon Turner's *History of the Anglo-Saxons* (1799–1805) Turner reports that 'in Whitaker's *Manchester*, part ii. Dr Whitaker was told that the cross had then lately been in the possession of Mr Chancellor Hughes, at Wells.' Sharon Turner, *The History of the Anglo-Saxons*, 3 vols (London: Longman, 1836), I, p. 293. Turner appears to have muddled up his source, for it is actually in Whitaker's *Life of St Neot* where the author claims to have been told by an old 'Ciceroni' at Glastonbury that Chancellor Hughes was the last known custodian of the cross. Whitaker, *Life of Saint Neot*, p. 39 n.

[103] *Britain* (1610), sig. T5v, p. 228; *Britannia* (1586), sig. I6r, p. 123.

[104] Camden sums up this sentiment in his preface: 'whereas conjectures are certain detections of things unknowne [...] I have always thought that they were to be accounted among the skuppers wherewith Time worketh and drawweth Veritie out of Democritus his deep dungeon.' *Britain* (1610) 'To the Reader', n.p. This frames time as an all-encompassing dungeon in which truths can easily be lost.

[105] Discussed above at p. 191–92.

[106] Ibid.

Camden goes further than Leland, however. Whereas Leland paints a detailed verbal description of Arthur's seal but includes no image, Camden prompts his readers to view the woodcut directly. Camden's decision to include a facsimile of the letterforms rather than simply the text of the inscription is an invitation to his readers to act as first-hand witnesses to the materiality of the object itself. The reason why Camden's approach is more successful than Leland's is because he exceeds Leland at conveying 'authenticity'. I use this term as it is employed by Stuart Jeffrey, whose research examines the failures of digital reconstructions in contemporary heritage interpretation.[107] By Jeffrey's definition, 'authenticity', which he deems to be lacking in most digital reconstructions, refers to the 'aura, patina and proximity that is attached to material objects'.[108] Digital visualisations lack the 'tactile, material traces of "age-value" that prompt emotional responses in the viewer'.[109] In the same way, Camden's exact replication of the cross's inscription, and the attention he draws to the letters 'being made after a barbarous maner, & resembling the Gothish Character, bewray[ing] plainly the barbarism of that age' (Barbarum quiddam et quasi Gothicorum prae se ferunt literae, et eius aetatis barbariem plane loquuntur), create the impression of authenticity which Jeffrey describes.[110] Though Leland's account of the archaeological finds at Cadbury and Padstow ('Camlan') attempt authenticity, the overall impression of his passage on Cadbury is perhaps closer to the digital projections that Jeffrey critiques, thanks in part to the Virgilian image of Troy that Leland projects over the Camp.

The authenticity of Camden's portrayal of Arthur's epitaph is reinforced when, in the expanded 1600 edition, the original image is replaced with one depicting the cross in its entirety (see Figure 7). Although it has previously been thought that Camden saw and copied the cross himself during his 1596 visit to the Glastonbury area, more recent research has uncovered a draft sketch of the cross in John Leland's notes, to which Camden had access.[111] As Oliver Harris has shown, the

---

[107] Stuart Jeffrey, 'Challenging Heritage Visualisation: Beauty, Aura, and Democratisation', *Open Archaeology*, 1.1 (2015), www.degruyter.com/view/j/opar.2014.1.issue-1/opar-2015-0008/opar-2015-0008.xml [accessed 7 March 2020]. Cited in Roberta Gilchrist, *Sacred Heritage*, p. 208.

[108] Gilchrist, *Sacred Heritage*, p. 208.

[109] Gilchrist, *Sacred Heritage*, p. 208, citing C. Holtorf, 'On Pastness: A Reconsideration of Materiality in Archaeological Object Authenticity', *Anthropological Quarterly*, 86.2 (2013), 427–43.

[110] *Britain* (1610), sig. T5v, p. 228; *Britannia* (1586), sig. I6r, p. 123.

[111] Richard L. DeMolen, 'The Library of William Camden', p. 328; Harris, '"Which I Have Beholden"'. Harris concludes that the sketch was probably produced by

sh Empire, seemeth even in this behalfe onely, most unfi
it with such a trumpetter, as might worthily have sounded
it. But behold the said Crosse and Epitaph therein.

Figure 7. Arthur's Cross in Camden's *Britain* (1610). Image courtesy of the University of Bristol Special Collections.

two individuals most likely to have been the original copyist of this cross were John Leland and John Stow.[112] Whilst Stow did not usually venture far in pursuit of antiquities, Leland visited the very church in Glastonbury to which the cross is believed to have been translated after 1539, and even claimed to have 'beholden [the cross] with most curiouse eyes and

---

either John Stow or John Leland, most likely Leland. The sketch is reproduced by Harris at p. 99.

[112] Harris, '"Which I have beholden"', pp. 100–02.

handled with fearful joyntes in each part'.[113] Rather than visiting the cross in person, it therefore seems more likely that Camden combined an earlier sketch of the letterforms (printed in the first edition of *Britannia*) with Leland's sketch to produce an approximation of the artefact in its entirety for the post-1600 editions of *Britannia*. Aside from demonstrating Camden's interest in increasing the Arthurian content of *Britannia*, this further underscores that Camden's Arthurian antiquarianism was a direct and conscious continuation of the work done by the 'old' antiquarians, like Leland, who came before him.

Poetry

Another clear continuity between Camden and Leland's Arthurian representations, and indeed the localised Arthuriana contained in fourteenth- and fifteenth-century *tabulae*, is their use of poetic extracts.[114] As in the Arthurian defences of Leland and Prise, the presentation of Arthurian material evidence in *Britannia* is always supported with textual witnesses of some sort. Whilst these routinely refer to canonical historiographies, Camden also makes use of more creative sources, such as poetry. The frequent use of these snippets is an extension of Camden's antiquarian tendencies: his interest in fragments was not limited to physical objects, but included textual titbits.[115] Camden's other major work, *Remaines Concerning Britaine*, contains five chapters dedicated to various kinds of textual 'remaines'.[116] In *Britannia*, Arthur is the subject of a disproportionately high number of poetic fragments from its later editions. Many of these have been lifted directly from Leland's writings. Frequently, the verse Camden cites appears obscure, fragmentary, and mysterious in origin, particularly when compared with his historiographic

---

[113] This is St John the Baptist parish church, situated today on Glastonbury's High Street; see Oxford, Bodleian Library, Bodleian MS Rawlinson B.416A, fol. 10v, and Carley, *The Holy House at the Head of the Moors Adventurous*, p. 178. Leland cited in Harris, '"Which I have beholden"', p. 96.

[114] The significance of poetry in Camden's work is a subject that is rather underappreciated and demands further attention. On Camden's poetry, see Vine, *In Defiance of Time*, pp. 103–05. An edition of the poems that Camden purportedly composed was published in 1975, though this includes poetry which Camden took from elsewhere. William Camden, 'Poems by William Camden: With Notes and Translations from the Latin', ed. George Burke Johnston, *Studies in Philology*, 72.5 (1975), iii–143. See also Herendeen, *William Camden*, pp. 180–242.

[115] Woolf, *The Social Circulation of the Past*, pp. 141–50.

[116] These include 'allusions' (wordplay based on adding and subtracting letters) (sig. T2v–V1r, pp. 140–45); anagrams (sigs V3v–X3r, pp. 150–57); 'wise speeches' (sigs Aa1r–Hh2r, pp. 177–235); and 'Certaine Poems, or Poesies, Epigrammes, Rythmes, and Epitaphs of the English Nation in Former Times' (sigs a1rh2v, pp. 1–59).

sources. Often, however, these verse fragments have been made to seem more mysterious or fragmentary than they really are through Camden's shrewd editing.[117] Without exception, the verse fragments appear in the chorographical second half of *Britannia* and therefore must be read regionally, as dictated by the work's structure; they are emplaced by Camden, just as his predecessor Prise rooted ancient manuscripts concerning Arthur in the places where he had found them.[118]

Camden's use of poetry in the pursuit of history reflects conversations about poetry taking place in his immediate intellectual environment.[119] Arthur B. Ferguson describes, in terms that echo Zerubavel's mnemonic bridges, how 'poesie historical' was used to plug evidential gaps in empirical histories:

> Basic questions regarding the still unresolved conflict between poetry and history [...] continued to hold hostage the idea of historical truth, especially as it applied to those reaches of the past where the possibility of finding empirical evidence became less and less likely, and where the historically conditioned imagination had increasingly to serve the purposes of interpretation. Awareness of the part played by poets in interpreting the most distant past gave rise to that unnaturally fertile hybrid known to contemporaries as 'poesie historical.' At a time of uneasily shifting epistemological positions, that concept acted [...] as a bridge between history proper and the quasi-history of myth and legend.[120]

The Italian scholar Lodovico Castelvetro produced a highly influential commentary on Aristotle's *Poetica* (1570) which framed poetry and history symbiotically as arts that could strengthen each other, should the poet decide to borrow from the techniques of the historian and vice versa.[121] Taking a closer look at Camden's immediate network, there is strong evidence of a long tradition of scholarly poetry flourishing in the intellectual circles in which he moved. This group of individuals included scholar-poets such as John Johnston, Edmund Spenser, and Michael Drayton.[122] To this list we can add Philip Sidney, author of the

---

[117] For more on Camden's doctoring of his poetic extracts, see Vine, *In Defiance of Time*, pp. 100–08.
[118] See above at pp. 180–83.
[119] There have been a number of broader studies concerning what George Puttenham termed 'historicall poesie': see Ferguson, *Utter Antiquity*, pp. 114–33; Chris Barrett, *Early Modern English Literature and the Poetics of Cartographic Anxiety* (Oxford: Oxford University Press, 2018).
[120] Ferguson, *Utter Antiquity*, p. 5.
[121] Lodovico Castelvetro, *Poetica d'Aristotele vulgarizzata e sposta*, ed. Werther Romani, 2 vols (Rome: Gius. Laterza, 1978–79).
[122] Camden mentions these men as examples of the poets of his day in *Remaines*.

Defence of Poetry, who Camden respected and held as a close friend.[123] Sidney's *Defence* made a case for the usefulness of poetry for the purposes of education, and whilst this has often been attributed to Sidney's humanistic outlook it should be noted that metrical forms appear to have been seen as appropriate for pedagogical purposes from a much earlier date, as A. G. Rigg has suggested.[124] Given that Sidney died in 1586, the year in which *Britannia* was first published, and that Camden's elegy for him appeared in the subsequent 1587 edition, it may be that the increase of poetic sources cited in subsequent editions was an intentional reflection on the late Sidney's philosophy.[125] John Leland, Camden's major source for *Britannia* and the provider of much of the poetry quoted within it, had himself dabbled in scholarly poetry within the context of humanist encomiastic verse – that is, verse dedicated to bringing deserved fame to its subject.[126] Arthurian poetry in *Britannia* takes on this encomiastic function, bringing fame to a subject believed by Camden and his predecessors to have been inadequately lauded in the writings (or absence thereof) of Arthur's contemporaries.

The Arthurian poetic excerpts in *Britannia* also work to memorialise Arthur. As this book's previous chapters demonstrate, verse extracts were already considered useful for commemorative purposes: fragments from metrical chronicles abound in fifteenth-century *tabulae* such as those at Glastonbury and York. At Arthur's Glastonbury tomb there seem to have been, over the years, a series of different epitaph verses that visitors copied down, and Elis Gruffydd recorded the tradition of a similar metrical epitaph on the tomb of Llewellyn the Great.[127] In Titus A.XIX a scribe copied Arthur's versified epitaph along with the metrical epitaph said to have adorned the tomb of Cadwallader, the last king of the Britons, at St Peter's basilica in Rome.[128] In *Remaines concerning Britain*, Camden

---

[123] On the relationship between Camden and Sidney, see H. R. Trevor-Roper, *Queen Elizabeth's First Historian: William Camden and the Beginnings of English 'Civil History'*, The Second Neale Lecture in English History (London: Jonathan Cape, 1971), p. 6; W. A. Ringler, *The Poems of Sir Philip Sidney* (Oxford: Oxford University Press, 1962), p. xviii; William Camden, 'Poems by William Camden', pp. 90–91, pp. 94–95, pp. 102–03.

[124] Rigg, *Book of British Kings*, p. 3.

[125] Herendeen goes so far as to call Sidney Britain's *genius loci* and the informing spirit of *Britannia*. Herendeen, *William Camden*, p. 188.

[126] James P. Carley, 'John Leland in Paris: The Evidence of His Poetry', *Studies in Philology*, 83.1 (1986), 1–50 (pp. 2–3).

[127] On the evolution of Arthur's verse epitaph(s), see above at p. 53. On Gruffydd's report of Llywelyn's tomb, see pp. 209–12.

[128] British Library, Cotton MS Titus A.XIX, ff. 114r–114v. See Krochalis and Stones, *The Pilgrim's Guide*, I, pp. 148–49.

included epitaphs under a section dedicated to epitaphs and other fragments pertaining to 'the English Nation in former times'.[129] Given the prevalence of short metrical extracts on tombs and *tabulae*, the verse snippets in Leland and Camden's writings might therefore be considered textual memorials that ape the qualities of their stone counterparts – a 'monument' could refer, after all, to both a physical commemorative structure *and* a written record. Places like Camlan and Cadbury, which Leland and Camden furnish with poetic extracts, probably did not have *tabulae* on display to commemorate their histories. Leland and Camden may therefore have considered their work to be filling this gap. Like physical *tabulae*, verse extracts functioned as a point of connection between written and oral traditions, and through their commemorative function provided a bridge between past, present, and future.

When using verse extracts to commemorate an Arthurian event, Camden's approach is akin to Leland's description of Arthurian sites in the *Assertio*. First, local geography is described, followed by a survey of archaeological evidence turned up in the area. Next, the 'common fame' of those living in the area concerning the site's ancient history is acknowledged. Finally, the description closes with a poetic extract imbued with the melancholy of loss. The description of Camlan in *Britannia* follows this model. Camden begins by repeating information lifted from Leland's *Assertio* – that Camlan stands at the head of the 'river Alan' in the village known as 'Camelford'.[130] Acknowledging Leland, Camden states that 'peeces of armour, rings, horse-harnesse of brasse' have been unearthed there by 'husbandmen', before remarking on local lore that reports a 'notable battell fought in this place'.[131] Finally, Camden turns to his textual authorities, citing an extract purportedly authored by an 'unknowen Poet living in the middle time' (in nescio quo medii temporis poeta), whose lines Camden elects to include 'because they may seeme to have beene written in no bad Poeticall vaine' (cum Musis non omnino inscripti videantur):[132]

---

[129] *Remaines*, sigs a1r–h2v, pp. 1–59.
[130] *Britain* (1610), sig. Q5v, p. 194; *Britain* (1586), sig. F6v, p. 76.
[131] 'For, as hee recordeth, peeces of armour, rings, horse-harnesse of brasse are otherwhiles [sometimes] digged up and turned out of the ground by husbandmen, and the common fame that continued for so many ages together reporteth that there was a notable battell fought in this place.' (Fragmenta etenim (ut prodit ille) armorum, annuli, aenea equorum ornamenta, nonnunquam ab agricolis ibi eruuntur, famaque tot saeculis conservata insignem hoc loco stragem factam fuisse praedicat.) *Britain* (1610), sig. Q5v, p. 194; *Britannia* (1586), sig. F6v, p. 76.
[132] Ibid.

> Then Cambula was sore agast, the nature chang'd to se
> Of his spring-head, for now the streame by this time gan to bee
> All mixt with bloud, which swelling high the banks doth overflow,
> And carry downe the bodies slaine, into the sea below.
> There might one see how many a man that swum and helpe did crave,
> Was lost among the billowes strong, and water was their grave.
>
> (------------------ Naturam Cambula fontis
> Mutatam stupet esse sui, transcendit inundans
> Sanguineus torrent ripas, & volvit in aequor
> Corpora caesorum, plures natare videres
> Et petere auxilium, quos undis vita reliquit).[133]

In fact, these lines come from *Gesta regum Britannie* (c. 1236), a metrical version of Geoffrey's *Historia* composed by William of Rennes.[134] It is unclear whether Camden knew this text in its entirety or just this excerpt, but he may have gained access to the witness owned by Robert Cotton.[135] The author of the *Gesta* sought to present Geoffrey's *Historia* – and consequently Arthur – in the same terms as classical epic. Whilst Geoffrey's text already exhibited epic qualities, these are amplified in the *Gesta*.[136] For example, the text opens with an invocation to the Muse Calliope, and the games that take place during Arthur's Caerleon celebrations are described in terms more classical than medieval.[137] Some scholars have identified parallels between the *Gesta*'s Arthur and classical presentations of Alexander the Great.[138] By citing the extract amid his description of the purported Camlan location, Camden immediately frames the battle, and therefore Arthur, in the epic mode, an association that becomes

---

[133] William Camden, *Britain* (1610), sig. Q5v, p. 194; *Britannia* (London: George Bishop & John Norton, 1607), STC (2nd edn) 4508, sigs M4v–M5r, pp. 140–41.

[134] William of Rennes, *The Historia Regum Britannie of Geoffrey of Monmouth V: Gesta Regum Britanniae*, 9.276-81. See above at p. 101.

[135] Wright's 'C' manuscript, London British Library Cotton MS Julius D.XI, ff. 2r–60v. This witness was part of Robert Cotton's library, probably sourced from the prolific antiquarian Thomas Allen (who also supplied Cotton with the Titus A.XIX manuscript). See William of Rennes, *The Historia Regum Britannie of Geoffrey of Monmouth V: Gesta Regum Britanniae*, pp. xcix–cii.

[136] See above at pp. 143–44.

[137] Putter, 'Latin Historiography', p. 96.

[138] Echard, *Arthurian Narrative in the Latin Tradition*, pp. 95–101. Previous scholars have suggested that Alexander may have influenced Geoffrey of Monmouth's Arthur, too; see Tatlock, *The Legendary History*, pp. 311–20; Antonio L. Furtado, 'Alexander of Macedonia to Arthur of Britain', *Arthuriana*, 5.3 (1995), 70–86; Padel, 'Recent Work', pp. 104–05.

clearer when Camden also cites Leland 'who writeth also that King Arthur our Hector was there slaine' (Lelandus [...] qui Arthurum Hectorem nostrum ibi cecidisse scribit).[139]

In this passage, the description of the large waves consuming the soldiers' bodies recalls the tone of the poetic extracts employed by Leland, characterised by loss and oblivion. Finally, Camden creates a sense of destiny and poetic circularity, remarking that 'if it bee true that Arthur here died, the same coast was destined unto him for his death, as for his birth' (et si verum sit Arthurum hic cecidisse, idem littus illi fuit fatale quod natale), before moving onwards to Tintagel, 'the native place of that great Arthur' (Arthuri illius magni incunabula).[140] In describing Tintagel, Camden cites two poetic extracts, both lifted from Leland's *Assertio*. The first extract, a quatrain, describes Tintagel from all angles, enabling the reader to imaginatively reconstruct the castle in their mind in three dimensions:

> There is a place within the winding shore of Severne Sea
> On mids a rocke about whose foote the tides turne-keeping play,
> Towry-topped Castle here farre thundreth over all,
> Which Cornishmen by antient name, *Tindagel* Castle call.
>
> (Est locus Abrini sinuoso littore ponti,
> Rupe situs media, refluus quem circuit aestus,
> Fulminat hic late, turrito vertice Castrum,
> Nomine Tindagium, veteres dixere Corini)[141]

This extract has no known source and may represent Leland's own composition. Rather than acknowledging that this fragment came from Leland, Camden again ascribes it to an unidentified 'late Poet', giving the impression that it is an antique fragment rather than a comparatively recent composition.[142]

Elsewhere, Camden goes further than simply misrepresenting his sources, and instead directly alters them. At these moments, Camden's

---

[139] *Britannia* (1586), sig. F6v, p. 76; *Britain* (1610), sig. Q5v, p. 196.

[140] *Britain* (1610), sig. Q5v, p. 194; *Britannia* (1586), sig. F7r, p. 77.

[141] *Britain* (1610), sig. Q6r, p. 195; *Britannia* (1586), sig. F7r, p. 77. Leland, *Assertio*, sig. B1v; Leland, *Learned*, sig. C1v.

[142] 'Of which a late Poet hath thus written' ([...] de quo quodam recens cecinit). *Britannia* (1586), sig. F7r, p. 77; *Britain* (1610), sig. Q5v, p. 196. Philip Schwyzer argues that 'late', despite ostensibly meaning 'recent', is sometimes used by early modern writers to introduce 'a nostalgic temporality capable of collapsing large stretches of time between the present and the lost object of desire'. Philip Schwyzer, '"Late" Losses and the Temporality of Early Modern Nostalgia', *Parergon*, 33.2 (2016), 97–113 (p. 99).

intentions to both historicise and commend Arthur become especially obvious. In the second poetic extract of the Tintagel section, a description of Uther's ravishment of Ygerne, Camden has cut lines from his source (John of Hauville's *Architrenius*). This dramatically alters the focus of the extract. A comparison with the fuller version in Leland's *Assertio* hints at Camden's intentions. The following uses Leland's *Assertio* as its base, with struck-through text indicating Camden's omissions:

> ~~The after coming youth, lightens the world of Coriney~~
> ~~With his three clouen sonne; & she that brought forth at that day~~
> ~~The fourth Phoebus, brought forth Arthur,~~ whilst the adulterer he
> Euen Tintagol so false of face brake in most wickedly,
> Neither Pendragon vanquished the flaming fire of Loue,
> But Merlins artes so manifold by counsel seekes to proue:
> And counterfeitees the Dukes attyre (as while the King did glose
> Thus) He put on the present face of absent Duke Gorlois.[143]

> (~~Hoc trisido mundum, Corinei postera sole,~~
> ~~Irradiat Pubes, quartique puerpera Phoebi,~~
> ~~Pullulat Arturum,~~ facie dum falso adulter
> Tintagoll irrumpit, nec amoris Pendragon aestum,
> Vincit & omnificas Merlini consulit artes.
> Mentiturque Ducis habitus & Rege latent,
> Induit absentis presenti Gorloys ora.)[144]

The overall effect of Camden's editing – which cuts off the text midway through a line – is that Arthur has been completely excised from his own morally and historically questionable conception story. Suddenly, this becomes an extract about another myth linked with Tintagel – Uther's ravishment of Ygerne – and Arthur is not mentioned at all. Thus, Camden drives a wedge between Arthur and his dubious Galfridian origins, shoring up Arthur's status as a real historical figure, rather than a figure associated with unrealistic mythologies.

Elsewhere in *Britannia*, Camden's shrewd editing places Arthur firmly in the spotlight. In the description of Glastonbury, Camden cites an excerpt from Joseph of Exeter's now-lost epic poem, *Antiocheis*.[145] To

---

[143] Leland, *Learned*, sigs C1v–C2r; corresponds to Camden, ibid.
[144] *Assertio*, sigs B1v–B2r; corresponds to Camden, *Britain* (1610), p. 194, sig. Q5v.
[145] *Britain* (1610), sig. T6r, p. 229. For a modern edition of the surviving fragment, see L. Gompf, *Joseph Iscanus: Werke und Briefe* (Leiden: Brill, 1970), p. 212. On Joseph's life and work, see Geoffrey B. Riddehough, 'A Forgotten Poet: Joseph of Exeter', *The Journal of English and Germanic Philology*, 46.3 (1947), 254–59; and Neil Wright, 'The Twelfth-Century Renaissance in Anglo-Norman England: William of Malmesbury and Joseph of Exeter', in *Latin in Medieval Britain*, ed. Richard Ashdowne and Carolinne White (Oxford: The British Academy, 2017), pp. 73–84 (pp. 79–83).

Camden's uninitiated readers, the fourteen-line extract appears to be an encomiastic poem in praise of Arthur. It is included as early as the 1590 edition of *Britannia*, and thus predates many of the other Arthurian poetry extracts, which are only added from the 1607 version. We cannot therefore dismiss it as a meretricious addition made in time for the benefit of a new generation of English readers in 1610. The excerpt appears immediately after the illustration of Arthur's cross, and is perhaps intended to supplement its textual inadequacy, acting as a kind of alternative epitaph. Although Camden admits that the extract is taken from *Antiocheis*, he does not elaborate on the nature of Joseph's work, which is not solely Arthurian in nature, in the 1590 edition of *Britannia*. We are simply told that Joseph sang of Arthur 'long ago' in his '*Antiocheide*' (olim in sua Antiocheide in Arthurum cecinit).[146] Camden gives slightly more detail in the English 1610 edition.[147] Most significantly, this is only half of the surviving fragment of *Antiocheis*. John Leland includes the full twenty-six-line fragment in the *Assertio*.[148] In the following quotation, struck through text indicates the parts of the surviving fragment that Camden excises in *Britannia*.

> -- ~~Posterity has shone forth~~
> ~~brightly famed for such great leaders, rich in so many nurslings,~~
> ~~abounding in so many men who could conquer the world by~~
>   ~~their strength~~
> ~~and even the ancients by their fame. Hence it was that~~
>   ~~Constantine took possession~~
> ~~of an empire, he held on to Rome and enlarged Byzantium.~~
> ~~and overwhelmed its strongholds with all-conquering flames.~~
> ~~From this grew Scaeva, a not insignificant partaker in civil strife,~~
> ~~who single-handedly killed a mass of opponents and withstood~~
>   ~~Pompey the Great,~~
> ~~standing alone as a superior wall of protection in front of Caesar.~~
> For famous death, and happie birth, hence flourish'd next in
>   place,
> Arthur the flower of noble Kings: whose acts with lovely grace
> Accepted and admired were, in peoples mouth and eare,
> No lesse than if sweet hony they, or pleasant musicke were.
> See former Princes, and compare his worth even with them all:
> That King in Pella borne, whom we great Alexander call,

---

[146] *Britannia* (1607), sig. O4v, p. 160, translation mine.
[147] '[…] his Poem *Antiocheis*, wherein he described the warres of the Christians for recoverie of the *Holy Lond*, and was there present with King Richard the First, speaking of Britaine'. *Britain* (1610), sig. T6r, p. 229.
[148] *Assertio*, sigs K1r–v; *Learned*, sigs L2r–v.

250 LOCAL PLACE AND THE ARTHURIAN TRADITION

> The trumpe of fame doth sound aloft. The Roman Stories eke
> Much praise and honour both, of their Triumphant Cæsars seake,
> And Hercules exalted is for taming Monsters fell:
> But Pine-trees, hazels low, (as Sunne the Starres) doe farre excell:
> Both Greeke and Latine Annals read: no former age his Peere,
> Nor future time his match can shew. For this is plaine and cleere,
> In goodnesse hee and greatnesse both, surmounts Kings all and some,
> Better alone, than all before, greater than those to come.
>
> (*Historia Britannicae Defensio*, p. 241; *Britain* [1610], sig. T6r, p. 229)
>
> (------------------------------~~Inclyta fulsit~~
> ~~Posteritas ducibus tantis, tot diues alumnis,~~
> ~~Tot faecunda viris, premerent qui viribus orbem,~~
> ~~Et fama veteres. Hinc Constantinus adeptus~~
> ~~Imperium, Romam tenuit, Byzantion auxit.~~
> ~~Hinc Senonum ductor captiua Brennius vrbe,~~
> ~~Romuleas domuit flammit victricibus arces.~~
> ~~Hinc & Scaeua satus, pars non obscura tumultus~~
> ~~Ciuilis, Magnum solus qui mole soluta~~
> ~~Obsedit, meliorque stetit pro Caesare murus,~~
> Hinc celebri fato foelici claruit ortu
> Flos regum Arturus, cuius cum facta stupori,
> Non micuere minus: totus quid in aure voluptas,
> Et populo plaudente fauus. Quaecunque piorum
> Inspice, Pelaeum commendat fama tyrannum.
> Pagina Caesareos loquitur Romana triumphos,
> Alcidem domitis attollit gloria monstris.
> Sed nec pinetum corili, nec sydera solem
> Aequant, Annales Latios, Graiosque reuolue.
> Prisca parem nescit, aequalem postera nullum,
> Exhibitura dies. Reges supereminet omnes
> Solus, praeteritis melior, maiorque futuris.)[149]

As with *Britannia*'s other poetic fragments, Camden seems to have lifted the *Antiocheis* extract directly from Leland without crediting him. In *De uiris illustribus*, Leland describes his efforts to hunt down Joseph's

---

[149] The struck-through English translation given here is Ceri Davies' modern English translation of Prise's *Historiae Britannicae Defensio*; the remaining English lines are from *Britain* (1610). Davies translates "Brennius" as 'all-conquering flames', but I would instead suggest that this indicates the legendary British king Brennius, who was said to have conquered Rome according to Geoffrey of Monmouth and traditions that followed his work. William Camden, *Britannia* (London: George Bishop, 1590), STC (2nd edn), sig. L8v, p. 160.

Antiocheis to no avail, finding only a fragment in the dusty library at Abingdon.[150] Camden may have read the fragment in full in Leland's *Assertio*, or perhaps had access to a copy in Leland's collections.[151] At any rate, Camden knew of the uncut fragment: he published it in full in *Remaines concerning Britaine* five years prior to *Britannia*'s 1610 English translation, and two years prior to the expanded 1607 edition, both of which nevertheless include the shortened extract. Whilst it is possible that Camden and his editors simply overlooked the extract when updating *Britannia* (the short version had been present from the 1590 edition), this seems unlikely given the attention paid to expanding Arthurian material in the later *Britannia* editions.

This raises the possibility that Camden made a conscious decision to omit the first half of the extract, an alteration that has a major impact on the text's reading. The cropped version reads as a standalone praise-poem for Arthur, with the opening line focusing on his 'famous death and happie birth'. The following lines ebulliently affirm Arthur's superiority, placing him at the head of a roll call of classical heroes: two conquerors (Alexander the Great; Julius Caesar) and one demi-God (Hercules).[152] With the exception of Hercules, these figures were unquestionably accepted as real by Camden's contemporaries. In contrast, the uncut version of the extract reads as a list of noble men remembered in posterity for their military prowess, with Arthur appearing somewhere in the middle. Before the subject of Arthur is even broached, Joseph mentions Constantine's imperial rule over Rome and Byzantium, Brennius' domination of Rome, and Caesar's monster-slaying. By cropping the

---

[150] 'I have sought for this brilliant work by Joseph as diligently as possible in many places, but have not found it. Only a fragment of the great work has recently come into my hands, while I was clearing out the dust and moths of the library of Abingdon.' (Hoc ego tam undecunque luculentum Iosephi opus diligentissime multis in locis quaesiui, nec inueni. Tantum fragmentum magni operis nuper mihi ad manus uenit, cum excuterem puluerem et blattas Abbandunensis bibliothecae.) *De uiris illustribus*, I, pp. 406–07.

[151] Another twist in this investigation of sources is John Prise's inclusion of the fragment in full in his *Historia*. Prise claims to have encountered it in Leland's *Assertio*, though of course we know that the pair were sharing sources (see above at pp. 180–81. John Prise, *Historiae Britannicae Defensio*, pp. 239–41.

[152] There are some parallels in the romance tradition of these comparative interreferential lists, and Chaucer even appears to send up this romance trope in the opening of *Sir Topas*. Whilst many examples compare the romance protagonist favourably to the heroes of other romances (Guy, Lybeus), others turn to classical figures like Hector, Alexander, and Charlemagne, as in the opening to *Richard Coeur de Lyon*. These lists are discussed in Megan G. Leitch, 'Introduction', in *Romance Rewritten: The Evolution of Middle English Romance: A Tribute to Helen Cooper*, pp. 1–24 (pp. 4–15).

poem, Arthur becomes the centre rather than the periphery. Moreover, by emphasising Arthur's 'death' and 'birth' in this way, Camden's readers are reminded of the Cornish sites associated with them (Camlan and Tintagel), mentioned elsewhere in *Britannia*, and therefore Arthur's West Country associations beyond the bounds of Glastonbury. A chain of association is therefore created linking Arthur's south-western places with each other, and with the noble acts that justify his imperial status on the European stage. By situating this extract firmly in the Somerset chapter – Arthur's centre according to Leland – rather than elsewhere, Camden grounds Arthur and his superlative deeds in his native places.

Camden uses other poetic extracts with distinctly south-western origins to shore up Arthur's connections with the West Country. Present in the opening Cornwall chapter from the 1607 edition is a snippet of verse attributed to 'Michael, a Cornish Poet, and of Rhymers in his time the chiefe.'[153] This is Michael of Cornwall (*fl.* 1243–55), responsible for a series of competitive flytings against Henry d'Avranches.[154] In one flyting Michael responded to Henry's slurs against his Cornish heritage by invoking King Arthur's appreciation for the Cornish. He claims that Arthur considered Cornwall to be invincible, unlike Normandy.[155] As with Joseph's *Antiocheis*, Camden may have discovered Michael's barbed flytings thanks to Leland's leads: Leland describes finding the work in 'the library at Salisbury'.[156] Camden visited Salisbury during his West Country itinerary, and subsequently included extracts from Michael's riposte in the 1607 *Britannia* and in *Remaines Concerning Britaine*, albeit not Michael's Arthurian material.[157] In *Remaines*, Camden refers to Michael as 'Merie Michael' rather than Michael of Cornwall. Here, on the other hand, Camden emphasises both Michael's Cornishness and his praise of Arthur. Camden cites Michael thus:

---

[153] *Britain* (1610), sig. Q1v, p. 186.

[154] These flytings were battles of wit conducted in elaborate Latin verse, reminiscent in their witty, combative spirit and metrical virtuosity of the poetry slams and rap battles of the present day. Rigg, *A History of Anglo-Latin Literature, 1066–1422* (Cambridge: Cambridge University Press, 1992), pp. 193–208.

[155] Rigg, *A History of Anglo-Latin Literature*, p. 194.

[156] 'Since I have mentioned John of Cornwall, it seems worth pointing out that a certain Michael of Cornwall wrote a barbed poem against Henry of Avranches, which is found in the library at Salisbury.' (Et quoniam in Cornubiensium mentionem incidimus, lubet ostendere Michaelem quondam Cornubiensem scripsisse aculeatum carmen contra Henricum Abrincatensem, quod in Seueriana extat bibliotheca.) Leland, *De uiris illustribus*, I, p. 389. For an edition of Michael and Henry's flytings, see Alfons Hilka, 'Eine mittellateinische Dichterfehde. Versus Michaelis Cornubiensis contra Henricum Abricensem', in *Mittelaterlich Handschriften [...] Festgabe zum 60. Geburtstag von Hermann Degering*, ed. Aloys Bömer and Joachim Kirchner (Leipzig: Hiersemann, 1926), pp. 123–54.

[157] William Camden, 'Rythmes', in *Remaines*, sigs D3r–D3v, pp. 21–22.

Moreover, that poet Michael, when as in the excessive commendation of his countrymen he had with gigging rimes resounded how Arthur in his battels gave them the honour to give the first charge, he thus courageously concludeth in rime:

> What frighteth us? If footing sure we have on steady ground
> (Barre crafty sleights) there is no force but we can it confound.
>
> (*Britannia* [1610] sig. P6v, p. 186)

(Poeta etiam ille Michael cum in suorum lauden profusior, illis primos ictus in pr[a]elis Arthurum concessisse tinnulis versibus docuisset, animose concludit.

Quid nos deterret? Si firmiter in pede stemus,
Fraus ni nos superset, nihil est quod non superemus.)

(*Britannia* [1607], sig. M2r, p. 135)

Camden echoes Leland and Prise by couching native British tradition in terms of honesty (and perhaps ignorance). Moreover, Camden connects Arthur directly with Cornwall and the people who still live there, just as Leland draws connections between Arthur and the *Murotriges* of Cadbury. By using his source selectively, Camden emphasises Arthur's connections with Cornwall and the Cornish people.

To conclude, Camden's selective use of physical and textual sources suggests that Arthur was a subject of more than passing interest to him. Long-held attitudes towards 'old' and 'new' antiquarianism have meant that the continuities between the interests and methodologies of Camden and his antiquarian predecessors have often gone unnoticed, and this has radically affected the way that we think about Camden's Arthuriana. Rather than reading Camden as an Arthurian sceptic, we should view Camden's *Britannia* afresh as an effective response to Leland's urgent appeal to his fellow antiquaries to do something about Polydore's displacement of Arthur. The reasons why Camden succeeded where his forbears did not are twofold. The most significant factor in Camden's successful defence of Arthur is the *Britannia*'s geographical structure, which grounds Arthur in the places where he was said to have existed. This effectively conjures the impression of eyewitness experience, a phenomenon further amplified by Camden's detailed description of the Glastonbury Abbey environs, the 'authentic' facsimile replication of Arthur's epitaph inscription, and later the cross in its entirety. By arranging Arthur geographically rather than narratologically, Camden reinforces Arthur's attachment to real, recognisable places clustered together in the South-West, continuing the work that Leland had started and effectively undoing the Arthurian displacement that Polydore Vergil was seen to have carried out.

Another successful element in Camden's defence of Arthur is his embedding of shrewdly edited poetic fragments in his descriptions of Arthurian places. These fragments act as newly erected monuments for places such as Cadbury and 'Camlan' which were not clearly and unambiguously located in canonical Arthurian texts such as Geoffrey's *Historia*, and were likely not supported with materials such as *tabulae*. For other sites, such as Glastonbury, these poetic fragments performed a restorative as well as a commemorative function. Camden would have been aware that Arthurian commemoration at the Glastonbury Abbey had previously been well-maintained, based on his access to Leland's notes. By Camden's time of writing, however, the abbey had been dissolved. Much of the demolition work was likely carried out in the late sixteenth and early seventeenth century at the same time that *Britannia* was being written, rewritten, and translated.[158] By the time the first edition of *Britannia* was published in 1586, the *magna tabula* and plaque were in the hands of Camden's fellow antiquarians.[159] Thus, the poetic extracts which Camden relates to Arthurian Glastonbury might be read as 'memorials of memorials'.[160] Camden's rendering of Arthurian Glastonbury represents an effort to revive and preserve the impression of the abbey as a site where Arthur was still commemorated, as it would have previously appeared to visitors like John Leland, William Worcester, and perhaps John Hardyng. There is therefore a poignancy in Camden's push to replicate a first-hand eyewitness experience of Arthurian Glastonbury. Whilst Leland invited his readers to share in his personal experience of Arthurian places, Camden can only invite his reader on a resurrected and virtual tour of Arthurian Glastonbury as it might have looked fifty years prior, before the abbey's dissolution and the dispersal of its artefacts, *tabulae*, and plaques.

---

[158] Adam Stout has argued that the main demolition of the Abbey probably took place in the late sixteenth and early seventeenth centuries. See Adam Stout, 'After the End: Glastonbury Abbey, 1539–1825', *Somerset Archaeology and Natural History*, 157 (2014), 72–93 (p. 79); Gilchrist, *Sacred Heritage*, pp. 169–70.

[159] On the fate of the *magna tabula* and plaque after the Dissolution, see above at pp. 62–63.

[160] Philip Schwyzer has shown how memorials to memorials flourished in post-Reformation England, citing literal examples at the Abbey of St Albans. Philip Schwyzer, '"A Tomb Once Stood in This Room": Memorials to Memorials in Early Modern England', *Journal of Medieval and Early Modern Studies*, 48.2 (2018), 365–85.

Camden's Arthurian legacy

This book ends where it began: at Glastonbury, but with the abbey's ruination rather than its restoration. Camden forms a fitting end point because his work was undertaken at a pivotal moment in the history of Arthur's localisation. In Camden's living memory, it had once been possible to witness Arthurian Glastonbury in person, with the full and unadulterated guided experience enabled by the monks, the *tabulae*, and the visual imagery on site. By the time Camden came to write *Britannia* this had changed. Unlike his predecessors, Camden did not experience Glastonbury's plaque and *tabula* at the abbey, but rather at the homes of the antiquarians who had recovered them. Camden's approach to writing Britain geographically by employing a chorographical structure partly represents an attempt at responding to the dislocation of the Dissolution. The *Britannia*'s structure allowed Camden to virtually replace displaced artefacts such as Arthur's cross and the two pyramids at the Glastonbury site. By using poetic excerpts as virtual memorials, Camden even created a similar effect to that produced by the *tabulae* that had once been displayed at religious houses like Glastonbury.

This had a powerful effect for Camden's inheritors, who were not able to experience Glastonbury as Camden and his predecessors had done. For them, *Britannia* provided the most evocative and effective reconstruction of the abbey as it had previously looked. The tone of subsequent antiquarians writing about Glastonbury was highly emotive, the sense of loss palpable. Many recorded the destruction as it was still ongoing. After acknowledging Glastonbury's glory in its medieval heyday, William Stukeley powerfully described the main abbey church reduced to a thatched stable in his 1724 *Itinerarium*, lamenting that 'every week a pillar, a buttress, a window jamb, or an angle of fine hewn stone is sold to the best bidder. Whilst I was there [at Glastonbury] they were excoriating St. Joseph's chappel for that purpose.'[161] Stukeley tries, in vain, to employ the same visual strategies used by Camden to recuperative ends: when an unscrupulous local pulls down the 'arms and cognisances of the great Saxon kings and princes, founders, and [...] abbots' from the old abbot's lodging and re-uses them awkwardly 'over his own doors and windows', Stukeley ensures that a drawing of the antiquities taken by his friend is 'put in its proper place' within the *Itinerarium* at plate 37. This is just one example of the extensive engravings Stukeley included in his work, which range from facsimiles of individual fragments to panoramic views over Glastonbury and its ruins.

---

[161] Stukeley, *Itinerarium* (1724), p. 145.

The impact of Camden's *Britannia* on the antiquarians who came after him cannot be overstated. These later antiquarians viewed 'the immortal Camden' as a patriotic hero, the 'sun whereat our modern Writers have all lighted their little Torches', in the words of eighteenth-century antiquarian and churchman William Nicholson.[162] As Thomas Roebuck has pointed out, Camden was distinguished from his forbears by how accessible he made antiquarianism as a practice: 'he became a kind of shorthand for "antiquarianism" itself, a way of looking at the world which anyone in Britain with an interest in antiquities could adopt'.[163] As the seventeenth century waned and the eighteenth century dawned, antiquarians had a new goal in mind: the 'continuing, editing, or publishing' of older antiquarian works.[164] Reissues of Camden's *Britannia* such as the much expanded and improved edition of Edmund Gibson (1695) formed a major part of this tradition, and in some senses Camden's text became the new blueprint for antiquarian writing. As the ruined abbeys and historical sites recorded by Camden in his original *Britannia* were irrevocably dismantled, Camden's champions began considering him as a kind of eyewitness to the 'old' Britain in terms reminiscent of how Leland and Camden themselves had viewed the people who lived around ruined Arthurian sites. In the 1693 proposal for the *Britannia*'s reprinting, a key addition planned for the volume was the 'places mentioned by Cambden, inserted, tho' many of them have by time been quite destroyed, and the Degrees of Longitude and Latitude Marked on the Sides'.[165] When the otherwise highly sceptical Daniel Defoe visited Glastonbury in the early eighteenth century, the experience of being shown a copy of Camden's *Britannia* by a tour guide at the site of the White Thorn tree was enough to convince him that the legends of Joseph of Arimathea and Arthur's burial at Glastonbury were authentic.[166]

Many of the figures who looked up to Camden as their model, including Edward Lhwyd and William Stukeley, brought fresh unreported local Arthurian traditions to the public's awareness. Lhwyd, a key contributor to Gibson's 1695 *Britannia*, was especially prolific in gathering and recording Arthurian place associations in Wales, and it

---

[162] Cited in Sweet, *Antiquaries*, p. 36.
[163] Thomas Roebuck, 'Edmund Gibson's 1695 Britannia and Late-Seventeenth-Century British Antiquarian Scholarship', *Erudition and the Republic of Letters*, 5.4 (2020), 427–81 (p. 468).
[164] Roebuck, 'Edmund Gibson's 1695 Britannia', pp. 431–32.
[165] *New proposals for printing by subscription, Cambden's Britannia, English newly translated, with large additions* (April 20th 1693), Wing (2nd edn) C373, sig. 1v.
[166] Daniel Defoe, *A Tour Thro' the Whole Island of Great Britain*, vol. 2 (London: G. Strahan, 1725), pp. 29–30.

is thanks to Lhwyd that many of these associations made it into print for the first time.[167] If Camden was innovative in crowd-sourcing his material for *Britannia* from a vast network of correspondents, Lhwyd took this collaborative approach and systematised it. Across Wales, Lhwyd distributed 4,000 copies of a questionnaire that asked for 'Roman ways, pavements, stoves, or any underground works: crosses, beacons, stones pitched on end in a regular order', giving a list of examples including 'Buarth Arthur' and 'Koeten Arthur'.[168] As Scott Lloyd puts it, this was rather 'a leading question', perhaps betraying Lhwyd's own interests; and in fact the greatest wealth of Arthurian place associations in Wales generated by Lhwyd came from his own itinerant notes, taken during his tours of Wales.[169]

Of course, it is possible that some of the Arthurian Welsh place attestations that returned from these questionnaires were actually influenced by texts like Camden's *Britannia*.[170] In the case of Camden's predecessor, John Leland, we know that at least one new piece of local Arthurian folklore likely emerged as a result of Leland's Arthurian writings. In his *Assertio*, Leland states that Guinevere was first buried at Amesbury before her remains were relocated to Glastonbury to join Arthur. Leland may have taken this piece of information from a lost text, or perhaps he elided his knowledge of Guinevere's retirement to Amesbury in Malory's *Morte* with information that he had read or heard during his trip to Amesbury.[171] It is impossible to know whether Amesbury held a connection to Guenevere prior to Leland's *Assertio*, but it is clear that Leland's description of Guenevere's Amesbury burial had a legacy. In the early seventeenth century a grave belonging to an unknown noblewoman was discovered during building works at Amesbury, and this was soon attributed to Guenevere by the architect Inigo Jones, who pointed to Leland's writings as evidence of her burial there.[172] The earls of Hertford, who held the Amesbury Abbey site at this point, took a personal interest in the grave goods, and even appear to have exhibited the grave site to interested visitors for several decades.[173] This demonstrates not only the considerable impact of Camden and Leland's work, but also the ways in which writings about Arthur's places could feed powerfully back into

---

[167] Lhwyd's Arthurian places are mapped in Lloyd, *The Arthurian Place Names of Wales*, as 'map 2'.
[168] Lloyd, *The Arthurian Place Names of Wales*, p. 108.
[169] Lloyd, *The Arthurian Place Names of Wales*, pp. 108–09.
[170] Scott Lloyd, 'Arthurian Place-names of Wales', p. 235.
[171] Discussed above at pp. 187–88.
[172] Bateman, 'A Grave Discovery?', passim.
[173] Ibid.

local tradition, blurring the boundaries between the textual and the oral just as Geoffrey's *Historia* that had helped to spawn new Arthurian places centuries earlier.

In the following century, William Stukeley was also inspired by Camden's work, as well as the antiquarian researches of John Bale and John Leland. In a letter to a friend, published with the second edition of his *Itinerarium Curiosum*, Stukeley describes his method: 'it is to be wished this branch of learning should revive among us, which has lain dormant since the great Camden'.[174] Like Edward Lhwyd, Stukeley modelled his collaborative and collegial approach to antiquarian praxis on Camden, so much so that he could not resist, during his travels, a half-mile trip out of his way to Conington, where Robert Cotton and 'the great Camden have often sat in council upon the antiquities of Britain'.[175] A clergyman and a Freemason, Stukeley is distinguished by his religious fascination with druidry in early Britain, and pioneered the study of prehistoric monuments such as Stonehenge and Avebury. It is Stukeley we have to thank for passing down a number of Arthurian place associations and local folklore. Some of these instances have already been described in this book, such as the tale connecting Lancelot's fight with the giant Turquin at Mayburgh Henge and Brougham Castle.[176] Others include the tradition, oddly reminiscent of the ley-lines projected over the Somerset landscape today by New Age believers, that Arthur had petitioned 'some saint' to prevent any 'serpent or venomous creature' from coming with the triangle created between the hills of Cadbury ('Camalet castle'), Glastonbury Tor, and Montacute.[177] Evidently, Stukeley is building on the Arthurian tradition at Cadbury that he inherited from John Leland and William Camden. He adds new details to Leland's evocative description of the hillfort and its ruined cottages: a road across the field where corn will not grow called 'K. Arthur's hunting causey', and a 'never-failing spring call'd K. Arthur's well' which the locals claim is surrounded with 'subterraneous vaults'.[178] Here, as with Edward Lhwyd's Welsh correspondents, it is difficult to know to what extent these new iterations of local Arthurian tradition owe their existence to the broad popularity of Leland and Camden's works. Stukeley also witnessed ruined Arthurian sites that, in Camden's day and before, had been entire, such as the site of

---

[174] Stukeley, *Itinerarium Curiosum* (1776), I, p. 35 (Iter 2)
[175] Stukeley, *Itinerarium Curisoum* (1724), p. 77.
[176] See above at pp. 131–34 (Brougham Castle and Mayburgh).
[177] Stukeley, *Itinerarium* (1724), p. 142.
[178] Stukeley, *Itinerarium* (1724), pp. 142–43.

Arthur's 'fam'd Round Table' at Winchester that had by then been pulled down during the reign of Charles II.[179]

In sum, Camden's local Arthurian representation was so successful that it continues to fundamentally shape how we view Arthurian places today. In turn, Camden's local Arthur was a product of what had come before. *Britannia* is more than just a replication of Camden's journey to Arthurian places; it is also instilled with the locative experiences of John Hardyng, John Rous, John Prise, and John Leland, whose works were sources for Camden. The work of previous itinerant antiquarians may have even been the catalyst for Camden's own travels. When we read *Britannia* we are seeing not only a single man's experience of Arthurian sites, but the accretive layering of several different perspectives on Arthur's places.

---

[179] Stukeley, *Itinerarium* (1724), pp. 183–84.

Map 5. William Camden's Arthurian places.

Coda: Arthur's local renaissance?

This book's central line of enquiry has been to investigate how Arthur became localised in England and Wales between the fourteenth and seventeenth centuries, and to understand the role played by local places in defending the impression of Arthur's reality. Ultimately, the ideas still held today about Arthur's local places can be traced back to on-site encounters with Arthur in the later Middle Ages. These continuities challenge the assumption that the local Arthur emerging at the end of the period was a sign of the king's waning importance. How do we define what is important? If we take "importance" to mean something that not only endures but continues to grow organically, then we might well say that the local Arthur is more important than Arthur the national or imperial symbol. Most people today cannot identify with the idea of Arthur as a conqueror of Europe, nor as an imperial icon, but they can identify with the Arthur of the landscape, of Iron Age camps, of their hometown legends: a local Arthur. Modern-day pilgrims still flock to Glastonbury to look at Arthur's grave and experience the new Arthurian associations that have appeared in and around the town since Camden's time of writing. The localisation of Arthur was not a retreat, but a renaissance.

No longer can we simply say that Arthur grew increasingly unpopular from the end of the Middle Ages, nor can we refer dismissively to his localisation as a retreat into unimportance. Rather, this was the time in which the local Arthur as we most often recognise him today emerged. The continuities between local experiences of Arthurian sites in the fifteenth century, defences of Arthur in the sixteenth century, and the major chorographical works of the late sixteenth and early seventeenth centuries partly concern the geographies themselves – the Arthurian locations that were handed down and became established – but they also relate to the ways in which Arthurian places were experienced. Writers used their personal experiences of Arthurian sites to shape their work alongside the writings of their contemporaries and predecessors who had also visited such locations. Thus, the local visions of Arthur that we inherit today are inflected with the echoes of Camden's own site experiences, those of his predecessors, and the antiquarians who came after and read their work.

The use of place in defence of Arthur began *in situ* at Arthurian sites themselves. Religious houses like Glastonbury were of fundamental importance to Arthur's localisation because experiencing a place connected with an illustrious figure like Arthur in person has a powerful effect due to the mnemonic bridging that occurs when we experience what Zerubavel calls 'constancy of place'.[1] The evidence of tour guiding at Glastonbury and Dover, York and Cirencester, and the numerous other hints at Arthurian *tabulae* across England and Wales demonstrate that those charged with managing Arthurian places made a concerted effort to choreograph their guests' transportive experiences. Visitors to Arthurian places were affected by the 'constancy of place' that they felt during their visits, an experience that was compounded, in the case of churches and abbeys, by the sanctity of those sites beyond their Arthurian associations. We know that visiting pilgrims were powerfully affected because they have left us traces of their experiences in the copies they made from *tabulae* and epitaphs, as attested by manuscripts such as Cotton MS Titus A.XIX, Cotton MS Cleopatra C.IV, and MS Royal 20 B.XV. This copying represented an attempt to preserve *in situ* experiences to return to at a later time, and sometimes also to furnish new textual projects, allowing a new generation of readers to experience Arthur's places vicariously through the medium of text.

There were various reasons why certain places came to be associated with Arthur in the first place. Much of this book is concerned with asking how Arthur became localised; but it is also worth asking how some places became 'Arthured', as the two processes are interrelated. The fifteenth century seems to have been the crucial point in time when local site histories entered broader textual tradition, and the second chapter of this book focused on Arthurian place claims that were current during the century: the site of his conception; his coronation and festal crowning; his burial; the city (or cities) of the legion; and the locations where Arthur held his court or convened the Round Table. Several factors could contribute to a site's association with Arthur. First, and perhaps most obviously, a location's prior appearance in major Arthurian texts, even if not connected directly with Arthur, could contribute to the 'Arthuring' of a particular location. Arthurian places could be upgraded, as it were: Dover, a battle site in Geoffrey's *Historia*, was transformed into an Arthurian court by Hardyng (and also, it seems, by the custodians of Dover Castle). Ambiguous toponyms originating in the *Historia Brittonum* or the *Annales*, such as Badon and Camlan, left space for adaptation,

---

[1] Zerubavel, *Time Maps*, p. 41.

contradiction, and occasionally duplication by their interpreters. Sometimes, Arthurian places appear to have been duplicated due to errors in scribal transmission, the misunderstanding of little-known toponyms, or the misattribution of sources. Naturally, too, matters of local pride would also have contributed to the identification of Arthur's places: Higden's pride in his local Chester, and Rous's in his native Warwick, led them to claim these places as cities of the legion. Politics could also cause a place to become connected with Arthur. Finally, distinctive landscape features, or visibly ancient remains, could also prompt a site to be associated with Arthur. Striking landscapes might include complex cave systems (the Nottingham cave network), extinct volcanoes (Arthur's Seat in Scotland), and conspicuous monoliths (as in the *Vera historia*, perhaps). Ancient remains could include earthworks (the amphitheatres at Caerleon, Cirencester, and Silchester; Arthur's Round Table in Cumbria) as well as inscribed rubble rebuilt into more recent architecture (as in the examples at Hereford, Carlisle, Dover, and Brougham Castle). Visible markers of antiquity help to transform a place into a *lieu de mémoire* because they perform a mnemonic function, reminding their onlookers of the site's antiquity.

The third chapter of this book turned to the issue of how Arthurian regions could be created by considering how one figure in particular, John Leland, called an Arthurian region into being in the West Country that would go on to have a long legacy. Leland's attempts to manipulate Arthur's geography mark a shift in the defensive use of place. The abbeys, churches, castles and towns of the fourteenth and fifteenth centuries largely fostered their Arthurian connections in order to shore up their prestige and antiquity. In contrast, Leland manipulated places to shore up Arthur's historicity. By sculpting and pruning Arthur's geography, Leland created the impression of a realistic area where a king might have had his seat, with a centre – Arthur's court at Cadbury – and a periphery. By comparing Leland's *Itineraries* with his later Arthurian defences, we can see which Arthurian places made it into his defence and which were rejected. There is already an indication of Leland's English biases in the *Itineraries*, which distinguish sites that 'sum caulle' Arthur's Round Table in Wales from their more certain English equivalents.[2] This is confirmed by Leland's downplaying of Arthur's Welsh sites in the *Assertio*. Leland's inconsistent critical approach makes it even clearer where his biases lie. Previous scholars have argued that Leland's *Assertio* has a clear anglocentric imperial agenda, and while this is not untrue,

[2] Leland, *Itineraries*, III, p. 99.

Leland's downplaying of Arthur's distant conquests suggest that he is more interested in Arthur's native places.

Of course, Leland can only provide a single perspective on Arthur's places; but his Arthurian localisation profits from being set side-by-side with the Arthurian geographies of other writers, such as John Prise and Elis Gruffydd. For Leland and Prise in particular, Arthurian places were important tools in defending the king's existence. All three writers had their own ideas about their respective identities, and they oriented Arthur differently according to how they saw themselves. Across the board, they saw the attack on Arthur's historicity as foreign in origin. Leland and Prise considered the "Roman" Polydore to be the foreign aggressor. On the other hand, Elis Gruffydd, who suffered suppression for speaking his native Welsh, clearly identifies the assault on the British History and the fabulation of Arthur's true history as English in origin. These authors' texts suggest that Arthur's native monuments are the best indicators of his true existence; but for each defender Arthur is to be found in different places.

Finally, I made the case for reclaiming William Camden as an Arthurian defender, placing him alongside the authors whose works are explored earlier in this book. There are clearly more continuities between the work of Camden and the 'old' antiquarians than previous scholarship has suggested. The writings of John Rous, John Leland, Humphrey Llwyd, and John Hardyng were all consulted by Camden in the preparation of *Britannia*, but Camden did more than simply use these earlier authors as his sources. Nor is Camden similar to his forebears only on account of his itinerant approach to research. Rather, Camden's rhetoric surrounding Arthur's places is strikingly reminiscent of Leland's own accounts of the same sites. Both Camden and Leland turn to physical topography, the impression of eyewitness experiences, descriptions of local lore, and the inclusion of poetic fragments in order to convey the transportive experience of Arthurian places. The reason why Camden's Arthurian localisation is seen to have succeeded where others failed is that his powerful descriptions of Arthur's places are organised geographically. The chorographical structure of *Britannia* effectively grounds Arthur in the places with which he was associated. Camden's shrewd use of visual imagery gave his readers the impression that they were visiting Arthur's places alongside him. The success of Camden's defence therefore lay in its effective harnessing of the rhetoric of place. Rather than taking offence at Polydore Vergil's denial of Arthur places, as Leland and Prise had done, Camden weaponised these places, turning them from sentimental refuges into evidence, and erecting virtual monuments in the form of poetic extracts to support places such as Cadbury, Camlan, and the recently dissolved Glastonbury.

Throughout this book, the significance of human contact during visits to Arthurian places has been a recurrent theme. Fifteenth- and sixteenth-century guests were not simply left to their own devices when they visited places connected with Arthur. They were shown around, and this human connection contributed to the numinosity experienced at Arthurian places. Monks, castellans, and chaplains guided visitors, helping them to interpret the visual and architectural features of the spaces in question. More learned guests like Worcester, Leland, and perhaps Hardyng, who were engaged in significant projects, were welcomed into abbey libraries or civic muniments rooms where they were encouraged to read and copy from the collections. We are not dealing here simply with lonely researchers isolated in dusty libraries. Figures like Dom. Murelage at Glastonbury were on hand to act as librarians or archivists in explaining the collections. Not all guiding appears to have been official: William Worcester was shown Cirencester Abbey by one 'Potsawe', and there is no indication by title or description that Potsawe was a monk, as is the case with the various 'Doms' that Worcester met at Glastonbury. This pre-empts Whitaker's description, some three centuries later, of the 'honest and knowing Ciceronii' who showed him round Glastonbury Abbey.[3] The unknown guide claimed to have personally seen the Glastonbury pyramids still standing in his own lifetime, and shared rumours as to the whereabouts of Arthur's cross.[4] Whitaker's description of the 'Ciceronii' evinces another aspect of human encounters at Arthurian sites: the framing of local inhabitants as eyewitnesses. Leland's report of the Murotriges' traditions or the people living around Camlan function in this way. Local people are often a fundamental part of Arthurian *lieux de mémoire*, either framed as eternal witnesses to an unbroken Arthurian connection, or else interpreters of the spaces and their Arthurian associations.

Though I hope to have demonstrated the worth of local Arthuriana in its own right, another central aim of this book was to challenge the shibboleth that local and national Arthurs were separate constructions. Rather, they relied upon each other. After leaving an Arthurian location, site visitors did not simply forget about the notes they had made. Some incorporated the content they had copied from paraphernalia such as *tabulae*, or from the holdings of on-site libraries, into broader textual projects. A significant proportion of these projects were nationalistic

---

[3] Whitaker, *Life of St Neot*, p. 39.
[4] Whitaker, *Life of St Neot*, p. 35, p. 39.

in nature. John Hardyng sought out Arthurian localities in order to strengthen the impression of England's sovereignty in his *Chronicle*. For John Rous, researching local Arthurian history was a crucial element of writing his *Historia regum Angliae*, a project of obvious national significance. John Leland made the national import of his local researches explicit in the package of promises he delivered to Henry VIII as part of his New Year's Gift.[5] Polydore Vergil's doubts regarding sites like Glastonbury and Badon prompted a series of histrionic responses whose authors clearly saw the defence of Arthur's local places as a matter of native pride. Finally, William Camden paid close attention to Arthur's sites in writing and revising *Britannia*, a work that strove to resurrect Britain as a newly realised nation. This all suggests that site visitors saw local Arthurian histories as something to be taken seriously. Not only were local histories considered interesting enough to be noted down in personal miscellanies, but also reliable and powerful enough to be worked into larger-scale national projects. In sum, local Arthurian places were consistently foregrounded in national projects from the fifteenth to seventeenth centuries, and national pride was visibly wounded when Arthur's sites were brought into question. This all demonstrates that a local Arthur did not mean an unimportant Arthur, and that Arthur the national symbol was (and still is) inextricably connected with the Arthur of local places.

This is not to say that all of Arthur's local manifestations enjoyed a long and lasting legacy. Philip Schwyzer describes his experience, in his own research, of feeling 'haunted by John Prise' because of Prise's ability to appear in surprising places.[6] While writing this book, I have felt haunted by the shadows of local Arthurian traditions. Over and over again, the ghosts of local Arthurian traditions seem to momentarily appear: Worcester's description of being guided around Arthurian Cirencester; Hardyng's references to Arthurian courts in obscure and surprising locations; the circumstantial evidence for tailor-made Arthurian romances at Glastonbury; the adaptations made to *Stafford's Chronicle* that place Arthur in Brougham, Cumbria; the inexplicable thirteenth- and fourteenth-century royal visits to Cadbury. These are just a few of the hints attesting to localised Arthurian traditions. Some Arthurian localities found their way into the wider tradition, helped along by their inclusion in texts such as Hardyng's *Chronicle*, Leland

---

[5] For a description of the 'Gift' and its promises, see Carley, 'The Manuscript Remains of John Leland', pp. 112–13.
[6] Schwyzer, *Literature, Nationalism and Memory*, p. 85.

and Prise's Arthurian defences, or Camden's *Britannia*. The increased awareness of certain Arthurian locations due to their publication in print, and especially in the vernacular, may explain why they gained an enduring place in Arthur's geography.

Other Arthurian localities were not immediately taken up into the wider tradition. Some, such as the Nottingham caves or Guenevere's grave at Amesbury, sank into obscurity. Others, perhaps, lay dormant (at least to our eyes) in their respective locations until their collection at a much later date by antiquarians such as Edward Lhwyd, William Stukeley, or their Victorian successors. A major challenge that I have faced in writing this book is the sense that the gap between the hints at lost traditions described above and the local Arthuriana first recorded by later antiquarians like Stukeley cannot, with current evidence, be easily closed. This is a common problem for those whose research touches on the intersection of oral and written traditions. Concerning the medieval carol, another research subject in which the connections between the danced, oral, and written carol cannot be discerned, David Fallows declares that:

> the picture must be built on a series of widely separated stepping-stones – or more precisely, on a scattered group of stones peeping up from the river and perhaps never intended to pave a way across.[7]

Fallows' stepping-stone analogy echoes the ruptures we face in studying Arthurian localisation, and also the ruptures in time that visitors to Arthurian places, in history and today, have felt. The localities explored in this book are therefore as much *lieux de mémoire* for the Arthurian scholar as they were for the early modern antiquarians who visited them, and perhaps for the people who lived around them. Yet these sites give a powerful impression of permanence, even when their foundation trenches or rubble declare otherwise. Ruined as they are, they remain visible. Unlike manuscript texts which can be invented, copied, transported from place to place, forged, palimpsested, and interpolated, 'rocks and engraved witnesses' instead give the impression of immobility and permanence, the constancy of place that Zerubavel argues is so vital to building mnemonic bridges to connect the present with the past.[8]

---

[7] David Fallows, 'English Song Repertories of the Mid-Fifteenth Century', *Proceedings of the Royal Musical Association*, 103.1 (1976–77), 61–79 (p. 61).
[8] See above at pp. 22–26.

Bibliography

Manuscripts and maps

Aberystwyth, National Library of Wales, MS 3035
Aberystwyth, National Library of Wales, MS 3054Di–ii
Aberystwyth, National Library of Wales, MS 5276Di–ii
Cambridge, Cambridge University Library, Atlas.2.61.1, 'Somerset'
Cambridge, Cambridge University Library, MS Ee.4.26
Cambridge, Corpus Christi College, MS 50
Cambridge, Corpus Christi College, MS 210
Cambridge, Corpus Christi College, MS 311
Cambridge, Gonville and Caius College, MS 72/39
Cambridge, Trinity College, MS R. 5. 33
Cardiff, Cardiff Central Library, Cardiff MS 1.362
Cardiff, Cardiff Central Library, MS 3.4
London, British Library Cotton MS Otho C.XIII
London, British Library, Cotton MS Caligula A.IX
London, British Library, Cotton MS Cleopatra A.IV
London, British Library, Cotton MS Cleopatra B.VI
London, British Library, Cotton MS Cleopatra C.X
London, British Library, Cotton MS Cleopatra D.III
London, British Library, Cotton MS Julius 106
London, British Library, Cotton MS Julius D.V
London, British Library, Cotton MS Titus A.XIX
London, British Library, Cotton MS Vespasian A.XII
London, British Library, Egerton MS 3028
London, British Library, Harley MS 565
London, British Library, Harley MS 661
London, British Library, Lansdowne MS 204
London, British Library, Lansdowne MS 212
London, British Library, Maps C.44.d.90
London, British Library, MS Add. 19709
London, British Library, MS Add. 27879

London, British Library, MS Add. 32151
London, British Library, MS Royal 20 B.XV
London, British Library, Arundel MS 220
London, College of Arms, Arundel MS 29
Oxford, Bodleian Library, Bodleian MS 565
Oxford, Bodleian Library, Bodleian MS 956
Oxford, Bodleian Library, Laud MS misc. 750
Oxford, Bodleian Library, MS Lat. Hist. A. 2
Oxford, Bodleian Library, MS Rawlinson B.169
Oxford, Bodleian Library, MS Arch. Selden B.10
Oxford, Bodleian Library, Dodsworth MS 125
Oxford, Bodleian Library, Bodleian MS 487
Oxford, Bodleian Library, MS Rawlinson B.416A
Oxford, Jesus College, MS 111
Paris, Bibliothèque Nationale nouv. Acq. Fr. 1415
San Marino, CA, Huntington Library, MS Huntington 132
Stratton-on-the-Fosse, Somerset, Downside Abbey, Downside 78291
Warminster, Longleat House, MS Longleat 55
York, York Minster, L1/1

Primary sources

Adams, Alison, ed. and trans, *The Romance of Yder* (Cambridge: D. S. Brewer, 1983)

Alfred of Beverley, *Aluredi Beverlacensis Annales, sive Historia de Gestis Regum Britanniae Libris IX,* ed. Thomas Hearne (Oxford: Sheldonian Theatre, 1716)

Bale, John, *The laboryouse journey and serche of Johan Leylande, for Englandes antiquitees* (London: S. Mierdman, 1549), STC (2nd edn) 15445

Bale, John, *Scriptorum illustrium maioris Brytannie* (Basel: Ioannem Oporinum, 1557–59), STC (2nd edn) 1296

Bale, John, *Index Britanniae Scriptorum,* ed. Reginald Lane Poole and Mary Bateson (Oxford, 1902)

Barbour, John, *The Bruce,* ed. A. A. M. Duncan, revised edn (Edinburgh: Canongate, 2007)

Bede, *Ecclesiastical History of the English People,* ed. Bertram Colgrave and R. A. B. Mynors (Oxford: Clarendon Press, 1969)

A Book of British Kings 1200BC–1399AD [*Stafford's Chronicle*], ed. A. G. Rigg (Toronto: PIMS, 2000)

Bromwich, Rachel, ed., *Trioedd Ynys Prydein* (Cardiff: University of Wales Press, 1963)

Brooke, Ralph, *A discouerie of diuers errors published in print in the much commended Britannia, 1594* (London: J. Windet, 1599), STC (2nd edn) 3834.5

Camden, William, *Britannia* (London: Ralph Newbury, 1586), STC (2nd edn) 4503

Camden, William, *Britannia* (London: Ralph Newbury, 1587), STC (2nd edn) 4504

Camden, William, *Britannia* (London: George Bishop, 1590), STC (2nd edn) 4505

Camden, William, *Britannia* (London: George Bishop, 1594), STC (2nd edn) 4506

Camden, William, *Britannia* (London: George Bishop, 1600), STC (2nd edn) 4507

Camden, William, *Remaines of a greater worke, concerning Britaine* (London: Simon Waterson, 1605), STC (2nd edn) 4521

Camden, William, *Britannia* (London: George Bishop and John Norton, 1607), STC (2nd edn) 4508

Camden, William, *Britain,* trans. by Philemon Holland (London: George Bishop and John Norton, 1610), STC (2nd edn) 4509

Camden, William, *Britannia: or a chorographical description of Great Britain and Ireland* (2nd edn) (London: Edmund Gibson, 1722)

Camden, William, *Britannia* (London: Richard Gough, 1789)

Camden, William, 'Poems by William Camden: With Notes and Translations from the Latin', ed. by George Burke Johnson, *Studies in Philology*, 72 (1975), iii–143

Carew, Richard, *The Survey of Cornwall* (London: S. Stafford, 1602), ESTC 4615

Churchyard, Thomas, *The Worthines of Wales* (London: G. Robinson, 1587), STC (2nd edn) 5261

Defoe, Daniel, *A Tour Thro' the Whole Island of Great Britain*, vol. 2 (London: G. Strahan, 1725)

Drayton, Michael, *Poly-Olbion* (London: Humphrey Lownes, 1612)

Enguerrand de Monstrelet, *Chroniques d'Enguerrand de Monstrelet,* ed. Jean-Alexandre Buchon, 8 vols (Paris, 1826)

Froissart, Jean, *Oeuvres,* ed. Kervyn de Lettendove, 25 vols (Brussels: Devaux, 1867–77)

Garnier, Joseph and Louis-Émile Bougad, eds, *Chronique de l'abbaye de Saint-Bénigne de Dijon* (Dijon: Darantiere, 1875)

Geoffrey of Monmouth, *The History of the Kings of Britain: An Edition and Translation of De Gestis Britonum (Historia Regum Britanniae)*, ed. Michael D. Reeve and trans. by Neil Wright (Woodbridge: Boydell, 2007)

Gerald of Wales, *Giraldi Cambrensis Opera*, ed. J. S. Brewer, James F. Dimock, and George F. Warner, Rolls Series 21, 9 vols (Cambridge: Cambridge University Press, 2012)

Gerald of Wales, *A Journey Through Wales*, ed. and trans. by Lewis Thorpe (London: Penguin, 1978)

Gray, Thomas, *Scalacronica*, ed. Joseph Stevenson (Edinburgh: The Maitland Club, 1836)

Guidott, Thomas, *A discourse of Bathe, and the hot waters there* (London: Henry Brome, 1676)

Gruffydd, Elis, *Tales of Merlin, Arthur, and the Magic Arts, From the Welsh Chronicle of the Six Ages of the World*, ed. Jerry Hunter, trans. Patrick K. Ford (Oakland, CA: University of California Press, 2023)

Hakluyt, Richard, *The Principal Navigations, Voiages, Traffiques and Discoueries of the English Nation*, 2 vols (London: George Bishop and Ralph Newberie, 1589)

Hardyng, John, *The chronicle of Ihon Hardyng* (London: Richard Grafton, 1543), STC (2nd edn) 12767

Hardyng, John, *The Chronicle of John Hardyng, Together with the Continuation by Richard Grafton*, ed. Henry Ellis (London, 1812)

Hardyng, John, *John Hardyng's Chronicle: Edited from London British Library MS Lansdowne 204*, ed. Sarah Peverley and James Simpson, TEAMS (Kalamazoo, MI: Medieval Institute Publications, 2015), http://d.lib.rochester.edu/teams/publication/simpson-pevereley-hardyng-chronicle [accessed 30 July 2018]

Higden, Ranulph, *Polychronicon Ranulphi Higden*, ed. Joseph Rawson Lumby, Rolls Series 41, 10 vols (London, 1665–85)

Holinshed, Raphael, *Chronicles*, The Holinshed Project, http://english.nsms.ox.ac.uk/holinshed/ [accessed 13 October 2017]

Jean de Wavrin, *Recueil des chroniques et anchiennes istories de la Grant Bretaigne, à present nommé Engleterre*, ed. William Hardy, 3 vols, 2nd edn (Cambridge: Cambridge University Press, 2012 [1864])

Johannis de Londonia, 'Commendatio Lamentabilis in Transitu Magni Regis Edwardi', in *Chronicles of the Reigns of Edward I and Edward II*, ed. William Stubbs, 2 vols (London: Rolls Series, 1882–83), I, pp. 1–22

John of Glastonbury, *Cronica sive antiquitates Glastoniensis Ecclesie/The Chronicle of Glastonbury Abbey: An Edition, Translation and Study of John of Glastonbury's Cronica of c.1342*, ed. James P. Carley (Woodbridge: Boydell, 2009)

Joseph of Armathy (London: Wynkyn de Worde, 1507)

Krochalis, Jeanne, ed., 'Magna Tabula: The Glastonbury Tablets', in *Glastonbury Abbey and the Arthurian Tradition*, ed. James P. Carley, 2nd edn (Cambridge: D. S. Brewer, 2001), pp. 435–567

Lambarde, William, *Archaionomia sive de Priscis Anglorum Legibus libri* (London: John Day, 1568), STC (2nd edn) 15142

Laȝamon, *Layamon's Brut*, ed. G. L. Brook and R. F. Leslie, 2 vols, Early English Text Society, Original Series 250, 277 (London: Early English Text Society, 1963–78)

Lapidge, Michael, ed., 'The *Vera historia de morte Arthuri*: A New Edition', in *Glastonbury Abbey and the Arthurian Tradition*, ed. James P. Carley, 2nd edn (Cambridge: D. S. Brewer, 2001), pp. 115–41

Leland, John, *Assertio inclytissimi Arturii Regis Britanniae* (London, 1544), STC (2nd edn) 15440

Leland, John, *A Learned and True Assertion*, trans. by Richard Robinson (London, 1582), STC (2nd edn) 15441

Leland, John, *Commentarii de scriptoribus Britannicis*, ed. A. Hall, 2 vols (Oxford: Theatro Sheldoniano, 1709)

Leland, John, *Joannis Lelandi Antiquarii de Rebus Britannicis Collectanea*, ed. Thomas Hearne, 6 vols (London: William and John Richardson, 1770)

Leland, John, 'Codrus sive laus et defensio Gallofridi Arturii contra Polydorum Vergilium', in *Joannis Lelandi Antiquarii de Rebus Britannicis Collectanea*, ed. Thomas Hearne, 6 vols (London: William and John Richardson, 1770), V, pp. 2–10

Leland, John, *Leland's Itinerary in England and Wales: In or about the Years 1535–1543*, ed. Lucy Toulmin Smith, 5 vols (London: George Bell, 1906–10)

Leland, John, 'Assertio inclytissimi Arturii', in *The famous historie of Chinon of England, together with The Assertion of King Arthure*, ed. William Edward Mead, Early English Text Society, Original Series 165 (Oxford: Oxford University Press for the Early English Text Society, 1925)

Leland, John, 'The Assertion of King Arthure', trans. by Richard Robinson, in *The famous historie of Chinon of England, together with The Assertion of King Arthure*, ed. William Edward Mead, Early English Text Society, Original Series 165 (Oxford: Oxford University Press for the Early English Text Society, 1925)

Leland, John, *De uiris Illustribus = On Famous Men*, ed. and trans. by James P. Carley, 2 vols (Oxford: The Bodleian Library, 2010 [I] and forthcoming [II])

Lhwyd, Edward, 'An account of some Roman, French, and Irish inscriptions and antiquities', *Philosophical Transactions*, 22.269 (1700–01), 790–92

Llwyd, Humphrey, *Commentarioli Britannicae Descriptionis Fragmentum* (Cologne, 1572)

Llwyd, Humphrey, *The Breviary of Britayne*, trans. by Thomas Twyne (London, 1573), STC (2nd edn) 16636

Llwyd, Humphrey, *The Breviary of Britain*, ed. and trans. by Philip

Schwyzer, MHRA Tudor & Stuart Translations (London: Modern Humanities Research Association, 2011)

Llwyd, Humphrey, *Cronica Walliae*, ed. Ieuan M. Williams (Cardiff: Cardiff University Press, 2016)

Llwyd, Humphrey, *Commentarioli Britannicae Descriptionis Fragmentum: A Hypertext Edition*, ed. Dana F. Sutton, The Philological Museum (Irvine, CA: University of California, 2005), www.philological.bham.ac.uk/llwyd/ [accessed 13 March 2020]

Lybeaus Desconus, ed. Maldwyn Mills, Early English Text Society, Original Series 261 (Oxford: Oxford University Press, 1969)

The Lyfe of Ioseph of Armathia (London: Richard Pynson, 1520)

Maffei, Raphael *Commentariorum urbanorum XXXXIII libri [...]* (Lyon: Sebastianus Gryphius, 1552)

Malory, Sir Thomas, *Works*, ed. Eugène Vinaver (Oxford: Clarendon Press, 1977)

Mannyng, Robert, *The Chronicle*, ed. Idelle Sullens (Binghamton, NY: Binghamton University, 1996)

Marvin, Julia, ed. and trans., *The Oldest Anglo-Norman Prose Brut Chronicle* (Woodbridge: Boydell, 2006)

Michael of Cornwall, 'Versus contra Henricum Abricensem', ed. A. Hilka, in *Mittelalterlich Handschriften [...] Festgabe zum 60. Geburtstag von Hermann Degering*, ed. Aloys Bömer and Joachim Kirchner (Leipzig: Hiersemann, 1926), pp. 123–54

New proposals for printing by subscription, Cambden's Britannia, English newly translated, with large additions (April 20th 1693), Wing (2nd ed) C373

Nitze, William A. and T. Atkinson Jenkins, eds, *Le Haut Livre du Graal; Perlesvaus*, 2 vols (Chicago, IL: University of Chicago Press, 1932–37)

Parker, Martin, *The most admirable historie of that most renowned Christian worthy Arthur King of the Britains* (1660), STC (2nd edn) R181453

Percy, Thomas, *Reliques of Ancient English Poetry*, 3 vols (London: J. Dodsley, 1765)

Powel, David, *The Historie of Cambria, now called Wales* (London: David Powel, 1584), STC (2nd edn) 4606

Prise, Sir John, *Historiae Brytannicae defensio* (London: H. Binneman, 1573)

Prise, John, *Historiae Britannicae Defensio / A Defence of the British History*, ed. and trans. by Ceri Davies (Toronto: PIMS, 2015)

Purvis, J. S., ed., 'The Tables of the York Vicars Choral', *The Yorkshire Archaeological Journal*, 41 (1966), 741–48

Putter, Ad and Kate McClune, 'The Geographies of Later Medieval Arthurian Literature in England and Scotland', in *La matière arthurienne tardive en Europe 1270–1530*, ed. Christine Ferlampin-Acher (Rennes: Presses Universitaires de Rennes, 2020), pp. 1049–58

Raine, James, *The Historians of the Church of York and Its Archbishops*, 2 vols (London: Longman, 1886)

Raine, James, ed., 'Aliud chronicon metricum ecclesiae Eboracensis', in *The Historians of the Church of York and Its Archbishops*, ed. James Raine, 2 vols (London: Longman, 1886), pp. 464–87

Rastell, John, *Pastyme of People* (London: John Rastell, 1530), STC (2nd edn) 20724

Rigg, A. G., ed., *A Book of British Kings 1200BC–1399AD* (Toronto: PIMS, 2000)

Rous, John, *The Rous Roll*, ed. Charles Ross (Gloucester: Sutton, 1980)

Rous, John, *Joannis Rossi Antiquarii Warwicensis Historia Regum Angliae*, ed. Thomas Hearne, 2nd edn (Oxford: Sheldonian Theatre, 1745)

Ryd, Valerius Anselmus, *Catalogus annorum et principum geminus ab homine condito* (Bern, 1550)

Spelman, Henry, *Concilia, decreta, leges, constitutiones in re ecclesiarum orbis Britannicis* (London: Richard Badger, 1639)

Sidney, Philip, *An Apology for Poetry (Or the Defence of Poesy)*, ed. R. W. Maslen, 3rd edn (Manchester: Manchester University Press, 2002)

Skeat, W. W., ed., *Joseph of Arimathie: Otherwise Called The Romance of the Seint Graal or Holy Grail*, Early English Text Society, Original Series 44 (London: Early English Text Society, 1871)

Smith, Thomas, 'Life of Camden' in *Camden's Britannia*, ed. and trans. by Edmund Gibson (London: F. Collins, 1695)

Stamp, A. E., ed., *Calendar of Close Rolls: Henry IV, 1399–1402* (London: His Majesty's Stationery Office, 1927)

Stow, John, *The Chronicles of England from Brute vnto this present yeare of Christ* (London: Ralph Newberry, 1580)

Stow, John, *Survey of London*, ed. C. L. Kingsford (Oxford: Oxford University Press, 1908)

Stukeley, William, *Itinerarium Curiosum. Or, an account of the antiquitys, and remarkable curiositys in nature or art, observ'd in travels thro' Great Brittan* (London, 1724)

Stukeley, William, *Itinerarium Curiosum: or, an Account of the Antiquities, and Remarkable Curiosities in Nature or Art, Observed in the Travels Through Great Britain*, 2 vols (London: Baker and Leigh, 1776)

Trithemius, Johannes, *Compendium sive Breviarum* (Mainz: Schöffer, 1515)

Twyne, John, *De rebus Albionicis* (London: Richard Watkins, 1590)

Ussher, James, *Britannicarum Ecclesiarum Antiquitates* (Dublin: Societatis Bibliopolarum, 1639)

Ussher, James, *The Whole Works*, ed. Charles Richard Elrington, 16 vols (London: Whitaker, 1847)

Vergil, Polydore, 'Polydore Vergil's English History, from an Early Translation', ed. Sir Henry Ellis (London: The Camden Society, 1846)
Vergil, Polydore, *Anglica Historia (1555): A hypertext critical edition*, ed. and trans. by Dana F. Sutton, The Philological Museum (Irvine, CA: University of California, 2005), www.philological.bham.ac.uk/polverg/ [accessed 1 September 2017]
Wace, *Wace's Roman de Brut: A History of the British*, ed. and trans. by Judith Weiss (Exeter: University of Exeter Press, 2002)
William of Malmesbury, *The Early History of Glastonbury / De antiquitate Glastonie Ecclesie*, ed. John Scott (Woodbridge: Boydell, 1981)
William of Malmesbury, *Gesta Regum Anglorum*, ed. R. M. Thomson and M. Winterbottom, 2 vols (Oxford: Oxford University Press, 1998–99)
William of Rennes, *The Historia Regum Britannie of Geoffrey of Monmouth V: Gesta Regum Britanniae*, ed. and trans. Neil Wright (Cambridge: D. S. Brewer, 1991)
Worcester, William, *Itineraries*, ed. and trans. by John H. Harvey (Oxford: Clarendon Press, 1969)
Zettl, Ewald, ed., *An Anonymous Short English Metrical Chronicle*, Early English Text Society, Original Series 196 (London: Early English Text Society, 1935)

Secondary sources

Abrams, Lesley, *Anglo-Saxon Glastonbury: Church and Endowment* (Woodbridge: Boydell, 1996)
Ackerman, Robert W., *An Index of the Arthurian Names in Middle English* (Stanford, CA: Stanford University Press, 1952)
Adrian, John M., *Local Negotiations of English Nationhood, 1570–1680* (New York: Palgrave Macmillan, 2011)
Alcock, Leslie, *Arthur's Britain: History and Archaeology AD 367–634* (London: Allen Lane, 1971)
Alcock, Leslie, *'By South Cadbury is that Camelot…': The Excavation of Cadbury Castle 1966–1970* (Aylesbury: Thames and Hudson, 1972)
Alcock, Leslie, 'Cadbury-Camelot: A Fifteen-Year Perspective', *Proceedings of the British Academy*, 68 (1983), 355–88
Anderson, Benedict, *Imagined Communities: Reflections on the Origin and Spread of Nationalism*, 3rd edn (London: Verso, 2006)
Anderson, Earl, 'Malory's Camelot, Winchester, and "the Chirche of Seynte Stevins"', *Neuphilologische Mitteilungen*, 92.2 (1991), 211–13
Anglo, Sydney, 'The "British History" in Early Tudor Propaganda', *Bulletin of the John Rylands Library*, 44 (1961), 17–48

Anthony à Wood, *Athenae Oxonienses, An Exact History of All the Writers and Bishops who Have Had Their Education in the University of Oxford. To which are Added the Fasti, Or Annals of the Said University*, ed. Philip Bliss, 2 vols (London: F.C. & J. Rivington, 1815)

Appadurai, Arjun, 'The Production of Locality', in *Modernity at Large: Cultural Dimensions of Globalization* (Minneapolis, MN: University of Minnesota Press, 1996), pp. 178–204

Apsimon, A. M., 'King Arthur's Cave, King Arthur's Hall and the Giant's Skeleton', *Proceedings of the University of Bristol Spelaeological Society*, 20.1 (1994), 75–76

Arber, Edward, ed., *A Transcript of the Registers of the Company of Stationers of London; 1554–1640AD*, 5 vols (London, 1875–94)

Archibald, Elizabeth, 'Lancelot as Lover in the English Tradition Before Malory', in *Arthurian Studies in Honour of P. J. C. Field*, ed. Bonnie Wheeler (Cambridge: D. S. Brewer, 2004), pp. 199–216

Archibald, Elizabeth, Megan G. Leitch, and Corinne Saunders, eds, *Romance Rewritten: The Evolution of Middle English Romance: A Tribute to Helen Cooper* (Cambridge: D. S. Brewer, 2018)

Archibald, Elizabeth, 'Malory and the Post-Vulgate Cycle', in *Romance Rewritten: The Evolution of Middle English Romance: A Tribute to Helen Cooper*, ed. Elizabeth Archibald, Megan G. Leitch and Corinne Saunders (Cambridge: D. S. Brewer, 2018), pp. 115–32

Armbrecht, Ann, *Thin Places: A Pilgrimage Home* (New York: Columbia University Press, 2009)

Armstrong, Dorsey and Kenneth Hodges, *Mapping Malory: Regional Identities and National Geographies in Le Morte Darthur* (London: Palgrave Macmillan, 2014)

Arnold, Jonathan, '"Polydorus Italus": Analyzing Authority in Polydore Vergil's Anglica Historia', *Reformation and Renaissance Review*, 16.2 (2014), 122–37

Ashe, Geoffrey, *A Guidebook to Arthurian Britain* (London: Longman, 1980)

Ashe, Geoffrey, 'The Origins of the Arthurian Legend', *Arthuriana*, 5.3 (1995), 1–24

Ashe, Geoffrey, 'Origins', in *An Arthurian Handbook*, ed. Geoffrey Ashe and Norris J. Lacy, 2nd edn (New York: Garland, 1997), pp. 1–56

Ashe, Laura, *Fiction and History in England, 1066–1200* (Cambridge: Cambridge University Press, 2007)

Ashe, Laura, 'Holinshed and Mythical History', in *The Oxford Handbook of Holinshed's Chronicles*, ed. Felicity Heal, Ian W. Archer, and Paulina Kewes (Oxford: Oxford University Press, 2012), pp. 153–70

Aston, Margaret, 'English Ruins and English History: The Dissolution and

the Sense of the Past', *Journal of the Warburg and Courtauld Institutes*, 36 (1973), 231–55
Auerbach, Erich, *Mimesis: The Representation of Reality in Western Literature*, ed. and trans. W. R. Trask (Princeton, NJ: Princeton University Press, 2003)
Aurell, Martin, 'Henry II and Arthurian Legend', in *Henry II: New Interpretations*, ed. C. Harper-Bill and N. Vincent (Woodbridge: Boydell, 2007), pp. 365–94
Baddeley, Welbore St Clair, *A History of Cirencester* (Cirencester: Cirencester Newspaper co., 1924)
Bakhtin, Mikhael, 'Forms of Time and of the Chronotope in the Novel: Notes towards a Historical Poetics', in *The Dialogic Imagination: Four Essays*, ed. Michael Holquist, trans. by Jay Wright (Austin, TX: University of Texas Press, 1981), pp. 84–258
Barber, Chris and David Pykitt, *Journey to Avalon: The Final Discovery of King Arthur* (York Beach, ME: Samuel Weiser, 1997)
Barber, Peter, 'England II: Monarchs, Ministers, and Maps, 1550–1625', in *Monarchs, Ministers, and Maps: The Emergence of Cartography as a Tool of Government in Early Modern Europe*, The Kenneth Nebenzahl Jr. Lectures in the History of Cartography (Chicago, IL: University of Chicago Press, 1992), pp. 57–98
Barber, Richard, 'Was Mordred Buried at Glastonbury?: Arthurian Tradition at Glastonbury in the Middle Ages', in *Glastonbury Abbey and the Arthurian Tradition*, ed. James P. Carley, 2nd edn (Cambridge: D. S. Brewer, 2001), pp. 145–59
Barber, Richard, 'The *Vera Historia de Morte Arthuri* and Its Place in Arthurian Tradition', in *Glastonbury Abbey and the Arthurian Tradition*, ed. James P. Carley, 2nd edn (Cambridge: D. S. Brewer, 2001), pp. 101–13
Barrett, Chris, *Early Modern English Literature and the Poetics of Cartographic Anxiety* (Oxford: Oxford University Press, 2018)
Barron, W. R. J., ed., *The Arthur of the English* (Cardiff: University of Wales Press, 2001)
Barrett Jr, Robert, *All England: Regional Identity and Cheshire Writing, 1195–1656* (Notre Dame, IN: University of Notre Dame Press, 2009)
Bartlett, Robert, *The Making of Europe: Conquest, Colonization and Cultural Change 950–1350* (London: Penguin, 2003)
Bartlett, Robert, 'Gerald of Wales [Giraldus Cambrensis, Gerald de Barry] (c. 1146 –1220x23)', *Oxford Dictionary of National Biography*, www.oxforddnb.com/view/10.1093/ref:odnb/9780198614128.001.0001/odnb-9780198614128-e-10769 [accessed 7 December 2018]
Bartlett, Robert, *England Under the Norman and Angevin Kings: 1075–1225* (Oxford: Oxford University Press, 2013)

Bateman, Mary, 'A Newly-Discovered Latin Prose *Brut* Manuscript at Downside Abbey', *The Downside Review*, 137.4 (2019), 166–181

Bateman, Mary, '"The Native Place of That Great Arthur": Foreignness and Nativity in Sixteenth-Century Defences of Arthur', *Arthurian Literature*, 35 (2019), 152–72

Bateman, Mary, 'A Grave Discovery?: Guinevere's Death and Burial at Amesbury in Medieval and Early Modern Tradition', in *The Arthurian World*, ed. Victoria Coldham-Fussell, Miriam Edlich-Muth, and Renée Ward (London: Routledge, 2022), pp. 413–28

Batt, Catherine, *Malory's Morte D'Arthur: Remaking Arthurian Tradition* (London: Palgrave, 2002)

Bautz, Friedrich Wilhelm, 'Anshelm, Valerius', in *Biographisch-Bibliographisches Kirchenlexikon*, ed. Friedrich Wilhelm Bautz (Hamm: Bautz, 1975), I, col. 188

Beal, Jane, 'Mapping Identity in John Trevisa's English Polychronicon: Chester, Cornwall and the Translation of English National History', in *Fourteenth Century England III*, ed. W. M. Ormrod (Woodbridge: Boydell, 2004), pp. 67–82

Beckett, John, *Writing Local History* (Manchester: Manchester University Press, 2007)

Beecham, K. J., *History of Cirencester and the Roman City of Corinium*, ed. David Verey, 2nd edn (Dursley: A. Sutton, 1978 [1886])

Berard, Christopher Michael, 'Edward III's Abandoned Order of the Round Table Revisited: Political Arthurianism After Poitiers', *Arthurian Literature*, 33 (2016), 70–109

Berard, Christopher Michael, *Arthurianism in Early Plantagenet England* (Woodbridge: Boydell, 2019)

Béres, Laura, 'A Thin Place: Narratives of Space and Place, Celtic Spirituality and Meaning', *Journal of Religion and Spirituality in Social Work: Social Thought*, 31.4 (2012), 394–413

Berg, Lawrence D. and Jani Vuolteenaho, eds, *Critical Toponymies: The Contested Politics of Place Naming*, ed. Lawrence D. Berg and Jani Vuolteenaho, 2nd edn (London: Routledge, 2016)

Biddle, Martin, 'The Painting of the Round Table', in *King Arthur's Round Table: An Archaeological Investigation*, ed. Martin Biddle (Woodbridge: Boydell, 2000), pp. 425–74

Biddle, Martin, 'The Making of the Round Table', in *King Arthur's Round Table: An Archaeological Investigation*, ed. Martin Biddle (Woodbridge: Boydell, 2000), pp. 337–92

Biddle, Martin, 'The Hanging of the Table', in *King Arthur's Round Table: An Archaeological Investigation*, ed. Martin Biddle (Woodbridge: Boydell, 2000), pp. 393–424

Blake, N. F., 'Caxton Prepares His Edition of the *Morte Arthur*', in *William Caxton and English Literary Culture*, ed. N. F. Blake (London: Hambledon, 1991), pp. 199–212

Blenner-Hassett, Roland, 'Geoffrey of Monmouth's *Mons Agned* and *Castellum Puellarum*', *Speculum*, 17.2 (1942), 250–54

Bly Calkin, Siobhain, *Saracens and the Making of English Identity: The Auchinleck Manuscript* (London: Taylor and Francis, 2013)

Boon, George C., *St Mary the Virgin, Silchester* (Basingstoke: Ridgeway Press, 1989)

Bowden, Sarah and Susanne Friede, 'Introduction: Sacred Space and Place in Arthurian Romance', *Arthurian Literature*, 36 (2021), 1–12

Bowman, Marion, 'Drawn to Glastonbury', in *Pilgrimage in Popular Culture*, ed. Ian Reader and Tony Walter (London: Palgrave Macmillan, 1993), pp. 29–62

Bowman, Marion, 'Procession and Possession in Glastonbury: Continuity, Change and the Manipulation of Tradition', *Folklore*, 115.3 (2004), 273–85

Bowman, Marion, 'Arthur and Bridget in Avalon: Celtic Myth, Vernacular Religion and Contemporary Spirituality in Glastonbury', *Fabula*, 48.12 (2007), 16–32

Bowman, Marion, 'Going with the Flow: Contemporary Pilgrimage in Glastonbury', in *Shrines and Pilgrimage in the Modern World: New Itineraries into the Sacred*, ed. Peter Jan Margry (Amsterdam: Amsterdam University Press, 2008), pp. 241–80

Bowman, Marion, 'Restoring/Restorying Arthur and Bridget: Vernacular Religion and Contemporary Spirituality in Glastonbury', in *Vernacular Religion in Everyday Life: Expressions of Belief*, ed. Marion Bowman and Ulo Valk (London: Routledge, 2012), pp. 328–49

Bradley, Laura, 'Nicolas Cage Lived *National Treasure* by Searching for the Holy Grail', *Vanity Fair*, 7 August 2019.

Bradley, R. and P. Topping, 'The Penrith Henges: A Survey by the Royal Commission of the Historical Monument of England', *Proceedings of the Prehistoric Society*, 60 (1992), 285–324

Bradner, L., 'Some Unpublished Poems by John Leland', *Publications of the Modern Language Association*, 71 (1956), 827–36

Breeze, Andrew, 'The Historical Arthur and Sixth-Century Scotland', *Northern History*, 52.2 (2015), 158–81

Breeze, Andrew, 'The Early Welsh Cult of Arthur: Some Points at Issue', *Studia Celtica Posnaniensia*, 1.1 (2016), 1–13

Breeze, Andrew, 'Legionum Urbs and the British Martyrs Aaron and Julius', *Voprosy Onomastiki*, 13.1 (2016), 30–42

Brewer, J. S., ed., *Letters and Papers, Foreign and Domestic, of the Reign of Henry VIII* (London, 1920)

Brinkley, Roberta Florence, *Arthurian Legend in the Seventeenth Century* (London: Cass, 1932)

Brinley Jones, R., 'Humphrey Llwyd (1527–1568), Antiquary and Map Maker', *The Oxford Dictionary of National Biography* (Oxford: Oxford University Press, 2004), www.oxforddnb.com/view/10.1093/ ref:odnb/9780198614128.001.0001/odnb-9780198614128-e-16867?rskey=yiP7G5&result=2 [accessed 12 March 2020]

British History Online, www.british-history.ac.uk/ [accessed 20 November 2018]

Broadway, Jan, *'No historie so meete': Gentry Culture and the Development of Local History in Elizabethan and Early Stuart England* (Manchester: Manchester University Press, 2006)

Brooke, C. N. L., *The Church and the Welsh Border in the Central Middle Ages* (Woodbridge: Boydell, 1986)

Brooke, Christopher, 'The Archbishops of St Davids, Llandaff and Caerleon-on-Usk', in *Studies in the Early British Church*, ed. Nora K. Chadwick (Cambridge: Cambridge University Press, 1958), pp. 201–42

Bromwich, Rachel, 'Pedwar marchog ar hugain llys Arthur (The Twenty-Four Knights of Arthur's Court)', *Transactions of the Honourable Society of Cymmrodorion*, 1956, 126–32

Bromwich, Rachel, 'Gwalchmei m. Gwyar', in *Gawain: A Casebook*, ed. Keith Busby and Raymond H. Thompson (London: Routledge, 2006), pp. 95–102

Bromwich, Rachel, A. O. H. Jarman, and Brynley F. Roberts, eds, *The Arthur of the Welsh* (Cardiff: University of Wales Press, 1991)

Brown, Michelle P. and James P. Carley, 'A Fifteenth-Century Revision of the Glastonbury Epitaph to King Arthur', in *Glastonbury Abbey and the Arthurian Tradition*, ed. James P. Carley, 2nd edn (Cambridge: D. S. Brewer, 2001), pp. 193–203

Brown, P., C. David, and Alan D. McWhirr, 'Cirencester, 1966', *The Antiquaries Journal*, 47.2 (1967), 185–97

Brown, Peter, 'Journey's End: The Prologue to the Tale of Beryn', in *Chaucer and Fifteenth-Century Poetry*, ed. Julia Boffey and Janet Cowen (London: Kings College Centre for Late Antique and Medieval Studies, 1991), pp. 143–74

Brown, Stewart, 'Glastonbury Abbey St Joseph's Crypt Archaeological Evaluation 2014', unpublished report for the Trustees of Glastonbury Abbey (Glastonbury, 2014)

Broyles, Paul, *'Errare* in Romance', New Chaucer Society Conference (London, 13 July 2016)

Bruce, Christopher W., *The Arthurian Name Dictionary* (New York: Garland, 1999)

Bruce, Mark P. and Katherine H. Terrell, eds, *The Anglo-Scottish Border and the Shaping of Identity, 1300–1600* (London: Palgrave Macmillan, 2012)

Burckhardt, Jacob, *The Civilization of the Renaissance in Italy: An Essay*, ed. and trans. by L. Goldscheider, 4th edn (London: Phaidon, 1951)

Burgess, Glyn S. and Karen Pratt, eds, *The Arthur of the French* (Cardiff: University of Wales Press, 2006)

Burton, Janet and Karen Stöber, eds, *Abbeys and Priories of Medieval Wales* (Cardiff: University of Wales Press, 2015)

Butterfield, Ardis, *The Familiar Enemy: Chaucer, Language, and Nation in the Hundred Years War* (Oxford: Oxford University Press, 2009)

Butterfield, Ardis, 'National Histories', in *Cultural Reformations: Medieval and Renaissance in Literary History*, ed. Brian Cummings and James Simpson (Oxford University Press, 2010), pp. 33–55

Byrne, Aisling, *Otherworlds: Fantasy and History in Medieval Literature* (Oxford: Oxford University Press, 2016)

Camargo, Martin, 'Tria Sunt: The Long and the Short of Geoffrey of Vinsauf's Documentum de Modo et Arte Dictandi et Versificandi', *Speculum*, 74.4 (1999), 935–55

Capulli, Chiara and Raffaele Danna, 'Ughi's *Viaggio di Fiandra ed Inghiterra*: A Florentine Merchant Experiences Sacred Space in Canterbury, 1444 – Analysis of a Previously Unknown Autograph Diary', International Medieval Congress (Leeds, 1 July 2019)

Carley, James P., 'Melkin the Bard and Esoteric Tradition at Glastonbury Abbey', *The Downside Review*, 99 (1981), 1–17

Carley, James P., 'Polydore Vergil and John Leland on King Arthur: The Battle of the Books', *Interpretations*, 15 (1984), 86–100

Carley, James P., 'The Manuscript Remains of John Leland, "The King's Antiquary"', *Text*, 2 (1985), 111–20

Carley, James P., 'John Leland and the Contents of English Pre-Dissolution Libraries: Glastonbury Abbey', *Scriptorium*, 40 (1986), 107–20

Carley, James P., 'John Leland in Paris: The Evidence of His Poetry', *Studies in Philology*, 83 (1986), 1–50

Carley, James P., *Glastonbury Abbey: The Holy House at the Head of the Moors Adventurous* (Woodbridge: Boydell, 1988)

Carley, James P., 'Arthur in English History', in *The Arthur of the English*, ed. W. R. J. Barron (Cardiff: University of Wales Press, 2001), pp. 47–57

Carley, James P., ed., *Glastonbury Abbey and the Arthurian Tradition*, 2nd edn (Cambridge: D. S. Brewer, 2001)

Carley, James P., 'The Discovery of the Holy Cross of Waltham', in *Glastonbury Abbey and the Arthurian Tradition*, ed. James P. Carley, 2nd edn (Cambridge: D. S. Brewer, 2001), pp. 303–08

Carley, James P., 'A Glastonbury Translator at Work', in *Glastonbury Abbey and the Arthurian Tradition*, ed. James P. Carley, 2nd edn (Cambridge: D. S. Brewer, 2001), pp. 337–45

Carley, James P., and Pierre Petitmengin, 'Pre-Conquest Manuscripts from Malmesbury Abbey and John Leland's Letter to Beatus Rhenanus Concerning a Lost Copy of Tertullian's Works', *Anglo-Saxon England*, 33.1978 (2004), 195–223

Carley, James P., 'John of Glastonbury and Borrowings from the Vernacular', in *Interstices: Studies in Middle English and Anglo-Latin Texts in Honour of A. G. Rigg*, ed. Richard Firth Green and Linne R. Mooney (Toronto: University of Toronto Press, 2004), pp. 55–73

Carley, James P., 'Arthur and the Antiquaries', in *The Arthur of Medieval Latin Literature*, ed. Sian Échard (Cardiff: University of Wales Press, 2011), pp. 149–78

Carley, James P., '"Many Good Autors": Two of John Leland's Manuscripts and the Cambridge Connexion', *Transactions of the Cambridge Bibliographical Society*, 15 (2014), 27–56

Carley, James P., 'John Leland', *The Oxford Dictionary of National Biography*. www.oxforddnb.com/view/10.1093/ref:odnb/9780198614128.001.0001/odnb- 9780198614128-e-16416 [accessed 7 December 2018]

Carlson, David, 'King Arthur and Court Poems for the Birth of Arthur Tudor in 1496', *Humanistica Lovaniensia*, 36 (1987), 147–83

Carpenter, David, *The Reign of Henry III* (London: Hambledon, 1996)

Castelvetro, Lodovico, *Poetica d'Aristotele vulgarizzata e sposta*, ed. Werther Romani, 2 vols (Rome: Gius. Laterza, 1978–79)

Cattell, David and Philip Schwyzer, 'Introduction: Visions of Britain', *The Seventeenth Century*, 33.4 (2018), 377–91

de Certeau, Michel, *The Practice of Everyday Life*, trans. by Steven Rendall (London: University of California Press, 1984)

Chambers, E. K., *Arthur of Britain* (London: Sidgwick & Jackson, 1927)

Chandler, John, ed., *John Leland's Itinerary: Travels in Tudor England* (Thrupp: Sutton, 1993)

Charles-Edwards, Thomas, 'The Early Welsh Arthurian Poems', in *The Arthur of the Welsh*, ed. Rachel Bromwich, A. O. H. Jarman and Brynley F. Roberts (Cardiff: University of Wales Press, 1991), pp. 15–32

'Chronicle written by a "British Tommy" awarded UN recognition', National Library of Wales, 9 June 2018 www.library.wales/information-for/press-and-media/press-releases/2018-press-releases/chronicle-written-by-a-british-tommy-awarded-united-nations-recognition/ [accessed 15 July 2019]

Clark, James G., 'Selling the Holy Places: Monastic Efforts to Win Back the People in Fifteenth-Century England', in *Social Attitudes and Political Structures in the Fifteenth Century*, ed. Tim Thornton (Stroud: Sutton, 2000), pp. 13–32

Clark, John, 'The King Lucius Tabula in St Peter Upon Cornhill Church, London', paper given at the Medieval and Tudor London Seminar, Institute of Historical Research, 2011 (revised 2014), available online www.academia.edu/6553953/The_King_Lucius_tabula_in_St_Peter_Upon_Cornhill_church_London

Clark, John, 'Trojans at Totnes and Giants on the Hoe: Geoffrey of Monmouth, Historical Fiction and Geographical Reality', *Report and Transactions of the Devonshire Association for the Advancement of Science, Literature and Art*, 148 (2016), 89–130

Clarke, Catherine A. M., *Literary Landscapes and the Idea of England, 700–1400* (Cambridge: D. S. Brewer, 2006)

Coates, Richard, 'Maiden Castle, Geoffrey of Monmouth and Hārūn Al-Rašīd', *Nomina*, 29 (2006), 5–60

Coates, Richard, 'Rethinking Romano-British *Corinium*', *The Antiquaries Journal*, 93 (2013), 81–91

Cohen, Jeffrey J., *Of Giants: Sex, Monsters, and the Middle Ages* (Minneapolis, MN: Minnesota University Press, 1999)

Collinson, Patrick, 'One of Us? William Camden and the Making of History', *Transactions of the Royal Historical Society*, 6th series, 8 (1998), 139–63

Cook, John, 'Events Set in Amber: Bakhtin's "Chronotope of the Castle" as Solidified Space-Time', *Australian Slavonic and East European Studies*, 28 (2014), 51–70

Cook, Murray, Hana Kdolska, Lindsay Dunbar, Rob Engl, Stefan Sagrott, Denise Druce, and Gordon Cook, 'New Light on Oblong Forts: Excavations at Dunnideer, Aberdeenshire', *Proceedings of the Society of Antiquaries of Scotland*, 140 (2010), 79–91

Cooper, Helen, 'The *Lancelot-Grail Cycle* in England: Malory and his Predecessors', in *A Companion to the Lancelot-Grail Cycle*, ed. Carol Dover, (Cambridge: D. S. Brewer, 2003), pp. 147–62

Cooper, Helen, *The English Romance in Time: Transforming Motifs from Geoffrey of Monmouth to the Death of Shakespeare* (Oxford: Oxford University Press, 2004)

Cooper, Helen, 'Lancelot, Roger Mortimer and the Date of the Auchinleck Manuscript', in *Studies in Late Medieval and Early Renaissance Texts in Honour of John Scattergood: The Key of All Good Remembrance*, ed. A. J. Fletcher and Anne-Marie D'Arcy (Dublin: Portland, 2005), pp. 91–99

Cooper, Helen, *Shakespeare and the Medieval World* (London: Arden Shakespeare, 2010)

Cooper, Helen, 'The Origins of the Early Modern', *Journal for Early Modern Cultural Studies*, 13.3 (2013), 133–37

Cooper, Helen, 'Arthur in Transition: Malory's *Morte Darthur*', in *Romance and History: Imagining Time from the Medieval to the Early Modern Period*, ed. Jon Whitman (Cambridge: Cambridge University Press, 2015), pp. 120–34

Coote, Lesley, *Prophecy and Public Affairs in Later Medieval England* (York: York Medieval Press, 2000)

Coyne, Kelly, 'The Eco-Tourist, English Heritage, and Arthurian Legend: Walking with Thoreau', *Arthuriana*, 23.1 (2013), 20–39

Crane, Robert, 'The Vogue of *Guy of Warwick* from the Close of the Middle Ages to the Romantic Revival', *Publications of the Modern Language Association*, 30 (1915), 125–94

Crick, Julia, *The Historia Regum Britannie of Geoffrey of Monmouth: Dissemination and Reception in the Later Middle Ages* (Cambridge: D. S. Brewer, 1991)

Crofts, Thomas H. Jr and Robert Allen Rouse, 'Middle English Popular Romance and National Identity', in *A Companion to Medieval Popular Romance*, ed. Raluca L. Radulescu and Cory James Rushton (Cambridge: D. S. Brewer, 2009), pp. 79–95

Cull, Marisa R., '"Prince of Wales by Cambria's Full Consent"?: The Princedom of Wales and the Early Modern Stage', in *Writing Wales from the Renaissance to Romanticism*, ed. Stewart Mottram and Sarah Prescott (Farnham: Ashgate, 2012), pp. 75–90

Cuming Walters, J., *The Lost Land of King Arthur* (London: Chapman and Hall, 1909)

Currie, C. R. J. and C. P. Lewis, eds, *English County Histories: A Guide* (Stroud: Sutton, 1994)

D., H. W. C., 'Short Notices', *English Historical Review*, 25.100 (1910), 804–34

Da Costa, Alexandra, 'Marketing the Shrine: Printed Pilgrimage Souvenirs, Guides, and Advertising', *Journal of the Early Book Society*, 16 (2013), 85–100

Dabundo, Laura, 'Maria Edgeworth and the Irish "Thin Places"', in *New Essays on Maria Edgeworth*, ed. Julia Nash (London: Routledge, 2006), pp. 193–98

Dale, Johanna, *Inauguration and Liturgical Kingship in the Long Twelfth Century* (York: York Medieval Press, 2019)

Daniell, Christopher, *From Norman Conquest to Magna Carta: England 1066–1215* (London: Routledge, 2003)

Darvill, Timothy, 'Grismond's Tower, Cirencester, and the Rise of Springhead Super-Mounds in the Cotswolds and Beyond', *Transactions of the Bristol and Gloucestershire Archaeological Society*, 132 (2014), 11–27

Davidson, Roberta, 'The "Freynshe booke" and the English Translator: Malory's "Originality" Revisited', *Translation and Literature*, 17.2 (2008), 133–49

Davies, Gareth, David Knight, Scott C. Lomax and Christopher Loveluck, 'From "House of Caves" to Nexus of Central England: Nottingham, c. AD 650–1250 – Future Research Directions', *Transactions of the Thoroton Society of Nottinghamshire*, 123 (2019), 55–76

Davies, R. G., 'Stafford, John (d. 1452), Administrator and Archbishop of Canterbury', *The Oxford Dictionary of National Biography* (Oxford: Oxford University Press, 2004), https://doi.org/10.1093/ref:odnb/26209

Davies, R. R., *The Matter of Britain and the Matter of England: An Inaugural Lecture Delivered before the University of Oxford on 29 February 1996* (Oxford: Clarendon Press, 1996)

Dean, Christopher, *Arthur of England: English Attitudes to King Arthur and the Knights of the Round Table in the Middle Ages and the Renaissance* (Toronto: University of Toronto Press, 1987)

DeMolen, Richard, 'The Library of William Camden', *Proceedings of the American Philosophical Society*, 128:4 (1984), 326–409

'Detailed record for Harley 1808', *British Library Online Catalogue of Illuminated Manuscripts*, www.bl.uk/catalogues/illuminatedmanuscripts/record.asp?MSID=6645&CollID=8&NStart=1808 [accessed 1 November 2019]

Dickinson, W. H., *King Arthur in Cornwall* (London: Longmans Green, 1900)

Digney, Stephen and Richard Jones, 'Recent Investigations at the King's Knot Stirling', *The Forth Naturalist and Historian*, 36 (2013), 129–48

Ditmas, E. M. R., 'The Cult of Arthurian Relics', *Folklore*, 75 (1964), 19–33

Ditmas, E. M. R., 'The Round Table at Stirling', *Bulletins Bibliographiques de La Société Internationale Arthurienne*, 26 (1974), 188–96

Diverres, A. H., 'Jean Froissart's Journey to Scotland', *Forum for Modern Language Studies*, 1.1 (1965), 54–63

Dobson, Barrie, 'The Later Middle Ages 1215-1500', in *A History of York Minster*, ed. G. E. Aylmer and Reginald Cant (Oxford: Clarendon Press, 1977), pp. 44–109

Dobson, Barrie, 'The English Vicars Choral: An Introduction', in *Vicars Choral at English Cathedrals*, ed. Richard Hall and David Stocker (Oxford: Oxbow Press, 2005), pp. 1–10

Dolmans, Emily, 'Locating the Border: Britain and the Welsh Marches in *Fouke Le Fitz Waryn*', *New Medieval Literatures*, 16 (2016), pp. 109–34

Dolmans, Emily, *Writing Regional Identities in Medieval England: From the Gesta Herwardi to Richard Coer de Lyon* (Cambridge: D. S. Brewer, 2020)

Donno, Elizabeth Story, 'Old Mouse-eaten Records: History in Sidney's *Apology*', in *Sir Philip Sidney: An Anthology of Modern Criticism*, ed. Dennis Kay (Oxford: Oxford University Press, 1987), pp. 147–67

Douglas Simpson, W., 'The Castles of Dunnideer and Wardhouse, in the Garioch, Aberdeenshire', *Proceedings of the Society of Antiquaries of Scotland*, 69 (1935), 460–70

Driver, Martha, 'Inventing Visual History: Re-Presenting the Legends of Warwickshire', in *Essays in Manuscript Geography: Vernacular Manuscripts of the English West Midlands from the Conquest to the Sixteenth Century*, ed. Wendy Scase (Turnhout, Belgium: Brepols, 2007), pp. 161–202

Drukker, Tamar, 'I Read Therefore I Write: Readers' Marginalia in Some Brut Manuscripts', in *Readers and Writers of the Prose Brut*, ed. William Marx and Raluca Radulescu (Lampeter: Trivium, 2006), pp. 97–130

Duffy, Eamon, *The Stripping of the Altars: Traditional Religion in England, c. 1400–c. 1580* (New Haven, CT: Yale University Press, 1992)

Dumville, David, 'Sub-Roman Britain: History and Legend', *History*, 62 (1977), 173–92

Echard, Siân, *Arthurian Narrative in the Latin Tradition* (Cambridge: Cambridge University Press, 1998)

Echard, Siân, '"Whyche Thynge Semeth Not To Agree With Other Histories...": Rome in Geoffrey of Monmouth and His Early Modern Readers', *Arthurian Literature*, 26 (2009), 109–30

Echard, Siân, ed., *The Arthur of Medieval Latin Literature* (Cardiff: University of Wales Press, 2011)

Edmunds, F., 'The Skeleton Found in King Arthur's Hall', *Transactions of the Woolhope Naturalists' Field Club*, 5–6 (1874), 28–31

Edwards, A. S. G., 'Notes on the *Polychronicon*', *Notes and Queries*, 25 (1978), 2–3

Edwards, A. S. G. and James Freeman, 'Further Manuscripts of Higden's Polychronicon', *Notes and Queries*, 63.4 (2016), 521–22

Edwards, Nancy, 'Welsh History Month: The Memorial Stone of King Cadfan of Gwynedd', *Wales Online*, 14 May 2013, www.walesonline.co.uk/lifestyle/nostalgia/welsh-history-month-memorial-stone-3812462 [accessed 1 April 2022]

Edwards, Nancy, 'Afterlives: Reinventing early medieval sculpture in Wales', *Archaeologia Cambrensis*, 169 (2020), 1–29

Eisenstein, Elizabeth L., *The Printing Revolution in Early Modern Europe*, 2nd edn (Cambridge: Cambridge University Press, 2012)

Ekwall, E., ed., *Etymological Notes of English Place-Names* (Lund: C. W. K Gleerup, 1937)

Elgenius, Gabriella, *Symbols of Nations and Nationalism: Celebrating Nationhood* (London: Palgrave Macmillan, 2011)

Ellis, Steven G., *Tudor Frontiers and Noble Power: The Making of the British State* (Oxford: Oxford University Press, 1995)

Evans, Arthur J., 'The Rollright Stones and their Folklore', *Folklore*, 6.1 (1895), 6–51

Fallows, David, 'English Song Repertories of the Mid-Fifteenth Century', *Proceedings of the Royal Musical Association*, 103.1 (1976–77), 61–79

Ferguson, Arthur B., *Utter Antiquity: Perceptions of Prehistory in Renaissance England* (Durham, NC: Duke University Press, 1993)

Field, P. J. C., 'Gildas and the City of Legions', *The Heroic Ages*, 1 (1999), www.heroicage.org/issues/1/hagcl.htm [accessed 25 October 2019]

Field, P. J. C., 'Searching for Camelot', *Medium Aevum*, 87.1 (2018), 1–22

Field, P. J. C., 'King Arthur: Hero or Legend?', in *The Arthurian World*, ed. Victoria Coldham-Fussell, Miriam Edlich-Muth, and Renée Ward (London: Routledge, 2022), pp. 25–34

Field, Rosalind, ed., *Tradition and Transformation in Medieval Romance* (Cambridge: D. S. Brewer, 1999)

Fitzpatrick-Matthews, Keith J., 'The xxuiii Ciuitates Brittannię of the Historia Brittonum: Antiquarian Speculation in Early Medieval Wales', *Journal of Literary Onomastics*, 4.1 (2015), 1–19

Fleming, Peter, 'Making History: Culture, Politics and *The Maire of Bristowe is Kalendar*', in *Reputation and Representation in Fifteenth Century Europe*, ed. Douglas L. Biggs, Sharon D. Michalove and Albert Compton Reeves (Boston, MA: Brill, 2004), pp. 289–316

Fletcher, Anthony and Diarmaid MacCulloch, *Tudor Rebellions*, 5th edn (London: Routledge, 2014)

Fletcher, Robert H., 'Some Arthurian Fragments from Fourteenth Century Chronicles', *PMLA*, 18.1 (1903), 84–94

Fletcher, Robert H., *Arthurian Materials in the Chronicles* (Boston, MA: Harvard University Press, 1906)

Flint, Valerie I. J., 'The Historia Regum Britanniae of Geoffrey of Monmouth: Parody and Its Purpose. A Suggestion', *Speculum*, 54.3 (1979), 447–68

Flood, John, *Poets Laureate in the Holy Roman Empire: A Bio-Bibliographical Handbook* (Berlin: de Gruyter, 2006)

Flood, Victoria, *Prophecy, Politics and Place in Medieval England: From Geoffrey of Monmouth to Thomas of Erceldoune* (Cambridge: D. S. Brewer, 2016)

Foister, Susan, 'Humanism and Art in the Early Tudor Period: John Leland's Poetic Praise of Painting', in *Reassessing Tudor Humanism*, ed. Jonathan Woolfson (London: Palgrave Macmillan, 2002), pp. 129–50

Fowler, Alastair, 'Perspective and Realism in the Renaissance', in *A Companion to Tudor Literature*, ed. Kent Cartwright (Oxford: Blackwell, 2010), pp. 339–49

Fowles, John, *Steep Holm: A Case History in the Study of Evolution* (Sherborne: Kenneth Allsop Memorial Trust, 1978)

Fulford, Michael, 'Calleva Atrebatum (Silchester, Hampshire, UK): An Early Medieval Extinction', in *Vrbes Extinctae: Archaeologies of Abandoned Classical Towns*, ed. Neil Christie and Andrea Augenti (Farnham: Ashgate, 2012), pp. 331–51

Fulford, Michael and Amanda Clarke, *Silchester Insula IX: Interim Reports 1–6* (Reading: The University of Reading, 1997–2004)

Fulton, Helen, 'Class and Nation: The English in Late-Medieval Welsh Poetry', in *Authority and Subjugation in Writing of Medieval Wales*, ed. Ruth Kennedy and Simon Meecham-Jones (London: Palgrave Macmillan, 2008), pp. 191–212

Fulton, Helen, 'Regions and Communities', in *The Oxford Handbook of Medieval Literature in English*, ed. Greg Walker and Elaine Treharne (Oxford: Oxford University Press, 2010), pp. 515–39

Fulton, Helen, 'Sir John Prise and His Books: Manuscript Culture in the March of Wales', *The Welsh History Review*, 31.1 (2022), 55–78

Furtado, Antonio L., 'Alexander of Macedonia to Arthur of Britain', *Arthuriana*, 5.3 (1995), 70–86

Gaines, Barry, 'Malory's Castles in Text and Illustration', in *The Medieval Castle: Romance and Reality*, ed. Kathryn Louise Reyerson and Faye Powe (Dubuque, IA: Kendell Hunt, 1984), pp. 215–28

Galbraith, V. H., 'An Autograph MS of Ranulph Higden's "Polychronicon"', *Huntington Library Quarterly*, 23.1 (1959), 1–18

Galloway, Andrew, 'Latin England', in *Imagining a Medieval English Nation*, ed. Kathy Lavezzo (Minneapolis, MN: 2004), pp. 41–95

Gellner, Ernest, *Nation and Nationalism* (Oxford: Blackwell, 1983)

Genet, Jean-Philippe, 'English Nationalism: Thomas Polton at the Council of Constance', *Nottingham Medieval Studies*, 28 (1984), 60–78

Gerould, Gordon, 'Tables in Medieval Churches', *Speculum*, 1 (1926), 439–40

Gibbs, Ray, *The Legendary Twelve Hides of Glastonbury* (Lampeter: Llanerch, 1988)

Gilchrist, Roberta, *Sacred Heritage: Monastic Archaeology, Identities, Beliefs* (Cambridge: Cambridge University Press, 2020)

Gilchrist, Roberta and Cheryl Green, *Glastonbury Abbey: Archaeological Investigations, 1904–79* (London: Society of Antiquaries of London, 2015)

Gillingham, John, 'Historians Without Hindsight: Coggeshall, Diceto and Howden on the Early Years of John's Reign', in *King John: New Interpretations*, ed. S. D. Church (Woodbridge: Boydell, 1999), pp. 1–26

Gillingham, John, *The English in the Twelfth Century: Imperialism, National Identity, and Political Values* (Woodbridge: Boydell, 2000)

Gillings, Mark, 'Chorography, Phenomenology and the Antiquarian Tradition', *Cambridge Archaeological Journal*, 21.1 (2011), 53–64, https://doi.org/10.1017/S0959774311000035

Glennie, J. S. Stuart, 'A Journey through Arthurian Scotland', *Macmillan's Magazine*, December 1867, pp. 161–74

Glennie, J. S. Stuart, *Arthurian Localities: Their Historical Origin, Chief Country and Fingalian Relations with a Map of Arthurian Scotland* (Edinburgh: Edmonston and Douglas, 1869)

Goldstein, R. James, *The Matter of Scotland: Historical Narrative in Medieval Scotland* (Lincoln, NE: University of Nebraska Press, 1993)

Gompf, L., *Joseph Iscanus: Werke und Briefe* (Leiden: Brill, 1970)

Goodall, John A., 'The Glastonbury Abbey Memorial Plate Reconsidered', in *Glastonbury Abbey and the Arthurian Tradition*, ed. James Carley (Cambridge: D. S. Brewer, 2001), pp. 185–92

Goodall, John A., 'The Chantry Chapel at Guy's Cliffe, Warwick', in *Coventry: Medieval Art, Architecture and Archaeology in the City and its Vicinity*, ed. Linda Monckton and Richard K. Morris (London: Routledge, 2011), pp. 304–17

Gornik, Vivian Beatrice, 'Producing the Past: Contested Heritage and Tourism in Glastonbury and Tintagel' (unpublished doctoral thesis, University of South Florida, 2018)

Gourvitch, I., 'The Welsh Element in the *Polyolbion*: Drayton's Sources', *The Review of English Studies*, 4.13 (1928), 69–77

Gourvitch, I., 'A Note on Drayton and Philemon Holland', *The Modern Language Review*, 25.3 (1930), 332–36

Gossedge, Rob and Stephen Knight, 'The Arthur of the Sixteenth to Nineteenth Centuries', in *The Cambridge Companion to the Arthurian Legend*, ed. Elizabeth Archibald and Ad Putter (Cambridge: Cambridge University Press, 2009), pp. 103–19

Gottfried, Rudolph B., 'The Early Development of the Section on Ireland in Camden's Britannia', *ELH [English Literary History]*, 10.2 (1943), 117–30

Gouttebroze, Jean-Guy, 'Melkin et Les Treize Boules de Cristal', *Journal of the International Arthurian Society*, 6.1 (2018), 70–94

Graesse, J. G., *Orbis Latinus: Lexikon lateinischer geographischer Namen des Mittelalters und der Neuzeit*, ed. Helmut Plechl and Sophie-Charlotte Plechl, 3 vols (Brunswick: Klinkhardt und Biermann, 1972)

Gransden, Antonia, 'Antiquarian Studies in Fifteenth-Century England', *The Antiquaries Journal*, 60.1 (1980), 75–97

Gransden, Antonia, *Legends, Traditions and History in Medieval England* (Cambridge: Cambridge University Press, 1992)
Gransden, Antonia, *Historical Writing in England*, 2 vols (London: Routledge, 1982)
Gransden, Antonia, 'The Growth of the Glastonbury Traditions and Legends in the Twelfth Century', in *Glastonbury Abbey and the Arthurian Tradition*, ed. James Carley, 2nd edn (Cambridge: D. S. Brewer, 2001), pp. 29–54
Grant, Alexander and Keith J. Stringer, eds, *Uniting the Kingdom? The Making of British History* (London: Routledge, 1995)
de Grazia, Margreta, 'The Modern Divide: From Either Side', *Journal of Medieval and Early Modern Studies* 37.3 (2007), 453–67
Green, Caitlin R., *Concepts of Arthur* (Stroud: Tempus, 2008)
Green, Caitlin R., *Arthuriana: Early Arthurian Tradition and the Origins of the Legend* (Louth: Lindes Press, 2009)
Green, Caitlin R., 'John Dee, King Arthur, and the Conquest of the Arctic', *The Heroic Age: A Journal of Early Medieval Northwestern Europe*, 15 (2012), www.heroicage.org/issues/15/green.php [accessed 25 January 2020]
Green, D. H., *The Beginnings of Medieval Romance: Fact and Fiction, 1150–1220* (Cambridge: Cambridge University Press, 2000)
Greenway, D. E., 'Henry [Henry of Huntingdon] (c. 1088–c. 1157), *Oxford Dictionary of National Biography*, www.oxforddnb.com/view/10.1093/ref:odnb/9780198614128.001.0001/odnb-9780198614128-e-12970 [accessed 7 December 2018]
Greenslade, M. W., 'Introduction: County History', in *English County Histories: A Guide*, ed. C. R. J. Currie and C. P. Lewis (Stroud: Sutton, 1994), pp. 9–25
Griffith, David, 'The Visual History of Guy of Warwick', in *Guy of Warwick: Icon and Ancestor*, ed. Rosalind Field and Alison Wiggins (Cambridge: D. S. Brewer, 2017), pp. 110–32
Griffith, Richard R., 'The Authorship Question Reconsidered', in *Aspects of Malory*, ed. Toshiyuki Takamiya and Derek Brewer (Cambridge: D. S. Brewer and Rowman & Littlefield, 1981), pp. 159–78
Grooms, Chris, *Cewri Cymru / Giants of Wales* (Lampeter: E. Mellen Press, 1993)
Gwenogvryn Evans, J., *Reports on Manuscripts in the Welsh Language* (London: Historical Manuscripts Commission, 1898–1910), I (1898)
Hadfield, Andrew, 'Spenser, Drayton, and the Question of Britain', *The Review of English Studies*, 51.204 (2000), 582–99

Hahn, Thomas, ed., *Sir Gawain: Eleven Romances and Tales*, TEAMS (Kalamazoo, MI: Medieval Institute Publications, 1995)

Haines, C. R., *Dover Priory: A History of the Priory of St Mary the Virgin, and St Martin of the New Work* (Cambridge: Cambridge University Press, 1930)

Haines, R. M., 'Canterbury versus York: Fluctuating Fortunes in a Perennial Conflict', in *Ecclesia Anglicana: Studies in the English Church of the Later Middle Ages*, ed. R. M. Haines (Toronto: University of Toronto Press, 1989), pp. 69–105

Hakluyt, Richard, *The principal navigations, voiages and discoveries of the English nation*, 2 vols, ed. David Quinn (Cambridge: Hakluyt Society, 1965)

Hale, Amy, 'Representing the Cornish: Contesting Heritage Interpretation in Cornwall', *Tourist Studies*, 1.2 (2001), 185–96

Hale, John R., *England and the Italian Renaissance: The Growth of Interest in its History and Art*, 4th edn (London: Blackwell, 2005)

Hammer, Jacob, 'Une version métrique de l'*Historia Regum Britanniae* de Geoffroy de Monmouth', *Latomus*, 2.2 (1938), 131–51

Hanna, Elizabeth, 'A "Scottish Monmouth"? Hector Boece's Arthurian Revisions', in *The Impact of Latin Culture on Medieval and Early Modern Scottish Writing*, ed. Alessandra Petrina and Ian Johnson (Kalamazoo, MI: Medieval Institute Publications, 2018), pp. 105–26

Hanning, R. W., '*Inventio Arthuri*: A Comment on the Essays of Geoffrey Ashe and D. R. Howlett', *Arthuriana*, 5.3 (1995), 96–100

Harper-Bill, Christopher, 'Dean Colet's Sermon and the Nature of the Pre-Reformation Church', *History*, 73 (1988), 191–210

Harris, G. L., 'Humphrey, Duke of Gloucester (1390–1447)', *Oxford Dictionary of National Biography* (Oxford: Oxford University Press, 2004), www.oxforddnb.com/view/article/14155 [accessed 15 August 2017]

Harris, G. L., *The Pre-Reformation Church in England*, 2nd edn (London: Longman, 1996)

Harris, Oliver D., '"Motheaten, Mouldye, and Rotten": The Early Custodial History and Dissemination of John Leland's Manuscript Remains', *Bodleian Library Record*, 18.5 (2005), 460–501

Harris, Oliver D., 'John Leland and the "Briton Brykes"', *The Antiquaries Journal*, 87 (2007), 346–56

Harris, Oliver D., 'William Camden, Philemon Holland and the 1610 Translation of Britannia', *The Antiquaries Journal*, 95 (2015), 279–303

Harris, Oliver D., '"Which I Have Beholden with Most Curiouse Eyes": The Lead Cross from Glastonbury Abbey', *Arthurian Literature*, 34 (2018), 88–129

Harrison, Frederick, *Life in a Medieval College: The Story of the Vicars-Choral of York Minster* (London: J. Murray, 1952)
Harvey, P. D. A., *The History of Topographical Maps: Symbols, Pictures and Surveys* (London: Thames and Hudson, 1980)
Haverfield, F., 'Voreda, the Roman Fort at Plumpton Wall', *Transactions of the Cumberland and Westmorland Antiquarian and Archaeological Society*, 13.2 (1913), 177–99
Hay, Denys, *Polydore Vergil: Renaissance Historian and Man of Letters* (Oxford: Clarendon Press, 1952)
Heard, Kate, 'A Glazing Scheme for Archbishop John Stafford', *Journal of Ecclesiastical History*, 60.4 (2009), 263–88
Heers, Jacques, *Le Moyen Age: Une Imposture* (Paris: Perrin, 1992)
Helgerson, Richard, 'The Land Speaks: Cartography, Chorography, and Subversion in Renaissance England', *Representations*, 16 (1986), 50–85
Helgerson, Richard, *Forms of Nationhood: The Elizabethan Writing of England* (Chicago, IL: Chicago University Press, 1992)
Heng, Geraldine, 'The Romance of England: Richard Coer De Lyon, Saracens, Jews, and the Politics of Race and Nation', in *The Postcolonial Middle Ages*, ed. Jeffrey Jerome Cohen (New York: Palgrave Macmillan US, 2000), pp. 135–71
Herbert McAvoy, Liz, 'Anchorites in Medieval Wales', in *Anchoritic Traditions of Medieval Europe*, ed. Liz Herbert McAvoy (Woodbridge: Boydell, 2010), pp. 195–216
Herendeen, W. H., 'Wanton Discourse and the Engines of Time: William Camden – Historian Among Poets-Historical', in *Renaissance Rereadings: Intertext and Context*, ed. Maryanne Cline Horowitz, A. J. Cruz, and Wendy Ann Furman (Champaign, IL: University of Illinois Press, 1988), pp. 142–56
Herendeen, W. H., *William Camden: A Life in Context* (Woodbridge: Boydell, 2007)
Herklotz, Ingo, 'Arnaldo Momigliano's "Ancient History and the Antiquarian": A Critical Review', in *Momogliano and Antiquarianism: Foundations of the Modern Cultural Sciences*, ed. Peter N. Miller (Toronto: University of Toronto Press, 2007), pp. 127–53
Hiatt, Alfred, 'Forgery at the University of Cambridge', *New Medieval Literatures*, 3 (1999), 95–118
Hiatt, Alfred, *The Making of Medieval Forgeries: False Documents in Fifteenth-Century England* (Toronto: University of Toronto Press, 2004)
Higham, N. J., *King Arthur: Myth-Making and History* (London: Routledge, 2002)
Hilka, Alfons, 'Eine mittellateinische Dichterfehde. Versus Michaelis

Cornubiensis contra Henricum Abricensem', in *Mittelalterlich Handschriften: Paläographische, kunsthistorische, literarische, und bibliotheksgeschichtliche Untersuchungen; Festgabe zum 60. Geburtstag von Hermann Degering*, ed. Aloys Bömer and Joachim Kirchner (Leipzig: Hiersemann, 1926), pp. 123–54

'Hill of Dunnideer, fort, platform settlement and tower (SM95)', Historic Environment Scotland, 1934, amended 2003, http://portal.historicenvironment.scot/designation/SM95 [accessed 5 November 2019]

Hiscock, Andrew, *Reading Memory in Early Modern Literature* (Cambridge: Cambridge University Press, 2011)

Hobsbawm, E. J., *Nations and Nationalism Since 1780: Programme, Myth, Reality* (Cambridge: Cambridge University Press, 1990)

Hodges, Kenneth, 'How King Arthur Invented Christmas: Reimagining Arthur and Rome in Early Modern Scotland and England', *Arthuriana*, 29.3 (2019), 25–42

Holbrook, Sue Ellen Holbrook, 'Malory's Identification of Camelot as Winchester', in *Studies in Malory*, ed. James W. Spisak (Kalamazoo MI: Western Michigan University Press, 1985), pp. 13–27

Holtorf, C., 'On Pastness: A Reconsideration of Materiality in Archaeological Object Authenticity', *Anthropological Quarterly*, 86.2 (2013), 427–43

Hosington, Brenda M., '"If the Past is a Foreign Country": Neo-Latin Histories, Their Paratexts, and English Cultural Translation', *Canadian Review of Comparative Literature*, 41.4 (2014), 432–55

Housman, John E., 'Higden, Trevisa, Caxton and the Beginnings of Arthurian Criticism', *Review of English Studies*, 23 (1947), 209–17

Howell, Raymond, 'The Demolition of the Roman Tetrapylon in Caerleon: An Erasure of Memory', *Oxford Journal of Archaeology*, 19.4 (2000), 387–95

Howell, Raymond, 'Roman Past and Medieval Present: Caerleon as a Focus for Continuity and Conflict in the Middle Ages', *Studia Celtica*, 46.1 (2012), 11–21

Hughes, Jonathan, *Arthurian Myths and Alchemy: The Kingship of Edward IV* (Stroud: Sutton, 2002)

Hunt, R. W., 'The Need for a Guide to the Editors of Patristic Texts in the Sixteenth Century', *Studia Patristica*, 17.1 (1982), 365–71

Hurlock, Kathryn, *Medieval Welsh Pilgrimage, c.1100–1500* (Manchester: Palgrave Macmillan, 2018)

Ingham, Patricia Clare, *Sovereign Fantasies: Arthurian Romance and the Making of Britain* (Philadelphia, PA: University of Pennsylvania Press, 2001)

Isidore of Seville, *The Etymologies of Isidore of Seville*, ed. Stephen A. Barney (Cambridge: Cambridge University Press, 2006)

Iqbal, Nosheen, 'A Bridge Too Far at Tintagel? Not According to English Heritage', *The Guardian*, 11 August 2019

Jackson, K. H., 'Nennius and the Twenty-Eight Cities of Britain', *Antiquity*, 12 (1938), 44–55

James, M. R., *The Ancient Libraries of Canterbury and Dover* (Cambridge: Cambridge University Press, 1903)

Jarman, A. O. H., 'Cerdd Ysgolan', *Ysgrifau beirniadol*, 10 (1977), 51–78

Jeffrey, Stuart, 'Challenging Heritage Visualisation: Beauty, Aura, and Democratisation', *Open Archaeology*, 1.1 (2015), www.degruyter.com/view/j/opar.2014.1.issue-1/opar-2015-0008/opar-2015-0008.xml [accessed 7 March 2020]

Jenkins, John, 'Modelling the Cult of Thomas Becket in Canterbury Cathedral', *Journal of the British Archaeological Association*, 173 (2020), 100–23

Johnson, D. P., 'Bishops and Deans: London and the Province of Canterbury in the Twelfth Century', *Historical Research*, 86.234 (2013), 551–78

Jones, G. H., *Celtic Britain and the Pilgrim Movement* (London: The Honourable Society of Cymmrodorion, 1912)

Jones, G. R. J., 'The Site of Llys Aberffraw', *Transactions of the Anglesey Antiquarian Society* (1957), 1–4

Jones, G. R. J., 'Early Territorial Organization in Gwynedd and Elmet', *Northern History*, 10.1 (1975), 3–27

Jones, G. R. J., 'Early Customary Tenures in Wales and Open-Field Agriculture', in *The Origins of Open-Field Agriculture*, ed. Trevor Rowley (London: Routledge, 1981), pp. 202–25

Jones, G. R. J., 'Some Donations to Bishop Wilfrid in Northern England', *Northern History*, 31.1 (1995), 22–38

Jones, Norman L. and Daniel Woolf, *Local Identities in Late Medieval and Early Modern England* (New York: Palgrave Macmillan, 2007)

Jones, Thomas, 'A Sixteenth Century Version of the Arthurian Cave Legend', in *Studies in Language and Literature in Honour of Margaret Schlauch*, ed. Mieczyslaw Brahmer, Stanislaw Helsztynski, and Julian Krzyzanowski (Warsaw: PWN, 1966), pp. 175–85

Jones, Thomas, 'Chwedl Huail ap Caw ac Arthur', in *Astudiaethau Amrywriol a Gyflwynir i Syr Thomas Parry-Williams* (Cardiff: University of Wales Press, 1968), pp. 48–66 (pp. 55–56)

Juhász-Ormsby, Ágnes and James P. Carley, 'Survey of Henrician Humanism', in *The Oxford History of Classical Reception in English*

Literature, ed. Rita Copeland (Oxford: Oxford University Press, 2016), I, 583–605

Kalinke, Marianne E., ed., *The Arthur of the North* (Cardiff: University of Wales Press, 2011)

Kantorowicz, Ernst, *The King's Two Bodies: A Study in Medieval Political Theology*, ed. Conrad Leyser and William Chester Jordan, 3rd edn (Princeton, NJ: Princeton University Press, 2016)

Kaufman, Peter I., 'Polydore Vergil and the Strange Disappearance of Christopher Urswick', *Sixteenth Century Journal*, 17 (1986), 69–85

Kedourie, Elie, ed., *Nationalism* (London: Hutchinson, 1960)

Keeler, Laura, *Geoffrey of Monmouth and the Late Latin Chroniclers 1300–1500* (Berkeley, CA: University of California Publications in English, 1946)

Keith, W. J., 'Thomas Hardy and the Literary Pilgrims', *Nineteenth-Century Fiction*, 24 (1969), 80–92

Kelly, Susan, 'Place-Names in the *Awntyrs off Arthure*', *Literary Onomastic Studies*, 6 (1979), 1–38

Kendrick, T. D., *British Antiquity* (London: Methuen, 1950)

Kennedy, Beverley, 'Gawain and Heroic Knighthood in Malory', in *Gawain: A Casebook*, ed. Keith Busby and Raymond H. Thompson (London: Routledge, 2006), pp. 287–96

Kennedy, E. D., 'Malory's Use of Hardyng's *Chronicle*', *Notes & Queries*, 16 (1969), 167–70

Kennedy, E. D., 'Malory's Use of Hardyng's *Chronicle*: A Reconsideration', *West Virginia Philological Papers*, 54 (2011), 8–15

Kennedy, E. D., 'John Hardyng and the Holy Grail', *Arthurian Literature*, 8 (1989)

Kennedy, E. D., 'Sir Thomas Malory's (French) Romance and (English) Chronicle', in *Arthurian Studies in Honour of P. J. C. Field*, ed. Bonnie Wheeler (Cambridge: D. S. Brewer, 2004), pp. 223–34

Kennedy, William J., *The Site of Petrarchism: Early Modern National Sentiment in Italy, France, and England* (Baltimore, MD: Johns Hopkins University Press, 2003)

Ker, N. R., 'Sir John Prise', *The Library*, 10:1 (1955), 1–24

Ker, N. R., *Medieval Libraries of Great Britain: A List of Surviving Books*, 2nd edn (London: Royal Historical Society, 1964)

Ker, N. R. and A. J. Piper, *Medieval Manuscripts in British Libraries* (Oxford: Clarendon Press, 1977)

Kerby-Fulton, Kathryn, *The Clerical Proletariat and the Resurgence of Medieval English Poetry* (Philadelphia, PA: University of Pennsylvania Press, 2021)

Kerr, Julie, *Monastic Hospitality: The Benedictines in England, c. 1070–c. 1250, The Administrative Structure* (Woodbridge: Boydell, 2007)

Kestemont, Mike, F. Karsdorp, E. de Bruijn, M. Driscoll, K. A. Kapitan, P. Ó Macháin, D. Sawyer, R. Sleiderink, and A. Chao, 'Forgotten Books: The Application of Unseen Species Models to the Survival of Culture', *Science*, 375 (2022), 765–69

Kewes, Paulina, ed., *The Uses of History in Early Modern England* (San Marino, CA: Huntington Library, 2006)

Kewes, Paulina, Ian W. Archer, and Felicity Heal, eds, *The Oxford Handbook of Holinshed's Chronicles* (Oxford: Oxford University Press, 2013)

Kimball Smith, Donald, *The Cartographic Imagination in Early Modern England: Re-Writing the World in Marlowe, Spenser, Raleigh and Marvell* (Farnham: Ashgate, 2008)

King, Andrew and Matthew Woodcock, eds, *Medieval Into Renaissance: Essays for Helen Cooper* (Cambridge: D. S. Brewer, 2016)

Kingsford, C. L., *English Historical Literature in the Fifteenth Century* (New York: Burt Franklin, 1927)

Klausner, David N., 'The Historical Arthur: Dryden's Great Leap Backwards', *Restoration: Studies in English Literary Culture, 1660–1700*, 34.1–2 (2010), 21–32

Knight, Jeremy, 'Welsh Stones and Oxford Scholars: Three Rediscoveries', *Bulletin of the Institute of Classical Studies*, 44.S75 (2000), 91–101

Knight, Stephen, *Arthurian Literature and Society* (London: Palgrave Macmillan, 1983)

Koebner, Richard, '"The Imperial Crown of this Realm": Henry VIII, Constantine the Great, and Polydore Vergil', *Bulletin of the Institute of Historical Research*, 26.73 (1953), 29–52

Kooper, Erik, 'Longleat House MS 55', in *The Prose Brut and Other Late Medieval Chronicles: Essays in Honour of Lister M. Matheson*, ed. Jaclyn Rajsic, Erik Kooper and Dominique Hoche (York: York Medieval Press, 2017), pp. 75–93

Krochalis, Jeanne, 'Magna Tabula: The Glastonbury Tablets', in *Glastonbury Abbey and the Arthurian Tradition*, ed. James P. Carley, 2nd edn (Cambridge: D. S. Brewer, 2001), pp. 435–567

Krochalis, Jeanne and Alison Stones, *The Pilgrim's Guide: A Critical Edition*, 2 vols (London: Harvey Miller, 1998)

Lacy, Norris J., 'The Arthurian Legend Before Chrétien', in *A Companion to Chrétien de Troyes*, ed. Norris J. Lacy and Joan Tasker Grimbert (Cambridge: D. S. Brewer, 2005), pp. 43–51

Lagorio, Valerie M., '*Joseph of Arimathie*: English Hagiography in Transition', in *Medievalia et Humanistica*, New Series, 6 (1975), 91–101

Lagorio, Valerie M., 'The Glastonbury Legends and the English Arthurian Grail Romances', *Neophilologische Mitteilungen*, 79.4 (1978), 359–66

Lagorio, Valerie M., 'The Evolving Legend of St Joseph of Glastonbury', in *Glastonbury Abbey and the Arthurian Tradition*, ed. James P. Carley, 2nd edn (Cambridge: D. S. Brewer, 2001), pp. 55–81

Lamont, Margaret, 'Becoming English: Ronwenne's Wassail, Language, and National Identity in the Middle English Prose *Brut*', *Studies in Philology*, 107.3 (2010), 283–309

Lancaster, 'Edward Bisse (c. 1588–by 1647), History of Parliament Online, www.historyofparliamentonline.org/volume/1604-1629/member/bisse-edward- 1588-1647 [accessed 2 August 2018]

Lapidge, Michael, 'An Edition of *De vera historia de morte Arthuri*', *Arthurian Literature*, 1 (1981), 79–93

Lapidge, Michael, 'Additional Manuscript Evidence for *De vera historia de morte Arthuri*', *Arthurian Literature*, 2 (1982), 163–68

Lavezzo, Kathy, ed., *Imagining a Medieval English Nation* (Minneapolis, MN: University of Minnesota Press, 2004)

Lavezzo, Kathy, *Angels on the Edge of the World: Geography, Literature, and English Community, 1000–1534* (Ithaca, NY: Cornell University Press, 2006)

Lavezzo, Kathy, 'Nation', in *A Handbook of Middle English Studies*, ed. Marion Turner (London: Wiley, 2013), pp. 363–78

Lawson, J., 'Chronotope, Story, and Historical Geography: Mikhail Bakhtin and the Space-Time of Narratives', *Antipode*, 43.2 (2011), 384–412

Leach, Stephen, 'King Arthur's Round Table Revisited: A Review of Two Rival Interpretations of a Henge Monument Near Penrith, in Cumbria', *The Antiquaries Journal*, 99 (2019), 417–34

Lee, Alexander, Pierre Péporté, and Harry Schnitker, eds, *Renaissance? Perceptions of Continuity and Discontinuity in Europe, c. 1300–c. 1550* (Leiden: Brill, 2010)

Legassie, Shayne Aaron, *The Medieval Invention of Travel* (Chicago, IL: University of Chicago Press, 2017)

Leitch, Megan L., 'Introduction', in *Romance Rewritten: The Evolution of Middle English Romance: A Tribute to Helen Cooper*, ed. Elizabeth Archibald, Megan G. Leitch, and Corinne Saunders (Cambridge: D. S. Brewer, 2018), pp. 1–24

Levelt, Sjoerd, 'Citation and Misappropriation in Geoffrey of Monmouth's *Historia Regum Britannie* and the Anglo-Latin Historiographical Tradition', in *Citation, Intertextuality and Memory in the Middle Ages and Renaissance*, ed. Giulino Di Bacco and Yolanda Plumley (Liverpool: Liverpool University Press, 2013), II, pp. 137–47

Levy, F. J., 'The Making of Camden's Britannia', *Bibliothèque d'Humanisme et Renaissance*, 26 (1964), 70–97

Levy, F. J., 'Sir Philip Sidney and the Idea of History', *Bibliothèque d'Humanisme et Renaissance*, 26:3 (1964), 608–17

Levy, F. J., *Tudor Historical Thought* (San Marino, CA: Huntingdon Library Publication, 1967)

Lindley, Phillip, *Tomb Destruction and Scholarship: Medieval Monuments in Early Modern England* (Donington: Shaun Tyas, 2007)

Liu, Yin, 'Building History in the English Rous Roll', *Viator – Medieval and Renaissance Studies*, 42.2 (2011), 307–20

Loades, David Michael, *Power in Tudor England* (New York: Palgrave Macmillan, 1997)

Loomis, R. S., 'From Segontium to Sinadon: The Legends of a Cité Gaste', *Speculum*, 22.4 (1947), 520–33

Loomis, R. S., 'Edward I, Arthurian Enthusiast', *Speculum*, 28 (1953), 114–27

Loomis, R. S., 'Scotland and the Arthurian Legend', *Proceedings of the Society of Antiquaries of Scotland*, 89 (1955), 1–21

Loomis, R. S., 'Arthurian Tradition and Folklore', *Folklore*, 69 (1958), 1–25

Lloyd, Scott, *The Arthurian Place Names of Wales* (Cardiff: University of Wales Press, 2017)

Lloyd, Scott, 'Arthur Place-names of Wales', in *Arthur in the Celtic Languages*, ed. Ceridwen Lloyd-Morgan and Erich Poppe (Cardiff: University of Wales Press, 2019), pp. 231–44

Lloyd-Morgan, Ceridwen, '*Breuddwyd Rhonabwy* and Later Arthurian Literature', in *The Arthur of the Welsh*, ed. Rachel Bromwich and Brynley F. Roberts (Cardiff: University of Wales Press, 1991), pp. 183–209

Lloyd-Morgan, Ceridwen, 'Oral et Écrit Dans La Chronique d'Elis Gruffydd', *Kreiz 5: Études Sur La Bretagne et Les Pays Celtiques*, 49.165 (1996), 179–86

Lloyd-Morgan, Ceridwen, 'From Ynys Wydrin to Glasynbri: Glastonbury in Welsh Vernacular Tradition', in *Glastonbury Abbey and the Arthurian Tradition*, ed. James Carley, 2nd edn (Cambridge: D. S. Brewer, 2001), pp. 161–77

Lloyd-Morgan, Ceridwen, 'Narratives and Non-Narratives: Aspects of Welsh Arthurian Tradition', *Arthurian Literature*, 21 (2004), 115–36

Lloyd-Morgan, Ceridwen, 'Welsh Tradition in Calais: Elis Gruffydd and his Biography of King Arthur', in *The Fortunes of King Arthur*, ed. Norris J. Lacy (Cambridge: D. S. Brewer, 2005), pp. 77–91

Lloyd-Morgan, Ceridwen, 'Crossing the Borders: Literary Borrowing in Medieval Wales and England', in *Authority and Subjugation in the*

Writing of Medieval Wales, ed. Ruth Kennedy and Simon Meecham-Jones (New York: Palgrave Macmillan, 2008), pp. 159–74

Lloyd-Morgan, Ceridwen, 'Writing Without Borders: Multilingual Content in Welsh Miscellanies from Wales, the Marches, and Beyond', in *Insular Books: Vernacular Manuscript Miscellanies in Late Medieval Britain*, ed. Margaret Connolly and Raluca Radulescu (London: The British Academy, 2015), pp. 175–92

Lloyd-Morgan, Ceridwen, 'Later Hybrid Narrative Texts in Middle Welsh', in *Arthur in the Celtic Languages*, ed. Ceridwen Lloyd-Morgan and Erich Poppe (Cardiff: University of Wales Press, 2019), pp. 203–13

Lloyd-Morgan, Ceridwen and Erich Poppe, eds, *Arthur in the Celtic Languages* (Cardiff: University of Wales Press, 2019)

Luders, Alexander, Sir T. Edlyn Tomlins, J. France, W. E. Taunton, and J. Raithby, eds, *The Statutes of the Realm III: 1509–1545* (London: The Record Commission, 1817)

Luft, Diana, Peter Wynn Thomas, and D. Mark Smith, eds, 'Rhyddiaith Gymraeg 1300–1425' (2013), www.rhyddiaithganoloesol.caerdydd.ac.uk/en/project.php [accessed 14 October 2019]

Lupack, Alan, 'The Arthurian Legend in the Sixteenth to Eighteenth Centuries', in *A Companion to Arthurian Literature*, ed. Helen Fulton (Oxford: Blackwell, 2012), pp. 340–54

Luxford, Julian M., *The Art and Architecture of English Benedictine Monasteries, 1300–1540: A Patronage History* (Woodbridge: Boydell, 2005)

Maccoll, Alan, 'The Construction of England as Protestant "British" Nation in the Sixteenth Century', *Renaissance Studies*, 18.4 (2004), 7–13

Maccoll, Alan, 'The Meaning of "Britain" in Medieval and Early Modern England', *Journal of British Studies*, 45.2 (2006), 248–69

Macht, Claire, 'Changes in Monastic Historical Writing Throughout the Long Fifteenth Century', in *The Fifteenth Century XVI: Examining Identity*, ed. Linda Clark (Woodbridge: Boydell, 2018), pp. 1–26

Mann, Sylvia and David Kingsley, 'Playing Cards Depicting Maps of the British Isles, and of the English and Welsh Counties', *Map Collectors' Series*, 87 (1972), 3–35

Marchant, Alicia, 'John Hardyng's Scotland: Emotional Geographies and Forged Histories in the Fifteenth Century', in *Historicising Heritage and Emotions: The Affective Histories of Blood, Stone and Land*, ed. Alicia Marchant (London: Routledge, 2019), pp. 51–66

Marks, Richard, 'Picturing Word and Text in the Late Medieval Parish Church', in *Image, Text and Church, 1380–1600: Essays for Margaret*

Aston, ed. Linda Clark, Maureen Jurkowski and Colin Richmond (Toronto: PIMS, 2009), pp. 162–88

Martin, Molly, *Castles and Space in Malory's Morte Darthur* (Cambridge: D. S. Brewer, 2019)

Marvin, Julia, 'Arthur Authorized: The Prophecies of the Prose Brut Chronicle', *Arthurian Literature*, 22 (2005), 84–99

Marvin, Julia, *The Construction of Vernacular History in the Anglo-Norman Prose Brut Chronicle: The Manuscript Culture of Late Medieval England* (Woodbridge: Boydell, 2017)

Mason, David, 'Writing on the Wall: Chronicles Written for Public Display at St Paul's Cathedral, London', *The Medieval History Journal*, 26.1 (2023), 23–56

Massey, Doreen, *Space, Place, and Gender* (Minneapolis, MN: University of Minnesota Press, 1994)

Massey, Doreen, *For Space* (London: SAGE, 2005)

Matheson, Lister M., *The Prose Brut: The Development of a Middle English Chronicle* (Tempe, AZ: Arizona Centre for Medieval and Renaissance Studies, 1998)

Mathivet, Stephanie, 'Alice Buckton (1867–1944): The Legacy of a Froebelian in the Landscape of Glastonbury', *History of Education*, 35.2 (2006), 263–81

Mayger Hind, Arthur, 'A Historical Pack of Playing Cards', *British Museum Quarterly*, 13 (1938–39), 2–4

McEachern, Claire, *The Poetics of English Nationhood, 1590–1612* (Cambridge: Cambridge University Press, 1996)

McKibben, Sarah E., 'In Their "Owne Countre": Deriding and Defending the Early Modern Irish Nation after Gerald of Wales', *Eolas: The Journal of the American Society of Irish Medieval Studies*, 8 (2015), 39–70

McKinstry, Jamie, *Middle English Romance and the Craft of Memory* (Cambridge: D. S. Brewer, 2015)

McKisack, May, *Medieval History in the Tudor Age* (Oxford: Clarendon Press, 1971)

McLaren, Mary-Rose, *The London Chronicles of the Fifteenth Century: A Revolution in English Writing* (Cambridge: D. S. Brewer, 2002)

McRae, Andrew, *God Speed the Plough: The Representation of Agrarian England, 1500–1660* (Cambridge: Cambridge University Press, 2002)

Meacham, Thomas, 'Exchanging Performative Words: Epistolary Performance and University Drama in Late Medieval England', *Medieval English Theatre*, 22 (2010), 12–25

Mehl, Dieter, *The Middle English Romances of the Thirteenth and Fourteenth Centuries* (London: Routledge & Kegan Paul, 1968)
Mendyk, Stan, 'Early British Chorography', *The Sixteenth Century Journal*, 17 (1986), 459–81
Merkle Sorrell, Jeanne, 'Listening in Thin Places: Ethics in the Care of Persons with Alzheimer's Disease', *Advances in Nursing Science*, 29.2 (2006), 152–60
Millican, E. B., *Spenser and the Table Round*, 2nd edn (London: Cass, 1967)
Moll, Richard, 'Another Reference to John Hardyng's "Mewyn"', *Notes and Queries*, 245 (2000), 497–98
Moll, Richard, *Before Malory: Reading Arthur in Later Medieval England* (Toronto: University of Toronto Press, 2003)
Moll, Richard, 'Ebrauke and the Politics of Arthurian Geography', *Arthuriana*, 15.4 (2005), 65–71
Momogliano, Arnaldo, 'Ancient History and the Antiquarian', *Journal of the Warburg and Courtauld Institutes*, 13 (1950), 285–315
Moore, William H., 'Sources of Drayton's Conception of "Poly-Olbion"', *Studies in Philology*, 65.5 (1968), 783–803
Morgan, Gerald, 'Welsh Arthurian Literature', in *A History of Arthurian Scholarship*, ed. Norris J. Lacey (Cambridge: D. S. Brewer, 2006), pp. 77–84
Morgan, J. R., 'Make-believe and Make Believe: The Fictionality of the Greek Novels', in *Lies and Fiction in the Ancient World*, ed Christopher Gill (Liverpool: University of Liverpool Press, 1993), pp. 175–229
Morgan, Prys, 'Elis Gruffudd of Gronant: Tudor Chronicler Extraordinary', *Journal of the Flintshire Historical Society*, 25 (1971–72), 9–20
Morgan, Victor, 'The Cartographic Image of "The Country" in Early Modern England', *Transactions of the Royal Historical Society*, fifth series, 29 (1979), 129–54
Morgan Evans, Dai, '"King Arthur" and Cadbury Castle, Somerset', *The Antiquaries Journal*, 86 (2006), 227–53
Morland, John, 'Pomparles, Glastonbury', *Proceedings of the Somerset Archaeological and Natural History Society*, 58 (1912), 53–59
Morland, Stephen C., 'Hidation on the Glastonbury Estates: A Study in Tax Evasion', *Proceedings of the Somerset Archaeological and Natural History Society*, 114 (1970), 74–90
Morland, Stephen C., 'Glaston Twelve Hides', in *Glastonbury, Domesday and Related Studies*, ed. Stephen C. Morland (Glastonbury: Glastonbury Antiquarian Society, 1991), pp. 61–84
Morris, John, *The Age of Arthur: A History of the British Isles from 350 to 650* (London: Weidenfeld and Nicolson, 1973)

Mottram, Stewart, 'Empire, Exile, and England's "British Problem": Recent Approaches to Spenser's *Shepheardes Calendar* as a Colonial and Postcolonial Test', *Literature Compass*, 4.4 (2007), 1059–77

Mottram, Stewart, '"An Empire of Itself": Arthur as Icon of an English Empire, 1509–1547', *Arthurian Literature*, 25 (2008), 256–73

Muir, Lynette, 'King Arthur's Northern Conquests in the Leges Anglorum Londoniis Collectae', *Medium Aevum*, 37 (1968), 253–63

Mulligan, Amy C., 'Moses, Taliesin, and the Welsh Chosen People: Elis Gruffydd's Construction of a Biblical, British Past for Reformation Wales', *Studies in Philology*, 113.4 (2016), 765–96

Munby, Julian, Richard Barber, and Richard Brown, eds, *Edward III's Round Table at Windsor: The House of the Round Table and the Windsor Festival of 1344* (Woodbridge: Boydell, 2007)

Myers, Anne M., *Literature and Architecture in Early Modern England* (Baltimore, MD: Johns Hopkins University Press, 2013)

Nash, Owain, 'Elements of Identity: Gerald, the Humours and National Characteristics', in *Gerald of Wales: New Perspectives on a Medieval Writer and Critic*, ed. A. Joseph McMullen and Georgia Henley (Cardiff: University of Wales Press, 2018), pp. 203–20

Noble, James, 'Tintagel: The Best of English Twinkie', in *King Arthur in Popular Culture*, ed. Elizabeth S. Sklar and Donald L. Hoffmann (Jefferson, NC: McFarland, 2002), pp. 36–44

Nora, Pierre, 'Between Memory and History: Les Lieux de Mémoire', *Representations*, 26 (1989), 7–24

Nora, Pierre, *Rethinking France: Les Lieux de Mémoire: Volume 1 The State*, ed. David P. Jordan (Chicago, IL: University of Chicago Press, 2001)

Norris, Ralph C., *Malory's Library: The Sources of the Morte Darthur* (Cambridge: D. S. Brewer, 2008)

Nuti, Lucia, 'Mapping Places: Chorography and Vision in the Renaissance', in *Mappings*, ed. Denis Cosgrave (London: Reaktion Books, 1999), pp. 90–108

O' Gorman, Richard, '*The Gospel of Nicodemus* in the Vernacular Literature of Medieval France', in *The Medieval Gospel of Nicodemus: Texts, Intertexts, and Contexts in Western Europe*, ed. Zbigniew Izydorczyk (Tempe, AZ: Medieval and Renaissance Texts and Studies, 1997), pp. 103–31

Orange, Hilary and Patrick Laviolette, 'A Disgruntled Tourist in King Arthur's Court: Archaeology and Identity at Tintagel, Cornwall', *Public Archaeology*, 9.2 (2010), 85–107

Orme, Nicholas, 'Place and Past in Medieval England', *History Today*, July 2008, pp. 25–30

Owen, Morfydd E., 'The Prose of the *Cywydd* Period', in *A Guide to Welsh*

Literature 1282–c.1550, ed. A. O. H. Jarman and Gwilyn Rees Hughes (Cardiff: University of Wales Press, 1997), II, pp. 319–29

Oxford English Dictionary, accessed online (Oxford University Press, December 2019), https://oed.com/ [accessed 3 February 2020]

Ovenden, Richard, and Stuart Handley, 'Howard, Lord William (1563–1640), Antiquary and Landowner', *The Oxford Dictionary of National Biography* (Oxford: Oxford University Press, 2004), https://doi.org/10.1093/ref:odnb/13947

Padel, Oliver J., 'Some South-Western Sites with Arthurian Associations', in *The Arthur of the Welsh* (Cardiff: University of Wales Press, 1991), pp. 227–48

Padel, Oliver J., 'The Nature of Arthur', *Cambrian Medieval Celtic Studies*, 27 (1994), 1–31

Padel, Oliver J., 'Recent Work on the Origins of the Arthurian Legend: A Comment', *Arthuriana*, 5.3 (1995), 102–14

Padel, Oliver J., 'Cornwall and the Matter of Britain', in *Arthur in the Celtic Languages*, ed. Ceridwen Lloyd-Morgan and Erich Poppe (Cardiff: University of Wales Press, 2019), pp. 263–80

Palmer, Kingsley, *The Folklore of Somerset* (London: B. T. Batsford, 1976)

Parins, Marylyn, ed. and trans, *Sir Thomas Malory: The Critical Heritage* (London: Routledge, 1987)

Parry, Graham, *The Trophies of Time: English Antiquarians of the Seventeenth Century* (Oxford: Oxford University Press, 1995)

Parry, J. D., 'Following Malory out of Arthur's World', *Modern Philology*, 95.2 (1997), 147–69

Passey, Joan, *Cornish Gothic, 1830–1913* (Cardiff: University of Wales Press, 2023)

Patterson, William, 'Oliver Castle, Upper Tweeddale', *The Journal of Scottish Name Studies*, 11 (2017), 93–102

Pearsall, Derek, 'The Idea of Englishness in the Fifteenth Century', in *Nation, Court and Culture: New Essays on Fifteenth-Century English Poetry*, ed. Helen Cooney (Dublin: Four Courts Press, 2001), pp. 15–27

Penman, M. A., *David II, 1329–1327* (London: Tuckwell, 2004)

Peverley, Sarah L., '"A Good Exampell to Avoide Diane": Reader Responses to John Hardyng's Chronicle in the Fifteenth and Sixteenth Centuries', *Poetica*, 63 (2005), 1–18

Piggott, Stuart, 'William Camden and the *Britannia*', in *Ruins in a Landscape: Essays in Antiquarianism* (Edinburgh: Edinburgh University Press, 1976), pp. 33–53

Pochoda, Elizabeth T., *Arthurian Propaganda: Le Morte Darthur as an Historical Ideal of Life* (Chapel Hill, NC: University of North Carolina Press, 1971)

Pocock, D. C. D., 'Haworth: The Experience of Literary Place', in *Geography and Literature: A Meeting of the Disciplines*, ed. William E. Mallory and Paul Simpson-Housley (Syracuse, NY: Syracuse University Press, 1987), pp. 135–44

Pocock, J. G. A., 'British History: A Plea for a New Subject', *The Journal of Modern History*, 47 (1975), 601–21

Pohl, Benjamin, 'When Did Robert of Torigni First Receive Henry of Huntingdon's *Historia Anglorum*, and Why Does It Matter?', *Haskins Society Journal*, 26 (2015), 143–67

Powicke, Maurice, 'William Camden', *Essays and Studies*, new series, 1 (1948), 67–84

Pryce, Huw, 'Gerald of Wales and the Welsh Past', in *Gerald of Wales: New Perspectives on a Medieval Writer and Critic*, ed. Georgia Henley and A. Joseph McMullen (Cardiff: University of Wales Press, 2018), pp. 19–45

Pryce, Huw, 'Sir John Prise', *The Oxford Dictionary of National Biography*, www.oxforddnb.com/view/10.1093/ref:odnb/9780198614128.001. 0001/odnb- 9780198614128-e-22752 [accessed 7 December 2018]

Ptolemy, *Ptolemy's Geography: An Annotated Translation of the Theoretical Chapters*, ed. and trans. A. L. Berggren and Alexander Jones (Princeton, NJ: Princeton University Press, 2000)

Purvis, J. S., ed., 'The Tables of the York Vicars Choral', *The Yorkshire Archaeological Journal*, 41 (1966), 741–48

Putter, Ad, 'Finding Time for Romance: Mediaeval Arthurian Literary History', *Medium Aevum*, 63 (1994), 1–12

Putter, Ad, *Sir Gawain and the Green Knight and French Arthurian Romance* (Oxford: Oxford University Press, 1995)

Putter, Ad and Jane Gilbert, eds, *The Spirit of Medieval English Popular Romance* (London: Routledge, 2000)

Putter, Ad, 'King Arthur at Oxbridge: Nicholas Cantelupe, Geoffrey of Monmouth, and Cambridge's Arthurian Foundation Myth', *Medium Aevum*, 72.1 (2003), 63–81

Putter, Ad, 'Latin Historiography After Geoffrey of Monmouth', in *The Arthur of Medieval Latin Literature*, ed. Siân Echard (Cardiff: University of Wales Press, 2011), pp. 85–108

Putter, Ad, 'Gerald of Wales and the Prophet Merlin', *Anglo-Norman Studies*, 31 (2012), 90–103

Radulescu, Raluca L., '"Talkyng of cronycles of kinges and of other polycyez': Fifteenth-Century Miscellanies, the Brut and the Readership of Le Morte Darthur', *Arthurian Literature*, 18 (2001), 125–42

Radulescu, Raluca L., 'The Percy Folio', in *The Encyclopedia of Medieval Literature in Britain*, ed. Siân Echard and Robert Rouse, 4 vols (London: Wiley-Blackwell, 2017), pp. 1512–515

Rahtz, Philip, *Glastonbury* (London: Batsford, 1993)

Raine, James, *The Historians of the Church of York and Its Archbishops*, 2 vols (London: Longman, 1886)

Ralph, Karen, 'Medieval Antiquarianism: The Butlers and Artistic Patronage in Fifteenth Century Ireland', *Eolas*, 7 (2014), 2–27

Rees, David, *The Son of Prophecy* (London: Black Raven Press, 1985)

Regan, Paul, 'Cartography, Chorography and Patriotic Sentiment in the Sixteenth-Century Low Countries', in *Public Opinion and Changing Identities in the Early Modern Netherlands: Essays in Honour of Alastair Duke*, ed. A. C. Duke, J. Pollmann, and A. P. Spicer (Leiden: Brill, 2007), pp. 49–68

Richardson, Henry Gerald, 'The Coronation in Medieval England: The Evolution of the Office and the Oath', *Traditio*, 16 (1960), 111–202

Richardson, R. C., 'William Camden and the Re-Discovery of England', *Transactions of the Leicestershire Archaeological and Historical Society*, 78 (2004), 108–23

Richland, J. B., 'Sovereign Time, Storied Moments: The Temporalities of Law, Tradition, and Ethnography in Hopi Tribunal Court', *PoLAR*, 31.1 (2008), 8–27

Riddehough, Geoffrey B., 'A Forgotten Poet: Joseph of Exeter', *The Journal of English and Germanic Philology*, 46.3 (1947), 254–59

Riddy, Felicity, 'Glastonbury, Joseph of Arimathea, and the Grail in John Hardyng's Chronicle', in *Glastonbury Abbey and the Arthurian Tradition*, ed. James P. Carley, 2nd edn (Cambridge: D. S. Brewer, 2001), pp. 269–84

Riddy, Felicity, 'John Hardyng in Search of the Grail', in *Arturus Rex: Acta Conventus Lovaniensis 1987*, ed. Willy Van Hoecke, Gilbert Tournoy, and Werner Verbeke (Leuven: Leuven University Press, 1991), II, pp. 419–29

Rigg, A. G., *A History of Anglo-Latin Literature, 1066–1422* (Cambridge: Cambridge University Press, 1992)

Ringler, W. A., ed., *The Poems of Sir Philip Sidney* (Oxford: Oxford University Press, 1962)

Roberts, Julian and Andrew G. Watson, *John Dee's Library Catalogue* (November 2009 update), item 1686, www.bibsoc.org.uk/sites/www.

bibsoc.org.uk/files/John%20Dee%27s%20Library%20Catalogue%204. pdf [accessed 1 August 2018]

Roberts, P. R., 'The Union with England and the Identity of "Anglican" Wales', *Transactions of the Royal Historical Society*, 22 (2007), 49–70

Roberts, Tomos, 'Welsh Ecclesiastical Place-Names and Archaeology', in *The Early Church in Wales and the West*, ed. Nancy Edwards (Oxford: Alan Lane, 1992), pp. 41–44

Robinson, J. Armitage, *Two Glastonbury Legends* (Cambridge: Cambridge University Press, 1926)

Rockett, William, 'The Structural Plan of Camden's Britannia', *Sixteenth Century Journal*, 26.4 (1995), 829–41

Roebuck, Thomas, 'Edmund Gibson's 1695 Britannia and Late-Seventeenth-Century British Antiquarian Scholarship', *Erudition and the Republic of Letters*, 5.4 (2020), 427–81

Roland, Meg, 'The Rudderless Boat: Fluid Time and Passionate Geography in (Hardyng's) Chronicle and (Malory's) Romance', *Arthuriana*, 22 (2012), 77–94

Rollason, David, 'From Tintagel to Aachen: Richard of Cornwall and the Power of Place', *Reading Medieval Studies*, 38 (2012), 1–23

Rollison, David, 'A Turning Point: The Generation of 1400', in *Commune, Country and Commonwealth: The People of Cirencester, 1117–1643* (Cambridge: Cambridge University Press, 2011), pp. 60–63

Romer, Frank E., ed. and trans, *Pomponius Mela's Description of the World* (Ann Arbor, MI: University of Michigan Press, 1998)

Rouse, Robert, 'Walking (between) the Lines: Romance as Itinerary/Map', in *Medieval Romance, Medieval Contexts*, ed. Rhiannon Purdie and Michael Cichon (Cambridge: D. S. Brewer, 2011), pp. 135–48

Rouse, Robert, *The Idea of Anglo-Saxon England in Middle English Romance* (Cambridge: D. S. Brewer, 2012)

Rouse, Robert, 'Reading Ruins: Arthurian Caerleon and the Untimely Architecture of History', *Arthuriana*, 23.1 (2013), 40–51

Rouse, Robert, 'What Lies Between?: Thinking Through Medieval Narrative Spatiality', in *Literary Cartographies: Spatiality, Representation, and Narrative*, ed. Robert T. Tally Jr (New York: Palgrave Macmillan, 2014), pp. 13–30

Rouse, Robert and Cory Rushton, *The Medieval Quest for Arthur* (Stroud: Tempus, 2005)

Rouse, Robert and Cory Rushton, 'Arthurian Geography', in *The Cambridge Companion to the Arthurian Legend*, ed. Elizabeth Archibald and Ad Putter (Cambridge: Cambridge University Press, 2009), pp. 218–34

Rowlands, Ifor W., 'King John and Wales', in *King John: New Interpretations*, ed. S. D. Church (Woodbridge: Boydell, 1999), pp. 273–87

Ruddick, Andrea, '"Becoming English": Nationality, Terminology, and Changing Sides in the Late Middle Ages', *Medieval Worlds*, 5 (2017), 57–69

Rudolph, Conrad, 'The Tour Guide in the Middle Ages: Guide Culture and the Mediation of Public Art', *Art Bulletin*, 100 (2018), 37–67

Rundle, David, 'Humanist Eloquence among the Barbarians in Fifteenth-Century England', in *Britannia Latina: Latin in the Culture of Great Britain from the Middle Ages to the Twentieth Century*, ed. Charles Burnett and Nicholas Mann (London: Warburg Institute, 2005), pp. 68–85

Rundle, David, 'Instaurations: John Leland and the Process of the Renaissance in England', Centre for Medieval and Early Modern Studies Seminar (University of Kent, 3 February 2022)

Rutter, Russell, 'William Caxton and Literary Patronage', *Studies in Philology*, 84 (1987), 440–70

Salmon, Arthur, *Dorset*, Cambridge County Histories (Cambridge: Cambridge University Press, 1910)

Sargent-Baur, Barbara N., 'Veraces Historiae aut Fallaces Fabulae?', in *Text and Intertext in Medieval Arthurian Literature*, ed. Norris J. Lacy (New York: Routledge, 1996), pp. 2–39

Scarisbrick, J. J., *Henry VIII* (Berkeley, CA: University of California Press, 1968)

Schichtman, Martin B. and James P. Carley, eds, *Culture and the King: The Social Implications of the Arthurian Legend. Essays in Honor of Valerie M. Lagorio* (Albany, NY: State University of New York Press, 1994)

Schramm, Percy Ernst, *The History of the English Coronation*, trans. by L. G. Wickham Legg (Oxford: Clarendon Press, 1937)

Schroëder, Horst, *Der Topos der Nine Worthies in Literatur und bildender Kunst* (Göttingen: Vandenhoeck & Ruprecht, 1971)

Schwyzer, Philip, 'British History and "The British History": The Same Old Story?', in *British Identities and English Renaissance Literature*, ed. David J. Baker and Willy Maley (Cambridge: Cambridge University Press, 2002), pp. 11–23

Schwyzer, Philip, *Literature, Nationalism and Memory in Early Modern England and Wales* (Cambridge: Cambridge University Press, 2004)

Schwyzer, Philip, 'Archipelagic History', in *The Oxford Handbook of Holinshed's Chronicles*, ed. Paulina Kewes, Ian W. Archer, and Felicity Heal (Oxford: Oxford University Press, 2013), pp. 593–608

Schwyzer, Philip, '"Late" Losses and the Temporality of Early Modern Nostalgia', *Parergon*, 33.2 (2016), 97–113

Schwyzer, Philip, 'Fallen Idols, Broken Noses: Defacement and Memory after the Reformation', *Memory Studies*, 11.1 (2018), 21–35

Schwyzer, Philip, '"A Tomb Once Stood in This Room": Memorials to Memorials in Early Modern England', *Journal of Medieval and Early Modern Studies*, 48.2 (2018), 365–85

Schwyzer, Philip, 'The Age of the Cambro-Britons: Hyphenated British Identities in the Seventeenth Century', *Seventeenth Century*, 33.4 (2018), 427–39

Seaman, A., 'The Church of Julius, Aaron, and Alban at Caerleon', *The Monmouthshire Antiquary*, 34 (2018), 3–16

Schmolke-Hasselmann, Beate, 'The Round Table: Ideal, Fiction, Reality', *Arthurian Literature*, 2 (1982), 41–75

Sharrer, Harvey L., 'The Passing of King Arthur to the Island of Brasil in a Fifteenth-Century Spanish Version of the Post-Vulgate Roman Du Grall', *Romania*, 92.365 (1971), 65–74

Shenton, Caroline, 'Royal Interest in Glastonbury and Cadbury: Two Arthurian Itineraries, 1278–1331', *The English Historical Review*, 114.459 (1999), 1249–55

Shrank, Cathy, *Writing the Nation in Reformation England, 1530–1580* (Oxford: Oxford University Press, 2004)

Simon, Jesse, 'Chorography Reconsidered: An Alternative Approach to the Ptolemaic Definition', in *Mapping Medieval Geographies: Geographical Encounters in the Latin West and Beyond, 300–1600*, ed. Keith D. Lilley (Cambridge: Cambridge University Press, 2013), pp. 23–44

Simpson, Aislinn, 'Winston Churchill Didn't Really Exist, Say Teens', *The Telegraph*, 4 February 2008, www.telegraph.co.uk/news/uknews/1577511/Winston-Churchill-didnt-really-exist-say-teens.html [accessed 7 February 2020]

Skene, William Forbes, *Four Ancient Books of Wales*, 2 vols (Edinburgh: Edmonston and Douglas, 1868)

Slevin, John Patrick, 'The Historical Writing of Alfred of Beverley' (unpublished doctoral thesis, University of Exeter, 2013)

Smith, A. H., *The Place-Names of Gloucestershire*, 4 vols (Cambridge: Cambridge University Press, 1964–65)

Sønnesyn, Sigbjørn Olsen, *William of Malmesbury and the Ethics of History* (Woodbridge: Boydell, 2012)

Stapleton, James P., 'King Arthur, Badon Hill, and Iconoclasm in Milton's History of Britain', *Renaissance Papers*, 18 (2013), 147–59

Starkey, David, 'King Henry and King Arthur', *Arthurian Literature*, 26 (1998), 171–96

Stevens, John, *The History of the Antient Abbeys, Monasteries, Hospitals, Cathedral and Collegiate Churches*, 2 vols (London: Thomas Taylor, 1722)

Stevenson, Katie, *Chivalry and Knighthood in Scotland, 1424–1513* (Woodbridge: Boydell, 2006)

Stevenson, Katie, 'Chivalry, British Sovereignty and Dynastic Politics: Undercurrents of Antagonism in Tudor-Stewart Relations, c.1490–c.1513', *Historical Research*, 86.234 (2013), 601–18

Stock, Brian, 'The Middle Ages as Subject and Object: Romantic Attitudes and Academic Medievalism', *New Literary History*, 5 (1974), 527–48

Strickland, Matthew, *Henry the Young King, 1155–1183* (New Haven, CT: Yale University Press, 2016)

Spenser, Edmund, 'The Ruines of Time', in *The Yale Edition of the Shorter Poems of Edmund Spenser*, ed. William A. Oram, Einar Bjorvand, Ronald Bond, Thomas H. Cain, Alexander Dunlop, and Richard Schell (New Haven, CT: Yale University Press, 1989), pp. 381–406

Steadman, Philip, *Vermeer's Camera: Uncovering the Truth Behind the Masterpieces* (Oxford: Oxford University Press, 2001)

Stout, Adam, 'After the End: Glastonbury Abbey, 1539–1825', *Somerset Archaeology and Natural History*, 157 (2014), 72–93

Stout, Adam, 'Savaric, Glastonbury and the Making of Myths: A Reappraisal', *The Antiquaries Journal*, 96 (2016), 101–15

Stout, Adam, *Glastonbury Holy Thorn: Story of a Legend* (Glastonbury: Green and Pleasant, 2020)

Summerson, Henry, Michael Trueman, and Stuart Harrison, *Brougham Castle, Cumbria: A Survey and Documentary History* (Kendal: Cumberland and Westmorland Antiquarian and Archaeological Society, 1998)

Summers, David A., 'Re-fashioning Arthur in the Tudor Era', *Exemplaria*, 9.2 (1997), 371–92

Swann, Marjorie, *Curiosities and Texts: The Culture of Collecting in Early Modern England* (Philadelphia, PA: University of Pennsylvania Press, 2010)

Swanson, R. N., *Church and Society in Late Medieval England* (Oxford: Blackwell, 1989)

Sweet, Rosemary, *Antiquaries: The Discovery of the Past in Eighteenth-Century Britain* (Oxford: Bloomsbury Academic, 2004)

Tahkokallio, Jaako, *The Anglo-Norman Historical Canon: Publishing and Manuscript Culture* (Cambridge: Cambridge University Press, 2019), pp. 38–46

Tarlow, Sarah and Susie West, eds, *The Familiar Past?: Archaeologies of Later Historical Britain* (London: Routledge, 1999)

Tatlock, J. S. P., 'Caradoc of Llancarfan', *Speculum*, 13.2 (1938), 139–52

Tatlock, J. S. P., *The Legendary History of Britain* (Berkeley, CA: University of California Press, 1950)
Taylor, John, 'The Development of the Polychronicon Continuation', *The English Historical Review*, 76.298 (1961), 20–36
Taylor, John, *The Universal Chronicle of Ranulf Higden* (Oxford: Clarendon Press, 1966)
Taylor, Jane, *Rewriting Arthurian Romance in Renaissance France* (Cambridge: D. S. Brewer, 2014)
Tite, Colin C. G., '"Lost or Stolen or Strayed": A Survey of Manuscripts Formerly in the Cotton Library', *British Library Journal*, 18 (1992), 107–47
Toorians, Lauran, 'Wizo Flandrensis and the Flemish Settlement in Pembrokeshire', *Cambridge Medieval Celtic Studies*, 20 (1990), 99–118
Toorians, Lauran, 'Flemish in Wales', in *Languages in Britain and Ireland*, ed. Glanville Price (Oxford: Blackwell, 2000), pp. 184–86
Towry Whyte, E., 'Brougham Castle, Westmorland', *Archaeologia*, 58 (1903), 359–82
Trevor-Roper, H. R., *Queen Elizabeth's First Historian: William Camden and the Beginnings of English 'Civil History'*, The Second Neale Lecture in English History (London: Jonathan Cape, 1971)
Trice Martin, Charles, *The Record Interpreter: A Collection of Abbreviations, Latin Words and Named Used in English Historical Manuscripts and Records*, ed. David Iredale, 3rd edn (Plymouth: Phillimore, 1982 [1892])
Tuan, Yi-Fu, *Space and Place: The Perspective of Experience* (Minneapolis, MN: University of Minnesota Press, 1977)
Tudor-Craig, Pamela, 'Iconography of the Painting', in *King Arthur's Round Table: An Archaeological Investigation*, ed. Martin Biddle (Woodbridge: Boydell, 2000), pp. 285–333
Turner, Sharon, *The History of the Anglo-Saxons*, 3 vols (London: Longman, 1836)
Turville-Petre, Thorlac, *England the Nation: Language, Literature, and National Identity, 1290–1340* (Oxford: Clarendon Press, 1996)
Utz, Richard, 'Hic Iacet Arthurus? Situating the Medieval King in English Renaissance Memory', in *Studies in Medievalism XXXI: Memory and Medievalism*, ed. Karl Fugelso (Cambridge: D. S. Brewer, 2006), pp. 26–40
Vale, Juliet, 'Arthur in English Society', in *Arthur of the English*, ed. W. R. J. Barron (Cardiff: University of Wales Press, 2001), pp. 185–96
Van Dussen, Michael, 'Tourists and Tabulae in Late-Medieval England', in *Truth and Tales: Cultural Mobility and Medieval Media*, ed. Fiona Somerset and Nicholas Watson (Columbus, OH: Ohio State University Press, 2015), pp. 238–54
Van Hoecke, Willy, Gilbert Tournoy, and Werner Verbeke, eds, *Arturus*

Rex: Acta Conventus Lovaniensis 1987 (Leuven: Leuven University Press, 1991)

Varnam, Laura, *The Church as Sacred Space in Middle English Literature and Culture* (Manchester: Manchester University Press, 2018)

Ven-Ten Bensel, E. van der, *The Character of King Arthur* (Amsterdam: H. J. Paris, 1925)

Verweij, Sebastiaan, *The Literary Culture of Early Modern Scotland: Manuscript Production and Transmission, 1560–1625* (Oxford: Oxford University Press, 2016)

Voelcker, Adam, 'Llangadwaladr (St Cadwaladr)', in *Churches and Chapels in North-West Wales*, ed. Jonathan M. Wooding and Nigel Yates (Cardiff: University of Wales Press, 2011), pp. 102–03

Vine, Angus, *In Defiance of Time: Antiquarian Writing in Early Modern England* (Oxford: Oxford University Press, 2010)

Vine, Angus, 'Copiousness, Conjecture and Collaboration in William Camden's *Britannia*', *Renaissance Studies*, 28 (2014), 225–41

Vine, Angus, *Miscellaneous Order: Manuscript Culture and the Early Modern Organization of Knowledge* (Oxford: Oxford University Press, 2019)

Visser-Fuchs, Livia, *History as Pastime: Jean de Wavrin and His Collection of Chronicles of England* (Donington: Shaun Tyas, 2018)

Wade, James, *Fairies in Medieval Romance* (London: Palgrave Macmillan, 2011)

Wakelin, Daniel, *Humanism, Reading, and English Literature, 1430–1530* (Oxford: Oxford University Press, 2007)

Wakelin, Daniel, *Scribal Correction and Literary Craft: English Manuscripts 1375–1510* (Cambridge: Cambridge University Press, 2014)

Wakelin, Daniel, 'Not Diane: The Risk of Error in Chaucerian Classicism', *Exemplaria*, 29.4 (2017), 331–48

Waldron, Roger, 'Trevisa's Translation of Higden's *Polychronicon*, Book I, Chapter 38, *De Wallia*: An Edition', in *Authority and Subjugation in Writing of Medieval Wales*, ed. Ruth Kennedy and Simon Meecham-Jones (London: Palgrave Macmillan, 2008), pp. 99–136

Walkling, Andrew R., 'The Problem of "Rondolesette Halle" in the *Awntyrs off Arthure*', *Studies in Philology*, 100.2 (2003), 105–22

Waltham, A. C., 'Crown Hole Development in the Sandstone Caves of Nottingham', *Quarterly Journal of Engineering Geology*, 26.4 (1993), 243–51

Ward Henry, Bruce, 'John Dee, Humphrey Llwyd, and the Name "British Empire"', *Huntington Library Quarterly*, 35 (1972), 189–90

Warren, Michelle R., *History on the Edge: Excalibur and the Borders of Britain, 1100–1300* (Minneapolis, MN: University of Minnesota Press, 2000)

Watkin, Aelred, 'The Glastonbury "Pyramids" and St. Patrick's "Companions"', *The Downside Review*, 61 (1945), 30–41

Watkin, Aelred, 'Last Glimpses of Glastonbury', *The Downside Review*, 67 (1949), 83–86

Watkin, Aelred, 'The Glastonbury Legends', in *Glastonbury Abbey and the Arthurian Tradition*, ed. James P. Carley, 2nd edn (Cambridge: D. S. Brewer, 2001), pp. 13–28

Watson, A. G., *Catalogue of Dated and Datable Manuscripts c. 435–1600 in Oxford Libraries*, 2 vols (Oxford: Oxford University Press, 1984)

Watson, Nicola J., *The Literary Tourist: Readers and Places in Romantic Victorian Britain* (New York: Palgrave Macmillan, 2006)

Weinberg, Carole S., 'Caxton, Anthony Woodville, and the Prologue to the Morte Darthur', *Studies in Philology*, 102.1 (2005), 45–65

Wenthe, Michael, 'Beyond British Boundaries in the Historia Regum Britanniae', in *Cultural Diversity in the British Middle Ages: Archipelago, Island, England*, ed. Jeffrey Jerome Cohen (New York: Palgrave Macmillan, 2008), pp. 95–116

West, G. D., *An Index of Proper Names in French Arthurian Prose Romances* (Toronto: University of Toronto Press, 1978)

Wheatley, Abigail, 'King Arthur Lives in Merry Carlisle', in *Carlisle and Cumbria: Roman and Medieval Architecture, Art and Archaeology*, ed. Mike McCarthy and David Weston (Leeds: The British Archaeological Association, 2004), pp. 63–72

Whetter, K. S., 'Malory, Hardyng and the Winchester Manuscript: Some Preliminary Conclusions', *Arthuriana*, 22.4 (2012), 167–89

Whetter, K. S., *The Manuscript and Meaning of Malory's Morte Darthur: Rubrication, Commemoration, Memorialization* (Cambridge: D. S. Brewer, 2017), pp. 23–53

Whitaker, J., *The Life of Saint Neot* (London: Joseph Stockdale, 1809)

Whitman, Jon, 'National Icon: The Winchester Round Table and the Revelation of Authority', *Arthuriana*, 18.4 (2008), 33–65

Wiles, John, 'Aberffraw, Excavated Features, Rejected Roman Fort and Suggested Llys Site', NPRN 401126 (Royal Commission for Ancient and Historical Monuments of Wales, 2007), https://coflein.gov.uk/en/site/401126 [accessed 30 May 2022]

Wijsman, Hanno, 'History in Transition: Enguerrand de Monstrelet's Chronique in Manuscript and Print (c. 1450–c. 1600)', in *The Book Triumphant: Print in Transition in the Sixteenth and Seventeenth Centuries*, ed. Malcolm Walsby and Graeme Kemp (Leiden: Brill, 2011), pp. 199–252

Williams, Glanmor, *Harri Tudur a Chymru* (Cardiff: University of Wales Press, 1985)

Williams, Glanmor, *Renewal and Reformation: Wales c. 1415–1642* (Oxford: Oxford University Press, 1993)

Winwood, H. H., 'Summary of Proceedings for the Year 1889–99', *Proceedings of the Bath Natural History and Antiquarian Field Club*, 7 (1893), 67–95
Withrington, John, 'King Arthur as Emperor', *Notes and Queries*, 35 (1988), 13–15
Withrington, John, 'The Arthurian Epitaph in Malory's *Morte Darthur*', in *Glastonbury Abbey and the Arthurian Tradition*, 2nd edn (Cambridge: D. S. Brewer, 2001), pp. 211–48
Wood, Charles T., 'Guenevere at Glastonbury: A Problem in Translation(s)', in *Glastonbury Abbey and the Arthurian Tradition*, ed. James P. Carley, 2nd edn (Cambridge: D. S. Brewer, 2001), pp. 83–100
Woolf, Daniel, *The Social Circulation of the Past: English Historical Culture 1500–1730* (Oxford: Oxford University Press, 2003)
Wordsworth, C., *The Precedence of English Bishops and the Provincial Chapter* (Cambridge: Cambridge University Press, 1906)
Workman, Leslie J., ed., *Studies in Medievalism IV: Medievalism in England* (Cambridge: D. S. Brewer, 1992)
Wright, Neil, 'A New Arthurian Epitaph', in *Glastonbury Abbey and the Arthurian Tradition*, ed. James P. Carley, 2nd edn (Cambridge: D. S. Brewer, 2001), pp. 205–09
Wright, Neil, 'The Twelfth-Century Renaissance in Anglo-Norman England: William of Malmesbury and Joseph of Exeter', in *Latin in Medieval Britain*, ed. Richard Ashdowne and Carolinne White (Oxford: The British Academy, 2017), pp. 73–84
Wulf, Charlotte A. T., 'The Coronation of Arthur and Guenevere in Geoffrey of Monmouth's *Historia Regum Britanniae*, Wace's *Roman de Brut*, and Lawman's *Brut*', in *Reading Laʒamon's Brut: Approaches and Explorations*, ed. Rosamund Allen, Jane Roberts, and Carole Weinberg (New York: Rodopi, 2013), pp. 229–51
Yale, Elizabeth, 'With Slips and Scraps: How Early Modern Naturalists Invented the Archive', *Book History*, 12 (2009), 1–36
Xiezhen Zhao, 'Dreams in Medieval Welsh Literature' (unpublished doctoral thesis, University of Cardiff, 2021
Zeiders, Blaire, 'The Arthurian Book in Print: Reading the Debts and Desires of the Early Modern English Nation' (unpublished thesis, University of Wisconsin-Madison, 2013)
Zeiders, Blaire, 'Conjuring History: The Premodern Origins and Post-Truth Legacy of John Dee's Brytanici Imperii Limites', *Journal of Medieval and Early Modern Studies*, 49.2 (2019), 377–401
Zerubavel, Eviatar, *Time Maps: Collective Memory and the Social Shape of the Past* (Chicago, IL: University of Chicago Press, 2003)

Index

abbeys
   Cirencester 112–13, 265
   Cwmhir 209
   Glastonbury *See* Glastonbury, Abbey
   Westminster 26, 34, 45, 149, 151–52, 156, 184, 191, 207
Abbots of Glastonbury *See* Glastonbury, Abbots
Aberconway, Abbey of 98–100
Aberffraw 97
Abingdon 250–51
Acts of Union 20–21, 147, 171, 173, 176, 178
Alexander the Great 33, 92, 246, 251
Alfred of Beverley *See* Chronicles, specific chronicles/chroniclers
Aliud Chronicon Metricum 39, 45–47, 80
Amesbury 187, 235, 257, 267
Anglesey 20, 97
Anglica Historia *See* Polydore Vergil
Anguselus *See* Auguselus
Antiquarians *See* Antiquaries
Antiquaries 25, 62, 79, 118, 121, 232, 242, 254–55, 267
   after 1700 8, 160, 254–59, 262, 267
   definition of 64, 217–20
   early antiquarianism 37, 40–41, 64, 68–88 (Hardyng and Worcester), 130, 219, 222, 262
   interest in Arthur 15–16, 25, 89, 135, 160, 216–17, 222, 223, 224, 253, 262, 267

   new/old Antiquarians 30–31, 217–24, 242, 253, 264
   Society of 216–17, 220–21, 222–23
   specific antiquaries indexed by surname
archiflamines 116
archbishops
   early British 45–46, 95, 101
   Dubricius 105, 107, 100, 109–10, 120, 152, 181
   Fagan 45–46
   Piramus 45–46
   Samson 45–46
archbishoprics
   Caerleon 107, 110, 116, 152
   Canterbury 102, 115
   London 95, 102, 116
   St Davids 102
   York 45–46, 115, 116
Arthur
   battles
      Badon 190
      City of the Legion (Caerleon) 116, 120, 152
      Camlan 25, 50, 162, 164, 165, 218, 246–47
      Dover 38, 135, 165, 187, 263
      against Emperor Lucius 146
      in Europe 143, 144, 146–48, 150
      Glastonbury (acc. Elis Gruffydd) 201
      in *Historia Brittonum* 143, 162, 218
      Ireland 201

Arthur, battles *(continued)*
   Moray   128, 142
   Richborough   148
   in Ryd's *Catalogus*   149
   York   201
burial and grave   1, 3, 12, 32, 34,
     50, 53, 76–77, 94–103, 132,
     138–39, 187, 257, 262
   at Glastonbury   1, 12, 34, 49–50,
     51–54, 56–57, 75–77,
     94–95, 99–104, 137,
     138–39, 159–60, 189–90,
     192, 218, 224, 239–42,
     261
   in Gwynedd   94–103
conception and birth   92–94, 103,
     236, 247–48, 252, 262
conquests   106
   continental   29, 143, 146
   of Northern Europe   142–43,
     150, 152
   against Saxons   146
coronation   103–15, 118, 120–25,
     130, 147, 152, 153, 218, 262
death   94–95, 218, 236, 247–49,
     251–52
decline of interest in   8–9
dream of   52, 75, 159
as emperor   8, 21, 33, 105–06,
     141–43, 145, 148–50, 152,
     154, 168, 252, 261, 263
epitaph
   copies of   40, 59, 72, 244, 262
   on the lead cross   26, 50, 51, 56,
     63, 185, 191, 195, 211,
     238–42, 249, 253, 255,
     265
   versions of   53, 76–77, 209, 244
heraldic arms   47–48, 52
negative depictions of   203
objects
   Arthur's seal   26, 34, 142,
     148–52, 156–57, 164–65,
     181, 184, 191, 207, 220,
     239–40

   crystal cross   52
   lead cross   26, 50, 51, 56, 63,
     191, 195, 238–42, 249,
     253, 255, 265
   Winchester Round Table   34,
     75, 90, 124–25, 237, 259
places of Arthur
   Arthur's cave   129
   Arthur's crowning   103–15,
     118, 120–25, 130, 147,
     152, 153, 218, 262
     Caerleon   103–06, 110
     Chichester   110, 113
     Cirencester   103, 104,
       107–13, 130
     Gloucester   103, 113, 114
     Paris   103, 106,
     Silchester   103–10, 113
     Winchester   103, 114
   Arthur's court   25, 29, 34, 90, 115,
     121–35, 137, 152–53, 160,
     185, 205, 263
     Alclud   127, 128–29
     Avalon   127
     Bamburgh Castle   127
     Cadbury   30, 32, 122, 135,
       152–61, 164–65, 168,
       176, 236, 258, 263, 266
     Caerleon   34, 115, 121, 122, 123,
       125, 127, 130, 135, 152,
       153, 176, 236
     Caernarfon   127
     Caerwent   34, 123
     Caerwys   205
     Cardiff   127, 128
     Cardigan   121
     Carduel   121
     Carlisle   127, 128, 130, 132
     Camelot   34, 121, 122, 125, 126,
       135, 152–61, 176, 258
     Cornwall   127, 128
     Cumberland   127, 131
     Dalry (St John's Town)   127,
       128, 129
     Disnadaron   121

Dover 127, 128, 135
Dumbarton 127, 128
Dumfries 127, 129
Dunbar 127, 128, 129
Dundonald Castle 127
Dunnideer 128, 129, 130, 132
Edinburgh 127, 128, 129
Glastonbury 127, 128, 137
Hereford 127, 129, 130
London 127, 128, 176
Moray 128
Nannerch 205
Nantes 121
Orkney, City of 121
Paris 142, 176
Perth 127, 129
Quarrois 121
in romance 121–22
Stirling 127, 128, 134–35
Winchester 121, 122, 123–25, 127
York 127
Arthur's Gate 191
Arthur's Oven 237
Arthur's seat 129, 263
Arthur's stone 129
Arthur's tomb
  at Glastonbury 53–54, 66, 75–76, 101, 138, 187, 196, 209, 244
  in Gwynedd 96–97
Avalon 1, 49–52, 56, 69, 73, 75–76, 77–78, 80, 87, 95, 97–101, 103, 127, 158–59, 182, 187
Cair Arthur 191
Camelot 32, 34, 56, 121–26, 152, 154–57, 161–63, 176
City of [the] Legions 90, 110, 113, 114–21, 153, 176
  Caerleon 27, 30, 34, 38, 103–07, 114–15, 116–20, 121–22, 122–6, 128, 130–31, 135, 137, 146, 152–53, 175–76, 191, 201, 205, 223, 236, 246, 263

Chester 116–21
Exeter 153
Warwick 116–21
return of 21, 76, 94, 189–90, 206
Round Table
  earliest mention of 121
  knights of 184–87
  location(s) 90, 122, 126, 130–35, 153–54, 176, 192, 259, 262–63
  monuments 130, 132–35, 192
  oath/rule of 87
  Winchester Round Table *See* Arthur, Objects
scepticism of 2–3, 5–8, 9, 13, 15–17, 18, 21, 29, 31, 34, 94, 138–39, 149–50, 178, 189–90, 206, 226–27, 237, 53–54, 256, 266
seal *See* Arthur, objects
tomb *See* Arthur, places of Arthur
Auguselus 186
Avalon *See* Arthur, places of

Badon *See* Arthur, Battles
Bakhtin, Mikhail 23–24, 56–57, 87, 217, 236
Bale, John 28, 174, 179, 189, 258
Baldred Bisset 93
Bangor 95, 201
Barbour, John 134
Bardsey (*see also* Enlli) 99–100, 152
Bath (city) 115, 147, 234–36
Beckery 27, 52, 75
Bede 5, 93, 117
Bénigne of Dijon, St, chronicle of *See* chronicles, specific chronicles/chroniclers
Berkshire 113, 148
Beverley, Alfred of *See* chronicles, specific chronicles/chroniclers
Biket, Robert 111
Biondo, Flavio 228
bishops
  Henry Beaufort 43

bishops (*continued*)
   Thomas Bekynton   115
   Dubricius   See Archbishops
   Duvianus   110
   Francis Godwin   38
   Maugano   110
   Walter Skirlaw   47–49
bishoprics   114
   Bangor   95
   Glamorgan   95
   Menevia   95
   St Davids   117–18
   Silchester   110
   Warwick   120
   Winchester   110
Bouchard, Alain   185–86
Brecknockshire   21, 191, 234, 237
Brennius   250–51
Brent Knoll   27, 54
Britain
   anglocentrism of   18–19, 21, 74, 173–74, 175
   conversion of   45–47, 51, 54, 116
   definitions of   17–18, 173, 218
   descriptions of   28, 224–25, 231, 255
   early history   16–17, 18, 35, 45–47, 73, 97, 116, 143, 146, 153, 178, 183, 188–89, 193–94, 200, 209, 222, 234–36, 238, 244, 258
   early modern Britain   18, 21, 173–74, 183
   as empire   16, 21, 74, 142, 173–74, 175
   foundation myths   16–17, 18, 35, 143, 166, 171, 178, 226, 230
   island of   16, 21, 174–75, 183, 233, 237
   as Nation   10–11, 16, 18, 35, 172, 173–74, 175, 183, 195, 233, 237, 266
The British History   3, 17, 18–19, 30, 36, 58, 97, 98, 108, 138, 141, 174–75, 179, 181, 189, 194, 197, 199, 206, 208–09, 213, 219, 227, 244, 264 (*see also* Geoffrey of Monmouth)
British identity   13, 15, 17, 19, 35, 171–74, 175, 176–78, 180, 182, 183–84, 193, 200
The Britons   9, 19, 45, 47, 69, 76, 80, 107, 119, 130, 150, 156, 172, 176–77, 180, 183–84, 189, 204, 236, 244
   language of (*see also* Welsh)   19, 80, 176–77, 183–84, 198–99, 204
Brougham   132–34, 157, 258, 263, 266
Brutus   17, 18, 35, 166, 207, 208, 219, 221, 222, 223, 226–27
burial mounds   111, 191, 234, 236

Cadbury   24–25, 27, 30, 32, 135, 138, 152–54, 156–61, 162, 163, 164–65, 168, 176, 189, 191, 195, 220, 236, 239–40, 245, 253, 254, 258, 263, 265, 266
Cador   95, 186, 193
Cadwaladr   18, 98, 109, 146, 244
Caerleon   27, 30, 34, 38, 103–07, 114–15, 116–22, 122–26, 128, 130, 131, 135, 137, 146, 152–54, 175–76, 191, 201, 205, 223, 236, 246, 263
Caerwent   34, 123
Caerwys   205
Calais   177–78, 201–03
Cambridge, University of   150, 153
Camden, William   16, 18, 21, 26, 30–32, 38, 54, 58, 63, 89, 98, 121, 139, 161, 170, 173, 216–60, 261–62, 264, 266, 267
Camelot   See Arthur, places of
Camlan   See Arthur, Battles
Canterbury   102–03, 115, 147, 182
   Beckett's shrine at   41
   Canterbury Cathedral   1, 41

INDEX

Caradoc
  city of 168–69
  legendary king 34, 166, 186
  of Llancarfan 49–50
  mantle of 34
Carannog, St 202
Cardiff *See* Arthur, places, Arthur's court
Cardigan *See* Arthur, places, Arthur's court
Carduel *See* Arthur, places, Arthur's court
Carew, Richard 224, 228
Carlisle 122, 128, 130, 132, 263
Castle Grosmond, Cirencester 111–13
Castle Rous 237
Castle Time (see Bakhtin, Mikhael) 23–24, 56–57, 87, 217, 236
castles 3, 7, 29, 35, 128, 130, 132, 139, 218, 263
  Arthur's castle, Dumbarton 127
  Bamburgh 127
  Brougham 132–33
  Cadbury *See* Arthur, Places of, Arthur's court
  Castle of the Giants 132
  Castle of Maidens 127
  Chepstow 123
  Dover 6, 34, 37–38, 68, 88, 130, 135, 165–66, 191, 201
  Dundonald (Ayrshire) 127
  Dunnideer 128, 130
  Edinburgh 129, 135
  Grosmond 112–13
  Hewin 131
  Naworth 62
  Nottingham 91, 130, 135
  Plompton Castle *See* Plumpton Voreda
  Stirling 127–28, 133–35
  Tintagel 2, 93
  Walwyn's Castle, Rhos 167
  Warwick 120–21
  Winchester 124–25
  Windsor 134
cathedrals
  Canterbury 1, 41
  Llandaff 181–82
  Ripon 39
  St Davids 182
  St Paul's 28, 37–38, 40, 44–45, 65, 72, 74, 104, 140
    Rode at 74
  Westminster 26, 34, 149, 151–52, 156, 184, 191, 207
  York Minster 3, 28, 37–41, 44–49, 58, 99, 182
caves 42, 90–91, 129, 135, 158–61, 206, 263, 267
Caxton, William 5, 33–35, 122–24, 126, 146, 150, 166, 187–88
Cerdic 148
Chalice Well at Glastonbury *See* Glastonbury, Chalice Well
Chapel Ride episode 51, 57, 75
chapels
  All Souls College, Oxford 47
  The Black Chapel 75–76
  Capel Gwial 205
  The Chapel Ride 51, 57, 75
  Dover 165
  Guy of Warwick's chapel 42–43
  Lady Chapel, Glastonbury 65–67, 72, 75–78
  St Cecilia's, Cirencester 165, 111–12
  St George's, Windsor 40
  St Henry's, Yarmouth 37
  St Michael's Chapel *See* Glastonbury Tor
  In *Vera Historia* 95–96
Charlemagne 33, 251
Chaucer, Geoffrey 1, 251
Cheldric *See* Cerdic
Chester *See* Arthur, places of, City of the Legion
Chichester *See* Arthur, places of, Crowning
Chinnock, John (Abbot) 59–60

Chrétien de Troyes   121–22
Christianity   45–49, 51, 54, 58, 116
chronicles   56, 60, 70, 87
   Brut chronicles   92, 93, 105,
      109–10, 121
   local chronicles   35–36, 88
   metrical chronicles   29, 39, 88,
      90–91
   specific chronicles/chroniclers
     Adam of Damerham   27, 50
     Alfred of Beverley   5, 109
     Bénigne of Dijon, St, chronicle
       of   148–49
     Boece, Hector   93, 129, 141,
       162–63, 167
     Bower, Walter   93
     Dover chronicle   68
     Fabyan, Robert   74, 210
     Fordun, John   *See* Chronicles,
       specific chronicles/
       chroniclers
     Froissart, Jean   134
     Geoffrey of Monmouth   68, 137
       Historia regum Britanniae   2,
         8, 9, 17–18, 22, 29–30,
         32, 46, 49, 50, 51, 64,
         69, 80–81, 90, 92–95,
         98, 100, 104–18,
         121, 123, 128–29,
         133, 135, 141–48,
         152, 157, 162–66,
         168, 171, 176, 181,
         185–86, 193, 197–98,
         205, 223, 236, 250,
         254, 258, 262
        derivatives   70, 101, 126,
          246
        scepticism of   137, 152,
          207–80, 226–27
       Vita Merlini   51
     Gerald of Wales   49–50, 56, 77,
       100–01, 117–20, 153,
       191–92, 197–98, 204,
       231, 237

     Gervase of Tilbury   160
     Gildas   5, 49, 81, 117–18,
       202–04, 233, 236
       fabrication of   193, 204, 220
     Gray, Thomas   34, 114, 124–25,
       153, 165
     Gruffydd, Elis   15–16, 30,
       32, 158–61, 171–73,
       175, 177–78, 185, 191,
       200–14, 244, 264
     Hailes Chronicle   96, 99, 101–03
     Hardyng, John   28–29, 35, 44,
       68, 72–88, 89, 106, 110,
       120, 125, 128–35, 162,
       186, 193, 216, 219, 254,
       259, 262, 264–66
     Henry of Huntingdon   198
     Higden, Ranulf   5, 94, 100,
       118–20, 193, 197, 211,
       263
     Holinshed, Raphael   17, 21,
       189–90, 228
     Jean de Wavrin   114
     John of Allhallowgate   39,
       45–47, 80
     John of Glastonbury   51–60, 63,
       67–70, 72, 75, 77–81,
       85–87, 93, 187, 202
     Laȝamon   92, 109, 129
     Maffei, Raphael   150
     Mannyng, Robert (of
       Brunne)   109
     Margam Abbey, Chronicle
       of   50
     Pershore Abbey, Chronicle
       of   197
     Rous, John   16, 37, 40, 42–44,
       72–73, 79, 106, 110,
       116–21, 153, 216, 222–
       23, 259, 263–64, 266
     Ryd, Valerius
       Anselmus   148–49
     Stafford's Chronicle   70–72,
       131–32, 266

Trithemius, Johannes 150–51
Wace 92, 105, 109, 121, 146–47
William of Malmesbury 54–59, 77, 79, 99, 166–67, 187, 248
William of Rennes 101, 246
Wynchcombe, Thomas 116–18
and *tabulae* 4, 36–37, 44–49, 65, 74
churches
    All Saints, Huish Episcopi 66
    Abbey Church, Glastonbury Abbey 53, 64–66, 69, 72, 76–79, 87–88, 112, 187, 255
    Damerham 59
    Cornhill, London 37
    Llandaff 120, 152, 181
    Llangadwalladr 97–98
    Metropolitan Church, Canterbury 182
    St Christopher-le-Stocks, London 37
    St John the Baptist, Colchester 37
    St John the Baptist, Glastonbury 241–42
    St Julis and St Aaron, Caerleon 117
    Silchester 108
    Tavistock 37
Cirencester 103, 104, 107–13, 130
    Cirencester Abbey *See* Abbeys
City of [the] Legions *See* Arthur, Places of
Colchester 37
Colgrinus 107
consorts *See* queens and consorts
Corineus 73, 166
coronations 103–14
Cornhill *See* churches
Cornwall 5–6, 9, 16, 92, 95, 128, 147–48, 163, 165, 172, 201, 224, 228, 230–31, 233–34, 236, 247, 252–53
    Cornish Rebellion 147
Cotton, Robert 63, 246, 258

Cumberland 62, 127, 131, 132, 234, 237
Cwmhir Abbey *See* abbeys

Dacia/Dacians 142, 150–51
Damerham
    Church of 59
    Adam of *See* Chronicles, specific chronicles/chroniclers
Damian (Deruvian) 46, 51
David II *See* Kings
Dee, John 73, 174, 223–24
Deruvian *See* Damian
Dolorous Garde 91, 127
Domesday book 58
Dorchester 168
Dover 28, 34, 39, 68–69, 128, 135, 137, 157, 165–66, 168, 187, 262–63
    Castle 6, 34, 37, 68–69, 88, 130, 135, 165, 191, 201, 262
Drayton, Michael 30, 232, 243
Dubricius *See* archbishops
Dumfries *See* Arthur, places, Arthur's court
Dunideer *See* Arthur, places, Arthur's court
Dugdale, William 118

Eamont Bridge 133
earthworks (*see also* hillforts) 7, 25, 90, 97, 129–31, 133–34, 137, 168, 263
    The King's Knot, Stirling Castle 134
Edinburgh *See* Arthur, places, Arthur's court
Edward I *See* kings
Edward III *See* kings
Edward IV *See* kings
Edward the Confessor *See* kings
Elaine of Astolat 124
Elizabeth I *See* queens
Enlli (*see also* Bardsey) 99–100
    Enlli Abbey 100

Exeter   153
    Joseph of   248

Fabyan, Robert   *See* chronicles, specific chronicles/chroniclers
Fagan   45–46, 51
Faganus   *See* Fagan
folklore   *See* oral tradition
Fordun, John   *See* Chronicles, specific chronicles/chroniclers
France   106, 142, 145, 148–49, 163, 165, 218

Galahad (Galaad)   61, 77–78, 81, 85, 87
Ganarew   129
Gawain   8, 60, 61, 122, 186, 227
    burial site   137, 165–68, 187, 197, 201
    death   137, 187
    skull/bones of   34, 68–69,
Geoffrey of Monmouth   *See* chronicles, specific chronicles/chroniclers
geography   14, 31, 141–44, 217, 227–34, 253, 255
Gerald of Wales   *See* chronicles, Specific chronicles/chroniclers
Germany   107, 142, 150
Gervase of Tilbury   *See* chronicles, specific chronicles/chroniclers
giants   54, 97, 129, 132–33, 142, 148, 165–67, 192, 236–37, 258
Gildas   *See* chronicles, specific chronicles/chroniclers
Glastonbury   16, 26, 28, 30, 32, 40–59, 103, 112, 128, 131, 137–38, 156–60, 166, 181–82, 187, 189, 196, 201, 204, 206, 219, 232, 237–42, 248–49, 252, 255–57
    Arthurian origins   49–55
    Arthurian tourism at   1, 6, 28, 30–44, 55, 60–88, 160, 255–57, 261–62, 265
    as Avalon   49–51, 56
    Chalice Well   1, 27–28, 62

Glastonbury Abbey   1, 12, 28, 30–44, 49, 52, 54–57, 59–67, 72, 74–76, 79–80, 87–88, 99, 138–39, 141, 151–52, 159, 160, 178, 181–82, 183, 187, 191, 193, 201, 204, 209, 218, 237–38, 248–49, 253–54, 255–56, 265–66
    abbots
        Abbot Beere   63, 65
        Abbot Chinnock   59–60
        Abbot Henry of Sully   53
    Arthur's grave   *See* Arthur, places
    renovations   3–4
    Glastonbury Tor   1, 27, 51–52, 158–59, 206, 258
    Holy Thorn   27, 256
    Pomparles Bridge   27, 137, 159, 232
    New Age Culture of   1, 22, 158
    Pomparles Bridge   27, 137, 159, 232
    Tabulae at Glastonbury   30, 37, 40, 41, 49, 55–68, 69–72, 74–75, 79–88, 102, 187, 219, 244
    Wearyall Hill   27, 52,
Gloucester   103, 113–14
Good, William   65–66, 87
Grafton, Richard   72–73
Gruffydd, Elis   *See* Chronicles, specific chronicles/chroniclers
Guenevere   *See* Guinevere
guides   1, 3–4, 24, 35, 41–44, 47, 49, 55–56, 62, 67–69, 78, 88, 112, 219, 230, 255–56, 262, 265–66
Guildford   123, 137
Guinevere   50, 53, 67–69, 91, 106, 129, 135, 148, 187, 257, 267
Guy of Warwick   40, 42–43, 219
Guy's Cliffe   42
Gwynedd   94–8, 101–02
Gwyn ap Nudd   159

Hailes Chronicle   *See* Chronicles, specific chronicles/chroniclers

INDEX

Hardyng, John *See* Chronicles, specific chronicles/chroniclers
Hector 33, 247, 251
Henry I *See* kings
Henry III *See* kings
Henry VI *See* kings
Henry VII (Henry Tudor) *See* Kings
Henry VIII *See* kings
Henry of Huntingdon *See* chronicles, specific chronicles/chroniclers
Henry the Young King *See* kings
Hercules 250–51
heritage 2, 15, 42, 168, 240, 252
Hertford, earls of 258
Higden, Ranulf *See* chronicles, chronicles/chroniclers
Hillforts (*see also* earthworks) 7, 25, 129, 130, 154, 157, 159, 161, 167, 236, 258
Hoel of Brittany 128, 149, 185–86, 193
Holinshed, Raphael *See* chronicles, chronicles/chroniclers
Holy Grail 1, 44, 53, 55, 61–62
Holy Thorn *See* Glastonbury, Holy Thorn
Homer 143
Howard, William 62–63
Huail ap Caw 202–05
Hughes, Thomas 63
Hughes, William, Chancellor of Wells 240
humanism 16, 17, 184, 195, 197, 218, 221–24, 229, 244
The Humber 107, 148, 162

Ireland 112, 133, 142, 150–51, 178, 201, 224, 231–32
    saints of 74
Isabella of France *See* queens and consorts
Italy 16–17, 30, 171, 174–75, 178–79, 180, 188, 194, 197, 200, 208, 213, 218, 243

James IV *See* kings

Jean de Wavrin *See* chronicles, chronicles/chroniclers
Jean Froissart *See* chronicles, chronicles/chroniclers
John of Allhallowgate *See* chronicles, chronicles/chroniclers
John of Gaunt, tomb of 44
John of Hauville 248
Joseph of Arimathea *See* saints
Joseph of Exeter 248–52
Julius Caesar 33, 38, 194, 249–51
Juvenal 196, 227

Kempe, Margery 41
kings
    legendary or pseudo-historical
        Arthur *See* Arthur
        Arviragus 37–38, 58, 60, 70, 77, 80–81
        Aurelius Ambrosius 45
        Constantine/Constantinus 249, 251
        Lucius 37, 44–48, 54
        Mark of Cornwall 92–93
        Melwas 49
        Uther 45–46, 93, 104, 106–07, 114, 128, 248
        Vortigern 129
    historical
        Cadfan (Gwynedd) 98
        David II (Scotland) 12, 134
        Edward the Confessor (Wessex) 149, 223
        Edward I (England) 9, 12, 53, 124, 134, 141, 160, 191
        Edward III (England) 9–10, 91, 125, 134, 160,
        Edward IV (England) 9, 73
        Henry I (England) 112–13
        Henry II (England) 9–10, 105
        Henry III (England) 105, 114
        Henry VI (England) 73, 106
        Henry VII (England) 104–05, 172–74, 179
        Henry VIII (England) 9–10,

kings, historical (*continued*)
    19, 62, 140–43, 173–74, 177–79,
      220, 266
    Henry the Young King   104, 115
    Ine (Wessex)   99, 139
    James I/VI (England/
      Scotland)   220
    James IV (Scotland)   129
    John I (England)   97, 104
    Llwywelyn ap Gruffydd
      (Gwynedd)   172,
      209–11, 244
    Llywelyn ap Iorweth
      (Gwynedd)   97–99
    Offa (Mercia)   43–44
The King's Knot   *See* earthworks
knights
    Arthur's knights   *See* Arthur,
      Round Table, knights of
    in romance literature   23, 56, 61,
      87, 122
    of the Garter   *See* Order of the
      Garter

Lambarde, William   223–24, 228, 232
Lancaster, House of   73, 106, 172
Lancelot   61–62, 91, 133, 186–87, 201,
    227, 258
law
    ancient law, study of   223, 231
    Leges Edwardi Confessoris   223
legionary cities   *See* Arthur, places,
    City of the Legion
Leicester   116, 121, 147
Leland, John   3, 15–18, 21, 26, 29–32,
    38, 68, 73, 79, 80–81, 89, 93,
    114, 118, 120–22, 125, 127,
    135, 137–70, 171–215, 216–28,
    231, 236, 238, 239–42, 244–45,
    247–54, 256–59, 263–64,
    265–66
    itineraries   41, 53, 58, 64, 68–69, 77,
      100, 110, 112–13, 131, 135,
      140–41, 145, 152–54, 156,
      160, 167, 263
    The King's Antiquary   140, 220–21

Robinson's translation   *See*
    Robinson, Richard
Lhwyd, Edward   98, 256–58, 267
Llanasa   200, 211–12
Llangadwaladr   *See* churches
Llywelyn ap Gruffydd   *See* kings
Llywelyn ap Iorweth   *See* kings
Llywelyn the Great   *See* kings,
    Llywelyn ap Iorweth
Llwyd, Humphrey   168–69, 174,
    183–84, 199, 216, 238, 264
local history   7–11, 35–36, 89–90, 266
Lodovico Da Ponte   *See* Ponticus
    Virunius
Lollardy   28
London   37–38, 45, 95, 102, 104,
    115–16, 127–28, 152, 173, 176,
    185, 201, 223, 228
Lovelich, Henry   92
Lucan   196
Lucius
    British king   *See* kings, legendary
    Roman emperor   144, 193

Maffei, Raphael   *See* chronicles,
    chronicles/chroniclers
magna tabula   *See* Tabulae;
    Glastonbury, Tabulae at
Malory, Sir Thomas   2, 5, 29, 33–34,
    56, 92, 122–26, 128, 133, 137,
    166, 187–89, 193, 257
Mannyng, Robert   *See* chronicles,
    specific chronicles/chroniclers
Matthew Paris   93, 197
Mayburgh henge   133, 258
Melkin   57, 60, 65–67, 73–74, 78–80, 85
Merlin   57, 76, 79–80, 100, 118, 133,
    205, 206, 236, 248
Mewyn   *See* Melkin
Michael of Cornwall   252
monasteries (*see also* abbeys)   7, 34,
    36, 37, 43, 51, 52, 138, 151–52,
    179, 181
monks   1, 4, 28, 35, 41–42, 49–50,
    54–59, 67–68, 78, 87, 99, 100,
    103, 149, 151, 181, 193, 255, 265

INDEX 325

Dom. Murelage
    (Glastonbury)   193, 265
Mont St Michel   142, 148–49
Montacute   65, 258
Moray   128, 142,
Mordred   76, 93, 95, 132, 137, 148,
    162–63, 165, 182, 185, 201
Morris, Lewis   100
Mortimer, Roger   91

Nannerch   *See* Arthur, places,
    Arthur's court
Nantes   *See* Arthur, places, Arthur's
    court
national identity   10–13, 19, 31, 105,
    172, 175–80, 183–84
Naworth Castle   62–63
Neckham, Alexander   113
Nennius   116–17, 118, 120, 143, 162,
    236, 237, 262
Neville, Richard   43–44
New Age   1, 22, 158, 218, 258
North Wales   15, 30, 54, 94, 98, 116–17,
    119, 141, 172, 201, 203, 205,
Nottingham
    Castle   91, 135
        Caves   90–91, 135, 263, 267

oral tradition   24–25, 29, 32, 47, 56,
    69, 96–97, 112, 129, 155–61,
    164, 166, 178, 182, 185, 202–03,
    205–06, 208–09, 212, 220, 237,
    245, 257–58, 267
Order of the Garter   125, 134
Orkney   121, 142
Ortelius, Abraham   231

Padstow   27, 164, 240
Paris   103, 106, 121, 140, 142, 149, 152,
    176, 197
Penrith (*see also* Mayburgh)   131–35
Pershore Abbey, chronicle of   *See*
    Chronicles, specific
    chronicles/chroniclers
Picts   128, 129, 142, 162, 231, 234
pilgrims/pilgrimage   1–2, 4, 28, 36,
    41–46, 53, 65–66, 74, 100, 262
Piramus, Archbishop of York   *See*
    archbishops
Plumpton Voreda   132–33
    and Plompton Castle   132–33
Polden   27
Polydore Vergil
    accusations of forgery   197,
        203–04, 219–20
    Anglica Historia   30, 138–39,
        174–75, 197
    Arthurian scepticism   3, 16–17,
        138–39, 142, 207, 253
        overstatement of   5, 138–39,
            226–27
    influence on Holinshed's *Historie of*
        England (1586)   189–90
    publication of Gildas' *De excidio*
        (1525)   118, 203–04, 219
    responses to
        in general   3, 16–17, 138–39,
            174, 179, 189, 200, 208,
            266
        by John Leland   141–43, 152,
            163, 171, 175–76, 178–
            79, 183–84, 190, 193–94,
            196–97, 206, 213, 224,
            253–54, 264
        by John Prise   171, 176–77,
            178, 180–83, 193–95,
            197–200, 203–04, 206,
            213
Pomparles bridge (cf Pons
    Periculosis)   *See*
    Glastonbury, Pomparles
    Bridge
Ponticus Virunius   197
Pons Periculosis (Pomparles
    Bridge)   *See* Glastonbury,
    Pomparles Bridge
popes
    Eleutherius   45–47
Powel, David   197
Prise, John   3, 16, 21, 30, 118, 152,
    171–84, 191–204, 206–10,
    213–14, 216, 220–21, 226,

Prise, John (*continued*)
  238–39, 242–43, 250, 251, 253, 259, 264, 266–67
Protestantism   174, 178
Ptolemy   141, 229–31, 233
Pynson, Richard   81

queens and queen consorts
  Eleanor of Castile   53
  Elizabeth I   65, 216–17, 220, 222–23, 225
  Guinevere   *See* Guinevere
  Isabella of France   91
quests   23, 29, 56, 60, 61, 121–22, 144, 148

Rastell, John   96, 149–50, 206–09
regions   10–11, 13–16, 19–21, 27–28, 30–31, 89–90, 136, 137–41, 168, 172, 225, 227–36, 243, 263
relics   25–27, 43, 52, 55, 58, 60, 102, 217, 219
religious houses   *See* abbeys, monasteries
Renaissance   17, 34, 221–22
Rhos   137, 165–67
Richard of Cirencester   93
Richard of York   73
River Humber   107, 148, 162
Robin Hood   8
Robinson, Richard   70, 140, 151, 153–54, 157, 166–68, 175, 187–88, 196
Rome
  England's break from   193
  resentment towards   171, 193–200, 264
  ruins and remains   109, 123, 130, 132, 155–56, 164, 231, 234–35, 257
  The Romans   18, 97, 108, 146, 178, 193–200, 206, 218, 227, 250
romance   20, 23, 29, 34, 42, 51, 53, 55, 56–57, 60–62, 75, 78, 80–1, 86, 91–92, 121–24, 126, 128, 129, 134, 135, 137–38, 143–46, 160, 171, 185–87, 200–02, 206, 251, 266
Round Table   *See* Arthur, places
Rous, John   *See* chronicles, chronicles/chroniclers
ruins   7, 25, 26, 31, 34, 108, 126, 130–02, 157, 218, 236, 255–58, 267
Ruthin   203, 211
Ryd, Valerius Anselmus   *See* chronicles, Specific chronicles/chroniclers

St Albans   3, 43–44
St David's, Wales   102, 117–18, 182
St John's Town   *See* Arthur, Places of Arthur, Arthur's court
St Paul's Cathedral   *See* Cathedrals
St Peter's basilica   149
saints
  St Aaron   116, 121, 153
  St Alban   43–44
  St Amphibalus   153
  St Andrew   73
  St Cadog   202, 210
  St Carannog   202
  St Collen   159
  St David   63–67, 77
  St Dubricius   *See* archbishops
  St Dunstan   103–04
  St Dyfrig (Dubricius)   *See* archbishops
  St Edward the Confessor   *See* kings, historical
  St Gildas   *See* chronicles, specific chronicles/chroniclers
  St Henry of Uppsala   37
  St Joseph of Arimathea   53–88, 103, 139, 255, 256
    at Glastonbury   53–88, 103, 139, 256
    subterranean sanctuary   65
    well   66
  conversion of Britain   *See* Britain, conversion of

INDEX

cruets (*see also* Melkin) 57, 62, 66
   fountain of 62
   in romance 53
   son of 61–62, 69, 81, 87
St Julius 116, 121, 153
St Mauganus *See* bishops
St Mary (the Virgin Mary) 52, 76, 98
St Patrick 51, 59–60, 94
St Philip the apostle 58
St Sampson *See* archbishops
St Thomas Becket 1, 41
St William (York) 39
Welsh saints *See* Wales, Saints of
Salisbury 43, 133, 147, 236, 252
Samson (Archbishop) *See* Archbishops
The Saxons 53, 107, 146, 231, 238, 255
scepticism of Arthur *See* Arthur, scepticism of
Scotland 10, 12, 16, 18, 20, 74, 80, 89, 93, 126–35, 141, 142, 148, 162, 172, 224, 231, 237, 263
   The Scots 16, 74, 93, 128, 134, 142, 147, 149, 162, 231
Shakespeare 29, 133
Sidney, Philip 196, 244
Silchester *See* Arthur, places of, Arthur's crowning
Somerton 168
South-West England *See* The West Country
Speed, John 232, 235
Spelman, Henry 63
Spenser, Edmund 243
Stafford, John *See* chronicles, specific chronicles/chroniclers
Stow, John 37, 73, 122, 135, 161, 228, 241
Sully, Henry of 53
Stafford's Chronicle (cf. John Stafford) *See* chronicles, specific chronicles/chroniclers
Stirling Castle *See* castles, Stirling

Stonehenge 96, 234–36, 207, 238, 258
Strabo 229–31
Street, Somerset 137
Stukeley, William 108, 133, 160, 255–56, 258–59, 267
Surloes 201–02

tabulae
   in general 4, 24, 28–29, 35–47, 56, 60, 65, 68–69, 74, 80, 88, 105, 181, 220, 242, 244–45, 254, 262, 265
   at Glastonbury 37, 40–41, 49, 52, 55–56, 59–72, 74–75, 77–88, 102, 187, 219, 244, 254–55
   at St Paul's 38, 40, 44–45, 74, 80
   at York 37–49, 65, 80, 99, 219, 244
Tacitus 142, 169, 194, 196
tapestries 4, 43
tour guides *See* guides
Twyne, Brian 150
Tor (Glastonbury) *See* Glastonbury, Glastonbury Tor
thin places 22–23
Tintagel 1–2, 15, 27, 92–94, 103, 191, 236, 247–48, 252
tournaments 124, 134
Tristan 92
Trithemius, Johannes *See* chronicles, specific chronicles/chroniclers
Troy 33, 35, 155–56, 236, 240
The Tudors 147
   Elizabeth I *See* Queens and consorts
   Henry VII *See* kings, historical
   Henry VIII *See* kings, historical
   interest in Arthur 9–10
   as a time period 8
Tyndale, William 178

Ussher, James 62–63, 70, 148
Uther Pendragon *See* kings, legendary or pseudo-historical

Van Eyck   145
Vergil, Polydore   *See* Polydore Vergil
Volteranus (Raphael Maffei)   *See* chronicles, specific chronicles/chroniclers

Wace   *See* chronicles, specific chronicles/chroniclers
Wales   9, 16, 18, 19, 97–98, 116, 174, 193, 196, 200, 202, 212, 220, 224, 231–34, 236
  Arthurian places in (*see also* Arthur, places of Arthur) 1, 6, 8, 15, 20, 30–31, 33–34, 38, 55, 89, 91, 94, 97–100, 108–09, 116–17, 119–20, 123, 131, 137, 141, 145–47, 153, 165–67, 172–83, 185, 190–92, 200–206, 227, 236–37, 256–57, 261, 262, 263
  annexation to England   *See* Acts of Union
  Gerald of   *See* Chronicles, specific chronicles/chroniclers
  kings of   *See* kings
  literature of   52, 96, 108, 123, 159, 178, 185–86, 197, 200–02, 208, 211–13
    Welsh poetry   7, 21, 178, 209–11
  manuscripts of   176, 178–79, 183, 211–12
  The Marches   20–21, 141
  The Principality   20–21, 234
  Saints of   74, 159, 202
  Welsh identity   18–21, 30, 172, 176–78, 183–84, 200
  Welsh language   176–79, 183–84, 199, 200–02, 208–09, 212, 264
wall paintings   4
Walwyn's Castle   167
Warwick   16, 40, 79, 106, 114, 117–18, 120, 263

Guy of   *See* Guy of Warwick
  earls of   43–44, 106, 120
Warwickshire   40–42, 234
Wearyall Hill   *See* Glastonbury, Wearyall Hill
Wells, city of   59, 63, 115, 236, 239
Welsh kings   *See* kings
Welsh marches   *See* Wales, The Marches
The West Country   15, 19, 30–31, 136, 137–70, 171, 182, 231, 236–37, 252, 254, 263
Westminster   123
  Westminster Abbey   *See* abbeys
William of Malmesbury   *See* chronicles, specific chronicles/chroniclers
William of Rennes   *See* chronicles, specific chronicles/chroniclers
Winchester
  Arthurian connections   34, 75, 90, 103, 110, 114, 121–27, 237, 259
  Castle   *See* castles
  Round Table   *See* Arthur, objects
Windsor   125
  Castle   134
  St George's Chapel   40, 43
Worcester, William   28, 37, 41, 44, 53, 66–72, 88–89, 99, 111–14, 118, 129, 131, 134–35, 193, 219, 222, 254, 265–66
Wycliffites   28
Wynchcombe, Thomas   *See* chronicles, specific chronicles/chroniclers

Yder   54–55, 186–87
Ygerne   248
York   28, 37–49, 58, 65, 80, 99, 102–03, 115–16, 121, 127, 182, 201, 219, 244, 262
  Minster   *See* cathedrals

www.ingramcontent.com/pod-product-compliance
Lightning Source LLC
Chambersburg PA
CBHW051558230426
43668CB00013B/1896